Praise for *Considering Genius*

"Crouch's work not only reminds us of why he is one of the world's most important living jazz critics, but also why jazz remains an elemental component of our cultural identity."　　　—*Ebony*

"This collection is rich in detail, broad in scope, and worthy of the music to which it is dedicated."　　　—*The New York Sun*

"This collection of his jazz writings is noisy, tedious, and brilliant—all at the same time."　　　—*Buffalo News*

"Crouch has an ear for both music and language—'the slow and gooey low notes of a brood of pigeons'—but he deepens the thrill by telling the reader exactly what he'd say in his own kitchen. This show of respect is breathtaking, and unsettling. . . . I react with wonder and appreciation at his frankness. . . . *Considering Genius* is cause for celebration. Crouch invites us to throw open the windows in our heads, open our ears and enter into a deeper musical citizenship."
　　　—*The Plain Dealer*

"[Crouch's] assessments of Miles or Dizzy Gillespie, John Coltrane or Parker, or of the various other jazz legends dealt with in these pages, invariably come across as deeply felt and ardently argued."
　　　—*The Weekly Standard*

"Crouch is at the top of his game as he balances the drive for innovation in each of his subjects with the larger ramifications of the work. . . . Crouch writes with equal measures of authority and verve."
　　　—*The Miami Herald*

WRITINGS ON JAZZ

Considering Genius

Stanley Crouch

BASIC
CIVITAS
BOOKS

A Member of the Perseus Books Group
New York

Books published by Basic *Civitas* are available at special discounts for bulk purchases in
the United States by corporations, institutions, and other organizations. For more
information, please contact the Special Markets Department at the Perseus Books
Group, 11 Cambridge Center, Cambridge MA 02142, or call (617) 252-5298 or
(800) 255-1514, or e-mail special.markets@perseusbooks.com.

Designed by Brent Wilcox

The Library of Congress has catalogued the hardcover edition as follows:
Crouch, Stanley.
   Considering genius : writings on jazz / Stanley Crouch.
      p.   cm.
   ISBN-13: 978-0-465-01517-7 (alk. paper)
   ISBN-10: 0-465-01517-4 (alk. paper)
   1. Jazz—History and criticism.   I. Title.
   ML3506.C75   2006
   781.6509—dc22

                                                        2006002225

Paperback: ISBN-13: 978-0-465-01512-2: ISBN-10: 0-465-01512-3

10 9 8 7 6 5 4 3 2 1

Dedication: Two Great Souls

Joyce Alexander Wein, wife of jazz impresario George Wein, was laid to rest August 19, 2005, in New York. Born in 1928, Joyce Alexander was from the black middle class of Boston. She loved literature, knew much about painting, and was not a woman who made the mistake of thinking that refinement and soulfulness were opposed. Before and after she married her husband in 1959, Ms. Wein suffered neither the expected limitations nor the racism of her time in cooperative silence.

Joyce Alexander Wein, in every way, represented the best of jazz and the best of American womanhood because she took a back seat to no one. She sat in the front and brought as many people to the first row as she could whenever she could. That was her greatness, and that was what she stood for, because she believed much more in fairness than in favors. She was a model for our nation.

In the second week of March 2006, drummer Roy Haynes celebrated his eighty-first birthday with a six-night job at the Village Vanguard. Miraculously playing with the power and precision of a man forty years younger, he proved himself the elder living essence of jazz. One could hear every one of the very special people with whom he had played come dancing through his beat, his strokes, his use of the brushes and the mallets. There they were: Sidney Bechet, Louis Armstrong, Lester Young, Coleman Hawkins, Bud Powell, Charlie Parker, Miles Davis, Sarah Vaughan, Thelonious Monk, Sonny Rollins, Joe Henderson, Freddie Hubbard, Andrew Hill, and John Coltrane. In the on deck circle was his grandson, the remarkable nineteen-year-old Marcus Gilmore, who is ready to swing on those drums right now. There it is. The beat of joy goes on.

Contents

THOUGHTS

BATTLE ROYAL

DETOURS AHEAD

THE WAY IT WAS, THE WAY IT IS

Prologue
Jazz Me Blues

My interest in jazz began as a boy while growing up in my hometown of Los Angeles, where I was born in 1945. My mother had many old 78-RPM recordings of Louis Armstrong, Duke Ellington, and Fats Waller. It was in the middle fifties and the sound of jazz was rarely heard anywhere other than in the homes of record collectors and the clubs where musicians earned their livings in the underground world of the night life; for the most part, people listened to rhythm and blues. I did not become aware of jazz in its contemporary and popular style until high school, because Lou Donaldson was on the jukebox at Miss Harris's, where everyone went to buy hamburgers after Jefferson High School let out. The hamburgers were sold by a monstrously large woman who had a giant mole on her nose and probably could have balanced a glass of water on her backside with no difficulty. She took orders, served the burgers, and collected the money with such arrogance that the salt on the meat seemed an extension of her personality.

I believe "Blues Walk" and "The Masquerade Is Over" were often played by Bubble-Up, a track star, ladies' man, and serious rumbler if the occasion called for it. Bubble-Up was one of those young men who always seemed to know what was happening and he could even pass for twenty-one when he wanted. This meant that he even mentioned, while smoking a Salem cigarette, that he and "his boys" had gone to Hollywood, where he saw Miles Davis's band and the band of John Coltrane, whom I had heard referred to by an older jazz fan as "Johnny Coltrane."

Before I was out of high school I had started a jazz record club to which we would bring our recordings, listen to them, and discuss what we thought we were hearing. My homeroom teacher, who was also the choir director, sponsored the club and she would be there as we played our

records and discussed them. She was a big-legged white woman with tobacco stains on her teeth and, for all of her sophistication, such terrible
taste in clothes that she seemed always on the way to an audition for the
part of an eccentric. I remember her mentioning the great recording of
"Black and Tan Fantasy" that had just been made by Louis Armstrong and
Duke Ellington, which she always played at the end of a semester of her
music appreciation class. For that class's conclusion she borrowed *Charles
Mingus Presents Charles Mingus* from me in order to discuss what she thought
was the remarkable manner in which the bassist and drummer Dannie Richmond varied time and tempo on "All The Things You Could Be by Now If
Sigmund Freud's Wife Was Your Mother."

At that point I was not really a fan of Armstrong or Ellington, though I
had become enamored of Ellington's music through an album that my
mother owned. It was *In a Mellotone*. I was taken most by the mutes and the
power of Ben Webster, the satin lyricism of Johnny Hodges, and the deep
feeling of Ivie Anderson.

My mother was quite a handsome woman who had inherited Indian
blood from her mother by way of a Choctaw whom her great grandfather
had married in Mississippi some time after jumping ship. He was, before
taking his leave, working on a Portuguese vessel that took him into its employ during a visit to his native Madagascar. His ship was in America during the Battle of Vicksburg in 1863 and he later told his progeny that the
first thing he heard was the sound of "those big guns going off." Moms was
proud of the fact that she was often mistaken for an Asian Indian and she
loved Ivie Anderson's singing, which she had often heard at the Elk's Club
on Central Avenue when the great Duke's band came to Los Angeles. But,
alas, she dismissed Anderson as startlingly homely, no matter how good she
sounded. Yes, she could be competitive with other women and contemptuous of those she considered less than attractive, a tendency that remained
in place until the very end of her life.

In my mother's house, I found myself listening to those *In a Mellotone*
Ellington pieces over and over and over, imagining the world for which
they were originally made. Moms had told me about how wonderfully
Ellington dressed and the way the band looked under the lights and how
she and her high school classmates had gone to Union Station to meet his
train, only to find themselves awed by the fine suit, the elegant diction, and
those alligator shoes he wore. She also loved to say that someone had made
the observation that Duke Ellington's music was twenty-five years ahead of
its time, which intrigued me as it would anyone who grew up in a period

when popular entertainment was dominated by science fiction, which presented the future as magical in its technology or foreboding in its threats and dangers.

In my room, I imagined the dance halls across America that my mother spoke of with such joy and reverence. She loved to talk about how people would work hard all week and then get their hair fixed either in somebody's kitchen or a beauty parlor. Hair was cut and mustaches were trimmed in the barber shop, where lies were told, predictions of personal success were made, and the blue stories of men and women were nearly acted out with emphasis on humor, irony, and the pathos of heartbreak that sometimes led to violent tragedy. The two sexes would meet when the women put on some version of a dress that had been copied out of a fashion magazine while the men wore suits that had been bought "on time."

Once they were ready, the young men and the young women would go to those places like the Elk's Ballroom and become something much closer to what they felt they should always be. The women were as beautiful as they could make themselves and the men got as close to handsome as possible. Both took to the wooden heaven of the dance floor, ready for anything that felt good and was good. Out there, under the lights or off in the corners, they would do some rug-cutting and some romantic leaning, getting very close as they gently hugged each other, either talking or listening to a line of "trash" as bands like Duke Ellington and his men created aural fantasy lands of grace and glamour.

Those were some of my earliest experiences of the sort of paradise that aesthetic fluidity could inspire. It could exist as no more than the notes themselves, in the invisible world of audible math; or it could move someone to remember the solid facts and fantasies of the past. The music could produce in the listener responses to the tales told by those who were there, which became a stream of images that attached themselves to the notes. What was most important about the music then and is still most important to me now is the fact that artistry meets the need for beauty that is common to people with aesthetic sensitivity. In my mother's day, her generation met that music with their dreams, their wishes, their memories, and voted for elegance with their feet. Black, brown, beige, and bone in skin color, they had a ball. Since sex, either achieved or ached for, was always at the center of this ritual, paradise was not pure in the least human sense because it brought the wetness of flesh and the smells of perfume and cologne doing battle with the inevitable pungency resulting from activity on and off the dance floor, in public and in private. Yaz, yaz, yaz.

But at the time that I was being introduced to jazz—hearing the tales of its makers from the men and women in the neighborhood or in a record store—I discovered a truth that still applies: the Negro community, which has produced an extraordinary number of artists, has little or no value for art and will always, like most communities, drop to its knees before entertainment clichés or trends. Though I would later naïvely impose ethnic politics on the music (and would witness musicians who even more naïvely tried to remove themselves from the Western context in which they had developed and had obtained their truest aesthetic values), at this early time in my life the music had little ethnic meaning to me. I was attracted to the world of jazz purely as an art, and the art was there for whomever felt that need to play or hear the special elements that distinguished it.

My friends and I had that same appreciation for the art because it made us think of things beyond the simpleminded concerns of adolescence, which were dominated by the desire for popularity and a ready willingness to submit to the dictates and tastes of peer pressure. Our hormones were as hot as those of other young men and we were as obsessed with the females who were evolving from girls into women, but there was also a poetic feeling that was taking an ever-larger role in our collective sensibility. No matter how much we might identify with the adolescent thirst for release that we heard in the sincere rhythm and blues singing of Smokey Robinson and the Miracles, we realized that there was another quality of feeling being expressed by Miles Davis on *Sketches of Spain* or Charles Mingus on "Alice in Wonderland." In rhythm and blues, we never felt that we went beyond being teenagers, but in the world of jazz, we heard the thoughts and passions of men and women who traveled the country and who had been to Europe, or even Japan. We didn't really grasp what they were saying, but we did know that they were referring to bigger things and that those things just might have been better than anything we presently knew. That was the shared feeling.

In reading Nat Hentoff's liner notes for *In a Mellotone* and *Sketches of Spain*, I encountered a level of discussion that went far beyond any of the commentary that I had read in movie reviews, fan magazines, or the barely literate ones that were dedicated to rhythm and blues. I had read Hentoff on Ellington and he introduced me to new words such as "teleological," but the way he described Miles Davis and the deep song of Spanish culture struck a mortal blow against my unintended provincialism. I was impressed because I had never thought of a jet-black Negro like Miles Davis being connected to anything beyond the world of Negroes in America. Like everyone else, I was well aware of the fact that we were in the middle of a national crisis that had arisen because America had not begun to treat its Negro population with anything close to respect. I was already reading American literature and was aware of the work of James Baldwin and Richard Wright, but I never thought one could connect what they had to say with the statements of great artists who did not have a special case that they were pleading. I had yet to encounter the work of Ralph Ellison and Albert Murray; each a man who saw very clear connections between the sensibilities and the structures of jazz artists and *any* serious artists from the wide world at large.

No matter; at the time jazz was enough for me because it offered an alternative to the mediocrity, oafishness, and stupidity that loomed over my adolescence and did its best to hamper, break, or overcome every form of young or old vitality, intelligence, and sensitivity that showed itself in any way whatsoever. (There has always been a brutish and stupid aspect to Negro life that has nothing to do with ethnicity; it unites with every brutish and stupid inclination of the species to treat roughly or feel threatened by anything that suggests there is more to our existence than the life of the senses and something more than the most obvious trinkets symbolizing a thoroughly mediocre version of success.) The music was something that took place in public and could be purchased in record shops but that issued a language of secrets that could be shared by those who cared for this particular art of the invisible. In my early experience, it seemed that jazz was always something liked by people who had separated themselves from the trends and the crowds of the time. They were romantics or homemade nobles, or found refuge and solace in somebody's beat and somebody's instrument. The music created a condition and responded to the need for the moods of jazz, which were always expanding into areas of adult feeling and experience, whether specific or not.

The musicians themselves were representative of a way of saying no to everything that held you down or assumed you should accept a secondary place in the world. Once one declared war against the limitations of the home community, there were civil rights issues, and it was a long time before I was to know that Charles Mingus, Thelonious Monk, Miles Davis, Max Roach, and John Coltrane represented the blood on the knife of the music. These were not easily accessible artists. They specialized in the wounds that men had to live through, and that were somehow conquered and simultaneously purged if expressed in all their anguish and their anger.

But the open secret of the music was the poetic quality that could transform the beast of pain into an aspect of beauty. No one articulated anything like that, of course. The only statement might be, "Coltrane is really saying it, ain't he?" A nod was the answer, and that was that.

Meeting like conspirators against the humdrum qualities of our moment, we threw out theories about what somebody was saying, sometimes arguing nearly to the point of throwing blows. Or we resorted to the constant repetition of words that were perpetually elastic in the breadth of what they could mean. They were sure to turn up. Or they didn't turn up because merely saying the name of a renowned musician brought so many associations with it: the surname or first name or nickname was strong enough to introduce indisputable layers of meaning into a conversation. Miles. Monk. Sonny. Coltrane. Mingus. Horace. Blakey. Dizzy. We were in awe of those creators and felt another kind of awe for those among us who looked old enough to go to clubs and hear these men in person.

I believe Bubble-Up had gone to hear Coltrane and Eric Dolphy at the Renaissance Club in Hollywood, which was not so much a place as some land of lights and magical activities in that time when few Negroes ever went that far outside of our neighborhood without being bothered by the notorious Los Angeles Police Department, which saw part of its job as protecting the white and refined from the raw and uncool Negroes who had minds that—if they had minds at all—were those of savages. But we were all ready to take our chances and make that trip when we got old enough to get away with it, which is to say pass for twenty-one at the door, sit down, and pretend that we knew something about drinks. We either ordered beer or wine and tried to stay the night with that single drink.

That came after exploring the world of jazz listeners in the Negro community of what is now called South Central Los Angeles. With the exception of one or two, these were not aspirant intellectuals in the usual sense of those who read books and thought about them or looked for others with whom they could talk about what those books contained. Yet they had their thoughts and their interpretations of the music, which is how I came to know about Sonny Rollins, who was considered rough, street, and unconventional. One guy named Ronnie thought all this was made obvious by the suspenders he wore on the cover of *Duets*, the Dizzy Gillespie album on which he played half of the tunes with the great trumpeter, leaving the other ones to Sonny Stitt, whose virtuosity was acknowledged but was thought of as the more conventional of the two saxophonists. Ronnie told me that one man (whom I never met) was so taken by Rollins that, when this man was in the middle of losing a fist fight, the man called for his favorite saxophonist to save him, as if the startling horn player would appear as a saint or a spirit and vanquish his opponent! Ronnie also had Ornette Coleman's early Contemporary recordings and liked them primarily because they didn't contain the clichés he heard from so many other saxophone players: "He's different, and I like that."

That statement of Ronnie's influenced the way I began to listen to musicians. The more individual they were, the better, which is why I soon developed a contempt for the "funky" or "soul" jazz movement of the time, quickly tiring of the overuse of minor thirds, supposed gospel effects, and trills. Only Horace Silver and Art Blakey led bands that were considered part of that movement but used those devices with such individuality and invention that they moved along in a separate lane from the cliché mongers. This was the first time I encountered the strained version of black "authenticity" that would continue to appear every few years in the music just as it did in Afro-American culture, always coming down to just a few who took the proposition seriously and made something of it that followed the line of Duke Ellington, who had been the first to develop a broad aesthetic based on delivering "Negro feeling in rhythm and tune."

Some knuckleheads who moved into the house behind ours during that period spent most their time dropping "red devils" (Seconals) and smoking weed. When they made a long night of it, the droopy heads would add a little Benzedrine and Thunderbird to have one side of their consciousness going up while the other side was going down. Then the whist cards would come out and they would battle until dawn, music blaring all through the night. These were the men who introduced me to Thelonious Monk and John Coltrane. Sitting there in their undershirts and their processed hair, they loved to lean back and talk about the big-time musicians back east, where everything was going on *all the time*. Legends of Monk's weirdness in dress and manner were gone into as if they had been seen, though no one had ever been to New York. It was all folklore but, again, I heard it said that Monk was one of those musicians whose work was far ahead of his time and that *Thelonious in Action*, which had been recorded in performance at New York's Five Spot, would someday be a classic. "Just wait and see. You'll believe it then." Coltrane came to me through *My Favorite Things*, which one of these guys had bought on the very day it came out. That record was only played once those pill-heads and chronic weed-smokers ascended to the sort of high that would allow them, they thought, to appreciate the very new sound of the music.

It was like that, meeting jazz listeners here and there, and listening to their tales of the players. Those tales were usually something that they had heard and embellished until the tales were interesting enough to repeat, replete with personal inventions. These were all kinds of people: thugs, workers, college-boy types, and Negro scholars of the sort who lived alone in some rooming house with their books and their library card and who usually had dinner at some greasy spoon before heading home to a nip, a jazz record, and a book that was stared at with great reverence before it was opened. One of those jazz people—only one!—was a woman, who seemed crazy to me because she had Ornette Coleman's *Free Jazz* on the wall with its Jackson Pollock cover, the most far-out thing I had ever seen on a jazz record. The painting said nothing to me then and it says nothing to me now, but it did make clear that this woman was quite different from the majority of those I would run into during the course of my jazz explorations. I considered those encounters worthwhile if I met a new person and heard some music I had never known about or was made witness to an old classic or a new dimension in stereo equipment.

This sole female fan of the music always refused to play *Free Jazz* because she said that it was a sin to waste time on a person who was not ready for that advanced music. Her way of speaking was stilted and she made me think of a pretentious grade school teacher swirling through a condition of deranged senses. She was either drunk or full of pills or had so much weed in her head it was nearly coming out of her ears. Actually, the woman probably was not high at all; she was just a female who had made decisions and had tastes so out of the ordinary that the only way I could explain them to myself was to put her in the intoxicated category. After all, she was always reclining, either on the couch or on her bed. She was just getting up or just lying down. I do remember that she was the first one I ever heard say "incarcerated" to describe where her boyfriend resided.

During those years I began to read *Down Beat* and discovered that a big controversy was going on in the world of jazz and that Ornette Coleman and John Coltrane were in the middle of it. It was in that magazine that I discovered quite serious writing about jazz by people like Martin Williams, Harvey Pekar, Don Heckman, Ralph J. Gleason, Bill Mathieu, Ira Gitler, and others. But I enjoyed as much as anything the pictures of the musicians and the reviews of performances around the country, which provided a national sense of the music, a broader vision that extended to the world at large as concerts and tours through Europe were described.

I became aware of LeRoi Jones in the early sixties through a couple of poems he published in a *Down Beat* yearbook. They were unlike anything I had ever read and I had no idea that Jones was black and thought I had been given some insight when someone who knew French looked at his spelling of his name and said, "Oh. That means 'the king.' He must be proud of himself." By 1966, Archie Shepp had published "A View from the Inside" in *Down Beat* and I began to feel that my distance from the conventions of my immediate generation was being put into music in New York, or that someone somewhere was playing what that feeling of looking for something out of the ordinary came to mean.

Those were the years that I began to hear in person the remarkable men who make jazz, and I was there at the Monterey Jazz Festival in 1964 when Mingus turned everything out with "Meditations." I had become aware of Mingus because someone had written a review of his *Jazz Portraits* in the *Los Angeles Times* and said that his "Alice in Wonderland" was a major jazz composition. I bought that recording and listened to it over and over, then began to collect Mingus recordings and read things about this unusually proud musician, who seemed to have nothing to do with what I thought of jazz musicians other than the fact that he played jazz music and wrote jazz compositions. *Charles Mingus Presents Charles Mingus, Pithecanthropus Erectus, The Mingus Dynasty, Mingus Ah Um, Mingus, Blues and Roots,* and *Pre-Bird* dramatically expanded my taste and my expectations of structural adventure. They also introduced me to Eric Dolphy, Ted Curson, Jackie McLean, J. R. Montrose, Jimmy Knepper, Charles McPherson, Lonnie Hillyer, Mal Waldron, Booker Ervin, and Dannie Richmond. With the exception of Dolphy, those men were not part of the discussion in *Down Beat* and *Metronome* about what was going on in jazz. I did not know it yet but those are the kinds of musicians who make jazz an art. They may or may not be innovators who provide fresh material and set fresh directions, but their very seriousness and decided individuality give a breadth and depth to the music that a handful of trail blazers never could by themselves.

Charles Mingus was one of the reasons that I went to Monterey in 1964, especially when I found out that he and Thelonious Monk were to divide an afternoon. I was walking past the fairgrounds where the concerts were held one afternoon when I heard some music and climbed over the fence to see who was playing and perhaps learn a bit more about *what* they were playing. I walked in this room that I recall as a small auditorium with chairs and tables and there was Charles Mingus rehearsing his band. I went and sat as close as I could, which was just a few feet from the musicians. Trim and muscular, Mingus seemed like a yellow demon of power as he stood instructing the musicians and holding his bass upright by the neck. He wore a necklace of large pearls and many emotions would flicker through his face as he spoke in a voice that would change register to emphasize something or because it was pushed up or down by the passion that suddenly took over his delivery.

I soon discovered as he complained about the desolation of the moment that he had just fired the big band that had been provided for the premiere of a new piece. So he was now putting together an alternate strategy with a smaller group that included John Handy, Dannie Richmond, and Jaki Byard, whom Mingus kept harassing because he wasn't providing the kind of piano part that was necessary but could only be explained in terms of feeling, not notes. Frustrated, Byard finally stomped out with Mingus cursing at his back. At this point, two white women who had come in with Charles McPherson and Lonnie Hillyer chided Mingus for his cruelty. Mingus's eyes seemed to spew lava as they were promptly told to get the hell out of the rehearsal. The white woman who had given Mingus the pearl necklace protested and was told that she could also get out. He punctuated this by snatching the necklace from around his neck and throwing it on the floor, where it became just so many loose marbles.

I had never seen such fury in an aesthetic situation (though I had experienced it in fist fights and gang fights and had felt it most intensely when I took a thirty-seven ounce Louisville slugger to a guy who had intended to shoot me with bullets he was attempting to steal from my mother's garage). Getting a chance to step away from that heat is why I was somewhat relieved when Mingus, needing a drink, threw some money on the table in front of me and demanded that I go buy him a couple of quarts of red wine. By the time I returned, Mingus was in a much more pacific mood and the structure he was creating—which moved from chords in 4/4 to a waltz, a minor vamp, and a Spanish mode before closing out as a blues—was coming together. A satisfied charisma came over him and pushed aside the dilemma that had darkened his personality. I left with nothing more than an intensified feeling of awe for this great musician and the threatening aspects of his turbulent personality.

The next afternoon was Mingus's, though Thelonious Monk played well with his quartet before a dull large group of musicians joined him for uninspired versions of some of his songs. What I remember most was that while Monk was playing with his quartet a small plane flew over the fair-grounds and its motor turned in a rhythm that Monk picked up and played with until tenor saxophonist Charlie Rouse heard it and then drummer Ben Riley. It was the first time I heard something in person that I had noticed and always enjoyed when listening to *Eric Dolphy at the Five Spot*: When a someone knocks over a glass during Richard Davis's bass solo, he incorporates the rhythm of that accident into his improvisation. That taught me that an improvisor could truly control his environment at certain times, even incorporating or creating a dialogue with meaningless sounds that are transformed by the intent of the player.

Around that time I discovered the music of George Russell and spent many hours listening to his *The Outer View* because it contained a version of "You Are My Sunshine," which featured the singer Sheila Jordan. I had read about her stopping everyone's breath at a Newport Jazz Festival during a performance of that song with Russell's sextet. Through George Russell I became aware of Don Ellis, whose trumpet playing I liked and whose essays in *Down Beat* had had a deep influence. Ellis, though caught up in the empty avant-gardism of John Cage, had a deep regard for the tradition of sound that preceded the monochromatic tones of so many of those who came after Charlie Parker and John Coltrane. I am sure that he picked that up from his experience with Mingus and with George Russell. I enjoyed the version of "You Are My Sunshine" on *The Outer View*, but had much more fun listening to the title track and "D. C. Divertimento" as well as the other instrumentals on which Ellis and Paul Plummer were playing so much horn. Neither of them sounded like anyone else I had heard and both were swinging. To be individual and to swing as well, that was enough for me.

I could never tell at that point whether or not George Russell was white and I remembered asking my father, who looked at the jazz composer's picture on the cover of *The Outer View* and said, "Oh, yeah, he's one of us. No doubt about that." I imagine that Wilford Mellers shared the same problem with me because in his *Music In A Newfound Land*, the critic describes Russell as having the shortcomings of a white man whose experiments sound pretentious because they suffer the limitations that come from being at a remove from the Negro musical tradition. Here was an example of what *most* gets under a Negro's skin: A white man telling him, rightly or wrongly, that he lacks the credentials to be considered "authentic." How one arrives at knowing those credentials is always the question, especially since art is one part experience and one part imagination. Having the very worst luck with white people, women, gambling, or keeping a job is no guarantee that a Negro will be able to swing the blues as well as, for instance, Stan Getz, a pure and gifted musician from any perspective. Of course, I knew Negroes who had grown up in the roughest projects and were so straight and formal in manner and talk that no white person who thought like Mellers would have accepted them as being truly "natural," unless they were naturally breaking their necks trying to live up to supposed "alien" standards. Academics now call those the "white middle-class standards," as if the vision of manners and cultivation central to the middle class doesn't stretch across ethnic lines and can't have as much a chance of being vital as deracinated. This is a fundamental misconception that forces too many in the middle class to waste time trying to embrace what they consider the mud and guts of the lower class.

I was not grappling with any of those things at that point in my life because I was too busy trying to better understand jazz, along with all of the other things that brought prickles of intellectual and emotional illumination into my life. People such as Dizzy Gillespie and Charlie Parker became heroes to me once I could hear the details of the speed with which they played, though Parker was an early fascination because of the aura of folklore and super human feats of self-destruction that surrounded him. These were interpreted as functions of a dual rebellion against both racism and the lack of aesthetic sensitivity that defined the marketplace of American art. I dreamed of seeing Gillespie, the puff-jawed wind demon, in person—especially true after reading of how heroically he had performed at the Monterey Jazz Festival, where he played his upward tilted horn through two demanding extended pieces on one afternoon: Lalo Shifrin's *Gillespiana* and J. J. Johnson's *Perceptions*, each of which I already had or immediately bought and put on the merry-go-round of around-the-clock listening. When my father told me that he had witnessed two women listening to Parker in San Francisco who were so taken by his work that they refused to go to the bathroom while he was playing and wet their seats, I thought I had really missed seeing a master in person. He was made even more mythic and simultaneously greasy when my father took me to meet Emmery Byrd, for whom Parker had written "Moose the Mooch" and who sat there, ursine and jovial, in a wheelchair nodding as my father spoke of the old days, back when Moose sold heroin and my father shot it. I felt that I was sitting in a room filled with fog between the present and the past and that those two men could walk through that thick mist and see everything clearly that was blocked from my view. My father also deflated my romantic picture of Billie Holiday when I told him how beautifully she could sing a love song and he said, "You should have heard her singing one to a woman. That was when she was *really* singing. I saw her romancing a girl with her voice just a couple of blocks from here at an after-hours joint up near Adams Boulevard on Central Avenue. She was fine and mellow all right but she was in her element when she was trying to pull a girl up next to her."

Part of my belief in the power of words came through having read about Holiday and the various moods she created when singing. Those descriptions allowed me to know, without a doubt, when I first heard her on the radio, "that must be Billie Holiday." As the disc jockey announced her name I think I realized then that if a writer was good enough, he could prepare a listener to recognize the sound of an artist on first hearing. That might apply to certain singers but I don't really believe that is true of instrumentalists. Even so, it always remains a goal.

Part of what made those years stand out for me was the power of the Columbia Record Club. Through the club one could encounter certain recordings all over the community—*Duke Ellington at Newport*, *'Round About Midnight* by Miles Davis, Erroll Garner's *Concerts by the Sea*, and, down the popularity pike, Ahmad Jamal photographed at the piano from below on the Chess cover of the ubiqitous *But Not for Me*. In the better homes, the ones that didn't have cold beer or Ripple wine in the fridge and weed or its leavings in a shoe box cover under the sofa (which sometimes contained chicken bones of indeterminate age), you could see those records. They'd be sitting on the floor and leaning against the phonograph player across from the plastic-covered couches and the candy that was stuck together in glass dishes with handled tops that probably could have caught a reflection from the framed photographs on the wall that had been developed in black and white but could have been considered avant-garde because someone had gotten the bright idea of carefully painting them over in color. I also remember seeing Mahalia Jackson and Duke Ellington, looking like agents of majesty on the cover of the *Black, Brown, and Beige* recording, but I don't recall hearing it then. Most of the Ellington that I heard after my mother's *In a Mellotone* recording was too advanced for me until I got Columbia's *Jazz Poll Winners* release, which featured Dizzy Gillespie on UMMG (Upper Manhattan Medical Group) playing as much horn as anyone would want to hear. Most importantly, I heard various ways of playing jazz. The Miles Davis Sextet with John Coltrane, Cannonball Adderley, Bill Evans, the Dave Brubeck Quartet with Paul Desmond, the singing group of Lambert, Hendricks, and

Ross, and Gerry Mulligan's Quartet with Art Farmer were the ones I liked most, primarily because I preferred the Mingus rendition of Holy Ghost church music on *Blues and Roots* to the version on *Jazz Poll Winners*.

Those were the basics of my early development as a jazz listener. They were expanded when I was introduced to the Modern Jazz Quartet over at a friend's house, which led to my buying the two-volume *European Concert*. Those two volumes brought me to a Negro version of what could have been called cool jazz. Everything was so well controlled, which made it sound cool, but the ideas blossomed forward in a distinctive blue heat and a clarity of interplay that was decidedly unique and not at all cool. The thought that those men were playing like that in concert halls throughout Europe was very exciting to me, partially because the Modern Jazz Quartet seemed, from their photographs, to be sort of an improvising elite who were there to play something beyond the shallow funk music of the day while laying down as much blues and swing as you could hope for or get. But cool jazz was associated with white West Coast groups and particular players such as Chet Baker, Gerry Mulligan, and Stan Getz—none of whom were from the West Coast, by the way. I saw Shorty Rogers on television at the time and couldn't take him seriously, first because his music seemed tepid and, second, because he reminded me of a badger trying to play a trumpet. Getz towered over all of them to me, especially after I paid my marathon dues listening to that almost peerlessly inventive saxophone he was effortlessly executing on *Focus*. That was the recording on which Getz made most of his supposed peers on the tenor seem like they were improvising somewhere in grade school while he was prancing around with a Phi Beta Kappa key hanging from the bell of his horn. I had first heard *Focus* on the radio and was taken by his playing with Roy Haynes on "I'm Late, I'm Late," which I associated with *Alice in Wonderland*, like any reader of books would.

The quality and refinement of the Modern Jazz Quartet turned John Lewis into a private hero, which was furthered by the awe in which John Caballero held him. Cabellero was the conductor of my high school's band and also taught music appreciation. Caballero played piano and had been a student of Samuel Brown, who had led the legendary bebop high school band in which Dexter Gordon, Chico Hamilton, Billy Higgins, and Don Cherry had played. Brown was still at Jefferson but he had by then become disenchanted with teaching, students, and even the possibilities of music, or so it seemed to me at the time. I remember Caballero saying that the music John Lewis knew and wrote was "too deep" for most people.

The music on John Lewis's *The Wonderful World of Jazz* became a paean to lyrical emotions sung through instruments at length, both on originals and standards. I became interested in anything John Lewis was interested in and read everything about him that I could find. Following Lewis took me to *Third Stream Music*, and on to Gunther Schuller's *Jazz Abstractions*, which featured Ornette Coleman and Eric Dolphy, each of whom I thought were thrilling players full of surprises and possessed of great forward motion in their improvising. Before I realized how repetitious a player he was and that so many of his improvisations were dominated by a single phrase (which Don Ellis pinpointed in a *Down Beat* Blindfold Test), I thought that Dolphy was a superior player to Coleman. I had started to warm up to Coleman after reading things that Schuller had written about him and becoming a frequent listener to the swinging but metrically liberated interplay between the alto saxophonist and Ed Blackwell on *Ornette!* When Tootie Heath came through town with Sonny Rollins in 1969, he and I spent some time talking about how brilliantly Blackwell played on "T&T," the feature track Coleman had written for him on *Ornette!* "People don't talk about Blackwell but, even though you can hear his influences, like Buhaina and Max, he's playing his own stuff. That's Blackwell all the way, brother. Yessir: pure Africa coming through that New Orleans street beat. Blackwell is brilliant. He figured it out that way and he's got a hell of a pair of hands. And Blackwell's mind is full of *pure dynamite*."

After the Watts Riot in August of 1965, black nationalism swept through the younger generation like a hallucinatory fever of the intellect. I was later told in New York by the writer Larry Neal that the sheer size of the riot—forty square miles—with block after block set fire and the National Guard called in, shocked everyone on the East Coast. It appeared that the idea of violent black revolution was no longer just a lot of fat-mouthing. Looking at the television all those miles away in New York made it seem possible, and from that irrational sense of possibility came a tribal politics that so seriously retarded the intellectuals of the black community, most of whom have yet to recover from the harm done to them by uncritical worshiping of Africa, embracing the contrivances of separatism, and attempting to disconnect themselves from the fundamental presence of Western thought and Western ways, both of which have bloomed in the Black American sensibility over the last three and a half centuries or so and are now as essential as air is to the lungs. For all of the influence of Marxist ideology on these misinformed proceedings, Hegel's dialectic was not applied to American culture, where it might have done the most good. There it would have led the most serious to what Ralph Ellison and Albert Murray realized profoundly: America is a land of synthesis in which every ethnic or religious group tends, over time, to become part of every other. It is not so much a melting pot as it is a rich thick soup in which every ingredient both maintains its taste and also takes on the taste of everything else.

That realization was not to be. The tribal impulse took over and began to derange everything, moving strongly from the Nation of Islam's conception that the Negro was a "dead monkey" unaware of his identity and his true culture, which was African and Islamic. Most did not buy the Islamic part, but the women especially loved to be referred to, eventually, as "black, beautiful, and the queens of the universe." The men felt that growing their hair into "naturals" made them more purely black, something like the West Indian dreadlocks of today. In this ethnic Mardi Gras of superficial identity on parade, the robes, big earrings, sandals, and books that were usually potted history helped reassert the kind of ethnic narcissism that had ebbed and flowed among Negroes since at least the middle of the nineteenth century. In the sixties it made a bigger wave than ever.

The impact this ideology had on jazz cannot be denied. It cannot be swept under the rug like all of the racism of the early days of black studies. That flaming animus is conveniently forgotten by black intellectuals who now have tenure, or sense that a serious discussion of that period would make it harder to maintain self-righteousness in every academic exchange. Today they would not be comfortable discussing the hostile, segregated attitudes of black students during the sixties and the seventies in which white students, racist or not, were made to bear the burden of "payback." This usually meant being brow-beaten or, on occasion, screamed at by pompously ill-informed black students who thought that higher education was an opportunity for ranting one's way through college. White boys were too weak to do anything about it, and white girls were equally spineless bitches who could do nothing but whisper among themselves. But, of course, those young men and women were to learn that the so-called "white world" of work was not a college campus and, out there, Whitey remained as mighty as ever.

Those problems arrived in the jazz world in the form of ancestral worship, ethnic costumes, endless drones, and the willful shrieking that was intended to let the white man know that these were not happy entertainers under any circumstances. The philosophical overview largely came from one little man: LeRoi Jones. If one reads the highly influential *Black Music*, it is easy to see an interesting thinker devolve into an ideologue and eventually fall between the two stools of mindless avant-gardism and black nationalism into the spittoon of racism. Race becomes the most important distinction, hostility the highest form of engagement, and the obsession nationalists had with "black unity" leads Jones to call for, by 1966, a "unity music" in which jazz, rhythm and blues, and religious music—Christian or not—all come together. (It sometimes seems as though the final essay in that book, "The Changing Same," was nailed to the door of the invisible temple of the Chicago avant-garde, which gather under the name of the Association for the Advancement of Creative Musicians, popularly known as the AACM.) The point that Jones stressed was musicians should be about moving jazz out of its natural place—that of an art music that swung on dance rhythms—and making it into a chocolate-covered "red ark" in which all of the commonest ideas that came from lame brains like Lenin and Mao could be retooled for a "revolutionary" blackness.

The tribal appeal is always great and there is nothing more tempting to the most gullible members of a minority group than suddenly hearing that, merely by being born, one is not innately inferior to the majority but part of an unacknowledged elite. I was not so sophisticated that I could avoid the pull of those ideas and found myself reading all kinds of books about Africa, and African customs and religion, many of which I purchased at the Aquarian Bookstore. It was in the western part of the black community and specialized in ethnic materials of seemingly every sort, from the scholarly and anthropological to the fantastic and, beyond that, to the virtually insane, meaning the works of cultists like Elijah Muhammad.

At that time, which was about 1966, I would have been pulled all the way into the maw of subthought, from which it might have taken longer to emerge if Jayne Cortez hadn't introduced me to Ralph Ellison's *Shadow and Act*, a book that set off roman candles of excitement in my mind. Ellison was the first fully formed Negro American thinker in the world of aesthetics I had experienced thus far. He was deeply rooted in his experience and in his the concerns. Ellison delivered those thoughts to the door of every person who was not white and willing to read him, but he did not allow himself to be limited, or defined by the distortions that rattled the minds of those who were blocked from seeing or assuming the inevitable presence of humanity behind his color. Unlike those younger black people who were busy jettisoning their heritage as Americans and Western people—both of which brought the built-in option of criticism—Ellison took the place of his ethnic group and himself as firm parts of American life and a fresh development in Western culture.

I had never read a black man who strode so with such ease through the world of ideas. Nor had I known of one who was so confident about how deeply important the background from which he came was to understanding the United States in terms of its accomplishments, its potential, its ironies, and its shortcomings. Ellison's book also revealed a vital sense of humor and an impatience with narrow definitions, whether coming from white men like Irving Howe and Stanley Edgar Hyman or emerging voices like LeRoi Jones, whom he already recognized as given to theories that would simplify and dehumanize the people for whom Jones thought he was speaking. Ellison had a literary foot covered by an elegantly designed and raucous style. It was color-blind and ready to boot out of the door anyone who was passing off ideological flatulence for the thorny rose bushes of real thought. He knew that such hard thinking could be both beautiful and prickly and that it could reduce the opposition to a condition that was as bloody as it was slaphappy. Ralph Ellison became an immediate hero and I began to read him obsessively, over and over, enjoying the learning that came with looking up the references that he brought to his uniquely broad vision of American life.

I was then working as an actor and a playwright with Jayne Cortez, who had been in the front line of the Civil Rights Movement. Cortez had gone south to work for the Student Non-Violent Coordinating Committee, registering black voters in Mississippi. But she was then employed at Studio Watts and conducting drama workshops near 103rd Street, where I had been on Friday the Thirteenth of August 1965 and had seen the riot take off in full force. At Studio Watts, we did Jean Genet's *The Blacks* and original dramas that were collectively written, but Cortez was then wary of dogma, which was why Ellison appealed to her and why she read *Invisible Man* once a year.

During that period I bought a set of drums from Cortez's son, Denardo Coleman, and began practicing. I had always loved Max Roach, Philly Joe Jones, Art Blakey, Elvin Jones, Ed Blackwell, and Billy Higgins, to name some, but my focus was on playing like Sunny Murray because I had been convinced that it was time for a style that broke completely away from convention. I thought I had an idea of where things were going when I played an ESP record for bassist Wilber Morris who said of Murray, "Oh, I see. He doesn't play like a jazz drummer, he plays like a symphony drummer. He just colors things. He's not playing time." I also knew Errol Henderson, who had played with Albert Ayler, Norman Howard, Henry Grimes, and Sunny Murray on a record called *Spirits*. Henderson encouraged me to go as far away from the norm as possible. I went over to his house and we played long duets that were more about sound than bass lines or drum rhythms in straight time.

I was soon taken by Milford Graves and became interested in getting more timbres out of the drum kit than were usually expected. In this direction, I spent plenty of listening time focused on tabla players and African drummers. I was still more involved with the environment of a piece of music than I was with playing time. Errol thought that we should get Arthur Blythe in our band, which we did. Blythe was the featured soloist in Horace Tapscott's big band and his quintet, which used two bass players.

I had first heard Blythe when he was living in San Diego but had come up to Los Angeles for a gig with Tapscott on a one-woman show of Jayne Cortez's, which anticipated the many single black women across the country who soon did their versions of ethnic protest on stage. Blythe stood out immediately because he had a big, broad sound with a point on it that was pumped up by an unusual vibrato that put it at odds with the conventional sounds of alto players whose tones were Charlie Parker-derived. He had obviously listened to Coltrane but also had a very strong grasp of the time that could give way to pithy shouts and singularly dramatic outbursts in the lower register. Tapscott, who composed the modal music they played, was always in the middle of a lean at the keyboard. He responded to Blythe with big, stark chords and short melodies that gave lyrical direction with the percussive drive of riffs. Then there were his skittering, thumping, and orchestral solos, which were never lacking in the power that arrives through integrity. The bassist was David Bryant, who would just as soon pick up the bow and saw as pluck his way through a performance. Behind it all, or in the middle, or surrounding the whole tune, were the drums of Everett Brown, who was from Kansas City and one of the finest virtuoso masters of thunder I have ever heard. Capable of playing four meters at once, Brown had invented a style so personal and volatile I have never heard anything like it since. This was the small underground group that only rose into public awareness every now and then because Tapscott had community concerns that led him to squander his talent in neighborhood situations long after the taste for jazz among black people had begun to go the way of the buffalo. He kept looking over the parapet as if he was waiting for the troops that never came to relieve the men at the Alamo.

At the end, with Everett Brown no closer to New York than a rest home in Kansas City, I heard Tapscott give his last performance in Manhattan's

Iridium, across the street from Lincoln Center. Foreshadowing a fatal stroke, his right hand had stopped working one morning and he had to play all of his improvisations with his left, seeming at first to have invented a new style. But he was only standing up to the demands of his gig and giving all that he had, articulating each note with his left hand as though it would have to stand in for all that he knew and had lived in the world of jazz—good, bad, and otherwise. I have never heard more courage and confidence in the invisible art of music, nor will I ever forget the sheer verve of his improvising and the fearful exuberance that he brought to the swing of each phrase. It was a swan song, a big bird flying low before disappearing somewhere into the heavens, up where silence reigns and no more is left of the human presence than the memory of a tall man who loved music, had implanted his legend in the rhythms of many women, and was always looking for as big a laugh as he could get.

I had my doubts that we could get Blythe to play with us because we were too "out"—or wild and blatantly unconventional. But we did get him and then later recruited Bobby Bradford, David Murray, James Newton, Wilber Morris, and Mark Dresser to work with us. The personnel changed, as it does in all bands, and we had many high-flying gigs until I left for New York in the fall of 1975. I will never forget how it felt to hear Arthur Blythe and Bobby Bradford invent such strong melodic lines that would occasionally explode into pure energy, which was never an end in itself, only a strident color that was used sparingly. Also unforgettable was the surprisingly mature sound of David Murray, who arrived at my home ready to play on his eighteenth birthday. Then there was James Newton, who was practicing a Debussy flute piece one day at my house and I recognized a passage that John Coltrane played in his long, well-structured improvisation on his original *Crescent*. Mark Dresser became our sole bassist after Wilber Morris left for New York and Errol got messed up in some kind of theft with a local black nationalist witch and left town, fleeing the police. I never heard from him again but his stories of Albert Ayler and Norman Howard were prime.

Errol never assumed that they were equal to Coltrane, Ornette Coleman, or Sonny Rollins. He thought their value was in the energy and the boldness they brought to the music, and he was willing to bet on all of us getting that through the gauntlet. Once he smirked at the memory of Albert Ayler chuckling and repeatedly saying "Poor Sonny" when Rollins came through Cleveland. "Albert could play what he knew and that was cool, but he couldn't get up there and mess with Sonny, who was playing his ass off. I knew what Albert could do and what he couldn't do. He went down there the next night to play with Sonny and Cherry and I think Sonny put something on his head because he didn't have much to say about it. Then, I was the one chuckling. But, you know, Albert and Norman Howard were gunning for Ornette, too. When you got with them, Albert would say, 'I bet when he hears me, he's not gonna pick up that tenor again,' and Norman would say, 'Yeah, I know he ain't gonna fuck with no trumpet!' They were both wrong: Ornette didn't care what anybody else did. He was pulling his own wagon and just wanted people to get out of his fucking way."

When I arrived in New York, I had the Claremont Colleges behind me, where I had taught drama, the history of jazz, and literature from 1968 to 1975. In those colleges, with students from well-to-do backgrounds and the security of a steady job, I was able to practice a great deal and have many rehearsals and conversations with Bobby Bradford, who had not only played with Ornette Coleman at the Five Spot after Don Cherry left the band, but had also worked with a Coleman-derived band co-led by saxophonist John Carter and included Bruz Freeman, who had played in Chicago with Charlie Parker and was the brother of Von Freeman, the tenor legend. Bradford had a very detailed overview of the entire music, from New Orleans to what we were trying to do or, in my case, thought we were doing. Bradford was one of the most intelligent men I had ever known and his sophistication was greater than that of any musician I had met up to that point. Like Jayne Cortez, he was aware of the racial troubles in the nation but he had not bought into any simple-minded ideology and always had something original to say about whatever was going on. Getting to know and talk so much with him constituted one of the greatest pieces of luck I have ever had.

In September of 1975 I moved to Manhattan and shared a loft with David Murray on Second Street and the Bowery, where we played every day and worked in different ensembles. But New York was quite startling to me because I had never heard so many great musicians across styles and because I came to know both Albert Murray and Ralph Ellison, who had very different ideas from those in the East Village who considered themselves artists. Those downtown, latter-day bohemians usually didn't know much about art at large and were almost always in a battle with middle-class convention, or the conventions of art that they assumed were symbolic of the middle class. In far too many cases, being a bad boy or a bad girl was as important as any work they produced. In comparison to what I was surrounded by down there, the worlds of Murray and Ellison were not only more challenging but also much more interesting.

By the time I arrived in New York I had become friends with Larry Neal, one of the few black writers who had any interest in jazz and whom you could see in the clubs or at concerts. I had met him when I came back east for a black nationalist gathering of propagandists whom LeRoi Jones presented as poets at the Apollo in Harlem and at the Brooklyn Academy. I was shocked by the low level of talent that Jones so enthusiastically presented, and by the muddy level of intellect that was common to almost all with whom I talked, except Larry Neal and the big Chicagoan named Amus Moore, who turned out the Apollo with his "Poem for the Hip Generation," which included a perfectly sung excerpt from Lester Young's improvisation on "These Foolish Things."

Larry Neal had written insightfully about Ellison and introduced me to Murray, who was little known at that time and sat back in his chair like the monarch of an unknown kingdom that stretched out in all directions from his Harlem apartment. Neal had been one of the black nationalist critics close to LeRoi Jones but was tiring of the empty rants that could be called literature if they attacked the white people and called for the overthrow of the nation. As an ex-military man, Murray laughed at all of that and found it embarrassing, since he thought that such talk corroborated the presumptions of all racists who considered Negroes nothing but born fools. When we left his apartment, Larry and I were like two convicts who were planning to make it over the wall and back into free society. Larry had heard all of the "new music" but didn't talk much about it; he was more interested in the implications of Duke Ellington, particularly his startling blues compositions.

Inspired by Ellison and Murray, Larry was looking for a larger context in which he could put—and test—his experience and perspective. He was anxious to go out into that world that LeRoi Jones had turned his back on and was soon encircled by a cult of followers who seemed to have read no more than ten books among them, all bad. I was too young and too naïve to realize that the LeRoi Jones whom I admired for his early poetry, fiction, and essays was never to return: He had left the world of art for good. A two-legged, chameleon that might change colors from black and anti-white to red and anti-capitalist, Jones would will himself into a minor man, nothing but a clever maker of shrill placards from that point on. During those years, when a plethora of desperately bad ideas overtook us, I sometimes believed that Jones was like some others who felt like Jorge Luis Borges's German war criminal as he recalled spiritual pits of the Third

Reich, "[a]s individuals, my comrades were odious to me; I strove in vain to convince myself that for the high cause that had brought us all together, we were not individuals." Now I doubt it. I think he incinerated his mind and sensibility in the campfires of ideology, out on the endless hikes with all the other little boys who had deluded themselves into thinking that their adolescent games did any more than obfuscate the realities of that period. As his talent descended, Jones and I became more alienated from each other and finally met in a Battle Royal many years later at a jazz conference in Wisconsin that was sponsored by the Smithsonian Institution. The results of that event appear later in this volume.

But I drew many intellectual satisfactions from getting to know Ellison and Murray, the acknowledged past master and the unknown-but-ever-rising force. I had first encountered Ellison on the campus of New York University, walking along with a brown-skinned look of class and taste that reminded me of the best teachers I had had in public school, each of whom had put everything on the nose of his belief in the inner life and what it would provide him or what it would allow him to make as an offering to the world. Ellison wore a stingy-brimmed hat, a dark suit, some wing tips, and carried a tan trench coat over one arm. He appeared startled when I called his name, but smiled as I introduced myself and reminded him of some letters that I had sent his way about *Invisible Man*. He wished me luck as a new arrival in Manhattan and I was to next see him at a party given by Murray.

There Ellison complained of the quality of vermouth and pulled from his suit pocket a small bottle with an eye dropper in it from which he dispensed the appropriate level of vermouth for his martinis. His wife, Fanny, wore a white sweater dress and black boots. She was barely brown, had freckles like black stars, and was beautiful in an almost innocent but harsh way because there was so much fire in her personality that it seemed to be both warming and burning her from inside. Stately and petulant, she sat in a large chair with her legs crossed, one boot moved up and down like a metronome impatiently waiting for the music to begin. Fanny Ellison was deeply intelligent, incapable of small talk, and quite magnetic. She and Ellison made quite a couple.

It was through discussions with Murray—either on the telephone or in person—and with Ellison over the telephone that I sped up my exit from the strictures of any version of the miseducation that was Negro nationalism or left-wing politics. Each man was very different and seemed to have very different ambitions. Deeply envious of his friend's stature, Murray was determined to come out of Ellison's shadow and be recognized as his own man, which led him to produce so many books, almost all of them classics or at least very, very good. Apparently burdened by extraordinarily high expectations, Ellison did not produce much work of importance after his first novel and his first book of essays. That lack of productivity disturbed Murray, who seemed to want from Ellison the kind of dialogue that Hemingway wished to have with Fitzgerald, one in which their books would each be a literary way of "raising" the other just as poker players do.

When Murray wrote, in quick succession, *South to a Very Old Place*, *The Hero and the Blues*, *Train Whistle Guitar*, and *Stomping the Blues*, he might not have stepped out of Ellison's shadow but he had created the most original body of work other than Ellison's that I knew of, and that remains true even now. Most important to my developing aesthetic vision was the fact that his work and Ellison's placed the blues and jazz right in the middle of the new forms and ways of redefining the expression of human life that had been invented in the twentieth century. As I read them, I came to feel that all I had been taught as a child was being reinforced and extended by two great minds.

My mother's generation always thought that racism imposed a misunderstanding of life in which one assumed to know the unknown individual before coming in contact with the person and, therefore, also assumed to know what this unmet person could and could not do. As far as my mother was concerned, being a Negro woman from Mississippi was no more a barrier holding Leontyne Price back from the top of the opera world than being bicycle mechanics had boxed the Wright brothers out of being the first men to get a heavier-than-air object off the ground by making revolutionary use of aerodynamics, which is based upon the character and manipulation of thrust. The people of my mother's generation and the ones that preceded it all seemed to feel that the world was theirs and that they could—and should—identify with whatever each of them considered good. What was holding them back were the problems of petty power that allowed the white folks to unfairly condescend in so many minor situations but that, when put together, could add up to a rough day, since racism was not the same every day and did not turn up in the same place. Like all of life, it slid up and down, ebbed and flowed, sometimes missed you, sometimes barely touched you, sometimes took you down like a tidal wave if you did not move quickly enough or know how to improvise a surfboard and ride, occasionally enjoying the adventure of keeping your balance while the white people were doing their level best to lay you out deep in the wet.

Larry Neal and I used to talk a lot about the breadth of the aesthetic thought of Ellison and Murray. We recognized that both of them were capable of celebrating Negro American life without sinking down into defensive postures that were finally based in what one writer calls "the magic of the blood"—they did not believe that good or evil was determined by genes or that color necessarily told one anything at all. Like those of my mother's generation, they did not accept the dictates of segregation and did believe that anyone, within or without the group, had the right to demand it of you. Whether one agreed with everything they said and thought or not, all of their statements were those of men, not boys, and they were not at all related to the intellectually threadbare fraternities and sororities of ethnic politics that had so quickly become what Larry and I determined were no more than alternate versions of the Marxist "god that failed."

Some of what Larry and I talked about was how uncontrived and basic to black American life the new things we were learning could be. In Ellison and Murray there were ideas to be had about the arrival of aesthetic complexities that might come from no more than the big fun of Saturday night dances. For instance, Ellison had very provocative observations about how the exchange between musicians and dancers in the 1930s might have affected the style of Charlie Parker. He saw Parker's mentor, Buster Smith, playing alto saxophone with the Blue Devils at dances held in Slaughter's Hall, where the local people had a particularly interesting way of responding to the music. Ellison remembered, "It was a dance step called the 'two and one,' or the 'two in one.' It was a brisk rhythm in which they would dance with and against the rhythm of the bands. There was a lot of improvisation going on on the dance floor, and these Negroes would go into quite a series of steps that carried them very rapidly from one end of the hall to the other, almost in one huge sweep of feet and bodies in motion. Then they would turn and come back down just as fast as they had gone. Buster Smith then had that strange, discontinuous style that one could see was also a reaction to what he was looking at from the bandstand. That discontinuity was later heard in Charlie Parker. But it could easily have some of its roots in Slaughter's Hall."

The summer before I moved to New York I attended a sort of tutorial on jazz criticism that had been organized by the great Martin Williams and that featured Murray, whom Williams more or less deferred to on a number of levels. Murray was a fresh force to those in attendance who would go on to write about jazz. He was surprising because his level of sophistication did not perpetuate what had become an often acrimonious situation in "dialogue" that consisted of whites—who had done, by far, most of the scholarly research on jazz—being subjected to sadomasochistic rituals.

This usually amounted to no more than a whole lot of sore-headed teddy-bear growling from pretentious and possessive Negroes, so much so that one would have thought that whites had been blocking the expression of what was an actual interest in the music as an art among black people or black academics. According to a well-read hanger-on of Roy Eldridge's, the great trumpet player said that there was never any interest in jazz as an art among most Negroes, who just happened to like it when the music was popular and it functioned in the world of dance.

True or not, we can clearly see at this point that if there had been any interest in the art of jazz among the black academics who began to invade the academy when black studies took what was usually its dubious position on our college and university campuses, the entire history of jazz over the last thirty-five years might have been quite different. With the academy submitting to many of the wishes of those black academics and the easily riled-up black students, annual budgets could have been put together that would have provided a national touring circuit that could easily have challenged the one in Europe that had long supported most jazz musicians. Even if it had begun in a segregated way, there would have eventually been black musicians who hired white musicians, just as Archie Shepp did throughout even during his most vociferous period of black-power pouting and breast-beating. By now, all racial barriers should be down and jazz musicians of all hues would have before them a substantial touring circuit of hundreds of American colleges. There, they might not only make reasonable money but also have their work and their intentions documented in all the ways that academies are good at when there is serious interest. But, as Henry Louis Gates, Jr. and Cornel West have pointed out to me when I brought up the subject, there has never been any serious or sustained involvement in the arts because most of black studies has been devoted to history, sociology, and political science.

Martin Williams and Albert Murray were interested in none of that during that summer of 1975. They were trying to provide an aesthetic overview that would address the history of jazz, the fundamentals of fine art, and provide the sort of vocabulary that could help writers better communicate the power of the idiom. It was there that I began to realize with greater clarity how important Williams was as a force, a thinker, and a dedicated scholar of this music. I was also able to grasp how thoroughly Murray was organizing the thoughts that would turn his *Stomping the Blues* into the first poetics of jazz when it was released in the following year (and a book party was given for it that Ornette Coleman attended in a white leather suit). Both being Southerners, Williams from Virginia and Murray from Alabama, the two made quite a combination. They showed in their observations, their jokes, and their intellectual reach that jazz would always be served best by integrated teams of serious people, the only true protection against the provincial superstitions and condescension of the American musical establishment and the rhetorical wind-up toys of black nationalism. As Ellison said, most profoundly:

> What gets lost when you overstate race is the fact that people aren't always thinking about race. They might be thinking about style, about technique, about information that would allow them to do whatever it was that they were trying to do. Hell, when you went to the record store, you were looking for anything that could help you achieve your own aspirations; you weren't concerned about seeing yourself in the limited terms that someone else might. This is very important because there is a wide open sensibility in jazz, and that sensibility made it possible to express so many of the essentials of the national character in the sound and feeling of the music. You hear the wanderlust, you hear the hopes and the dreams; you are given a feeling for the inevitable disappointments and the equally inevitable humor. That is why those bands swinging that music had such significance. They existed in a ritual where the highly demanding aspects of the musical imagination and the dancing imagination frequently met, pulling together techniques and expressions of elegance from anywhere they could.

Though Williams and Murray said that in many different ways from Ellison, always adding takes that came from their individual experience and taste, the substance of that summer tutorial led by those two men was what made jazz an art and why. But neither Williams nor Murray, for all of their imagination, could have realized that during that very summer, way down yonder in New Orleans, a woolly-headed fourteen-year-old wunderkind of the trumpet was unknowingly preparing himself to become the most astounding force jazz would ever see in its struggle to achieve the highest possible ground in the world of fine art, both here and abroad.

I met Gary Giddins and his first wife through Williams that summer. He was then working for the *Village Voice* and was in the process of developing a reputation as one of the most capable younger jazz writers. Giddins directly helped me start publishing in the *Voice*, where whatever reputation I was to eventually have benefited immeasurably from the tough-minded editing skills and formal expertise of Robert Christgau, M. Mark, Ellen

Willis, and Karen Durbin, a quartet as fine at their craft as any individuals I have encountered since moving to New York.

Living in lower Manhattan by that fall, I was soon seeing so many fine musicians' work in person that I had to reconsider the so-called avant-garde since it was, in far more cases than not, below the level of the music that was being played here and there in almost every style that had come forward since the beginning of jazz. I learned this from conversations with the musicians, listening to their rehearsals, performing with some, and being a part of the scream-and-shout festivals that were put on downtown during what was called the "loft jazz" period. This movement of sorts took off and made its presence felt in the late seventies and early eighties. It was an alternative because, although the clubs wouldn't hire those musicians, they could play in private galleries and large rooms that served no alcohol but were legally allowed to present concerts.

My shift in taste was furthered by my getting a chance to book the Tin Palace, initially for Sunday afternoon performances of free music. That series introduced Air and the World Saxophone Quartet to New York, but it was hard to keep pulling an audience in, though one of the great pleasures was watching Henry Threadgill look on with astonishment as Arthur Blythe blew the bell off the alto and the paint off the walls one afternoon. I later saw Cecil Taylor look at Don Pullen in the same way when Pullen was performing at the Village Vanguard with George Adams in one of the extra fine small groups of the eighties. Adams knew the vocabularies of Pharaoh Sanders and Albert Ayler but had high command of the blues and could swing as hard as you might want to hear, boosted up by the bass of Cameron Brown and the drums of Dannie Richmond, who had created his first masterworks with Charles Mingus. Both Pullen and Adams had worked with Mingus, who was the structural mind behind the elastic conception of a range of styles dominating the music as opposed to just one approach. Unfortunately, the group's signal authority was never truly captured on record and remains only in the memories of those who were present and heard them on those nights when they turned the Village Vanguard into a red-carpeted fireplace. "These guys are incredible," tenor saxophonist Big Nick Nicholas said at the bar of the Vanguard one night, "they can stomp down or get low down in the blues, they can play pretty as you want to hear on a ballad, they can even play some of that crazy shit, then go all the way back to ragtime. This band is a bitch on roller skates, baby. You better watch out: they'll run over you if you ain't ready. I know that's right."

For perhaps a year, at the suggestion of the flutist Lloyd McNeil, I was hired to book the Tin Palace for the entire week. Then I got a chance to hear what I thought represented the best music available. It was also good to see the jazz audience of lay listeners and musicians, all of whom would arrive wherever it was claimed some swinging was going on. Those jazz people, from all over the world and almost all classes, were there to experience the revelations that result from improvisation when the groove arrives and the moment becomes pregnant, waiting for new life to be delivered by the musicians.

This experience is so strong that it can convert a staff that has never thought anything about jazz and is only happy to have a job in a joint where the pay is steady and the staff doesn't have to bend over or drop to its knees in order to get paid. Being in the presence of the music night after night made all of them connoisseurs much faster than I would have thought. That Tin Palace staff was a typical mix of Lower East Side types, from the aspirant long-haired rock star to the grotesquely voluminous Italian woman who amazed other women, first with her easy ability to move her tremendous girth, and second with her very handsome and devoted boyfriend. The owner loved to regale us with his decadent stories of great sex at Plato's Retreat but could be counted on to follow you into the street, ready to rumble or resort to hot lead if there was some obvious trouble that had to be moved outside, where it might be ended forever. One big black doorman had been done a favor by "the boys," who then demanded, as repayment, that he remain in their employ for the rest of his life, which also entailed doing uptown pickups of drug or numbers money. With a characteristically bitter look in his eye, he would offer tales of how he had seen "niggers uptown holler when they got shot, noisy as a fucking bitch having a baby."

Soon we had to turn away crowds and cabs were bringing people to the club who had said to the drivers that they were looking to hear some jazz. There were many extraordinary nights. A number of them took place when all of the customers were gone and only the staff, musicians, and insiders were there to hear the incredible raconteur and mimic we all knew as Philly Joe Jones. Jones was able to tell remarkable stories about himself and many musicians, could perfectly imitate the different accents of bobbies as opposed to upper-class Englishmen in tales about his life in London, and even explain how taken he was by Charles Wilcoxin, the writer of drum books. Jones had traveled to Wilcoxin's home in the Midwest and was put up in a little house so that every morning he and Wilcoxin could go through his latest book. I always imagined Philly Joe in a ribbed undershirt with his processed hair held inside of a handkerchief and Wilcoxin in a sweatshirt as the two of them went through those remarkable books of rudiments raised to the level of virtuoso études for the snare drum. However it actually went, those two men with their separate sticks and snare drums were the symbolic essence of the kinds of friendships and the camaraderie that come from the love of the art.

There were also wonderful nights of playing. One especially memorable performance took off around 2:00 a.m. The bandstand was crowded with musicians, all jamming in different styles on a blues, lifting up the bandstand and taking the listeners with them. It was an evening of pure steam and I remember little other than how startled I was to see Frank Wright—whom Philly Joe jokingly called "Frank Wrong"—standing up there fingering his tenor saxophone with a typical look of self-importance. (I was surprised because Wright was an arrogant incompetent who often talked himself up but stayed clear of bandstands where one had to know how to play. Yet Manhattan is what it is, and Frank Wright had his spirit broken by the fact that New York, unlike Europe, did not accept his squeaking and honking as "new music." People were not opposed to fresh ideas delivered with authority, but they were also no longer taken by the novelty of noise. On either that night or another, after the audience was gone, explaining to me how rough a customer he was, Wright had pulled a wooden handled Afro comb from his pocket. It had metal teeth that fit neatly into another piece of wood designed so that it looked harmless. It was not. "If they come up messing with me," Wright said, "I'll give them this," and suddenly smote the bar with the comb's naked teeth, which appeared at the speed of greased lightning. "Imagine if that was somebody's face," he said, with a quizzical snarl. Then, like a suddenly deflated balloon, the combative mask shriveled and Wright was hit with the dejected blues, wondering why no one liked his playing as he burst into tears, his nose stopping up and his voice rasping his trouble, almost sobbing that he was doing all he could do, that it was too late, that he didn't know how to do anything else.) The only other person I remember from that big late-night jam session was George Coleman, who then kept in shape by running track and bench-pressing many pounds at the gym. I believe Wright had created a lull in the jam session that was responded to by Coleman, who played twelve choruses, each in a different key. Big George illustrated what an actual master of the fundamentals could do, which was second nature to him. Coleman had played well through the cuttings and stabbings that he had seen at black dances while working as a big kid with B. B. King; he had brought grace to the high velocity experiments of Max Roach, and further proved himself during the extraordinary moments of great romance and express-train tempos he encountered in the Miles Davis Quintet, where he scaled rare balladic heights that were captured in performance on Davis's *My Funny Valentine*.

On other nights some of that exceptional jazz was created by giants like Philly Joe Jones and Billy Higgins, or surpassingly great individuals such as Coleman, Harold Mabern, Cedar Walton, Pharaoh Sanders, Clifford Jordan, Barry Harris, Dewey Redman, Gary Bartz, Kenny Barron, John Hicks, Arthur Blythe, Fred Hopkins, Steve McCall, Hilton Ruiz, and many others. Very little of it was what was called avant-garde because most of that music did not have or create the feeling of jazz. I was sure of that and, upon looking at the full rooms of jazz people, few associated with that movement approached me to hire them. Notable exceptions were Henry Threadgill, Jimmy Lyons, and the Revolutionary Ensemble.

When it wasn't inept or pretentious, most supposed avant-garde jazz was more an improvised version of European concert music. As such, it was often bathed and swaddled in rhetoric arriving from worlds as different as those of cultural anthropology, modernist aesthetics, and race politics. The basic argument was that artistic value was relative and that standards were not objective but rather contrived ways to both avoid embracing original expression and to also exclude "non-European" forms. For all that blather, there is no reason why someone should not play whatever he or she wants to play, but it seems to me that what gives an art its deepest identity is the quality of its dialogue with the past. The problem is not that a number of "avant-garde" musicians do not know the past, but that they do not *reimagine* it with enduring profundity as opposed to eccentricity.

One of the things that led me to that conclusion was that sometime during the late 1970s I noticed that I heard recordings of swinging or lyrical jazz played for pleasure by every vanguard musician whose home I visited. They loved it, but had not figured out how to reproduce that feeling in a new body of sound, which Charles Mingus, John Lewis, George Russell, Ornette Coleman, John Coltrane, and Miles Davis had done most brilliantly between the late fifties and middle sixties. Many things screwed up the development of the territories opened up by those frontiersmen. But, along the way, the sound of jazz kept replenishing itself through the art of dedicated players, many of whom this volume hopes to celebrate.

The musician who stands out most in my memory of all of those swinging nights I experienced in New York is Billy Higgins, whom I now consider the greatest drummer since 1960, and the symbolic hero of this book. Higgins did not innovate on the level that Elvin Jones, Tony Williams, and Ed

Blackwell did, but he had the greatest cymbal beat and the most flexible swing. When Higgins sat down, one realized that swing, at its essence, was the pulsation of good will. Higgins was so sympathetic to whomever he was playing with that he didn't impose his beat upon anyone else; he remained characteristically himself but played *their* interpretation of the beat. This is major, not minor. Most drummers and most players define themselves by the way they play the time, where they hear the entry point of every beat in a bar. Higgins was the freest of anyone I have ever heard. If you liked to play on the front of the beat, it was fine with him; if you preferred the middle, he could get with that; if you liked to lag in the caboose, he could get to that car and hang out all the way back there with you. The result was that he could swing with any bass player and support the individual pulse and rhythmic language of every featured player.

His precision was so refined that an arrogant and smart-alecky bassist who smirked while I was explaining this to him at the Jazz Standard one night suddenly changed his demeanor and became reverential at the mention of Higgins. He said, "[o]ne of the greatest moments of teaching in my life happened when Billy Higgins gave a master class at my college. He told us that you should be able to hear the four sixteenth notes that make up a beat and precisely adjust to any one of them. Yeah, well, that's easy to say. I'd like to see somebody do that. Well, Billy Higgins took a metronome and moved it over by a sixteenth of a beat four times and played his ride cymbal right there every time. He did it long enough so that we could hear exactly where he was. He could hear like that. Billy Higgins was about fitting in with everybody else." That he could make himself so compatible and remain such a great individual is the essence of the art of jazz.

Around 1980, I had given up the drums and devoted most of my time to being a writer. That decision had actually started forming while I was in California and the incredible Don Moye came to the Claremont Colleges and did a solo concert on which he exhibited so much mastery of African and jazz percussion that I was stunned, intimidated, and shaken. With Moye was Kunle Mwanga, a brilliant virtuoso of the music business who would bring the Art Ensemble of Chicago to New York, and would later manage David Murray, with whom he conceived some of the shrewdest presentations I have ever seen. He would then go on to represent Ornette Coleman. Mwanga, who recently began his memoir about life in the music business, should have many fresh things to tell us.

I began a friendship with Wynton Marsalis in 1980, when he was in the band of Art Blakey. Buster Williams had first told me about him one night at the Bottom Line. He said there was a kid down in New Orleans who was going to shake New York up when he got here. That was a rare statement from someone like Buster Williams, who had surely heard them come and heard them go. When I saw young Marsalis with Blakey, I thought his technique was sensational but I didn't hear that much jazz in what he was playing. He seemed to be cocky when we met, but that didn't bother me—in New York, who isn't? He also appeared to have more than average intelligence, which interested me.

I invited him to dinner at my house and discovered that he did not know much about Louis Armstrong, Thelonious Monk, Ornette Coleman, or Duke Ellington. When I played a Coleman record for him, "Bird Food," he said, "I never heard Charlie Parker play like that." That was how it began.

As we continued to talk, Marsalis showed genuine interest in understanding things about jazz that he did not know. So I loaned him a number of those recordings, gave him a copy of *Stomping the Blues*, which he read quickly and considered the most sophisticated thinking he had ever encountered about jazz as an aesthetic phenomenon. I introduced him to Albert Murray and Ralph Ellison, with both of whom the two of us had some gargantuan conversations, good food, and big laughs. We were never with the two men at the same time because, by then, Ellison had become angry at Murray and an icy distance set in that didn't thaw out until Murray went into the hospital for a back operation and picked up the phone while recuperating to hear the voice of his old buddy inquiring as to how he felt and how he was doing. No matter, Marsalis absorbed everything that came his way at the pace with which the especially talented learn.

As he developed his vision, Marsalis took a position against—with the exceptions of Ornette Coleman, Don Cherry, Dewey Redman, and Bobby Bradford—most of what was considered avant-garde jazz because it reminded him too much of the twentieth-century concert music he had played in orchestras under the batons of men like Gunther Schuller. Marsalis took his direction from Pablo Picasso, who had impressed him by investigating extreme abstraction during his cubist period. But, instead of staying on that road and leaving the life of the world behind, the greatest of twentieth-century artists had returned to his grand battle with form, using what he discovered to intensify his peerlessly diverse investigation of the fundamental themes of the portrait, the still life, the bullfight, dancers on the beach, artist and model, and so on. Marsalis concluded that, if an artist embraced the scientific and technological model of constant innovation as opposed to continually reimagining the basics as Picasso and Ellington had done, there was great danger ahead, which was what he thought that most European music after Béla Bartók had not avoided. From studying their interviews and talking with them, Marsalis decided that, unlike the generation that preceded the bebop development of World War II, the beboppers began to take seriously what was written and said about their art in ways that Armstrong, Hawkins, Ellington, and the others never had. This led some to believe that they had to "keep up" with the developments in European music instead of creatively building upon the legacy of melody, harmony, timbre, and rhythm that individuated jazz in so many styles and specific approaches. This was not a neoconservative vision as his detractors came to assert over and over: It was radical in that Marsalis went on to produce the broadest interpretation of his idiom since Charles Mingus, who also rejected the bulk of music that came after Ornette Coleman because he could not abide by the narrowness of its scope and the frequent incompetence of its practitioners.

As far as the contemporary antics of jazz musicians were concerned, Marsalis also stood up against the fusion or jazz-rock that had as its godhead Miles Davis. When he was interested in jazz, Davis had done so much for musicians that, even when he had abandoned jazz in favor of pop trends, it was such a no-no to talk against him that I recall one night in the Vanguard when a big saxophonist started to grab Marsalis because the upstart trumpeter would not accept *any* version of the idea that it was okay to lay out the stuff that Davis was playing because the former innovator was just reacting to the fact that black musicians never made any money. I was drinking a bottle of Heineken and seriously thought I was going to have to break it in the face of the saxophone player, but he calmed down and everything became almost mellow until Marsalis bent the minds of the musicians by saying that one had to take on the challenge of the greatest musicians in one's idiom, which was why Beethoven couldn't avoid the counterpoint that Bach had done better than anyone. If never before, I realized on that night that this young man truly saw no real difference between the demands facing those substantially engaged with European concert music and the ones arrayed before jazz musicians. This was also made more impressive because, unlike most who dismiss the sheer weight of accumulated artistry in European concert music, he was already one of the two or three greatest exponents of it on his instrument, a fact that impressed Ellison much more than it did Murray.

Ellison seemed to think that Marsalis could have left jazz behind him, while Murray thought that jazz could do no better than to have a world-class virtuoso who addressed the entire sweep of the music, from New Orleans to the present, and who could make academic contributions as well. Though I agree with Murray, I still have more value for Ellison's aesthetic achievements than I do his, as brilliant and heroically broad as his thinking about art might be. Even though Ellison wrote only two books of essays after his single novel, he was first and foremost an artist, while Murray, as all of his books and three of his four novels prove, is far more important and substantial as a thinker than he is as an artist. But perhaps I came to that conclusion because Ellison seemed to find it easier to address the tragedy at the center of life than Murray, who could talk about it in his essays but contrived grand—perhaps innovative—ways to avoid it in most of his fiction. I always put my money on the tragedian because, as Bessie Jones of the Georgia Sea Island Singers once said after asking an audience if anyone knew what it meant to be born, "All being born means is that you're going to die." As I once told Saul Bellow, whom I met through Ellison at the National Book Awards, that's as basic a sense of existentialism as any I've ever heard. Bellow was startled by its directness and thought it was pretty good, too.

One afternoon in the early eighties, as Marsalis and I were riding somewhere and rolling up the highway ramp close to the Waterside Towers near 23rd Street on the east side of New York, he said to me that if jazz ever had the essential support system of teachers who could really pass on the technical fundamentals of the aesthetic as well as Murray had laid them out conceptually in *Stomping the Blues*, and if they could also provide situations in which high school students would compete the way they do in European concert music, things would greatly improve for the music in a very short period of time. I thought that was an interesting idea but assumed that it had as much of a chance as a publicly declared Jew had of rising to the top of the Third Reich. But sometimes the darkness is only a blindfold that maintains power until dawn.

In 1987, Alina Bloomgarden, director of Visitor's Services at Lincoln Center, Marsalis, and I met because Bloomgarden wanted to start a series of summer concerts at Lincoln Center. Bloomgarden had done volunteer work at Barry Harris's Jazz Cultural Theater and was inspired by what she saw. This enthusiasm pushed her to meet with Nathan Leventhal, the president of Lincoln Center. At Bloomgarden's urging, Leventhal agreed to set aside the budget necessary to produce the summer series of jazz concerts.

Those concerts were so successful that they eventually grew into the department known as Jazz at Lincoln Center. That did not come out of nowhere. The suave Gordon Davis, a lawyer who had been a city commissioner and was then on the board of Lincoln Center, had the bright idea that the jazz series could—and should—become something much bigger than an annual summer event. From there, things began to build to the unprecedented point that the jazz program became a fully equal constituent with the other components of Lincoln Center—the New York Philharmonic, the Metropolitan Opera, New York City Ballet, and the Film Society of Lincoln Center. The air up there was very thin and the lungs of a program could give out if it wasn't ready. But Jazz at Lincoln Center made it.

The next step was to have a hall built that would, to Marsalis's specifications, be the first designed with the sound of jazz in mind. This had been a dream of his after playing the great opera halls in Europe, where the sound was superior to any concert halls he had played in America. What if an architect could be found who would design a performance space for jazz that was on the level of an opera house? Though it seemed barely possible, it was the right time to hold onto that high-minded dream. The old New York Coliseum in Columbus Circle was to be torn down and that real estate became the most competed for in the city. Licked chops were flying everywhere, and we had to see if we could get jazz up in there.

Rudolph Giuliani was in charge of it all, but Jazz at Lincoln Center got no response to its proposal for a hall or even a return of a single phone call. The word was that Giuliani wanted another opera house built in Columbus Circle. So Rudy did not seem interested. But there was a man in the mix who had been on a task force appointed by Giuliani to investigate police and community relations in the wake of a scandalous example of sadistic police force in Brooklyn. I had gotten along with Giuliani while on that task force, so I called his office and set up an appointment to talk with him. His press liaison was Christine Lategano, who sat in on the meeting.

Giuliani and I began by tossing around jokes about his thinning hair, his son, the Yankees, and the politicians in Albany who were always trying to give New York so much less than it deserved. After some laughs, he paused, as if to say, "You're on." I then said to him that the concerts, lectures, and film presentations of Jazz at Lincoln Center formed an innovation in American culture. He replied by saying that he thought Wynton Marsalis was doing a marvelous job in every way. I couldn't think of anything else to prepare the pitch, so I just went straight for it. I said that if Jazz at Lincoln Center got a space to build a hall in Columbus Circle, New York would have the very first place in the entire world that was built specifically for jazz. It would be an innovation in world culture. Giuliani leaned back in his chair, looked around, then sat forward with a hard twinkle in his eye. "It would also be one of my legacies to the city of New York, wouldn't it?" "Of course," I responded. The mayor then told Christine Lategano to call in the guy who had the plans from Lincoln Center. It was on.

Since 1987, what began with three people meeting to discuss putting on annual summer jazz concerts at Lincoln Center has grown far beyond what any one of us would have thought possible. Jazz at Lincoln Center has produced over 850 original concerts in the New York City area. It has produced over thirty-five tours featuring the Lincoln Center Jazz Orchestra, the Afro-Latin Jazz Orchestra, and other ensembles that have reached over three hundred cities in thirty-five countries on five continents. It has featured over 850 musicians; commissioned compositions and arrangements by over forty musicians; sent over fifty thousand copies of sixty previously unavailable Duke Ellington scores to over thirty-five hundred schools through the Essentially Ellington High School Jazz Band Competition and Festival; produced educational programs that have reached over five hundred thousand students, educators, and members of the general public; and produced more than 160 hours of the Peabody Award-winning Jazz From Lincoln Center radio program, hosted by Ed Bradley and broadcasted nationwide. The Lincoln Center Jazz Orchestra has collaborated on concerts with more than a dozen symphony orchestras around the world as well as a flamenco dance company and an African drum and dance ensemble. Beyond that, Jazz at Lincoln Center has collaborated in productions with more than forty arts organizations, music programs, and centers for the performing arts. I am more proud to have been involved with it than anything I have given my support to since my volunteer efforts for those in Los Angeles who were working to sustain the civil rights movement more than forty years ago.

Throughout everything that I have done in Manhattan since 1975, much of which falls outside of music, I have maintained my love for the unsurpassed variety of that inimitable sound, and have continued to evolve an ever-deeper feeling for what distinguishes it and how jazz became the uniquely great art form that it continues to be. This volume will take you across a wide territory of aesthetic thought, performance reviews, obituaries, battle royals, and an out-chorus in which I take the position that blues, in the swinging version we call jazz, is for today and for tomorrow and for all of us who have a need for that very special feeling of jazz, especially when it is elevated to the position of shining aesthetic order.

THE MAKERS

Miles Davis in the
Fever of Spring, 1961

I wear Brooks clothes and white shoes all the time
I wear Brooks clothes and white shoes all the time
Get three C's a D and think checks from home sublime

I don't keep dogs or women in my room
But I love my Vincent baby until the day of doom

Rhinehart, Rhinehart, I'm a most indifferent guy
Rhinehart, Rhinehart, I'm a most indifferent guy
But I love my Vincent, baby, that's no Harvard lie
  —"Harvard Blues"

So much was behind him on the Manhattan night of May 19 when he walked on that world-famous stage in 1961 and heard the applause of a full house. The audience was about half black and half white, ranging from sidewalk types to high society in the close rows and the boxes. What happened is now on *Miles Davis at Carnegie Hall*, the double compact disc containing the first full release of all the material played on that evening in its exact sequence. A signal moment in jazz took place, one in which so many aspects of American culture, stardom, personality, politics, and ethnic complexity were put on display or implied. The evening was a benefit for the Flying Doctors of East Africa, a humanitarian organization founded in 1957 by three plastic surgeons, one American and two British. Based in Kenya, the Flying Doctors provided medical assistance, surgery, and training to populations suffering from disease, deformities, and wounds brought about by accidents or violence. Outside the concert hall was an ambulance, newly purchased for the organization, that those attending the benefit could see and examine.

During that first spring of the youthful and doomed Jack Kennedy administration, there was a national feeling of invincible optimism undercut by the shock and despair that came from the country witnessing the barbaric Southern responses to the Civil Rights Movement, which was perceived by some Negroes as no more than one aspect of an international problem with race and colonialism that connected all black people. In that context, Davis would sum up all that had happened for him since he had made his comeback from drug addiction at the Newport Jazz Festival in 1955, perhaps all that had happened since he had begun playing with Charlie Parker ten years before that.

Now was his time, nobody else's. The trumpeter was ahead of the curve, holding a position that was much larger than the sound of anybody's music. His attire was under as much awed scrutiny as the notes he chose to play. He had been setting styles among Negro musicians and others for at least six years, defining what was hip and what was not. Philadelphia drummer Rashied Ali remembered how an album cover of the middle fifties with Davis in seersucker jacket, no shirt, and cap had kicked off a trend. Trumpeter Ted Curson observed how musicians laughed at white buck shoes until Davis wore a pair and let them know that those, too, were theirs for the having. Opening the way was his business. The attitude with which he carried himself, a chastening kind of arrogance, exuded something that made it possible for him, as trumpeter Bill Dixon recalled, to enter and change the context of a room as thoroughly as did Duke Ellington and Thelonious Monk, two other Negro men whose power took on a palpable condition in the atmosphere as soon as they came through the door. Davis didn't announce songs and he never seemed too happy to be *anywhere*. Geniality was verboten. Were his attitude reduced to one question, it would have been, "So?"

Some speculated that the nastiness of his attitude had been picked up from his hanging around with the dismissive and monumentally egotistical Sugar Ray Robinson, the greatest prizefighter of all time and one of the champion boxers who might be seen in the audience on any of the nights when the pugs decided to go downtown and hear their buddy blow his horn. Davis was surely quite impressed by Robinson's public demeanor, which was low-keyed, articulate, and matter-of-fact, even playful. Yet he was never caught wiping shit off his imperial grin. There was not the slightest hint of inferiority or intimidation in his manner. Quite the reverse: He was a king among men. The fighter was also highly regarded in the world of sports and show business for his powers as a negotiator of contracts; his smoothness, the fact that he demanded percentages of gates and the profits from radio and television or—with the fans in the seats and ready for the battle to start—Robinson would sit in the dressing room still in his street clothes ready to go home if the promoters didn't bend his way and put up some more money.

Robinson owned a number of businesses in Harlem, and one of them, Sugar Ray's, was the hottest bar uptown, where every black somebody who was *truly* somebody came to drink, talk, and be inside the black rhythm on its hippest tip. When the great boxer walked into his club, everything went his way and the energy shifted because the emperor of the evening had brought greater power to the night. Miles Davis noticed that, just as he had seen it with Charlie Parker and Duke Ellington. On an athletic level, the trumpeter so admired pugilists that he studied the high art of fisticuffs among them, loving the various punching bags as well as the jabs, punches, and feints that training gave destructive accuracy. He eventually had a boxing gym built in the basement of his home. There was sophistication in his soul and a taste for blood.

This small man with the big influence, he who would turn his back on his audience and walk off stage, gave the impression that the conventions of the entertainment business had never entered his mind and evolved into his own Sugar Ray. When sustained attention came his way, Davis was ready to hold power over others. He did this in a number of ways and for a number of reasons. Davis used his rasp of a voice at such a low volume that people had to pay close attention to understand what he was saying. They had to lean into a land of whispers. He made anybody, black or white, feel that nothing about him or her was automatically important or worthy of respect. You could be treated like mud no matter who you were. Yet another part of the awe musicians felt for him came from the fact that Davis had, as Dizzy Gillespie observed, revolutionized working conditions when he forced club owners to accept three sets a night, not the forty minutes on and twenty minutes off that began either at nine or ten and continued until closing time, which could be, in Manhattan, four 'o clock in the morning. The silly kinds of album covers art directors conceived with no images of Negroes weren't for him and he made this obvious when the cover of "Someday My Prince Will Come" had a head shot of his wife, Frances Taylor, a golden, big-eyed Negro beauty. Musicians had deep respect for his highly intelligent sense of overall musical engagement, which brooked no racial lines and went far outside of jazz in pursuit of scales and forms he could adapt to his music. One musician recalled noticing two things:

Miles was always surrounded by a lot of white people whenever I went over his house. They were giving him music and he was analyzing it with them. Once, now, I walked in on him talking to them whities and his voice was straight and normal, just like anybody. Loud. I heard it! Then when he saw me, he went back down into that frog voice everybody was used to. He thought that was hip. Made him seem like a gangster or something. That wasn't all of it either, I found out that another thing he was doing was he would be hanging with Gunther Schuller, John Lewis, and George Russell. They would be looking into some different stuff and discussing another whole level of music. These guys were into conceptions, not just how to play some hip notes on some chords everybody else played. Miles, John, and George, those Negroes were standing toe to toe with them whities, *intellectually*, and they were bringing home some *serious* bacon.

As handsome, jet-black matinee idol, the trumpeter was also—along with Nat Cole and Sidney Poitier—breaking down the color restrictions of sex appeal among Negroes and whites. He stood shoulder to shoulder on the plane of pretty boys with Billy Eckstine or Harry Belafonte, each the traditional, light-skinned version of an attractive Negro, a heartthrob palatable to the white and the black. Now, with cool Miles Davis, an extra look was added to those that raised bushfires below the navels of American women. The skin tone yoke of "if you're white you're all right; if you're brown stick around; if you're black stay back," was slipping off. To those yellow-loving Negro women who once said of men his color: "I've already got me one shadow, I don't need two," Miles Davis was starting to seem kind of sexy. Black motherfucker. For the white women, rich and famous, or rich and unknown, or just pretty and curious, or not pretty but still attracted, the black guy with the trumpet and the dark glasses became an embodiment of the primitive and the cultivated in one package. That stuff crosses the street: There is also the fact that extremely dark Negroes with superior abilities can put the white and the black under a spell, each group feeling that it is in the presence of something aboriginal. Wow-wow from back before way back. That, too, worked for cool Miles Davis. Oh, he had it going on.

His trumpet style, as deeply steeped in the Negro tradition as possible, was all his own, a cool mist or blast of blue flame full of insinuation, sensuality, remorse, and melancholy. That style was not the sound of a man walking on eggshells, as someone had described it. Saxophonist Jackie McLean reckons it more to that of a man sitting on a slowly floating block of ice at the North Pole, encircled by nothing but water as far as the eye can see, and unflinchingly telling his Harmon-muted story and the story of all he knows. Whatever the image his sound inspired, by 1961 Columbia Records, in its ads and through its record club, had promoted him in such a way that one could not feel *truly* sophisticated unless a recording or two of his work was in the collection. Moody and romantic, sailing up over the beat of his subtle to extremely swinging small group, or expanding the emotional range of his art in concerto situations devised by the trumpeter in conjunction with Gil Evans, the Miles Davis horn not only helped define the very best of American life; it helped purify our conception of what quality was possible within the arena of the popular. In that respect, he was a miniature Duke Ellington of his moment.

Though born in 1926 and but a week shy of his thirty-fifth birthday on that May night at Carnegie Hall, Davis had the knowledge of a man much older than he actually was. He had come up the privileged way and he had come up the hard way. His father was a quite-well-to-do dentist in East St. Louis and a gentleman farmer who raised prizewinning swine. The high life and the low life were equally familiar to the trumpeter and he now had democratic contempt for the pale, blue-veined wealthy who thought some line back to the *Mayflower* kept them from being sad, boring, pompous, unwitty pains in the booty; he had disdain for the immigrants who ran show business: and there was nothing in his heart but a feeling of rancor toward those Negroes struggling below who had allowed dissipation to tear them down from the proud glory of their talent.

In New York, Davis had learned about the lack of communication, the decadence, and the perversion that attended more than enough of the long-term wealthy and the nouveau riche. He looked somewhat askance when they appeared around him. Given his complexity, there was still an ease he had always shown toward these people, from the forties forward, when he might talk with them about horses, golf, hunting, the latest fashions for men and women, as well as the various painters and sculptors who were at the centers of discussion when the innovations of the century came into the conversation. Inky, as he was sometimes called by those Negroes ready to chide him, knew how to make the upper-class white people look up to him. The trumpeter was far from an anti-Semite or a bigot of any sort, but Davis knew that if America weren't so racist, Jewish entrepreneurs wouldn't have been able to corner so much of the market and move back and forth between the darkies in the basement and the white folks in the office buildings that nearly touched the sky. The Negro provided the fault

line that allowed plenty of despised Europeans of whatever religious backgrounds to stand in with the white crowd, to even carry themselves as
though they knew more about the United States than black Americans and
could serve as their guides into the greater society. They could kiss his ass
at high noon on the steps of City Hall. He enjoyed frustrating them and
playing hard to get, negotiating with the same sort of toughness Sugar Ray
was known for, letting it be known that he didn't really enjoy performing
that much and wanted to stay off the scene in order to investigate his other
interests. If there was going to be any begging connected to gigs, it wasn't
going to be on his part.

Once a shameless heroin addict himself, Davis would use the harshest
terms to describe those still pinned to the cotton by syringes. They were
barely above filth, even if they were his friends. He could knowingly describe to outsiders exactly how drug deals went down on the Manhattan
avenues where the dope was bought and the dope was sold. Anytime some
friend who was still tied up came by his swank home and borrowed money
for heroin, Davis would note "for drugs" on the remaining stub after writing the check and tearing it out of its book. The trumpeter became so opposed to anything pharmaceutical that he boasted of not even using as-
pirin. But every now and then he wavered and the neighborhood druggist
had to slip him some pills to handle his troubles. According to Philly Joe
Jones, Davis's drummer in the classic quintet of the fifties, the band-leader
would, here and there, use some heroin. After throwing up like a beginner,
Davis would go up on the bandstand and, emboldened by the drug, take
chances of a taller order than usual, bringing them off only because he had
done all the laborious technical homework necessary to capture and give
compelling logic to a spontaneous and formidable fantasy. Nothing, however, took him off of the career path he was on once he got a true sense of
where he wanted to go.

By the late fifties, polish and the good life were essentially what he was
after, but Davis had no intention of automatically accepting anybody else's
definition of what either of those two things meant. Clothes, food, cars,
and whatever else went with feeling the sheen of absorbed quality just
under the skin were what he wanted, first and foremost, when he wasn't
only obsessing over extending his musical abilities. Davis was a gourmet
cook who lived on the Upper West Side of Manhattan and would instruct
the women in his building on just how to prepare succulent meals, step by
step. If they got in jams, his door would either be knocked on in a panic or
he would get a frantic phone call. Then, in his signal rasp, the trumpeter

would talk them through the culinary crisis. Once, when preparing his legendary chili, Davis realized that something was wrong; it didn't yet have that perfect taste. Eventually, he took two teaspoons of water from the tap, stirred them in, tasted the chili, and announced to his friends that the offering had now crossed into the territory of the delicious. Davis had begun driving sports cars during the middle fifties after walking past a showroom window and seeing one of the small automobiles conspiratorially winking at him. The trumpeter stopped, paused, turned around, and saw, once more, the car wink. He knew then that there was no choice other than to buy it. What else could he do? The car wanted *him*.

At least that was what he told his friend Jean Bach, a beauty of the Grace Kelly visual strain who had been running around with Negroes and anybody else she damn well pleased for almost twenty years. Her sweet man as the Depression wound down was the musically combative trumpet giant Roy Eldridge. She rode around Chicago with the medium-brown, slick-haired bantam flamethrower in his car when such things certainly were not done by upper-class cutie pies groomed for positions of significance in what was then the certified, snow-white aristocracy of this land. Bach, a Vassar girl from Chicago, was also palsy with Duke Ellington and knew her way around the Manhattan she had migrated to and in which she found her own success in radio. She was an insider when she started to learn the ways of Davis in the middle fifties.

"Miles was very different from other jazz musicians I knew," Bach recalls. "When I met him at a party in Boston, he surprised me because he was such a good dancer. Very, very good. He knew all of the steps and was very graceful. This guy didn't step on your feet and stagger around. Oh, no. Completely at ease on the ballroom floor. Most musicians can't dance, of course, but he sure could. Miles knew how to lead and all he wanted to talk about at the time was Grace Kelly. He was fascinated by her, which might have been one of the reasons why we became close. I believe he liked my look and I was from that kind of background.

"His own look was very important and he explained to me that because he was very dark he picked all of his clothes quite carefully. He never wore white dress shirts, for instance, only off-whites, like eggshell and different shades of blue that complemented his skin. Details were important to him. Some of them were odd and some of them weren't. His star was on the rise and he had an absolutely charming balance of the cocky and the elfish in his humor. The things he would say. Oh, he was just such an *imp*. He wasn't funny; he was witty. But his wit could put you on the floor, I tell you. There was always an unusual angle to what he said and what he saw. He was sort of a handsome leprechaun. Small, beautifully built, and full of mischief. Things were panning out for him and he intended to enjoy himself. But there was always this kind of sadness about him. It was there and very penetrating. You knew he had been hurt by something or was sunk in some kind of deep melancholy. Miles could withdraw into his sadness and it could seem as if he wouldn't be able to come out of it. His unhappiness could trap him and hold him down. It really could. Depression was one of his struggles."

Davis was also struggling with his dislike of women, which began with his mother, whom he almost never brought into a conversation with Bach for any purpose other than to make fun of, or to serve as the wicked queen at the center of some bitter anecdote from his childhood. He wasn't very thrilled by black women and made them the butts of jokes for their lack of education or their bad taste or their huffy pretension or their provincialism or their palatial rumps. One Negro woman thrown out of his house nude and covered with cigarette burns made her way into the acidic cup of gossip that was passed around during those years. White women could be criticized for their hair clogging up the drain in his bathroom. In one case, after he had visited a young white woman in the hospital, reading Paul Lawrence Dunbar and James Baldwin aloud so she could get an equal black dose of rural and city feeling, her miscarriage of the child she carried by Davis was described as a clear example of her ineptitude: "Oh, she can never do *anything* right."

Conversely, there could be no more courtly man and no one more capable of expressing transcendent romantic emotion through his horn. As trumpeter Freddie Hubbard recalls: "That Negro was slick harmonically. He caught something playing with Bird. Charlie Parker taught him something. He learned it and he *edited* it. There was some hip, inside-the-chord stuff he worked out that let him make his statement with less notes. Then he had a *tone*. You hear me: a *tone*. It could touch anybody but it could do something different to women. Miles would hit a low note with that Harmon mute in his horn and the girls would move their legs like they had just got too hot to keep their thighs together."

Davis began learning from Charlie Parker when he was working on 52nd Street with him in the middle forties. The trumpeter had arrived in 1944 from East St. Louis with a suitcase of Brooks Brothers suits and plans to study at Juilliard and in the streets of jazz. Charlie Parker was the man Davis sought and he spent his first weeks in town looking for the alto saxophonist. Davis had heard Parker when he came through St. Louis with singer Billy Eckstine's band, which had needed a substitute trumpet player and hired the dark young man. In that band a new music was in the process of being made. It was soon known as bebop or rebop or bop. The style was far more intricate than normal and its texture was leaner, even abrasive, devoid of the lush vibrato that distinguished earlier schools. Essentially, Parker was its fountainhead. He was a phenomenon possessed of such magical muscle memory that he could teach his body to do almost anything at extreme velocities—throw with great accuracy, shoot pool, play golf, do card and coin tricks, assume very difficult yoga positions. That ability had allowed him to learn the saxophone far faster than even his legend had it. At seventeen, in 1937, he could barely play at all. In three years, he was a top-flight young alto player. In seven years, his abilities made the majority of jazz saxophone players want to hide under the bed. Davis knew from the first time that he heard Parker what kind of playing he wanted to do himself. He was equally taken by Dizzy Gillespie, who was the organizer of the style and a trumpet virtuoso to end virtuosi in jazz. While his tone was thin, Gillespie played with such slithering rhythmic daring and harmonic complexity that he, like Parker, redefined his instrument. Gillespie, who would one day look like a wind demon with his enormously puffed-out cheeks, also taught those anxious to know just how to play the new bebop style, including not only the brass and reed players but also the piano players, the bass players, the drummers. Parker had the language but Gillespie ran the homemade conservatory.

Davis found Parker in Harlem that fall of 1944. He was ragged and homeless, high on heroin, but always ready to live life his way, which came down to two words: *me first*. They roomed together for a bit and Davis studied what Parker and Gillespie did while taking classes at Juilliard. Sometimes, when the music coming from the many clubs on 52nd Street was at an end, he and the trombonist J. J. Johnson would sit in Grand Central Station and study the scores of twentieth-century composers that Davis had gotten from Juilliard's music library—Stravinsky, Ravel, Debussy, Bartok. That intellectual curiosity never left him. At the time, as Vernon Davis remembers his brother, "Miles was like Jack Armstrong on the radio, the All-American boy. He was sweet as pie. Do anything for you. My brother was cocky now. He got that on his *own*, not from my daddy, not from my mother, not from *anybody*. That came with him; that was his own thing. But he was still the sweetest kind of boy. Charlie Parker, New York, women, and all those kinds of things changed that over the years."

In essence, the 1944 Davis was then a country boy and would remain so for the rest of his life—regardless of how much he came to know, both intimately and conceptually. He was also another of the many spoiled, middle-class Negroes who had brought so much to jazz and had long been battering the one-dimensional stereotype of the impoverished, barefooted darkie wailing his woes from behind a stack of cotton bales. Duke Ellington, Coleman Hawkins, and Fletcher Henderson were men of his ilk, innovators all, each reared in comfort and thoroughly modern in taste and deportment. Davis, whose grandfather on his mother's side was an American Indian who wore his hair in two long braids, had been served by a maid in his father's Southern-style mansion on two hundred acres, where he learned to ride horses, fish, and hunt.

For all that, the ethnic skin game still revealed itself. As Vernon Davis recalls: "We lived in those times when it was all crazy. It was supposed to be segregated, but that was some shit. In the Negro school named after Abraham Lincoln we already had integration, you know. We had the blondes and the redheads and the ones with the blue eyes and the green eyes and the hazel eyes and the hair running all the way down their back and that sort of thing. They weren't considered white because they had people who looked like us in their families *some*place. So in the white schools, you had just white people. But *we*, you understand, had *everybody*. Once you saw all of that and you met people in your family looked as white as anybody in the movies, you knew this whole thing was fake. Color didn't mean anything. My brother didn't need to get to New York to find out a damn thing about that. He liked who you were. He didn't care what color you were. Miles didn't look up to you or to look down on you. You had to show him something. Then he made up his mind whether the two of you could hang out or you could go to hell."

In the bandstand sweatshop of high-velocity music-making that Charlie Parker preferred, the world swiftly moving by in glinting details, Davis got his first New York notice, sometimes struggling with the music, eventually finding his own way to fill in all the spaces. But he was soon looking for something of his own to play, a compressed breather from the cascading triplets that characterized Parker and his followers, no matter their instruments. Lester Young, Billie Holiday, and Louis Armstrong gave him strong clues. Each of them were whittlers. They cut things down and they sailed. Their music was whimsical, melancholy, spiritually weather-beaten, full of brave and gutter humor but, finally, dreamy and majestic in a decided manner. Davis liked what they did and learned from Thelonious Monk how to use stark materials that could, in their simplicity, create an inverse kind of dissonance against complex chords. If, as saxophonist, bandleader, and scholar Loren Shoenberg observes, the harmony itself is harsh, then a direct consonant melodic invention is dissonant. Uh oh.

His own first recording date as a leader, in 1947, used Parker on tenor, and Davis was heard moving in his own smooth direction. He was also in the process of working out what would become known as "cool jazz," an approach to sound that seemed "white" to a number of Negro musicians but, in its most popularized and deracinated version, might best be called suburban, soft and fluffy, rather light and flat in the ass. With a short-lived nine-piece band that used the tuba and the French horn, Davis helped spread into greater prominence the clouds of color that were identifiably central to the work of the white bandleader Claude Thornhill. The nonet used those musical tints and textures with what the trumpeter had learned from Parker and Gillespie. In that sense, the importance of what Davis was doing had a meaning beyond the notes that were being written, harmonized, and improvised.

The whole effort symbolized an interracial cooperation that had no real precedent in jazz history. White musicians had been influenced by many black musicians and Negroes had been influenced by a few white musicians; they had all jammed together on hundreds upon hundreds of nights; beginning with Benny Goodman's Quartet, featuring Lionel Hampton and Teddy Wilson, they had started working together in public; but close collaboration of the sort Davis and John Lewis had with Gerry Mulligan, Gil Evans, and Johnny Carisi had not happened before. Black and white musicians tended to pick up from each other what they picked up, or Negroes ghost-wrote material for white bands or, like impassioned extras, supplied "hot" features in white bands. The mutual attempt to consciously draw upon the evolving blues- and swing-based Negro American tradition as well as the art music of Europe was new; it was a kind of integration devoutly to be wished by many Americans, in and out of music.

Since Davis had gone to Juilliard, it was quite understandable that such a possibility would mean something to him. What he in particular sought was the sciously urbane, which, as Negro men like Benny Carter and Ellington had proven, could cross all lines of ethnicity and class. The goal was the profoundly sophisticated as opposed to the highly polished but depthless. Then a vital understanding of the rough-and-tumble streets could artistically coexist with the more subtle, the less obvious, the view from the top of the park, thus creating a much broader palette of human expression. This was equally symbolized by Negroes such as Billy Eckstine crossing over into the territory of the romantic balladeer, which had once been the exclusive domain of the alabaster pink-faced matinee idol, so much so that white record producers usually spurned the idea of Afro-American men singing anything other than the blues.

In "the quarter of the Negroes," as Langston Hughes called it, being "cool, calm, and collected" was also a form of protest against the rough and the unready, not only in racial terms but in the terms of living life itself. It rejected the overheated and the hysterical. For Negroes, cool had a very special aspect of ambitious rejection. It meant, when most realized, having the ability and the inclination to whip out the down-home grinds and bumps and all of their steamy traces at the drop of a hat, but the equal ability to move on out beyond the uneducated and the vociferous, lifting off free of the minstrel mask and the brutal, anti-intellectual elements Americans of all colors always found themselves threatened by, from within and from without. Cool in being and cool in music were about the Negro making off with what James Baldwin called "the sacred fire," the differentiations of flame that warmed the cultural penthouses of Western civilization as opposed to the oil drums full of flickering trash before which those without a clue to the broader doings of life warmed themselves. But in the hands of the least imaginative, the low-keyed style was the Lester Young extension drained free of the blues. As things may happen, the cool movement soon supplanted the biting complexity heard in one side of Parker and Gillespie. Correctly called "pipe-and-slippers jazz" by Gerry Mulligan himself, that kind of cool approach moved as far as possible from the feeling of the Negro and turned the tables on those who had measured the art by its heat, its rocking or sensually delicious swing, its updated Elizabethan depths of emotion. To know the white will of cool jazz at its fullest was to know a wisp.

Oddly, Davis was soon bumped out of something he had helped start and was scrounging around New York looking for dope. When he got jobs he was often too high to play as well as he could and he began to look the part of the addict, so much so that Billy Eckstine, as Jackie McLean remembers, once took Davis off the street and gave him a beautiful overcoat to replace the smudged and filthy one he was wearing. At that time in the early fifties, Davis was getting with the Harlem Sugar Hill crowd that included McLean, Sonny Rollins, and Art Taylor, all fellow talents, all fellow addicts, all destined to make their names known and respected. He was ascending in the music though sinking in his life. Swinging hard was on the trumpeter's mind but contrasted with a pliant lyricism. He wanted to bring the burning and the soothing together. All he had to do was get off the drugs and something strong would start to rise up out of him. But those years of drug addiction were quite a battle. The whole trouble with heroin began shortly after he returned to New York from a brief but successful trip to Paris in 1949 and found himself unemployed, bored, and frustrated. Since he couldn't free himself of the dope, one wealthy white woman from Detroit got him a psychiatrist, which didn't work. Nothing did the job until the trumpeter had been shamed, when his father made it clear that he knew his son was on drugs. Then, on a visit to his father's house, the trumpeter went through withdrawal, later telling Jean Bach that his entire body felt the way he did when his foot went to sleep: The sensation was a convergence of numbness and pins and needles.

By 1954, as Davis liberated himself from the hook of heroin addiction, he became the insider's truest post–bop trumpet player. Dizzy Gillespie was then less concerned with first-class bands and had expanded the entertainment side of his presentation, though he and Davis both did in Chet Baker when the dark blond supposed-wonder from the West Coast was brought to New York. Baker got top billing at Birdland over Gillespie one week and over Davis the next. Musically speaking, the two put the white hope's head in a bag and turned the bag flat, red, and sticky. Davis was especially angry because he saw Baker, whom he had so heavily influenced, as no more than another example of how some white guy could bite a chunk out of the neck of a Negro's style and set up residence in the bank, the blood from the chunk of meat in his mouth dripping a puddle that turned to gold at his feet. Downtown in 1956 at the Cafe Bohemia in Greenwich Village, Davis told one Harlem friend over drinks at the bar that he intended to "bust all of this up. Miles said that they had stopped him as long as they could and now he was coming for their ass and coming with his own kind of thunder." That might explain his unpredictable attitude toward white musicians. He could talk of Gil Evans as his best friend but might, given his mood, ask a white musician wanting to sit in with him, "Do you see anybody up here who looks like you?" When Stan Getz headed for his bandstand, Davis would tell this great player to leave or he would call Sonny Stitt in order to make sure that his ass got eaten up. These sorts of things made him aloof and caused white musicians and writers to feel they had achieved a victory if Davis spoke to them or gave the indication that he had any respect for what they did. Where Negro musicians had traditionally been accessible, Miles Dewey Davis was not.

In 1955, at the Newport Jazz Festival, Davis had made what was considered a comeback. It actually was not, since the trumpeter was getting very good reviews for public performances in 1954 and had them coming out to hear him when he performed at Manhattan record stores and night clubs. At Newport, Rhode Island, what actually happened was that a large number of people went ape wild for him as he played a set with Thelonious Monk, Gerry Mulligan, Zoot Sims, Percy Heath, and Connie Kay. The bootleg recording of that performance is neither particularly impressive nor the sound good enough to give us an impression of what kind of nuance was at work. Whatever the music actually sounded like, Davis was then cleaned up and ready to move out toward stardom. He convinced producer George Avakian that it was time to sign him to Columbia Records, devising a brilliant plan that would get him out of his contract with Prestige, where he had already made a number of highly regarded all-star group recordings. Davis wanted Avakian to approach Prestige with the idea that if the trumpeter signed with Columbia and made a small-group recording, the attention would shoot up the sales of the three or four small-group recordings he still had to do for Prestige in order to finish out his contract. Prestige went for it and Davis did a marathon session before the taping microphones with his great quintet of the time, which included John Coltrane, Red Garland, Paul Chambers, and Philly Joe Jones.

It all changed for him when 'Round About Midnight came out on Columbia. The pink-and-blue jacket showed Davis in dark glasses holding his horn, looking removed, unapproachable, a contemplatively hip man in his own world, one who had no time for entertainment, an elegant piece of coal squeezed into a diamond by the pressure of the times. The music is perfect, track to track, the band performing with superb locomotion and indisputable lyricism. Davis was now on board the gravy train and it was starting up for him. Avakian got the trumpeter a good manager in Jack Whittemore, who kept the band working so that Davis would have stable personnel and the latitude to keep the sound of the group developing. Avakian took Debbie Ishlon of the promotion department to hear him at the Cafe Bohemia. Ishlon had been responsible for getting Dave Brubeck on the cover of Time magazine. According to Avakian, Ishlon's experience of hearing and seeing Davis was pivotal:

Debbie flipped out and saw him as a new super-cool image. She was responsible for getting the editors of Town and Country interested in Miles. Otherwise, they would never have done anything with jazz, I'm sure. And it was during the Cafe Bohemia period that he started to do two things. He blew more and more solos with the mute right on top of the microphone, and then he would turn his back to the audience and even walk off. That got a lot of talk. Let's face it, Debbie helped exploit that with the image of the *artiste* who is all for his music, and the audience doesn't matter. But the main thing is that she got Miles into areas that no jazz artist had ever been in before, and that helped build him up quite rapidly.

The other thing is that we started a record club, and nobody knew how big that became. There were no record clubs at the time except the old Book of the Month Club deal with Victor Red Seal, which was for classical music only. So we ended up having a total monopoly on a phase of the business which nobody knew was really big. That was the secret behind people like Miles suddenly becoming big stars.

The next Columbia recordings couldn't be with small groups because Prestige was pushing out the quintet records the trumpeter made in order to complete his contract. Those Prestige recordings were very popular and Bill Cosby said at a New York memorial for the trumpeter that one could be considered extremely hip in Philadelphia during the fifties by just walking around with a Miles Davis Quintet album under one's arm. In a shrewd attempt to avoid being lost in a glut of small-band product, Avakian knew Columbia had to go for big. As part of that strategy, Davis then hooked up again with Gil Evans, spurning Avakian's suggestion that he use Gunther Schuller to write and conduct long works for him. Davis had already participated in Columbia recording experiments under the direction of Schuller, performing on pieces written by John Lewis and J. J. Johnson. He wanted something else and got it. Evans put Davis in the kind of context that almost all superior jazz musicians, beginning with Louis Armstrong, evolve toward, which is the concerto in idiomatic terms. What begins in small bands is almost always taken into a larger environment. This was true of Gillespie in his big bands and the longer works he commissioned during the bebop era of the late forties; with varying success, Charlie Parker had agreed to appear in formats broader than his quintets and quartets and wanted to perform with orchestras; Clifford Brown had recorded with strings. Davis, expanding upon his *Birth of the Cool* context, was in there again, ten years gone by and all kinds of fresh information and ideas behind his forehead.

The brilliantly promoted and highly successful *Miles Ahead*, *Porgy and Bess*, and *Sketches of Spain* are signal examples of his powers. The recordings were inclined toward the pallid textures that resulted from the impressionistic influences on Evans and from the disavowal of the varied Negro vocal inflections that had meant so much to the richest instrumental timbres of the idiom. Usually, when this was not the ongoing obsession with getting a pass into the European party of aesthetic seriousness, it was a psychological assertion on the part of white musicians who became fed up or bored with the assumption that they were less than authentically equal artists because of how far removed their cultural roots were from the Negro origins of the craft.

But that didn't really matter, finally, when it came to the collaborations between the little man from East St. Louis with the trumpet and the long, tall Canadian with the arranger's pen. Regardless of how indistinct some of the arrangements might have made jazz seem, Davis himself had those things in his playing and was never—even at his most puckish—very far from the stink and the grease of the gutbucket at the center of the art. From one perspective, we hear something like the suave, country-boy Negro in Harvard Yard, surrounded by all kinds of refined knowledge and pulling together the stuff with an equally refined angle that surprisingly aligns the conventionally astute and the down-home for yet another triumphant level of Americana. In fact, one could say that where Davis moved away from the cool school was in his grasp of the *blues* and all its myriad meanings, something that he also played with far greater authority than either of his most prominent trumpet rivals during the fifties, Gillespie and Clifford Brown. In fact, as the *Portrait of Duke Ellington* proves, Davis's collaborations with Evans had reawakened Gillespie, his former mentor, who was seeking to reach the levels of emotional depth, subtlety, and large-ensemble context that Davis was so good at expressing and devising with his best friend. Even Louis Armstrong approached Evans about writing something for him after he had heard *Porgy and Bess*. The Davis style, his sound, and the settings he chose for his horn were touching even the ambitions of his idols.

Style was one thing, bandleading another. His intelligence and his charisma made Davis one of the very greatest leaders in his peak years, and his bands were some of the most hard-swinging units in the music. Some had included Jackie McLean, who played the alto saxophone like a blow torch; Horace Silver, a pianist and composer who was a foot-stomping brigadier general in the war against tepid, West Coast jazz; Kenny Clarke and Art Blakey, two of the most swinging and innovative drummers in jazz history; Sonny Rollins and John Coltrane, the freshest tenor saxophonists of the day; Garland, Chambers, and Jones, the most highly regarded rhythm section; and Bill Evans, the man who would become one of the most influential pianists of the last forty years. Davis also, with *Kind of Blue*, made the strongest case for the modal movement of limited harmony and scalar manipulation that maintains affecting sway even to this moment.

Beginning with the classic band of the middle fifties that included Coltrane, Davis started to impose a perfect combination of the loose and the prepared. He didn't like music that sounded thrown together and wasn't very fond of the jam session context, where personality was reduced purely to improvisation and never expressed itself in overall shape. His popularity was connected to that sense of order and to his awareness of the nature of the public ear as well as some advice he had been given by his mother. Slow songs, medium-tempoed pieces, and bouncing numbers are usually what the public likes most. Extremely fast performances of the sort Charlie Parker loved were never popular. At one point, Vernon Davis remembers, the trumpeter's mother told him that if he wanted people to listen to what he was doing he needed to slow down and give them tunes that they could hum, some references, something that stuck in their minds, something that didn't just fly by like a succession of fastballs that struck out the audience's attention and its affection. Davis took heed. His repertoire still included quick-stepping bop tunes and all kinds of blues but was soon dominated by popular songs of the day, or older popular songs like "Bye, Bye Blackbird." Like the straw-hatted white woman in the yacht race on the cover of *Miles Ahead*, he was leaving spray in the faces of the other racers.

But Davis knew that there was always color trouble to be had, even if one wasn't looking for it. In 1959, while he was taking a break outside Birdland, a white cop saw him put a pink lady in a cab and told the trumpeter to move along. Davis, beautifully dressed as always, wanted to know why he was supposed to move along. The cop told him because he said so. Davis refused, saying he was just standing there getting some air. The cop threatened to get a little heavy. Davis told this representative of law enforcement that he was working downstairs with his band and that, if the cop looked, he could see that the picture on the wall was of *him*. The cop wasn't having any of that. As it always can be, one word, an attitude, a show of power, and a refusal to be bullied mixed themselves up rather quickly and Davis was soon struggling with the cop to keep him from using his billy club. There was a furor in the street as patrons ran up the stairs from Birdland when they heard the trumpeter was in a tussle; clubs started emptying and there was soon a large crowd.

Freddie Hubbard, who had come to New York in 1958, was going to hear Davis for the first time in person:

I lived in Brooklyn and was coming up out of the subway on 50th and Broadway. I walked up to Birdland, on 52nd, and I saw all of these people standing outside the club. I looked in the circle and saw Miles Davis fighting with two cops, plain clothesmen. They were swinging blackjacks at Miles and he had a pretty, white Italian suit on. He was boxing them and hit one of the guys right on the jaw and I'll never forget that sound of his fist before the cop went through one of those thick windows and broke the glass in what they called a Ham and Egger. Everybody cheered, "Oh." But the other guy continued to beat Miles on the head and it amazed me to see all of the people standing around, Coltrane, Cannonball, and it might have been Wynton Kelly or Red Garland watching this man getting beaten. They did not jump in. More cops came and eventually arrested Miles and blood was streaming down his head. The amount of blows that he took must have had a damaging effect. They were trying to knock him out. I wanted to break in and help the brother, but people said, "Don't go in there." When I asked his band why they didn't jump in to help the man, they said, "We can't get involved in *that*."

The police took Davis to the precinct house on 54th Street, where he was to be booked for assault and resisting arrest. The crowd followed them to the police station, where two Negroes told the detective who hit Davis over the head that if he thought he was so tough he could step outside and find out what it felt like to get a *real* ass-whipping. Realizing that the wrong Negro had been roughed up this time, the cops in charge interrupted the booking procedure and allowed Davis to get some medical treatment, which resulted in ten stitches. The trumpeter spent the night in jail and made the front pages the next day, blood spattering his sporty one-button jacket with no lapels.

The incident was very shocking to the jazz world at large because Davis had seemed so untouchable. Within his universe, the violence toward Davis took everyone almost as off guard as Kennedy's assassination did the country a few years later. This was New York City, not the South. Oh, really?

The trumpeter eventually won a suit against the City of New York, but was forever after convinced that no matter how high he might ever rise, unless a white man looking for a Negro to bully knew *exactly* who he was, Miles Dewey Davis III might find out what demonic forces kept the battleship of racism afloat and ready for action. Until the end of his life, the incident could suddenly pop up in a conversation with Davis that seemed to have no bearing on race. It stuck. The stardom that brought him top club and concert salaries, the sales of hundreds of thousands of records, his Mercedes Gold Wing, the fine home converted from a Russian Orthodox church, those lines upon lines of women ready to drop their drawers at his request, the musicians imitating his dress, his manner, and his attitude, as well as the jazz polls showing that he was the man of the hour were all smudged blue with irony as far as he was concerned. The blood stopped flowing but the thuds of the blackjacks reverberated.

By the spring of 1961, other kinds of blood were being drawn. Ornette Coleman had arrived in New York fifteen months earlier and was at the center of a controversy about so-called free jazz, which dispensed with harmony in favor of a shifting, quirky, angular, simplistic, and gripping rendition of the demons and the dreams in the disaffected soul of the time—the discomfort with the drab order of suburban suffocation, the desire to return to some kind of primitive purity, the anger at the facelessness of the individual in the cheese dip of melded Americana, that terror of the end of the world that could be brought about by a small number of men with unprecedented weapons of incalculable destruction, that lonely-boy shriek and sob that Coleman conjured up through his white plastic saxophone with such boundless determination. Some felt as though they were not so much listening as watching bricks passionately but fruitlessly thrown through the endless windows of a factory intent on making humanity no more than a mechanistic extension of a constricted sense of order and production. Coltrane, considered by his least-sympathetic listeners as no more than an incredibly long-winded and hysterical academic, went for the call of the wild, too, and the vastly intellectual blast furnace that he had brought to Davis's bandstand was now busy incinerating the distance between the academy and the outback—the blues cry jumbled up in all kinds of incantational rhythms, the simple but layered forms turning the piano and the bass into extensions of the scalding, polyrhythmic drums—with the saxophonist down on one knee, as often as not exhausting himself and his audience as he produced an auditory image that took his bedazzled listeners deeper and deeper into the horrors and the magic of the rain forest.

What was cool Miles Davis going to do about all of that?

Well, he was going to let all concerned know the difference between him and everybody else under hot discussion. Davis would come from strength, pure, complex, and simple. What he always possessed as a hole card was a personal epistemology, an individual way of knowing, and that code of knowing was formed at its source by all the thinking he had done about the trumpet, the tone he had discovered within it, his understanding of how much distinct colors could add to the communicative power of notes, what improvised rhythms of swing and of floating song meant to momentum and how harmony and accent could work together, meaning that an unexpected note didn't need to be given heavy emphasis because the element of surprise created the *illusion* of emphasis.

Then there was the epistemology of the blues, which he had heard Charlie Parker play backwards and forwards, which Ellington gave extraordinary plasticity, which Monk bent and thumped into new conditions on the keyboard, which most white men didn't feel comfortable playing and which far too many Negroes understood best in its store-bought form of cliché, self-pity, and overstatement, not in its deep song context that met the same devil in the midnight crossroads that flamenco did. The Miles Davis blues, his gutbucket authority, had a Spanish streak of violence, tragedy, and transcendent disregard for unearned happiness, sometimes delivered with the arrogance of a matador heckling a bull, sometimes as quietly and as darkly as a dying person taking in the final breaths that are so near silence it seems the animation of the life force is dissolving into a meager train of shriveling sighs.

There were also the epistemological boudoir discoveries Davis had made as an offstage romantic lead, as a pimp during his heroin days, as an experimenter in many shades of jade, as one whose teetering and tottering on the masculine-feminine line led to stories that were the gossip joy of his inferiors, especially those musicians who could not equal his success in any direction, on or off the bandstand. All of those two-heads-on-a-pillow experiences had taught him about frailty, about longing, about whispers and shouts, about giggles and cries, about smells and textures of skin, about all the forces and the shadings of translucent feeling that are liberated when the time is right or when the sun goes down and there's nobody else around. That density of romantic and erotic knowing gave his ballad renditions an intimacy that was laid on the air without the slightest tremor of apology. In a decidedly rowdy Negro club filled with hustlers and whores, Davis could bring quiet with his Harmon mute stuck in the bell of his horn as some love song lay under his musical and emotional microscope. He had the power to make an audience briefly become better than itself.

At that very first Carnegie Hall concert of his, with a well-rehearsed large band of sixteen white and three black musicians looking over their music, and the central force the Negro men of his own quintet—Hank Mobley, Wynton Kelly, Paul Chambers, and Jimmy Cobb—prepared to set each note afire, Miles Davis had all intentions of being even better than himself. The inky prince of jazz had trained and sought all of the strength necessary to flex his feeling and his will on the people in the seats of Carnegie Hall. He had been working on his horn for stamina and range— playing long improvisations, squealing into the upper register, tackling avant-garde ideas about pitch and color, and inventing completely unpredictable rhythms—as the indispensable two volumes of *Miles Davis in Person* reveal, recorded a month earlier at San Francisco's Blackhawk. But there may have been more than preparation for the big concert on his mind when he was playing all of that mighty horn. Drummer Jimmy Cobb was in the band at the time and has another perspective:

> As far as the way he was playing at the Blackhawk before we got to New York and did Carnegie Hall, all those long solos, and like that, they could have been because he was showing out for Marguerite Mays. He tried to tell her I couldn't play for looking at her but I told him to speak for himself, which is what he meant anyway. She was Willie Mays's wife. That woman was *as fine as possible*.

The trumpeter was introduced to that audience by the disc jockey Symphony Sid Torin, a Jewish hipster, pot-head, huckster, knucklehead, lover of jazz and jazz musicians and the position over them his radio broadcasts and on-the-air interviews had given him. Torin and Miles went back to the days of Charlie Parker, who condescendingly referred to the self-described "all night, all frantic one" as "Symphonic Sidney." Svelte and superbly tailored in the Manhattan town largely tamed by robber barons who had built libraries, museums, and concert halls to honor themselves, the suave country boy from East St. Louis was ready to let it rip. He intended to whip it until it turned red. He wanted to seduce it and tease all its clothes off. He wanted to ruminate about it and shoot a tragically informed arrow of song into the air before he closed the door and painted his address blue. Miles Davis was not there to bullshit. But he *was* anxious. Everyone remembers him being that way, and so was Evans, of whom Jimmy Cobb recounts:

> Gil said that he was petrified. He was really scared to do that concert. So he was drinking corn whiskey he had brought down from 125th Street. He had never been in front of that many people before. Gil said he would rather do a lot of other things rather than go out on that stage. Miles was nervous, too. It was a big deal for all of us. It was a social event. This guy

named Pete Long who worked in promotion up in Harlem at the Apollo was a friend of ours and he was kind of a promoter. I think he was part of that evening. I think it was his idea that every woman who came in got a rose. It was a high class event.

As a benefit for the African Medical Education and Research Foundation, it was also a political event. Not very long before the performance, a delegation of five or six people was brought to Davis's home by Max Roach, the great poetic genius of the drums and a close friend who had worked with the trumpeter in Charlie Parker's band. The delegation was convinced that the African Research Foundation was in cahoots with South Africa and other forces upholding colonialism. They were inclined to see race in broad, black nationalist terms that were rooted in the nineteenth century. Those conceptions ran through the Caribbean, and were, due to W. E. B. Du Bois, given the name Pan-Africanism, a politics of color based on the idea that a sin committed against any black person at any point on the globe by a representative of any kind of white racism or colonial power was a sin against all blue-black to bone-colored people anywhere. Race and its relationship to racism precluded all else. The men Max Roach brought to Davis's home urged him not to perform. Davis said, rather oddly, given what had happened to him not yet two years ago in front of Birdland, that if you had enough money you could buy your freedom. He was going to play. They left, he went about his business.

Davis had been interested for a while in having a concert at Carnegie Hall but didn't know exactly how to go about doing it, especially if such an event involved him approaching anybody. He wanted to be the one approached. Jean Bach became aware of this and made that information available to Dr. Tom Rees, whom she had known since 1945. Rees was one of the surgeons who had founded the Flying Doctors of East Africa, which was a division of the African Medical Education and Research Foundation. Begun in 1957, the Flying Doctors started building what is now a medical force of over four thousand people, more than 90 percent of them black Africans. At that time, Rees and his people needed a benefit in New York to help further the work they were doing. The doctor went to see the trumpet player. He had a surprise for Davis:

> When I was studying medicine I was a jazz musician, earning my way through school. I knew a white trumpeter, who played in the same band, named Doug Mettome, who ended up playing in the Billy Eckstine Band,

in which Miles played. In fact, Doug was the only white player in the band. He and Miles became very close. As you know, Miles was not very fond of white people. He was *not* fond of white people. But he loved Doug because, whenever they traveled in the South, the band, of course, in those days, had to stay in rickety hotels and stuff. Doug, being white, could have stayed in a nicer place, but he didn't choose to; he stayed with the band.

When I went to see Miles at his house he was very suspicious, almost antagonistic. What did I want? What was I doing there? I broke the ice by telling him I had been a pal of Doug Mettome. That melted him right away. He really loved Doug. I talked to him straight. You had to; that was how he talked. I told him that this organization was doing good for Africans, who had, otherwise, no medical care and we were devoted to providing medical training and teaching in Africa. I told him that our organization in New York was a mixed organization, that we had several black people as well as whites on our board. After several meetings and conversations with him, he finally thought it might be a pretty good idea. We spoke to Gil Evans about it and Gil thought it was a great idea. Along comes the night. We had a beautiful audience, about half white and half black audience. Everybody was dressed up. It was really quite a scene.

As the recording shows, Davis was in particularly powerful form. He had brought his own brand of virtuosity to high profile. There was nothing in his distinct style that he could not do on that night. Cobb remembers Evans being so nervous that the orchestral introduction to the first piece, "So What," began more slowly than it should have, meandering along, which meant nothing and even provided a fine contrast to the explosion of the quintet moving into position. Davis immediately let everyone know how much swing they were going to have to handle. As usual, there was his characteristic phrasing flotation, which made it possible for the hard groove of Negro muscularity to coexist with reflection. So we heard the optimum achievement of jazz—getting the triangle of the meat, the mind, and the emotions together; no separation. In a player like Davis, that sort of perfection was outstanding because his lyrical gifts and his freedom of line could carry along even the intelligent listener who had no comprehension of jazz. By keeping that song going on he could "call the children home" just as effectively for his time as Buddy Bolden had when jazz rose from the womb of the gutbucket around the turn of the century in good old funky-butt New Orleans.

Tenor saxophonist Hank Mobley was also aflame, though a more conventional player than Davis, and Wynton Kelly laid out some of the greatest improvised rhythm ever captured as his feature on "So What" preceded the ending of the tune. Davis then performed with the large ensemble, his "Spring Is Here" defined by a confident beauty based in the weight that his tone could give whatever note he played. Next he and the quintet did "Teo," a flamenco-influenced waltz with an Afro beat that found the trumpeter leaving no doubt that he was at the forefront of new sonic directions and new materials for his instrument, nearly shrieking into the upper register with repeated exclamations of a force the audience that night found shocking. After his second feature on the piece, Davis let Kelly dissolve the waltz before, almost suddenly, starting "Walkin'," now a fast blues that found him exhibiting some of the red-hot playing much more expected of someone like Roy Eldridge, emotion and drive pulling the rhythm section instead of being driven by it. Mobley, nobody's second-string bluesman, pushed his bell right into the cut of the groove; Kelly, never to be outswung, laid down swing upon swing, his final chords as percussive as Monk's; Chambers bowed his bass feature with no loss of momentum, and Davis and Cobb then took turns pitching and smacking back each other's balls of fire.

Davis turned another corner of feeling. He then stood in the middle of the Evans arrangements using his horn to create a different texture of intimacy on "The Meaning of the Blues" and "Lament" before prancing into the jaunty arrangement of pianist Ahmad Jamal's "New Rhumba." That Jamal number is a tribute to one of the trumpeter's signal influences. Every statement, each exchange with the orchestra, the shapes of his lines, the dramatic ascents into the upper register, the nuances of his rhythm are very nearly perfect. The first half of the concert concluded, Miles Davis had brought the cool and the hot into alignment, successfully daring to be the aesthetic link between extremes. He had it all going on, and everyone there knew it.

The audience during intermission was ecstatic. Then the second half began. On the recording a tune starts then ends mysteriously. Jimmy Cobb recalls:

Miles was playing "Someday My Prince Will Come." Then he suddenly took the tune out and walked off. I didn't know what was going on at first until the harp player asked me, "Is he supposed to be there?" I asked who she meant. And there was Max Roach squatted like an Indian holding up a sign saying "Africa for Africans." Then a stagehand came out and ushered Max off.

Some remember Roach being lifted and carried off, though the drummer says he walked off the stage and when he got into the wings, Davis told the stagehands, "Don't touch him." Tom Rees says that he went backstage to see what was happening because everyone was out front but there was no Miles Davis. The trumpeter's wife of six months, dancer Frances Taylor, and Gil Evans talked to Rees. They told him that Davis was finished for the night. He was going home, they couldn't convince him to do otherwise but Evans was willing to go out and get the job done with the orchestra. Rees found Davis seething behind a curtain, feeling that he had been set up and lied to by the doctor. When Rees said the opposite of anything racist was going on and that the proof was clearly the audience itself, black and white people in attendance come to hear him together, Davis peeked out but said that Max Roach was his friend and he couldn't go against someone he had known that long.

Rees got Davis to go outside with him, where they found Roach picketing with members of the delegation that had come to the trumpeter's home in an attempt to stop him from playing the benefit. As Rees talked with Roach, it became clear that neither he nor anyone else knew exactly what the Flying Doctors of East Africa actually did. There had been wrong information. Rees told the drummer that if there was anything racist about the organization he would be in protest against it as well. The doctor summarized what he and his team did. Rees also wanted to know why Roach almost destroyed the trumpeter's concert and so angered him that he would not go back on, which would lead to his being pulverized by the papers the next morning. It could unnecessarily hurt the career of Miles Davis. Finally, Roach relented and began to say that maybe there was a misunderstanding and that Davis should finish the concert. All the facts could be sorted out later. Davis was not immediately ready to go back out there. Perhaps his mood had been so jangled that he didn't want to try and recapture the concentration he would need to maintain the level of the first half. Upon considering that Gil Evans would have to pick up the slack and face the disappointment of the audience alone, Miles Davis, loyal to his best buddy, took his horn and went back on.

On the recording it's clear that his playing is not as consistently good as it was in the first half, though the rest of the band maintains the same standards of groove, stank, and swing they had set before intermission. Davis's

"Oleo" is as strong as a Gillespie set of razors run through the "I Got Rhythm" chord changes, but "No Blues" falls back on some pat material from the Blackhawk recordings. He sounds professional but distracted and may well have still wanted to go home. Then, with "I Thought About You," he recovers and the ballad artistry that had no trumpet equals since the arrival of Charlie Parker turns down the lights in the hall to the point where whispers get their best hearing. As a finale, Davis plays an excerpt from "Concierto de Aranjuez" with Evans and the orchestra. The piece has little to do with jazz and the arrangement is nothing of serious import for the idiom but there is a fascinating contrast between what the ensemble sounds like and how the blues knowledge that Davis imparts with such swing remakes the entire context every time he blows a note, either written or improvised. Even his far-from-subtle mistakes don't mar the overall effect of his aesthetic individuality. By the last note, the trumpeter has reasserted himself as an ordering conqueror of the present, which is what all jazz musicians aspire to, whether playing the music as written or as they think it ought to be.

The concert received a standing ovation, which was deserved. But it also represented, with the craft on the bandstand and the cooperation of the races, what was to be destroyed when the Civil Rights movement was overrun by the forces of Black Power. Neither Miles Davis nor Max Roach, each man a genius, could have imagined just how clearly the events of that evening summed up much of the music and the social texture that had come into being since they both performed with Charlie Parker on 52nd Street fifteen years earlier. Triumph and doom were in the air that night, the former symbolized later by the 1963 March on Washington, the latter by the Birmingham bombing murders of four little girls a few weeks later, then the assassination of Jack Kennedy two months following that Sunday morning explosion. From that point on, the destination was set and no one, regardless of how much money he or she possessed, would be able to buy any kind of freedom from all that. Not even Miles Davis.

1998

Bird Land

Charlie Parker, Clint Eastwood, and America

In the red and purple bric-a-brac that often passes for jazz criticism or jazz scholarship, Charlie Parker looms large. He is the rebel angel speared by the marksmen of the marketplace, and by the grand conspiracy of robed and unidentified klansmen. Parker was truly one of the most mysterious figures in American art. Six years ago I began the bedeviling job of writing Parker's biography. It quickly became clear that much of what was taken for granted about the alto saxophonist was a mix of near-truth, fabrication, and butt-naked lies.

Over the last few years, culminating in Clint Eastwood's very bad film *Bird*, there has been more attention than usual shown to Parker. Almost everything he ever recorded is now available, some of it reworked for sound vastly superior to the original releases. There is a coffee-table book, a video documentary, and a stack of glowing reviews of *Bird* that reveal the extent to which many who would be sympathetic to Negroes are prone to an unintentional, liberal racism. That racism reduces the complexities of the Afro-American world to a dark, rainy pit in which Negroes sweat, suffer, dance a little, mock each other, make music, and drop dead, releasing at last a burden of torment held at bay only by drugs.

It must be that melodramatic notion of suffering that makes Eastwood's film so appealing. Many film critics appear to have the same problem with the depiction of Negro life that many literary critics do. Too quick to prove that they really understand the plight of the caged coon, who would be a man if only the white world would let him, they often fall for condescending, ignorant, bestial images of Afro-Americans, feeling for them as visitors to Dr. Moreau's Island did, where the noble beasts of the jungle were mutilated into bad imitations of human beings in the mad surgeon's "house of pain." In *Bird*, Negro life is such an incredible house of pain that the dying Charlie Parker summons up, with one exception, only a montage of negative experience.

The exception is his friend Dizzy Gillespie, who proudly asks an audience just served up some sensational saxophone what they think about it. Otherwise Parker on his deathbed summons up a black doctor predicting that he will die from drugs, a black saxophonist laughing at him, a black musician throwing a cymbal at him in disgust during his early, ineffectual efforts at improvisation. All that remains for him, in Eastwood's account, are images of his smiling, vibrant, white lover Chan, and of his white trumpeter buddy Red Rodney. This is a Charlie Parker in no way connected to, in no way the product of, the Afro-American culture filled with the bittersweet intricacies that were given aesthetic substance so superbly in his music.

The movie makes a perfect companion to Chan Parker's *To Bird with Love*, a huge picture book now out of print that was done with the French archivist and producer Francis Paudras. Artfully organized and intimate (it includes bills, love notes, and poignant telegrams), one would never guess from the book that its author was the last of Parker's four wives, the first two black, the last two white. A famous photograph of Parker with his first wife, Rebecca, whom he married when he was fifteen, their son Leon, and her subsequent husband Ross Davis is cropped so that Rebecca doesn't exist. Those are the kinds of croppings that abound in Eastwood's film, which reportedly leans heavily on Chan's unpublished memoir, *Life in E-Flat*. All of the things that Chan knew little about, or preferred to ignore, remain outside the film.

Though Parker was well taken care of as a child, for example, and was quite attached to his mother, whom he called every weekend, she is only referred to once in *Bird*, when the soothsaying doctor tells that boy he better watch out for that dope. Chan is given a monologue about her own childhood and her own father and asks Parker about his early life, but he tells her in reply only about the day he discovered that he was addicted. So much for the complexity, or the vitality, of *his* past. His second wife, Geraldine, didn't play a large role in his life, and was only married to him a year; but Doris, the third, went to California in 1946 when Parker had a nervous breakdown there, visited him in Camarillo as often as she could, and returned with him in 1947 to New York, where they lived together until 1950. (Though Eastwood's stacking of the deck in Chan's favor elicits a remarkable performance from Diane Venora, there is something distasteful about the film's general slighting of black women, not least in light of Parker's friendships and working relationships with women such as Mary Lou Williams, Sarah Vaughan, and Ella Fitzgerald; only one on-screen speaking part is given to a black female, in a fictitious situation in which Bird recalls being told, when he was working his style out, "Nigger, don't be playing that shit behind me while I'm trying to *sang*.")

This film depicts not Negroes, but Negro props. No wonder, perhaps, in the light of Eastwood's comment to *Newsweek* that because he listened to a lot of rhythm and blues on the radio as a young man, "I think I was really a black guy in a white body." We get the young Parker playing a song flute as he rides on the back of horse, a teenaged Parker with a saxophone on the porch of an unpainted house, a couple of young Negroes smoking cigarettes near him. Had Parker grown up in New Orleans instead of Kansas City, he would almost certainly have been shown on a cotton bale.

Then the movie flashes forward to Parker in 1945, roaring through the chords of "Lester Leaps In." Forest Whitaker, who plays Parker, has been directed to hump and jerk and thrust his horn outward, exactly as Parker did not. "The thing about Bird," says Art Taylor, a drummer who played with him, "is that he didn't move. He just stood there almost still as a statue, and when he finished, there was a pool of water at his feet." (Whitaker obviously has the talent to get far closer to Bird than he did; but he was not asked to do much more than another version of the Negro manchild.)

Next Parker comes home, high, in 1954, and explains to Chan that he has just been fired from Birdland, the club named for him. As he gives the details, she talks to him as though he is a child who went off without his lock and got his bike stolen. Bird refers to himself as "an overgrown adolescent," angrily taunting her for trying to "work that psychology on him." He swallows iodine, falls to the floor, and Chan stands over him, saying, "[t]hat was stupid. Now I'll have to call an ambulance." From that point in the story until its bitter end, despite an outburst here and a joke there, this Charlie Parker is forever under somebody—his wife, his doctors, his agent, the white South, the narcotics police, the court system, the music business. He is always a victim: of the white folks, of the iron-hearted colored people, of himself. At best he is an idiot savant, in possession of natural rhythm, with little more than boyish charm and a sense of bewilderment. There is no sign of the sophistication, the curiosity, the aggressiveness, the regality, the guile, the charisma of which all who knew Parker still speak. Eastwood's Parker works only at getting high or not getting high.

Even the world of music is presented as something Bird isn't very involved in, other than as a way of making a living. He shows no real love for the saxophone or for jazz. There is no competitive feeling, no sense of threat, no arrogance, no appreciation of any of his predecessors. (As the

pianist Walter Davis Jr. told me: "You can't have a movie about Bird and
not have him run over *somebody*. This was a very aggressive man. He took
over and made things go *his* way. If you weren't strong, Charlie Parker
would mow you down like grass.") He's just a colored man with a saxophone, a white girlfriend, and a drug problem. When he dies, you are almost relieved.

The critics have made much of Eastwood's love of Parker's art, and even
more of the technology that he and his music director Lennie Neihaus used
to extract Parker's improvisations from their original recordings so that
contemporary musicians could overdub them for today's sound. That ac-
complishment, however, was a catastrophic mistake. The splendid remas-
terings that Jack Towers and Phil Schapp have done with Parker's own
work on Savoy and Verve are vastly superior to this gimmicky, updated
soundtrack. On the CD versions of *Savoy Original Master Takes* and *Bird: The
Complete Charlie Parker on Verve*, there are aesthetic details never heard before.
Moreover, as Doris Parker said to Eastwood after a screening of *Bird* at the
New York Film Festival: "Charlie didn't play by himself. When you take
him away from his real musicians, you destroy what inspired him to play
what he did." What the musicians play on Eastwood's soundtrack is often
incompatible, in fact, with what Parker's alto is doing; the music is mixed so
high that the saxophone almost never rises above the background, and the
drummer, John Guerin, does *not* swing.

The life of Charlie Parker was a perfect metaphor for the turmoil that exists in this democratic nation. It traversed an extremely varied world, including everything from meeting and talking with Einstein to attending
parties with Lord Buckley where Communists tried to turn him. Parker was
at once the aristocracy and the rabble, the self-made creator of a vital and
breathtakingly structured jazz vernacular and an anarchic man of dooming
appetites. He was always trying to stay in the good graces of those stunned
by his disorder. His artistic power was almost forever at war with the curse of
his gift for self-destruction. He was dead in 1955, at thirty-four, his remarkable musical gifts laid low by his inability to stop fatally polluting and tam-
pering with the flesh-and-blood source of his energy, with his own body.

Those musical gifts made it possible for Parker to evolve from an inept
alto saxophonist, a laughingstock in his middle teens, to a virtuoso of all-
encompassing talent who, by the age of twenty-five, exhibited an unprecedented command of his instrument. His prodigious facility was used not
only for exhibition or revenge, moreover, but primarily for the expression

of melodic, harmonic, and rhythmic inventions, at velocities that extended the intimidating relationship of thought and action that forms the mystery of improvisation in jazz. In the process, Parker defined his generation: He provided the mortar for the bricks of fresh harmony that Thelonious Monk and Dizzy Gillespie were making, he supplied linear substance and an eighth note triplet approach to phrasing that was perfectly right for the looser style of drumming that Kenny Clarke had invented.

The anomalies are endless. He performed on concert stages as part of Norman Granz's Jazz at the Philharmonic, traveling in style and benefiting from Granz's demand that all his musicians receive the same accommodations, regardless of race; but when he was at the helm of his own groups, Parker was usually performing in the homemade chamber-music rooms of nightclubs. "One night I'm at Carnegie Hall," he once told the saxophonist Big Nick Nicholas, "and the next night I'm somewhere in New Jersey at Sloppy Joe's." These shifts of venue paralleled the contrasts in his personality. The singer Earl Coleman, who first met Parker in Kansas City in the early 1940s, said of him:

> You could look at Bird's life and see just how much his music was connected to the way he lived. . . . You just stood there with your mouth open and listened to him discuss books with somebody or philosophy or religion or science, things like that. Thorough. A little while later, you might see him over in a corner somewhere drinking wine out of a paper sack with some juicehead. Now that's what you hear when you listen to him play: he can reach the most intellectual and difficult levels of music, then he can turn around—now watch this—and play the most low down, funky blues you ever want to hear. That's a long road for somebody else, from that high intelligence all the way over to those blues, but for Charlie Parker it wasn't half a block; it was right next door. . . .

It was not Parker's scope, however, but his wild living, and his disdain for the rituals of the entertainment business, that made him something of a saint to those who felt at odds with America in the years after World War II, who sought a symbol of their own dissatisfaction with the wages of sentimentality and segregation. Parker was a hero for those who welcomed what they thought was a bold departure from the long minstrel tradition to which Negroes were shackled. He was, for them, at war with the complicated fact that the Negro was inside and outside at the same time, central to American sensibility and culture but subjected to separate laws and depicted on stage and screen, and in the advertising emblems of the society, as a creature more teeth and popped eyes than man, more high-pitched laugh and wobbling flesh than woman.

Parker appeared at a point in American history when that bizarre image of the Negro had been part of many show business successes: minstrelsy itself, the first nationally popular stage entertainment; *Birth of a Nation*, the first epic film and "blockbuster"; "Amos 'n' Andy," the most popular radio program since its premiere in 1928; *The Jazz Singer*, where Jolson's Jacob Rabinowitz stepped from cantorial melancholy into American optimism by changing his name to Jack Robbins, changing the color of his face, and introducing the recorded voice to film; *Gone with the Wind*, Atlanta's plantation paradise lost; not to mention the endless bit parts in all the performing arts that gave comic relief of a usually insulting sort, or that realistically showed Negro women advising lovelorn white girls in their boudoirs. Parker offered an affront to that tradition of humiliation.

In fact, the jazzmen who preceded Parker had also addressed the insults of popular culture, and countered those stereotypes with the elegant deportment and the musical sophistication of the big bands. Parker turned his back on those bands, though; and not only because he preferred five-piece units. Manhandling the saxophone and Tin Pan Alley ditties, writing tunes that were swift and filled with serpentine phrases of brittle bravado, arriving late or not at all, occasionally in borrowed or stolen clothes so ill-fitting that the sleeves came midway down his forearms and the pants part way up his calves, speaking with authority on a wide variety of subjects in a booming mid-Atlantic accent, Parker nicely fit the bohemian ideal of an artist too dedicated to his art to be bought and too worldly to be condescended to. (Except, of course, when he chose himself to mock his own identity, as when he stood in front of Birdland dressed in overalls and announced to his fellow players that he was sure they must be jazz musicians because they were so well dressed.)

Historically, Parker was the third type of Afro-American artist to arrive in the idiom of jazz. Louis Armstrong had fused the earthy and the majestic, and had set the standards for improvisational virtuosity and swing; but he was also given to twisting on the jester's mask. Duke Ellington manipulated moods, melodies, harmonies, timbres, and rhythms with the grace of relaxed superiority, suavely expanding and refining the art in a manner that has no equal. Armstrong's combination of pathos, joy, and farce achieved the sort of eloquence that Chaplin sought; and Ellington commanded the implications of the Negro-derived pedal percussion that gave Astaire many of his greatest moments. But Parker was more the gangster hero, the charming anarchist that Cagney introduced in *Public Enemy*. The tommy-gun velocity of Parker's imagination mowed down the clichés he inherited, and enlarged the language of jazz, but like Cagney's Tom Powers, he met an early death, felled by the dangers of fast living.

In many ways, Parker reflected the world in which he was reared, the wild-west town of Kansas City, where everything was wide open and the rules were set on their heads. The mayor and the police were in cahoots with the local mob; liquor flowed during Prohibition, and gambling and prostitution were virtually legal. When the musicians went to bed, everybody else was getting up to go to work. Parker's mother was the mistress of a deacon considered an upstanding representative of the life led by those who lived by the Bible. These were, perhaps, the origins of Parker's conviction that finally there was no law; and the double standards of the racial terrain understandably added to that view.

Parker's father was an alcoholic drawn to the night life; his mother left him when the future saxophonist was about nine. Convinced that she could keep young Charlie away from the things her husband loved by giving the boy everything he wanted, she reared him as a well-dressed prince who could do no wrong. That treatment is far from unusual in the lives of Negro innovators. It gives them the feeling that they can do things differently from everyone else. But there was also a crippling side to it. As the bassist Gene Ramey, who knew the saxophonist from about 1934, remarks in the excellent oral history *Goin' to Kansas City*: "He couldn't fit into society, cause evidently his mother babied him so much, that he . . . was expecting that from everybody else in the world."

But when Parker, who was known for his laziness, became interested in music in the 1930s, he quickly discovered that the gladiatorial arena of the jam session made no allowances for handsome brats in tailor-made J. B. Simpson suits at the height of the Depression. He was thrown off many a stage. It was then that he decided to become the best. As Parker told fellow alto player Paul Desmond in 1953: "I put quite a bit of study into the horn, that's true. In fact, the neighbors threatened to ask my mother to move once when I was living out West. They said I was driving them crazy with the horn. I used to put in at least 11 to 15 hours a day. I did that for over a period of three or four years."

He practiced incessantly, and was in the streets, listening to the great local players. He was drawn especially to Buster Smith and Lester Young, though he told the younger saxophonist Junior Williams that it was when he heard Chu Berry jamming in Kansas City in 1936 that he actually became serious about the saxophone. (So serious, in fact, that he gave his first son Berry's name, Leon.) Berry was swift, articulate, and a great chord player; Smith had deep blues soul; Young preferred a light sound that disavowed the conventional vibrato and invented melodic phrases of spectacular variety and rhythmic daring. Parker was also taken by the trumpeter Roy Eldridge, whom he quotes (as saxophonist Lenny Popkin points out) in an early homemade recording, he studied the harmonic detail of Coleman Hawkins; and he was surely inspired by the unprecedented velocity of the pianist Art Tatum.

Velocity was essential to Parker's life. Everything happened fast. On the night that Joe Louis lost to Max Schmeling in 1936, fifteen-year-old Charlie Parker proposed to Rebecca Ruffin and married her a week later. He was a morphine addict by the summer of 1937, which suggests that he may have mixed in an upper-class circle, since there was no heavy drug trade in Kansas City at the time. By January 1938, Parker was a father. He was also anxious to see more of the world and "rode the rails" with hobos later that year, stopping in Chicago, then continuing on to New York, where he arrived with a nickel and a nail in his pocket. It was there that Parker found the beginnings of his own style. In 1940, he returned to Kansas City for his father's funeral and joined Jay McShann's big band, becoming the boss of the reed section and the principal soloist. In a few years he headed the movement that added new possibilities to jazz improvisation and was termed, much to Parker's chagrin, "bebop."

It was during Parker's three years with McShann that the intellectually ambitious personality began to take shape. Parker was interested in politics, mechanics, history, mathematics, philosophy, religion, languages, and race relations. He loved to mimic actors like Charles Laughton, was a prankster and a comic. His problems with dissipation became obvious, too; he told his wife Doris that he had never been able to stop, and recalled that his mother would have to come and get him from a hotel where he was using Benzedrine, staying up nights and going over music. These appetites made him unreliable, and McShann had to send him home for rest often, working with his mother to try and help him handle his addiction.

Parker was also, in fine modernist fashion, a man of masks. Gene Ramey, a member of the McShann band, recalled:

He shouldn't have been nicknamed Yardbird or Bird Parker; he should have been called Chameleon Parker. Man, could that guy change directions and presentations on you! But he also had a gift for fitting in—if he wanted to. That applied to his music most of all. Bird would sit in anywhere we went—Bob Wills, Lawrence Welk, wherever the local jam session was, anybody that was playing. . . . We used to practice together often, just saxophone and bass. We would take "Cherokee," and he would ask me to tell him when he repeated something so he could meet the challenge of staying fresh and fluent. Bird liked to take one tune and play it for a couple of hours. Then he would know every nook and cranny of the melody and the chords. He was very scientific about those things. . . . Now he might not talk about it, but don't let that fool you into believing he wasn't thinking about it.

But beneath the masks, beneath the obsession with music, the mimicry, and the involvement in the sweep of life, there was a need. McShann says that Parker had a crying soul that always came out in his playing; and his first wife, Rebecca, observed it when he was in his early teens:

It seemed to me like he needed. . . . He wasn't loved, he was just given. Addie Parker wasn't that type of woman. She always let him have his way, but she didn't show what I call affection. It was strange. She was proud of him and everything. Worked herself for him and all, but, somehow I never saw her heart touch him. It was odd. It seemed like to me he needed. He just had this need. It really touched me to my soul.

The refinement of Parker's rhythm and the devil-may-care complexity of his phrases came to early distinction during those barnstorming years with McShann, in his next job with Earl Hines, and in the laboratory for the new vernacular that was Billy Eckstine's big band. On "Swingmatism" and "Hootie Blues," recorded with McShann in 1941, Parker had already put together the things that separated him from the alto order of the day. His sound is lighter; he uses almost no vibrato; the songful quality of his lines have a fresh harmonic pungence; and his rhythms, however unpredictable, link up with an inevitability that seems somehow to back its way forward through the beat.

When McShann brought his band to New York in early 1942, Parker was able to spend time afterhours with the musicians who were stretching the language of jazz uptown in Harlem, usually in Minton's Playhouse or

Monroe's Uptown House. "When Charlie Parker came to New York, he had just what we needed," said Dizzy Gillespie. "He had the line and he had the rhythm. The way he got from one note to the other and the way he played the rhythm fit what we were trying to do perfectly. We heard him and knew the music had to go *his* way."

The importance of Parker's jamming with Gillespie, Monk, and the others has often been noted; but the importance of his big band experience cannot be overemphasized. In those bands, Parker learned not only how to blend with other musicians and how to lead a section, he also became a master of setting riffs, those spontaneous motifs that were repeated as chants. Riffs were what gave Kansas City's jazz its reputation; they compressed the essence of the music into one vital unit of rhythm and tune. By playing for dancers, Parker discovered the world of rhythms that Afro-American audiences had invented. Backing singers as varied as McShann's blues crooner Walter Brown, the romantic balladeer Eckstine, and the unprecedented virtuoso Sarah Vaughan, Parker had three distinctly different approaches to the voice to draw from, all of which were incorporated into the epic intricacy of his melodic inventions. Jazz had always demanded that the player think and play his ideas with exceptional speed and logic, but Parker proved that everything could be done even faster. Unlike Tatum, Hawkins, and Byas, who were excellent technicians given to harmonically sophisticated arpeggios, Parker was primarily a melodist; his work brought lyricism to the chords and made rhythmic variations that matched the best of Armstrong and Young.

By casting aside vibrato, Parker introduced a sound many considered harsh at the time. But the ballad performances on Warner Bros.' *The Very Best of Bird* (the famous Dial sessions of 1946–1947) establish that the hardness of his sound was modified by a charming skill for elucidating the riches of romantic fancy in a way that made his music both spiritual and erotic; this was the romantic talent that drew many women to this disordered but beguiling man from whom a high-minded sense of grandeur was delivered with imperial determination. That imperial aspect was also a part of his music's attraction: awesome virtuosity of the sort heard in "Warmin' Up a Riff" or "Koko" is always a protest against limitations. (Both performances are available on *Savoy Original Master Takes.*)

The small, curved brass instrument with cane reed and pearl buttons was throttled and twisted, until it allowed him to express a barely stifled cry that was ever near the edge of consuming rage, the pain of consciousness elevated to extraordinary musical articulation. Bird often sounds like a man torn from the womb of safety too soon. He resented the exposure that music demands, and yet he loved it, because there was no other way he could project himself. But this was no primal scream: The fearful force of Parker's music is always counterpointed by a sense of combative joy and a surprising maturity, by the authority of the deeply gifted. Parker brought the violent rage of the primitive blues (of Robert Johnson, for example) to the citadels of art inhabited by the music's greatest improvisors. For Parker, swing and lyricism were some sort of morale, the bars behind which the beast of hysteria was confined.

Will, in sum, was important to the art of Charlie Parker. He was, after all, a heroin addict. Those who know little about intoxication often fail to realize that the repetition of the condition is what the addicted love most. They seek a consistency that will hold off the arbitrary world. If a few glasses of whiskey, or a marijuana cigarette, or an injection of heroin will guarantee a particular state, the addict has something to rely on. As Parker told Doris: "When you have a bad day, there's nothing you can do about it. You have to endure it. When I have a bad day, I know where to go and what to do to make a good day out of it." Doris Parker also notes that the saxophonist often showed the strength to kick the habit, cold turkey, by himself at home. But the temptations ever present in the night world of jazz always overwhelmed him.

Charlie Parker's early fall resulted more from his way of making "a good day" than it did from race, the economic system, or the topsy-turvy world of his art. It was a tragedy played out along a dangerously complex front of culture and politics, something far more intricate than the crude hipster mythology of Eastwood's *Bird*. It was a fully American story of remarkable triumphs, stubborn misconceptions, and squandered resources that tells us as much about the identity of this country as it does about the powers of jazz.

1989

Papa Dip:
Crescent City Conquistador
and Sacrificial Hero
Louis Armstrong

For all the grandeur, mirth, and joy that Louis Armstrong—Papa Dip—gave to the world, he was essentially a sacrificial hero. Though he had contributed the essential successes that made jazz the most sophisticated performing art in Western history, by the bebop era the middle-aged innovator was frequently dismissed as no more than a wide-smiling entertainer, an Uncle Tom, even a walking aesthetic cadaver. But as long as an old lion has teeth and claws, it isn't safe to stick an arm in his cage. Armstrong was such a lion. His technique was pared down by time and by his fantastic exhibitions of stamina and bravura playing in the 1930s, when nothing was too difficult or too dangerous to try. Consequently, would-be hip listeners and musicians who focused on obvious virtuosity missed the new things that he had to offer. The wisdom and depth of experience of his later years was vastly different from the rebellious longing and the exhilaration of conquest heard when he was a young innovator.

One reason Armstrong's best late work is often overlooked is that his early achievements were so monumental. A quintessential twentieth-century man, Armstrong created a body of work that interacted perfectly with the technology of the age, when human motion was literally reproduced rather than described. Through the phonograph record, the radio, and film, his artistic *action* was captured as he took on convention and won a well-documented battle. He defeated the greatest gift, the ultimate measure, and the inevitable enemy: time. A character in Jean-Luc Godard's *The Married Woman* states an understandable European vision when she says, in a discussion about memory, the past, and discerning truth: "I prefer the present because I have no control over it." That woman would have been shocked to realize what Louis Armstrong had been doing all those years: ordering the present in the context of ensemble improvisation.

As Albert Murray has pointed out, the phonograph record gave musical artists the opportunity to leave truly accurate scores. We don't have to surmise intent: We can hear coherence and achievement or confusion and failure. In that respect, technology transcended the written manuscript in the same way that the jazz musician transcended the present. When Papa Dip was a youth aflame with a fresh musical world in his very cells, his recordings provided master classes: Aspiring jazzman and songwriters played Armstrong discs over and over in order to learn how artistic expression worked on the hoof and what the particulars of his transforming logic were.

Though he was by no means the first improvisor, Papa Dip took improvisation beyond embellishment and into full-fledged melodic invention, made charismatic by the vitality and sweep of his phrasing. He proved over and over that a musician could take a theme, no matter how trivial, and create variations that simultaneously transcended the point of inspiration and brought order to the present. Armstrong made the musical performance a work in progress much like a series of nudes or bathers in Picasso's work, where there is no *correct* version, only the variation or variations that most move the individual.

Armstrong thus broke away from European precedent by redefining and enriching the conception of the performer. Papa Dip's example inspired many musicians to be more than superb actors, which is what the best European concert performers are: They take texts created in the past and bring life to them in the present, making the composer the playwright and the performer the actor. Individuality expresses itself through pacing, rhythm, inflection, and timbre. Papa Dip, however, melded playwright and actor, and so opened the way for the most demanding performing art.

The short performances determined by the three-minute limits of the 78 RPM recording artistically parallel the role of the computer chip's effect on technology: an enormous amount of information in a small space. They have such poetic density that the number of ideas captured in those short durations often give the impression that Armstrong's recordings and those of other three-minute maestros are at least twice their actual length. Just as dullness enlarges the feeling of time, the clarity, passion, and audacity of Armstrong's early masterpieces had the same effect at the opposite end of the block.

Papa Dip's greatest contribution, however, runs contrary to conventional critical wisdom. As Max Roach points out: "Louis Armstrong proved that everybody could think and play at the same time. In European music, only one person *really* thinks—the composer. The other musicians only think *in-*

terpretively. Armstrong liberated everybody. Now you can hear a band, and everybody up there is thinking, playing, listening, fitting their ideas in with the other music that is being created on the spot." In other words, the notion that Papa Dip made jazz a soloist's art is absolutely wrong. When Armstrong's lines are transcribed and removed from the context in which they were created, his power is diminished, as is that of any important improvisor. The rhythm of swing that he brought to fruition and the logic of his inventions meant that *everyone* in a jazz band had to swing and invent logically. By example, he elevated the quality of collective creation, upping the ante for every musician in an ensemble. A pianist who comps brilliantly is speaking the language of Papa Dip; a bassist who walks inspired and inspiring lines is talking Armstrong talk; a drummer who colors and swings with sensitive precision is putting Satchmo's lessons into practice. In fact, the grand mastery that Max Roach brought to the drum solo is but another example of Armstrong's overwhelming significance. But the ultimate legacy of Louis Armstrong is an *ensemble* logic, regardless of how often he overcame the handicap of bands in which the musicians were vastly inferior to him in every way. That was his heroic gift, but only part of his message.

As maturity increases the speed of perception and experience becomes denser, fewer details are needed to recognize essential meanings. While the younger person is still contemplating, the old master has moved on to the next point, digesting through the shorthand made possible by the passage of many moons. In art, that law allows the individual gesture to take on greater resonance. The best of Louis Armstrong's work after fifty proves that his expressive ideas didn't reach their peak until he was nearly sixty. By the middle 1950s, Armstrong could shade a single pitch with a greater swell of nobility, a deeper sense of tragedy, a stoic nostalgia shaped by the facts, and a bittersweet richness born of the lessons he had learned about victory, ambivalence, and loss. Four collections that prove my point are *Louis Armstrong Plays W. C. Handy* (1954), *Satch Plays Fats* (1955), *Satchmo: A Musical Autobiography* (1956/57), and *Echoes of an Era: The Duke Ellington-Louis Armstrong Years* (1961). He was then like Escudero, the Spaniard whom Ralph Ellison described as growing to the point that he could reduce the entire vocabulary of his tradition to a few compelling twists of his fingers.

On the *Handy* record, the epic sense of Negro life that made Armstrong such an imposing artist is matched by material that encompasses tender romance, satire, tragedy, and triumph. His trumpet improvisations are masterfully colored, the rhythmic power of his swing has a breathtaking inevitability, and his emotion is sometimes so purely noble that it seems almost one with the elements. Every reading of melody has the measured authority of a gifted original summing up what he knows with a stately grace that can also rise to heroic power, as on the last laps of "Chantez-Les Bas" or "Atlanta Blues." The singing is as good as the playing: His delivery of "Beale Street Blues" is filled with elegance, awe, satire, mystery, and sorrow. It is a miniature made large by Handy's images and Armstrong's knowledge of a world much bigger and more vital than the lean pickings assumed by condescending liberals (hello, James Lincoln Collier). His "Yellow Dog Blues" has little of the pugnacious loss of Bessie Smith's. The opening is sympathetic but understated; then as we hear where the lover has disappeared to, Armstrong deepens the sorrow, slowly dissolving his sound as the man gets farther and farther away. Ironically, "St. Louis Blues" is one of the weaker selections, too long and overdone. Yet the overall quality makes for a great record. "Aunt Hagar's Blues" shows how well Handy understood the motion from sacred to secular art and the standard of grandeur set by religious ritual. After exquisitely singing the theme through his trumpet, Armstrong lays down the law. A deacon is telling his congregation "the way of living right." When he says "no winging, no ragtime singing," Aunt Hagar jumps up and defends a music that "just tells my feet to dance and I can't refuse/When I hear the melody called the blues." The children singing the blues in harmony are "like a choir from on high broke loose." As if describing his own career, Papa Dip dismisses the description of his art as "the devil's music" by proudly singing, "if the devil brought it, the good Lord sent it right on down to *me*."

The *Waller* recording is buoyant, good-humored, full of emotional contrasts, and impeccable in its swing. In fact, Armstrong *emphasizes* the variety within Waller's love songs, largely downplaying the "novelties" and clowning that overshadowed the composer's deeper work when he was alive. The different qualities of passion Papa Dip brings to "Squeeze Me" as opposed to "Keepin' Out of Mischief Now," or "I've Got a Feeling I'm Falling" as opposed to "Ain't Misbehavin'," and the way he swings "Honeysuckle Rose" through the roof, make it obvious that he was at a stripped-down but potent level of power. The trumpet and vocal of "Blue Turning Grey over You," though spliced together, is a classic Armstrong ballad. But that song is no more impressive than the transcendent nobility and tragedy of "Black and Blue," which rises above the racial specifics of the lyrics and expresses a mournful indignation at what life has dealt.

The *Musical Autobiography* finds Armstrong at the zenith of his mature technical and communicative powers. Papa Dip could still play an emotive high F, but there was an increase in intimacy as he reduced the overtly complex phrasing, the daredevil bursts, the lines that democratically started on any beat or between any, and the dragon-slaying rage at all limits. The outcome was a tone richer than ever and a microscopic precision of detail. Armstrong was again at the conceptual forefront of the music with his abbreviations in a period when Thelonious Monk and Miles Davis were beginning to shear away the prolixities of bebop.

Though some of the material was done earlier in the 1950s by one or another of Armstrong's working groups, the December 1956/January 1957 sessions, either with small bands or added personnel and arrangements by Sy Oliver or Bob Haggart, find the old master at a high point of glory. In feeling and ease, where invention is as much about emotional enrichment as technique, he frequently equals his own remarkable victories, and often surpasses them. For instance, the two-minutes-and-seven-seconds of playing that dominates "Wild Man Blues" is superior to the classic of thirty years earlier and shows how Armstrong had by then brought the instrument to the same level of expressiveness as Billie Holiday's voice at its best. Where the young Dippermouth pounded out the notes with a grainy tone of angry sorrow, then undercut himself with swift, liberating combinations, Satchmo the old simba uses a dark, heavy sound that is, magically, light and smooth at the same time. The melodic construction is stark and given to middle-register statements that evolve one into the other, filled with translucent whispers even as they are soberly declaimed. Melancholy and heat swell through the relaxed musical sentences and what were overt roughenings of pitch in 1927 are reduced to delicate flecks of sand like the minute distortions passion brings to a singer's voice. This is blues feeling at its most soulful and its most beautiful. Each of the breaks, especially the first, is eloquent, and as the emotion almost closes in on resignation, Papa Dip moves to the upper register with the militant cries of a battered spirit that will not be defeated. Like the romantic songs mentioned above, this piece contains a tenderness and a familiarity with the frailty of human life and happiness that no young man ever possesses to this degree. An inarguable masterpiece.

Though Papa Dip was in good-to-exceptional form on the small group performances, it is especially rewarding to hear him sailing over unobtrusive big band arrangements again. "I Surrender Dear," "Exactly Like You," "If I Could Be with You," "I Can't Give You Anything but Love," "Georgia on My Mind," "Memories of You," "Body and Soul," "I Can't Believe You're in

Love with Me," and "That's My Home" are new classics, detailed with delicacy and often including some of his finest singing. As one example from the love songs, "I Surrender Dear" offers stately trumpet phrasing, a surprisingly understated bridge both instrumentally and vocally, and concluding brass majesty with the added edge of great experience. The searing swing he lays down on "Hobo, You Can't Ride This Train" and "I'll Be Glad When You're Dead" shows him in possession of the deft power that avoids hysteria as it uplifts. Part of their relaxation comes from slower tempos than the originals. Any great artist would be proud of the number of accomplishments contained in the *Autobiography*. Essential Papa Dip.

By 1961, the harsh traveling schedule and the years of bearing down on himself and his horn had led to a decline in Armstrong's health. A severe heart attack in 1959 had forced him to pare his work down further. But there was still, as Alberta Hunter might say, "a lot of good tunes left in the old violin." The challenge of Duke Ellington, in top form, and a gathering of fresh material brought a point to the old conqueror's sword. The upshot was his last recording date of high consistency as instrumentalist and singer. Of the four sides, three are excellent. If the merely good third side is skipped, the listener finds twelve performances of excellent singing such as "I'm Just a Lucky So and So," driving trumpet such as "It Don't Mean a Thing," elevated melody-making such as "Solitude," and the unearthly lyricism that culminates on "I Got It Bad and That Ain't Good." It is a joy to hear the way Ellington responds to Armstrong, offering sophisticated suggestions that are ignored in favor of the pithy, then saving them for the masterful piano feature on "Don't Get Around Much Anymore." Unlike too many gatherings of giants, this one came off as a strong addition to the many accomplishments of each man.

Yes, Louis Armstrong was a real sacrificial hero, an innovator who led American music to a new land of artistry that he wasn't always able to enter himself, too often presented in circumstances so beneath him that even his extraordinary talent couldn't lift everything. Before his heart attack, when he was still at the height of his mature skills, his crude manager Joe Glaser blocked Papa Dip from working with Gil Evans on an album of concerto arrangements, something Armstrong wanted to do after he heard Evans's work with Miles Davis on *Porgy and Bess*. There was much more he could have done. When we hear him observe in song on the *Handy* record that "from milkless milk and silkless silk, we are growing used to soulless soul," there can be no doubt that Papa Dip is talking about things at the other end of the field from where he built his own monument, homemade and universal.

1985

Not So Dizzy
Dizzy Gillespie

When he died recently at seventy-five, Dizzy Gillespie wasn't in the middle of anything that had the jazz world hanging from the bell of his up-angled trumpet, but he was mourned because his was the last of the minds that had been central to the bebop movement of the middle 1940s. When Gillespie went, so did the memory of how it all came about; what he, Charlie Parker, Thelonious Monk, Kenny Clarke, Oscar Pettiford, and the others did in Harlem clubs, hotel rooms, apartments, and walking down the street as they talked music. Gillespie could see every room, every uniform, recall the smells, the colors, the meals, the ways the instruments gleamed or lay dully under the light, hear the chords as the unusual notes were added, recollect the styles of clothing and the way Negroes and whites wore their hair and talked during those years, how it felt to become the most recognized member of a movement that bloomed right out of his trumpet and Charlie Parker's saxophone, out of the different way pianos, basses, and drums formed the inspiring and supporting unit of the rhythm section. With their vibratoless tones, their willfully dissonant harmonies and their race horse tempos, the beboppers remade the small jazz unit and Gillespie led the first big band to make thorough use of what was the freshest material since Duke Ellington had come to power. Over the years, Gillespie worked in many formats, exploring his interest in exotic rhythms and making his own variations on the context of trumpet soloist and jazz orchestra that Louis Armstrong had pioneered in the early 1930s.

Gillespie is also mourned because he embodied the essence of his art. In his walk and his facial expressions, the movements of his hands, the sound of his laugh, the tonal flexibility of his voice, the bored to molten cast of his eyes, the way he danced on his bandstands, and the position his body went into when he was on fire and the trumpet had no limitations, Dizzy Gillespie carried and projected the moxie, the curiosity, the wit, and the pathos that enliven the world of jazz. Like Louis Armstrong, he was aware of the spiritual muscle necessary to hold still the gymnastic elegance of an iron cross with one hand in the ring of tragedy, the other in the ring of comedy. The travels, the parties, the endless train of nights across the globe when he was made welcome because of the heat he could put through a cold brass instrument, the high casualty list of talent he had seen knocked across the line into death by self-inflicted or social blows, and the humor both light and very dark were taken into Gillespie's electrons. When he arrived, the epic was there.

Like a number of the American geniuses who affirm the democratic ideal, Gillespie came not from the polished fish bowl of the academy, but, at least partially, from the ocean itself. He was homemade and a scholar of his art, a man who sweated his way to a pinnacle of velocity technique, harmonic sophistication, and rhythmic intricacy that hasn't been surpassed. With his cheeks swelling like those of a brown wind demon, he played the trumpet with such power and finesse that he took a position—after Louis Armstrong and Roy Eldridge and before Miles Davis and Clifford Brown— as one of the five most influential players of his horn in the history of the national music.

Even under ruthless scrutiny, Gillespie becomes a mythic figure because his accomplishments were so exceedingly large that they would seem to have been accomplished by some Crockett-like combination of fish and fowl, man and beast, sinner and saint, angel and devil, bear and antelope. He was a supreme musical intellectual, whose fire and evangelical willingness to personally deliver musical details made ensemble sense out of what might have been no more than an individual horn style. Many are the stories of his sitting down and showing piano players how to accompany and what chords to play, bass players the nature of the new harmony, and drummers the rhythms compatible with what he and Charlie Parker were playing. The Harlem apartment he had on Seventh Avenue during the 1940s was a conservatory where the young and curious came to find out what the increasingly formidable trumpet master was putting together. Fifteen or twenty musicians used to be seen walking with him through the streets, listening to his advice and singing the notes he was explaining to them.

In keeping with the necessities of the night world in which jazz was made and the wit that has carried the Negro through the protean configurations of our society, Gillespie was prepared. He became a professional in an environment where anything could happen. His humor was boundless. His temper was quick, and his response could cut to the bone. The pranks he loved to play and the confidence he had in his dissonant harmonic ideas sparked the antipathy of certain older musicians when Gillespie was making his way during his early twenties. But the young trumpet player who had first been influenced by Roy Eldridge continued to search the piano keyboard for what he needed to get him where he wanted to go. A bottle was thrown against his head because he refused to play something on the piano for a white man during a Southern tour with Earl Hines in the early 1940s. Above the Mason-Dixon line, that man might have experienced another side of Gillespie. He was good with his dukes. He carried a knife and once nearly slashed off the arm of a Northern redneck.

Bassist Al McKibbon worked with the trumpeter's bebop big band in the late 1940s and remembers a night they were playing a dance at the Savoy Ballroom in Harlem. McKibbon's wife was at the edge of the bandstand and Gillespie, ever spontaneous, jumped off the bandstand, took her in his arms and went on to win the jitterbug contest. Four or five years ago at a New York club, a woman in the audience turned out to be the same partner with whom he had won first prize in Manhattan's largest Latin dance contest two or three decades earlier. "Man, did we *practice!* Oooh. And when we got there, we were *ready*. I'll never forget that night. Oh, it was so wonderful."

Such Americans are both numerous and rare. They are numerous because so much of our national tale is the story of their arriving from such surprising places and so indelibly imprinting our culture with both their personalities and the impersonal facts of their accomplishments, proving their work both inimitable and beacons of universal possibility. They are rare because few of even the great American individuals have had as invincible an effect on the way we define ourselves as Gillespie did. He rose from the position of an odd fish to a star surfer riding the high, high curving water of a trend, then sank into the position of those miracles taken for granted, but periodically returned to view, dripping with new wisdoms, beckoning as others followed him at the risk of their own prestige and peril.

1989

At the Five Spot

Thelonious Monk

Though Thelonious Monk's stature is very clear now, his historical relationship to the music was for quite some time a very curious one. In many
ways, he was one of the founding fathers of the Bebop Revolution of the
forties, but more as a theoretician and instructor than a lickmaker. Dizzy
Gillespie admits to having learned a lot from him, Miles Davis went over to
his house to learn chords as did so many others, he composed songs that
many played, worked in a band with Coleman Hawkins, and maintained
enormous respect among the makers of the then-new music. Part of it had
to do with the fact that he was capable of teaching musicians inroads to a
music he himself wasn't interested in playing. He was, to use Regis Debray's
phrase, conducting a "revolution within the revolution." Where men like
Charlie Parker, Gillespie, Navarro, Powell, and others were inventing styles
that called for new levels of instrumental control in terms of rapid tempos,
passages dense with eighth notes, and complex syncopations, Monk was
repudiating it all.

It is almost as though Monk understood more quickly than anyone else
how the bebop style could be reduced to mannered chord-running and
rhythms that were far less varied than those of the musics that had preceded it. He seemed intent on forging a music that could make use of a variety of elements, including the call-and-response energy of New Orleans,
the updated antiphonal relationships between soloists and riffs or thematic
backgrounds heard in Ellington and Basie, the percussive nature of the Afro-
American piano tradition, and Jelly Roll Morton's dictum that a jazz pianist
should sound like a *jazz band*. And all of this telescoped through the syncopations, polyrhythms, and flirtations with the tempo of the Afro-American
dance tradition. There were professionals like the Nicholas Brothers, Bill
Robinson, the endless chorus lines with soloists that were the visual coun-
terparts of the large and small bands. There were also the dance hall ama-
teurs whose elegance, slides, twirls, bumps, and grinds had sparked and in-

spired more than a few bands. In other words, the problem that Monk presented was one of thoroughness: What made him avant-garde was his determination to sustain the *power* of the tradition rather than reduce it to clichés, trends, novelties, or uninformed parodies. Because of that decision, he had to wait almost twenty years before he could be heard in person on a regular basis rather than by what must have been the incredibly painful proxy of hearing his own songs played by others in clubs that would not hire him because he was "too bizarre."

Much of the problem Monk has presented has to do with the fact that he is the first Picasso of jazz, the first Afro-American musician to develop a style that willfully shunned overt virtuosity in favor of a control of the elements of the music in fresh ways. Monk may be a great aesthetic chef, but he is not a waiter: He may cook the food, but you have to get up and serve yourself. That is: Just as Picasso demanded that the viewer *do* something other than peruse a painted photograph or an *impression* of a photograph, Monk demands that the listener play the song along with him, fill in the holes he leaves, figure out where he is, understand what he's doing with the beat, or at least *sense* more than the ordinary. He understood early on that jazz requires each of its artists to develop his own version of four-four swing—fast, medium, slow; his own version of the blues, of ballads, and of the Afro-Hispanic rhythms misnomered as "Latin." All these things Monk did, but in such an original manner that many did not think he could play at all.

Actually, Monk has totally rethought the tradition. He has a great love for the whole legacy of Afro-American music as it has been translated through the piano keyboard and through guitars as well (there is more than a little mutuality to his manner of drive and relaxation and that of Charlie Christian, even to some of his dissonances echoing the tone and the attack of the great guitarist). In his playing, one can hear everything from the most sophisticated to the most "primitive." It is almost as though he (as Ornette Coleman was to do later) took everything he learned when playing with a revivalist or listening to the country-blues players, amateur or professional, and used that material as a screen through which he would strain the florid aspects of bebop, removing the bejeweled scabbard (to alter our metaphor) and presenting the constant jumps and jerks or lyrical glints of light on the blade. Replete with a profound understanding of motion, texture, weight, balance, and contrast. But that is to be expected, for Monk is the third man in the chain of major American composers working outside European concert-hall forms, the first two being Jelly Roll Morton and Duke Ellington.

It is as a composer on all levels—themes, improvisation, accompaniment thick with thematic abstractions, riffs, percussive grunts, startling shifts of register and polyphonic provocation—that Monk was to have his say and make his mark. In many ways, he taught musicians *and* listeners *and* critics how to *think*. Though he is a past master of subtlety, he never wanted you to miss anything he was playing or forget what the theme was once the improvising started. Oh, yes, Monk was in pursuit of the most virtuosic of possibilities: authority. He seemed to have realized that jazz was a music constantly at war with the overdone and the sentimental and that it was always in danger of being reduced to maudlin mannerisms, whether through ineffectual vibrato, obviousness, or clichés. Even the new technical levels of bebop could find themselves being shunted through quasi-European graveyards of gangrened pretension (as with those who thought "bop" was a Negroid mispronunciation of Bach). It was not that he was particularly at war with European expertise but simply that it was irrelevant to what he did. With Monk's determination to fuse the victories of Ellington, Basie, and Christian into a perceptible form that could give the small group the orchestral complexity that had not existed since New Orleans, he brought about a movement within a movement, with Miles Davis being his first great pupil. And not only did Monk inspire musicians but he provoked some of the finest critical writing and some of the bitterest fights between schools of writers and fellow practitioners. His performances scandalized pianists of every school and confounded listeners—not to mention the fact that his demeanor and dancing in front of the bandstand when he was finally "accepted" convinced some that he was no more than another flam artist embroidering the emperor's new clothes; or, at best, inept.

Monk's music was so far inside the tradition that he seemed to demand that the listener have a thorough enough knowledge of the African American legacy to appreciate how he was playing around with it, off it, and through it. What he was after was to make a small band take on the force of a big band, and two big bands in particular—Ellington's and Basie's, furthered by the riff power of Christian. What Ellington had was a thorough translation of the entire tradition through his band, including soloists like Barney Bigard who could take you from New Orleans to New York in the course of eight bars; while Basie had an understanding of the power of the musical rest so that the force of the rhythm section's motion could set up almost excruciatingly delicious anticipation and suspense in the mind and emotions of the listener; then Christian could have everything in motion in two bars. Also, it would seem that Monk understood the importance of a leader's organizing his soloists for contrasting melodic, rhythmic, timbral, and harmonic styles. Both Ellington and Basie had players who provided them with a collage of improvisational styles and both were cunning enough to have them play in sequences that would light things up. In answer to this, Monk developed a piano style that could emulate brass, reeds, guitars, and drums and that was capable of carrying you from the barrelhouse to the penthouse and *back*. His intent was to do as he had heard Ellington do: address ongoing thematic development rather than merely arrange "backgrounds." If you need references, listen to Ellington's *Skrontch* and *Chatterbox*, recorded in 1937 and 1938, respectively. The accents and the continual concern with the themes are clear antecedents to Monk compositions like *Evidence*, "Coming on the Hudson," and *Rhythm-a-ning*. But to understand their relationship to Monk, one must listen to the performances on *all* levels. For he quite possibly was the first musician of his generation to realize that he could reverse the process of taking solos down and orchestrating them by taking powerful syncopated accents (such as the brass figures on *Chatterbox*) as germs to be spaced with powerful notes into themes as stark and beautiful as *Evidence*, with intricate counterpoint provided either by his own runs or the interjections of his drummers. (This is why thematically oriented drummers like Haynes, who magnificently reiterates the melodic rhythms of *Evidence* under Griffin's solo and extends them as well, are so necessary to the fruition of Monk's music.)

Just as fascinating as Monk's relationships to the two greatest bandleaders is his relationship to Christian, a man whose talents were only glimpsed, however profoundly they affected the history of the guitar. I find Monk's solo on *Coming on the Hudson* particularly Christian-like in the way the eighth notes are spun out, the starts and stops, the sustained tones, the percussive chords, the badgering of the rhythm. But that is not the only one. On *Rhythm-a-ning*, he seems to have found a brilliant abstraction of the striding *furioso* of Basie and the booting, meddling, even rageful and simultaneously joyous strumming and plinking of the great guitarist, all undercut and measured by Monk's genius for rearrangement and startling sound-blocks. For those who would investigate, try "I Got Rhythm," "Stardust," and "Tea for Two" by the Charlie Christian Quintet, recorded in Minneapolis in 1939 (Columbia G–30779). Listening to those numbers makes it clear that Christian's spirit and sensibility pervade much of what Monk does and are beautifully redefined for the uses of an extremely unique and priceless musical mind.

By the time the recordings reissued here were made, Monk had been at the forefront of New York music for almost twenty years and had been lucky enough not only to have survived in mind, skin, and spirit, but to have continued growing in confidence and boldness. He had also been well documented on Blue Note, Prestige, and Riverside recordings, which gave his live performances a backdrop of one of the most significant bodies of musical work composed and performed in any context. His songs, such as 'Round Midnight, Straight, No Chaser, and Well, You Needn't, were being played by more than a few bands and three of his best students—Miles Davis, Sonny Rollins, and John Coltrane—were beginning to be looked at as major or important figures. Davis's subtle, spare, and non-European way of playing the trumpet was undoubtedly the result of having perceived the weight of Monk's conception. Rollins's fascination with endless timbres, percussive phrasing, rhythmic trickery, thematic improvisation, irony, and humor goes without saying. Coltrane discovered the value of the whole-tone scale and was to tell A. B. Spellman that the "sheets of sound" had in part come from his attempts to imitate Monk's runs while working with him at the Five Spot in 1957. And I would add that the shape and rhythm of Monk's composition *Trinkle Tinkle* was more than a bit helpful. Monk had observed it all and had had one chance, on *Swing Spring* on the famous session with Miles Davis in 1954, to show who the boss really was. In order to tell Monk that he loved him, even though he wouldn't allow him to play while he was soloing, Davis quotes some Monk licks in the trumpet section that precedes the piano solo. The rankled giant responds by taking the lick and building an incredible solo of virtuosic colors, turns, harmonies, and rhythms that seem to say, "Excuse me, young man, but if you intend to piddle around with my stuff, see if you can get to *this!*" By no means was Monk to be undone or outdone. He was ready and had been ready for a long, long time.

The Five Spot had begun its music policy in 1956 with the band of Cecil Taylor, a vanguard pianist whose linear rhythmic style can be almost totally traced to *Work*, a composition performed by Monk in the early fifties. The following summer Monk came into the club with a quartet that included John Coltrane, tenor saxophone; Wilbur Ware, bass; and Shadow Wilson, drums. The group played to packed houses and the engagement was considered a major event. Unfortunately, it was never recorded in public performance, but three studio tracks exist (reissued on Milestone M–47011). It is equally sad that the two records in the present reissue set were met with critical derision when they were initially released (probably because Johnny Griffin and the rest of the members constituted a *different* band). To my ears, these recordings are excellent and every member of the band rises to the opportunities provided, particularly what must be called the reed and percussion *sections*.

With a quartet that included a tenor saxophonist with the intellectual, emotional, and technical skills of Johnny Griffin, Monk was able to realize his orchestral desires by using the entire range of the horn, pivoting the motion of the band off the bass, with the piano and trap drums creating an ongoing arrangement of textural, harmonic, and melodic development. Griffin could give Monk the clarinet, alto, tenor, and upper-baritone ranges, often suggesting in tandem with Monk's particularized and sonorous voicings more than one horn (as had been done brilliantly elsewhere by Gigi Gryce's alto on *Gallop's Gallop*, a Monk performance and composition that still looms over contemporary music). Malik gave first-class bass from start to finish, walking the chords with a melodic direction and a powerful, steady swing that could get hankty and tricky on tunes like *Rhythm-a-ning*. Roy Haynes, one of the all-time giants, played as if in training for the belt every second, with poise, class, fire, and taste, underwoven by superb execution. Each cymbal and each drum is used something like a dancer in an extremely complex fabric of sonic choreography—elaborating, paraphrasing, shifting the beat, giving it different ranges by use of timbral variation and often working up to a magical one-man ensemble in which the drums function as a big band would, filling the roles of chanting brass and weaving, feathery or double-timing reeds—replete with plungers, mutes, and alternate fingerings! A superb orchestrator of the musical ideas as they are extemporized about him, Mr. Haynes is arguably as great—if not greater—than any drummer in combination with Monk. All in all, obviously one of Monk's finest working groups. Again: a four-man orchestra.

Without the precedence of Duke Ellington's *The Mystery Song* of 1931, I cannot imagine compositions like *Light Blue* or "Coming on the Hudson" existing, each of which is one of the "mood" or "blue" numbers that, as Gunther Schuller has pointed out, Ellington invented as categories. The manner in which Ellington uses the piano throughout both takes also prepares one quite well for the way in which Monk works as an under- or counter-voice in the rhythm section. *Light Blue* as performed by this quartet is a stripped-down, elegant, and unsentimental ballroom number of great romance, wisdom, and dignity. As with all the performances, there is a powerful dance feeling to it. In the improvisation, Griffin is very melodic, songful, attentive to the line's contours and weights, its joy and emaciated lyricism. Monk's solo jags, darts, and dangles over the dancing cymbals of Haynes and Malik's Wellman Braud-like solemn beauty, creating a masterful composition-within-a-composition and an arrangement-within-an-arrangement. "Coming on the Hudson" is full of despair, pain, and a perseverance of stoic dignity. Griffin brilliantly organizes his arpeggios with thematic and Monkish ideas, rounding out a fusion of Coleman Hawkins, Lester Young, Charlie Parker, and the big blue shout of the Chicago tenor school. Monk's thematic rearrangement seems a paean to courage and responsibility, taking care of the business of being one's self, regardless of the odds and the sorrow. Although *Rhythm-a-ning* is more than strongly related to a passage in Lawrence Brown's opening solo on *Ducky Wucky* (an observation passed on to me by Gary Giddins), at least in terms of certain notes, its rhythmic character is more about Charlie Christian. There is a joy to the statement of the line, the interjections of Griffin that are echoed by Monk, and the improvisation that epitomizes the sensibility of swing. Griffin and Haynes really stretch out in the long tenor solo, always listening to each other and buoying the music up over the driving bass line. Monk's solo was spoken of earlier. Malik carries the music into a solo by Haynes that is not only melodic, but is a *good* melody. "Epistrophy," the band's closing theme, ends the first side as it does the second, each side of the original album having been intended to suggest a club set.

Blue Monk is a classic blues theme that receives a fine rendition. One of the interesting structural aspects of the improvisation is how Monk begins his section with a variation on Griffin's last phrase and fades his own solo into an accompaniment for the bass improvisation, thereby avoiding a break in musical feeling. Excellent musician that he is, Haynes begins his drum solo with a variation on Malik's last phrase. Other notable aspects are Griffin's blue authenticity and Monk's ability to capture the essence of the form and sensibility without relying on clichés.

Evidence achieves great power and Griffin's range on his horn allows the melody to build with extreme tension. Griffin's melodic imagination, his arpeggios, and the excellent ways in which he uses the ideas presented to him by the rhythm section keep a focus on the theme that belies facility for the sake of exhibition. Monk is, again, cogent and muscular, creating a spare melody of acidic colors before submerging his thematic arabesques into the environment for Malik. Haynes takes another solo that is as well thought out as one of Monk's.

Nutty, Blues Five Spot, and *Let's Cool One* are all very interesting Monk themes. *Nutty* takes on a lyricism at Griffin's hands that makes it an affectionate portrait of something while maintaining the rhythmic surprise and genius, with Monk's paraphrases and satiric asides seeming on occasion to descend through the meter. The control of Monk's solo and the motion of the band is outstanding. *Blues Five Spot* is an example of how an exceptional musician can take a very traditional phrase and get the feeling of more than one horn by subtle shifts of register. Griffin overflows with ideas and notes, then eloquently plays the last two choruses *a cappella* before Monk's entry with the rhythm section. Just as the band sound has been varied before by Monk's laying out and letting Griffin stroll with bass and drums, the whole rhythm section's leaving him out there does the same thing and extends the conception of the break as well. Monk is especially skillful in his solo as he reiterates the theme in abstraction and builds in complexity to then contract the melody to a series of oddly syncopated jabs that are marvels of implication because, before one knows it, one is filling in the rest of the theme on his own. As with his solo on *Blue Monk*, Haynes gives the sound and feeling of hand drums but builds an original percussion melody that illustrates his imagination and his personalizing of things that Art Blakey would seem to have begun bringing to the drums in the early fifties. *Let's Cool One* begins almost as a march in abstraction before developing in rhythm and line to a beautiful melody with a supremely sophisticated bridge tinted with blues. Griffin holds onto the theme throughout his improvisations, with and without the rhythm section, playing particularly beautiful bridges and, in his unaccompanied two choruses, giving possibly his best playing of the record. The composer's playing is another splendid thematic venture characterized by bittersweet and jolting harmonies.

In Walked Bud is one of the best selections of the entire two volumes. First, it is a fascinating example of how well Griffin had captured Monk's ideas and transmuted them for his own devices, as when the trills, oblique scalar melodies, thematic paraphrases, and register leaps come off sounding more Monkian than anything else. But Griffin is doing more than aping Monk, for the swing, the drive, the sound, and the juggling of the dense runs over the wonderful rhythm section are definitely his. When Monk enters, the fire is way up and he proceeds to push the smoke button on his own, rippling and building a solo that drives and drives, breathes, makes fine uses of repetition, and builds, again, a new composition. Malik takes his finest solo of the recording, deftly anticipating the later popularity of Eastern musical approaches. Haynes bats a beautiful clean-up and the bouncing, swinging theme burns its way out. The rendition of *Just a Gigolo* has recently struck me as a Monkian recasting of the piano solo that appears on an Armstrong version of the song done in the thirties. On *Misterioso*, another classic blues that closes the recording, Griffin's lovely and biting blues melodies are shouting, sophisticated, and powerful, yet free of the hysteria of imitation or spiritual mimicry. Monk's last solo of the package is quite a fitting one: It shows off the resources of a musical master who can take the most basic of forms and bring a range of moods and techniques that gives it freshness while refusing to sell it out.

In closing, I would like to say that you have in your hands the documentation of a wonderful musical unit and some of the best improvising ever captured in performance. It is part of the legacy of one of the finest of American and world artists, a man whose gifts to the spirit, the mind, and the emotions of the mass of strangers all over the world who listen to him have been given unselfishly. The work of Thelonious Monk personifies one of the closing passages in Albert Murray's masterwork on Afro-American music, *Stomping the Blues*:

> What it all represents is an attitude toward the nature of human experience (and the alternatives of human adjustment) that is both elemental and comprehensive. It is a statement about confronting the complexities inherent in the human situation and about improvising or experimenting or riffing or otherwise playing with (or even gambling with) such possibilities as are also inherent in the obstacles, the disjunctures, and the jeopardy. It is also a statement about perseverance and about resilience and thus also about the maintenance of equilibrium despite precarious circumstances and about achieving elegance in the very process of coping with the rudiments of subsistence.

For those who would experience the wisdom, courage, and clarity of a great twentieth-century artist, listen closely.

1977

Ahmad Jamal

Though no musician since 1945 has dominated the jazz scene with quite the overwhelming impact of Charlie Parker, it is also true that no single artist after the great alto saxophonist has been more important to the development of fresh form in jazz than Ahmad Jamal. As a virtuoso Pittsburgh pianist, he is in the luminous order of titans that includes Earl Hines, Mary Lou Williams, and Errol Garner. But as a conceptualist Jamal is in another line altogether. Having sought more than a distinctive style, Jamal must be listened to as one of the pianists whose work had significance far beyond his vision of the keyboard. Jamal has to be considered along with Jelly Roll Morton, Fletcher Henderson, Duke Ellington, Art Tatum, Count Basie, Thelonious Monk, Horace Silver, and John Lewis, all thinkers whose wrestling with form and content influenced the shape and the texture of the music and whose ensembles were models of their musical visions.

For those acquainted with jazz histories, the inclusion of Jamal in that list might sound farfetched. Even though he has received fulsome praise from musicians, Jamal has often been dismissed by jazz writers as no more than a cocktail pianist, a player so given to fluff that his work shouldn't be considered seriously in any artistic sense. Claims for his influence, however, aren't even vaguely exaggerated. In fact, it is now much easier to see how broad and deep his effect has been. There were elements in his music even thirty-five years ago that are still profound ideas about the way a small ensemble should—or could—function. And perhaps the reason that what he had to offer wasn't perceived as clearly as it should have been is that too many might have been looking for literal emulation when what Jamal had to give jazz was as much conceptual as it was literal. Jamal, like Monk, had ideas that could function free of the specific ways in which he applied them, meaning that once one understood the concept it wasn't necessary to ape his manner of execution.

Those ideas reached fruition and had such influence because Jamal was a superb student of jazz tradition, as are all true innovators. He not only understood the fundamentals of the idiom and the achievements of his predecessors and his peers, Jamal also heard implications within them that led him to introduce fresh ideas about group form. Rather than state a tune in one tempo and improvise, however well, over an expected kind of accompaniment, Jamal sought orchestral effects and might turn an individual piece into an idiomatic symphonette. Riffs, interludes, linear developments, harmonic substitutions, vamps, modulations of tonality, of meter, of tempo, and of timbre were arranged so intelligently that a single song could become an excursion into form that was as surprising as the most inventive improvisation in a standardized format. In fact, it might be more accurate to say that Jamal often heard rhapsodies, since the definition of one is "a musical composition of irregular form having an improvisatory character." But his arrangements had such interest because they took on the ensemble freedom of direction a listener is accustomed to hearing in an unaccompanied piano performance. To bring that kind of surprise to playing by three performers was truly an innovation.

Yet none of it would have worked had Jamal not also been a swinger of the first order, a player whose control of the beat allowed for exceptional freedom of phrasing. That case was matched by his delightful variety of attack. He could slide a light, silvery tone from his instrument; one darker and more vocal; yet another darker still and more percussive. In a given performance he might call upon all of those timbres, or a phrase might move across the keyboard in twists of different color. It is probable that the blues, which he plays with the tickling charm and confidence of the downhome masters, is what attuned him to such distinctions of color, since blues feeling is as much about texture as it is about anything. One could go even further by observing that the insinuation so basic to the charisma of the slow blues never lies very far below the surface of Jamal's music, which can move as well into the idiomatic humor and idealism heard in virtuosi as different as Waller, Tatum, and Wilson. A signal aspect of his talent was Jamal's ability to so skillfully combine the fleet and the fluid with the spare and the suggestive that each stylistic reference was an immediate event or part of a *form*, not just a manner of phrasing or attack. Block chords, staccato statements, airy lines, trills, arpeggios, and so on were frequently isolated and used as the basis of movements within given pieces. Devices were elevated to forms, or elements of form.

As these performances often show, Jamal was concerned with organic detail to such an extent that his imagination expressed itself in approaches that dissolved any significant distinction between foreground and background. Through the use of space and changes of rhythm and tempo, Jamal invented a group sound that had all the surprise and dynamic variation of an imaginatively ordered big band. His spare and subtle ideas set up grooves and riffs with a low-keyed but jaunty magnetism quite reminiscent of Count Basie: They cunningly prepare for dramatic changes of dynamics and direction. Piano, guitar, and bass function much like brass and reeds, harmony and rhythm, allowing the leader to create tension and release in a number of ways, few of them conventional. The piano is the lead voice and the guitar is sometimes the counter-voice; the piano will slip under the guitar and supply accompaniment by taking over the very same figures heard previously from that guitar, which is presently *stating another melody*, a riff— or improvising! It is also important to note that Ray Crawford was bringing an almost unprecedented degree of nuance to his guitar playing, making use of expressive timbres that ranged from a willfully tinny and nearly whining quality to round, glowing tones that curved and bent with the miniscule precision of a vocalist. Jamal rarely missed an opportunity to make the most of what each of his players could do, and the results brought qualities of group sound that were as impressive as those achieved by George Kirby's classic sextet.

Those qualities were admittedly admired by Miles Davis, who was taken by Jamal's ensemble approach and his repertoire. "I think," says bassist Todd Coolman, "that what Miles liked about Ahmad was the level of excitement that he achieved without being obvious. What he does *not* play allows the listener to be involved on a level that was unprecedented. He has such a very refined use of tension and release that he brings off a roller coaster effect by almost seeming to just let things slowly build to these high points of tension that are released just like they are on a roller coaster when you get to the top and the car suddenly plunges down. Ahmad has as much technique as anybody out here and always has had it but he chooses to play only as much of it as will work. Miles learned from that, which was a big lesson for someone who came up hearing Bird, Dizzy, and Bud Powell. The other thing that Miles got from Ahmad was the idea of using musical form as a compositional device, where you take a certain portion of a time and use it as an interlude, milking all the music possible out of it. Ahmad's appreciation of the bass line was superior; he understood the function of the bass line to such a degree that he allowed the sound of the band to function as a whole. And Israel Crosby's understanding of the bass line as melodic counterpoint was equal to anybody's in any music that I know about. His lines are so good they could be songs in themselves. Because

Ahmad valued that, he was able to create trio music that had more levels of interaction than we are accustomed to hearing."

Davis recorded six of the songs included on this album after he heard Jamal play them. His sense of ensemble was forever changed by the pianist, and when he did his own studio version of "A Gal in Calico," he even got Philly Joe Jones to use his cymbals in emulation of the rhythm Ray Crawford plays on the body of his guitar with Jamal, turning his instrument into a percussion section. As I once wrote of the relationship of the trumpeter to the pianist: "In June of 1955, when Davis recorded with Red Garland, Oscar Pettiford, and Philly Joe Jones, the Jamal influence was overt. In 'Will You Still Be Mine' Davis's phrasing shows the impact of the pianist—the pungent phrases that appear in the middle of fleet bursts, the determination to make each idea different from the last, the understanding of how overall shapes are achieved through the understanding of the song's basic structure, allowing for reiteration of central elements, whether melodic or harmonic, rhythmic or textural. As Philly Joe Jones once told me: 'Miles used to study Jamal. Once when we were in Chicago listening to Jamal when he didn't use a drummer. We kept hearing an accent on the fourth beat, but there wasn't no goddamn drums up there anywhere. Miles kept looking and noticed that Ray Crawford was hitting the guitar with his thumb on the last beat, swinging the hell out of the band. Miles said to me, 'Joe, if you took your drumstick and hit the rim of the snare on four, it would swing the band to death'."

Jamal was born in 1930, so he was only twenty-five when the last session included here was recorded, a fact that makes the independent nature of his intelligence that much more imposing. In a period when Art Tatum and Bud Powell so overshadowed the keyboard that theirs seemed the two most magnetic directions, Jamal was able to draw from them and combine what he liked in their work with that of Nat Cole and Errol Garner, covering the most important piano and trio conceptions of his time, but bringing something quite unique to his own work. As this album shows, Jamal had a vision of restraint that could express itself in the puckish good humor and perfect swing of pieces like "Old Devil Moon," "Billy Boy," "The Surrey with the Fringe on Top," and "A Gal in Calico"; in the meditative entrancement of "Crazy He Calls Me" or tenderness of the sort heard in "Will You Still Be Mine." "Poinciana" has the exotic dreams of hypnotic vamps and the mobile-like turning of emphasis from one voice or texture to another (if only for his rhyming responses to the textures around him during his feature following Crawford, Jamal would be a musician of extremely subtle precision). There are moments during the B section of "Aki and Ukthay" that clearly predict the rhythmic feeling of the mature Coltrane ballad style.

But perhaps the most interesting group pieces are "Slaughter on 10th Avenue" and "Pavanne." The former shows the twenty-one-year-old Jamal already seeing past the way most bands approached a song and going for signal contrasts of rhythm, tempo, and timbre. "Pavanne," though, is something of a shocker. The quality and scope of the formal overview is remarkable. It is built around a vamp that also forms a motivic cornerstone. Introduced by Jamal, it is played beneath the piano as he improvises on a melody we have yet to hear, using another rhythm as a release from the tension of the vamp. When Jamal picks up the vamp himself again, it sits beneath the melody line Crawford introduces, which has the same structures as "So What?" and is the theme Coltrane used for "Impressions." Then the piece moves through an interlude and becomes a blues, with Jamal playing a chorus, Crawford crooning a few, and the band turning back around for riffs that not only summon Kansas City but are variations on the vamp-motif that opened the piece!

Jamal's influence on pianists is no small achievement, since his work touched Red Garland, Bill Evans, Herbie Hancock, and McCoy Tyner, either as players or as bandleaders or both. As he grew from the point heard on this recording, Jamal developed hand signals that allowed him spontaneously to reorder the pieces he was playing, shifting interludes and sections around as he heard them on the spot, which brought a truly revolutionary spontaneity to group playing. One can see Betty Carter using her own versions of those signals with her band today and can even observe them in the rock-and-roll band of Miles Davis, whose greatest days are long behind him but who is still deeply affected by the pianist, even in decline. The cues Wynton Marsalis applies are rooted in Jamal, as are the vamps Keith Jarrett now spontaneously pivots off of when playing standards with Gary Peacock and Jack DeJohnnette. His influence is still seminal, even when the players under his conceptual sway aren't aware of it. When one listens to this record closely, the discretion and joyous intelligence of Ahmad Jamal are charismatically evident. That he produced all of these ideas between the ages of twenty-one and twenty-five proves that this bandleader is one of the most gifted in the history of this music.

1989

Himself When He Was Real
The Art of Charles Mingus

Charles Mingus was born in 1922 and, by his death in 1979, had proven himself a musician of multiple gifts—as instrumentalist, composer, band-leader, creator of structures for improvisation, and rethinker of the rhythm section. Those talents and the ways in which he used them to make his mark on his instrument, his writing, and his ensembles affected jazz on a number of levels. The very best of his work triumphantly resolves the op-posites of primitive intensity and high sophistication into a language that freely manipulates the vast resources of jazz in ways few others attempted before this adventurous artist forged his identity from the smithy of his dis-cipline and imagination.

1. The Bassist

He was the next great virtuoso bassist who rose to fierce artistic authority after Jimmy Blanton, Oscar Pettiford, and Ray Brown, all of whom made their invincible reputations before Mingus arrived in New York in the early fifties. When Mingus hit Manhattan, jazz bassists had already developed a fresh percussive-harmonic identity for the instrument. In European music, the bass is almost always played with the bow and is never utilized with the freedom heard in jazz, where the bull fiddle is almost always plucked.

The improvisational significance and the stamina demanded of the jazz bassist are signal victories for Western music. The jazz bassist interprets the various structures of songs through the invention of bass lines, chorus after chorus, while the meter and the tempo are defined, usually in a two-bar phrasing cycle of quarter notes in 4/4 time. The bass notes and rhythms are responses to a number of things—the chordal forms, the modes, or the har-monically free creations of the other members of the rhythm section and the ideas of the featured player. The physical power is a melding of the aes-thetic and the athletic; a combination essential to meeting either the heated challenges of sustained ensemble inspiration or to handling the long hours of traditional jobs worked in dances and night clubs. In fact, it is easy to prove that the jazz bassist gave the instrument a pizzicato eloquence far beyond any that ever existed in European music. This contribution still stands. The greatest pluckers and distance runners of the bass are jazz musicians.

Even so, Mingus threw sand in the Vaseline of expectations. He was hot to play long phrases like those of the bebop horn players and worked on his facility until he could move across the instrument with a velocity and weighted force that are still far from common. The blessing of extremely large hands and powerful fingers allowed him to execute things that are still quite difficult for most bassists.

His innovations were many. Mingus improvised his features by approaching the bass as though it were a guitar, a jazz cross-breeding of concert and down-home blues guitar. He named Segovia as an influence and wasn't kidding, especially since the speed and accuracy of his work by the middle fifties had no precedent. When he was inspired, superbly phrased melodic inventions moved from the bottom of the instrument all the way to the top, sometimes even breaking into double lines of contrary motion that sprinted or stomped past each other, one going up, the other down—a technique those gargantuan fingers made possible but that no one other than Mingus would have conceived.

Unlike too many of those who came after him, Mingus never lost the thick, dark sound of the bass register or the strength of the long, heavy bass string. Even when the master bassist followed an idea into the extreme upper register, his instrument maintained its identity, never sounded like a cello. While Mingus increased the expressive possibilities of his instrument, his artistic needs giving voice to a wide sweep of emotions made musically logical, he didn't reduce the bass to a four-stringed extension of skittering castrati.

His control and sweep of nuance were as important as his velocity technique. The uses Mingus made of his bass strings for vocalized effects easily remind one of the colors heard from bottle-neck blues guitarists, who seek the melismatic slides, the whines, the howls, the tremolos, and the percussive pings basic to impassioned Negro singing, either in secular or religious music, from the field holler to the sanctified shout. It is also true that he sought the caustic melancholy of flamenco and could summon his impression of that Andalusian third cousin of the blues with startling strummings and Spanish scales. As bassist Vishnu Wood recalls, Mingus's concert training resulted in an authority with the bow that made it possible for him to give a spontaneous three-hour lesson to Wood, Doug Watkins, and Paul Chambers, leading them from a bar to his home and dazzling the younger men with his command.

Perhaps under the influence of Charlie Parker or Lennie Tristano, Mingus often phrased outside of the normal bar divisions used by other musicians. Trumpeter Tommy Turrentine once told this writer that he remembered practicing with Mingus sometime in the fifties. "All we did," Turrentine said, "was work on getting away from playing in two-, four-, and eight-bar phrases. We were trying to phrase either shorter than usual or longer than usual. Get out of that rut. Mingus wanted to make it so that your phrase would just be about itself, not the form breaks or the way people usually started and stopped. He was a man who hated clichés. Mingus believed if you worked on it, you could end up at the place where you could naturally hear your way outside of tired formats in your playing."

Mingus was also the first bassist to spontaneously move out of the harmonic-percussive-metric position in the rhythm section and use his instrument for the periodic tensions and releases of improvised counterpoint—little riffs and melodies that moved up alongside the line of the featured improvisor or emulated the obbligatti horn players invented in response to blues or ballad singers. This eventually inspired in so many young bassists such a decadent and self-indulgent disregard for swing that Mingus verbally disavowed it and forcefully returned to almost straight 4/4 time-keeping! Even so, by 1960 Mingus had so completely rethought the musical possibilities of the bass that his conception divides its history into those who came before his innovations and those who came after them.

2. The Composer

Like Ellington before him, Mingus would invent his own structures whenever those common to jazz and popular music made impossible the fulfillment of his imagination. He wrote many extremely fine melodies, often long and chromatic lines that transferred the swooping shapes, rhythmic subtleties, and intensities of jazz improvisation to the written page. In doing so, Mingus personalized a technique as old to jazz as what arrangers had done with the Louis Armstrong inventions of melody and rhythm that laid down the laws of swing. But instead of following the convention of writing fresh themes to fit familiar harmonies, Mingus often allowed his melodic lines to go their own distances and shaped his forms in submis-

sion to their risings and fallings. The regular 12-, 16-, and 32-bar forms
were of no intrinsic interest to him, however much he loved certain standard tunes—like "I Can't Get Started"—and returned to them throughout
his career.

Even something as basic as the short, repeated melodic chant of a riff
could get an unusual treatment. Building upon the best of Fletcher Henderson and Count Basie—whether or not he studied them particularly—
Mingus might stack up a number of blues riffs in overlapping durations so
that they went beyond conventional antiphony to create thick and dissonant polyphony; short melodic extensions of the polyrhythmic percussion
effects heard in African music, where the individual part, static and simple,
increases the complexity of the whole. The difference, however, was that
his music was rooted in harmony, something absent in African music. That
was but one of the many ways in which Mingus rethought blues melody,
blues timbre, the dissonances of blues harmony, or the combination of dou-
ple and triple metric feeling so central to the blues beat.

Mingus so astutely worked at reinterpreting the jazz tradition because
he had performed or jammed with Louis Armstrong, Kid Ory, Duke Ellington, Lionel Hampton, Charlie Parker, Art Tatum, Bud Powell, Thelonious
Monk, Miles Davis, Thad Jones, Dizzy Gillespie, Max Roach, Elvin Jones,
Roy Eldridge, Lennie Tristano, Red Norvo, and many others. This range of
musical encounters somehow freed him from the attraction to a single style
and inspired him to fuse techniques and schools. Because Mingus didn't
turn his back on anything that touched him deeply, the sectional textures
and musical codes of expression he used in a number of his pieces gave his
music much more tonal richness, breadth of emotion, and rhythmic variety
than the conventional bebop material that dominated the art of his generation. His performances demanded that the musicians he employed put on
and pull off musical masks of startling aesthetic contrast with what became
trademark confidence as the Mingus approach gained mature authority.

James Newton, virtuoso flutist, composer, and scholar observes: "The
depth and the expression of the music Mingus created is something we are
not used to in the work of anything less than the great jazz composers,
such as Jelly Roll, Ellington, Strayhorn, and Monk. What he had to express
caused him to use a broad range of the tradition. It was extremely brilliant,
the way that Mingus used the tradition and the material he got from Duke
and Bird. He organized all of these things in a way that you sometimes find
shocking because they are so profound in their understanding of this music
in so many ways.

"The upper harmonic extensions of the 9ths, 11ths, and 13ths that Bird had heard from Tatum and made into a new language was what Mingus understood and put into the forms of his music in a way different from what Charlie Parker and Dizzy Gillespie and Bud Powell did. Maybe from listening to Charlie Parker's contrapuntal ideas in "A-Leu-Cha" and "Chasing the Bird," he started thinking about the kind of counterpoint that he developed to such a brilliant and complex extent. The time that Mingus spent with Max Roach, when they worked together in the fifties, also had a lot of influence on the way that man wrote his rhythms. His accents were transfers and variations on the kinds of beats Max plays on his snare drum. Mingus obviously learned from Duke the importance of pulling in everything you knew and testing your imagination on it until something came out that was yours."

There are obvious and profound precedents for Mingus's stylistic range in Ellington works such as *Black, Brown, and Beige* (where the Joycean range of approaches used in *Ulysses* is brought to jazz), *The Tattooed Bride*, and *The Controversial Suite*, but it is a credit to Mingus's artistic esteem that he, alone of the musicians of his generation, called upon the scope of jazz for the projection of his own epic. In the work of Mingus, the polyphony of New Orleans is reinterpreted, the plungers that disappeared with bebop are retained, the scalding incantation of the Negro American church is put to secular use, the rich textures of Ellington are personalized, the swift, twisting chromatic intervals of Tristano are mixed in, the harmony of Tatum and the improvisational principles of Parker are made compositional, while the flexibility bebop brought to the rhythm section is expanded upon with heated daring.

3. The Bandleader

It was not unusual for Mingus to perform a piece in which a steady 4/4 might switch over to a Charleston beat, then metrically modulate into some version of a waltz (3/4 or 6/4), break down to a gutbucket pulse, spin into a flamenco vamp, and sail out with a lyric shout chorus. Such changes of direction, whether set or improvised, were part of a conception that individualized his work and served the higher purposes of getting beyond both staid formats and the limitations of the musicians at hand. That is: The various devices Mingus brought to many of his compositions could make extended performances interesting and less dependent on super improvisors. When successful, those techniques also spared the listener that arena of aesthetic damnation where the athletic quality of jazz sinks into the boringly facile and reveals the arrogance of self-indulgent and uninspired performers who don't know when to stop. In effect, Mingus's finest music was so rich that it could challenge and inspire the most talented or subordinate the mediocre players he made do with from the beginning of his career to the end.

Mingus was also a pioneer in the use of one- and two-chord foundations for improvisation, a decided turning away from the successions of complex chords favored by the beboppers. With works like *Pithecanthropus Erectus* and *Love Chant*, he got there in the middle fifties, before Miles Davis and John Coltrane, both of whom later popularized such modal structures. Nearly twenty years ago, Mingus said to this writer: "When I told Miles and Monk and the other cats about one chord, they thought I was crazy." He realized that the traditional three-chord harmony of the blues could be reduced even further and, with an appropriately charismatic rhythmic foundation, a piece could avoid monotony and achieve incantation, a force he was attracted to in musics as far removed as those of the sanctified Negro church and flamenco. When his efforts were successful, Mingus created musical and listening experiences that became, like all extraordinary moments, aspects of the sensibility from that point forward.

4. Rhythm Section Innovator

As radical as any of Mingus's contributions was his reinterpretation of the rhythm section. The emotion and the command of pulsation central to the art of the rhythm section are often misunderstood by those outside of jazz. This is especially true of the statement of the tempo and the meter, which, in European concert music, is carried within the theme-and-variation phrasings of the strings, brass, and woodwinds themselves. Jazz expands upon that method of musical statement.

In its own language, jazz brings together the thematic and harmonic development of Western art music with the incantational techniques heard in so much Third World music, where repetition and percussion create hypnotic effects that exist in place of compositional development. This is possible because the thematic and/or harmonic variations of the featured improvisor function within the incantational context of the rhythm section, a percussive-harmonic unit of piano, bass, and drums that carries the form and subtly orchestrates it.

That spontaneous orchestration is innovative: The form becomes active as the members of the rhythm section bring evolving animation to the structure, interpreting it by the chorus and reacting to both the improvisations of the featured player and to the inventions within the rhythm unit itself. This creates a very complex but often extremely refined polyphonic dialogue in which chords, colors, registers, motifs, and rhythms form the words.

In European music, the meter and the tempo have no meaning in themselves and say nothing; in jazz, the meter and the rhythm speak through the rhythm section. The rhythm unit gives emotional and artistic coherence to the very shape of the tempo and the pulsation—the statement and the interpretation of the meter itself, the underlying, syncopated divisions of motion through musical space—the *time*. The fractional measurements of existence are given aesthetic life.

That is the syncopated point of the ride cymbal's carrying of the beat and the meshing of the bass's quarter note with it. The momentum of swing and the quality of rhythmic statement known as a groove arrive when the bass note is perfectly placed and rings sufficiently with hums just long enough to subtly link with the reverberation of the ride cymbal, an effect as essential as it is virtually immeasurable. Upon the varied nuances and adjustments of this rhythm grounding, the tensions and releases of jazz improvisation are built.

Where the rhythm section of piano, bass, and drums traditionally supported and inspired the featured player within the context of chorus form and tempo, Mingus's rhythm unit took startling liberties with the form itself. (Musician and scholar Andrew Homzy calls this "plastic form.") The bassist saw the rhythm section as an entity that could double and triple its speed in the same way featured players ran fast passages of eighth and sixteenth notes over the basic quarter note. The spontaneous accellerandos and decellerandos thereby became as basic to his music as the double- and triple-timing of players from Coleman Hawkins and Art Tatum to Charlie Parker and John Coltrane. Mingus also introduced the spontaneous varying of meters, moods, and materials. He thusly took what might have been his own impatient or neurotic relationship to the supposedly subordinate role of the rhythm section and transformed it into flexible and exciting music. If a featured player was leaning on the laurels of his own clichés, the bassist didn't just stand and listen to the same tired patterns over and over; he moved to do something about it.

The Mingus rhythm section would challenge the featured player, even assert a combative relationship, throwing up obstacles that, when appropriately handled, increased the variety and the heroic quality of the improvisation. As bassist Mark Dresser observes: "The way Mingus functioned compositionally as a bassist was a radical departure. He was the first bassist I know of who wasn't concerned with making the soloist comfortable. In some ways, he was functioning the way the drummer would function, lighting the fire from the bass. People didn't expect that kind of power from that low register. Mingus was ready to change the feeling of the bottom register, give it a whole new intensity so that he could drive and push the band himself. He wasn't afraid to stick his foot in the band, and he had the strength, the technique, and the imagination to do it. That could make him uncomfortable to drummers and soloists."

At any moment, Mingus might change keys, shift meters, drop the chords in favor of a modal vamp or pedal point, stop playing and silence the piano, leaving the horn out there with only the drummer. He might sing out a riff that was picked up by the other horns, or benefit from having previously encouraged his fellow rhythm players to so understand the rate and flow of the beat that they could help him create situations in which the triangle of the rhythm section had staggered relationships to the downbeat, neutralizing straight time and creating an ambiguous momentum. For all of that, Mingus would often bring everything back home to the blues or to stomping swing, using the gutbucket or the groove as the traditional resolution of all experimentation. The recorded results are, as is true of Mingus at large, erratic, but the many successes are indelible additions to the possibilities of jazz performance.

1994

Blues for the Space Age

Ornette Coleman

In 1959, when Ornette Coleman arrived in New York and opened on the Bowery with the quartet that included Don Cherry, Charlie Haden, and Billy Higgins, there was no talk of a harmolodic system. He spoke of playing with natural raw feeling instead of technical obsession, yet Coleman proved to have the most comprehensive grasp of improvised order outside of preconceived form that we have heard in the jazz avant-garde. Coleman brought a conception to the music that Wallace Roney explains perfectly: "Ornette wanted to get the same kind of freedom he heard in Charlie Parker but discovered that the only way he could do that was to move away from chords and count on his melodic imagination to get him where he wanted to go."

Most of Coleman's greatest recordings are either on Atlantic or Blue Note and were made by 1965. With Cherry, Freddie Hubbard, Eric Dolphy, Haden, Jimmy Garrison, Scott LaFaro, David Izenzon, Higgins, Ed Blackwell, and Charles Moffett, he laid down what remains the heaviest body of purely avant-garde jazz. Just a few years ago, when the saxophonist performed with Haden and Higgins at Lincoln Center, it was obvious that Coleman is still the boss and that when he has actual jazz musicians up to the task of playing his concept with absolute authority, his vision of group improvising is far, far beyond that of those who claim to have extended upon what he brought to the Five Spot in 1959.

Coleman's signal achievement is that one does not have to have a panel discussion to argue about whether or not he is a jazz musician. The sound of blues is central to his alto-saxophone tone and to the passion of his music because, at heart, Coleman is a sophisticated country-blues player, the most highly developed to arrive in jazz after Thelonious Monk, Charlie Parker, Miles Davis, and John Coltrane. The grandest example of thematic improvisation unbound by harmony, Coleman creates variations both subtle and explosive. His phrases are often conversational, traveling the length of inspiration rather than two-, four-, or eight-bar phrases. Emotion can determine tempo and create another kind of syncopation, one in which velocity arrives as unexpectedly as accents outside of the expected. A master at getting everything in, Coleman can turn from very complex chromatic passages that feel devoid of any metric direction, then fall right into a succession of stark but protean riffs delivered with a level of fiery swing that none of those who purported to follow him have ever equaled.

Like all professional improvisers, Coleman proves himself an intellectual because artistic improvisation is contemplation in motion that seeks to achieve high-quality aesthetic success, not just the kind of venting one can hear after asking a roomful of children to improvise. The professional has to recognize the elements in the musical environment—the notes, the rhythms, the registers, the colors—respond to them, create a design, and achieve form. In Coleman's case, that form has great plasticity, protean possibilities, but it arrives in music quite like the Picassos that mix the figurative with abstraction.

Technically speaking, the most important thing about Coleman is that he proved how much jazz could do with its own tradition in order to "advance." It did not have to use academic methods borrowed from the European avant-garde as the basic foundation with which to marginalize the jazz idiom and the distinctive emotion of the music. It also did not need the exotica of Indian or African music or the pretensions that too often attend the rhetoric of those devoted to something "non-Western." Jazz could build on its Negro-American origins while maintaining its universality. Negro-American, of course, means the national mix with a certain interpretation informed by parade music, blues, spirituals, gospel, dance tunes, street chants, and so on. As Coleman said in the early 1960s: "Many people don't realize it, but there is a real American folklore music in jazz. It's neither black nor white. It's the mixture of the races, and the folklore has come from it." That realization is what anchors his achievement. He believes that anything he hears is his if it can fit what he's doing and come through his personality in an aesthetically natural manner.

The astonishing sweep of liberated form and emotion in his music is made obvious in his remarkably symphonic improvisation on "The Ark," from his 1962 Town Hall concert with bassist Izenzon and drummer Moffett, both of whom brilliantly respond to and inspire Coleman's creation of long movements based on the theme rather than choruses. In the process, they make his trio perhaps the most spontaneously flexible we have ever heard. Inspired, Coleman moves with absolute ease in and out of straight time, moods, keys, meters, tempos, and dynamics.

For all of Coleman's abstractions, he's much like a blues singer, stretching from tender whispers to exultant shouts, from mystical whines to angry growls swirled around by gloom or closely wrapped in midnight-hour erotic memories. At times, Coleman also relates to Izenzon's arco playing in ways that makes us rethink the idea of "third stream"—the fusing of jazz and European music—as if he decided that what Gunther Schuller and John Lewis proposed should provide another color that could spontaneously give wider sonic and emotional range to his music.

Ornette Coleman is that magical combination of the primitive, the great thinker, the virtuoso, and the brave singer of songs. We are lucky to have him among us.

                                                                    2002

Titan of the Blues

John Coltrane

Like all serious jazz musicians, John Coltrane invented a remarkable personal style, but his status also stems from the fresh conception he developed for an entire band. Probably his most artistically successful period as a bandleader was between 1961 and 1965, when he fronted the classic quartet, which included drummer Elvin Jones, pianist McCoy Tyner, and bassist Jimmy Garrison. At its best, the art of that ensemble at least equals the finest music written for or performed by any foursome, regardless of idiom. Over the last year, MCA has reissued digital versions of Coltrane albums made between 1961 and 1964. Of the reissues, *Impressions* finds the saxophonist experimenting with differently sized ensembles, while *Coltrane*, *Crescent*, and *A Love Supreme* best capture the quartet's contribution. That contribution was the fusion of passion and intellectual depth that distinguishes jazz from the music of the concert or popular worlds, neither of which offers the combination of the inflamed soul and the mind in such perfect synthesis.

So much enduring music was produced by Coltrane's group because he grasped how essential *hearing* is to improvising. It is at the center of the *action* that is improvising, the source of vitality. Detailed hearing draws upon the aesthetic feeling that brings music alive and separates it from the academic and merely virtuosic. Hearing is the way knowledge, experience, and technique are given structure and function. It informs taste, sensitivity, and passion; determines the clarity of the melodic, harmonic, rhythmic, and textural choices available. Given the necessary discipline, those who hear best sound best.

But one can hear well enough to become an extraordinary improviser, as did Art Tatum or Don Byas, and still have a style that is compatible with the conventions of group playing. In fact, most jazz musicians organize bands around chemistry, and though the individual styles included might be unique, the ensemble approach is usually generic in the best sense of the word. The listener experiences personal versions of different schools—New Orleans, swing, bebop, etc. Yet with Coltrane's quartet, the saxophonist and his musicians could hear their way through the materials and make collective variations on them that redefined the strategic aspects of the aesthetic. That is the difference between an individual and a group conception—the former, however wonderful, is but one musician's way; with the latter the means must be sufficiently large to include roles for traditional ensemble instruments (especially the rhythm section, if the music is jazz). The upshot was the redefinition of blues, swing, ballads, 4/4 (fast, medium, and slow), and what Jelly Roll Morton called "the Spanish Tinge," which had evolved by the 1960s to include African-derived rhythms and elements of Third World music from as far east as India.

No musician of Coltrane's era was better prepared to extend the jazz aesthetic. Born September 23, 1926, he had worked with many masters, learning the particulars of their music from the inside. Everything he drew from Eddie "Cleanhead" Vinson, Dizzy Gillespie, Earl Bostic, Tadd Dameron, Johnny Hodges, Miles Davis, and Thelonious Monk was put to specific use with such expanding facility that saxophone technique was revolutionized. Coltrane wanted to have every register, corner, fingering, overtone, and possible note on call at will. By working through blues, swing, bebop, and the architecture of Monk, as well as the precise ensemble conceptions of Miles Davis, Coltrane synthesized a broad range of music with an inherent scope missing from almost all so-called avant-garde jazz. Unlike most associated with the avant-garde, he knew what the essences of the tradition were—blues, idiomatic lyricism, and swing—and was able to remake them rather than avoid their demands.

Coltrane's appetite for freedom of expression drove him to learn all that he did, yet his understanding of and feeling for the blues made him a giant. From working with blues singers and with supreme blues instrumentalists (Hodges, Davis, and Monk), Coltrane obviously concluded that the blues essentials could provide the foundation upon which to build his saxophone style and the style of his band. In blues, the form is simple, the harmony limited, and the expression often arrives through overt and subtle use of texture and rhythm. With such insight, Coltrane separated himself from other saxophonists who also used sweeping arpeggios by bringing an increasing complexity of timbre to his epic sashes of notes—the keening to grunting to rasping to wailing colors of the blues. In that sense, saxophone and all, Coltrane became the champion blues shouter of his era, a man whose enormous harmonic resources were made idiomatic by their order and the molten timbres that coated them.

Just as Miles Davis once made simple, songful phrases more musically and emotionally intricate by calling on the tonal resources trumpeters had so superbly refined before the bebop era, Coltrane made his own dense passages earthy through blues coloration and blues intensity. And as he matured, Coltrane took advantage of the blue *mood* that had been brought into jazz by Ellington (and where better to hear that source than in the band of Hodges?). The melancholy, sophistication, and bittersweet swing of that mood had been best personalized in the wake of the bebop era by Monk and Davis. In fact, the greatest contribution of Davis's influential *Kind of Blue* was conceptual: If limited harmony and scales were to replace numerous chords and arpeggios, then modal jazz should ground itself in the three elements mentioned above—blues, idiomatic lyricism, and swing.

Aware of all of that, Coltrane had to find musicians whose hearing and invention were passionate enough to both inspire him and also express their own personalities. Though his players have often said that he never told anyone what to do, it is obvious that Coltrane knew how important personnel is to composition. Therefore, if his musicians *hadn't* been doing what he wanted, they would have been fired. For his purposes, the fact that a conception is an imaginative way of using knowledge meant that he had to hire musicians whose sensibilities fitted the vision he was pursuing.

Because Ahmad Jamal's group conception was as important to Coltrane as it was to Miles Davis, enlisting McCoy Tyner was pivotal. On *Coltrane Plays the Blues* (Atlantic), one hears the vamps, block chords, and uses of rhythms other than those conventionally used to swing a band. Hearing it right after Jamal's *But Not for Me* is illuminating. Then one can easily notice how Tyner made his own style out of Bud Powell, Jamal, Red Garland, and Wynton Kelly. The percussiveness of his distinctly original accompanying style moved the music closer to a point at which the roles of drums and harmony instruments were profoundly reinterpreted. Tyner took on the role of a percussionist with tonal resources in the rhythm section, sharing heavily rhythmic vamps with the bass, which supplied the dominant ground beats upon which Coltrane and the drummer built their own improvisations (hear "Out of This World" and "Tungi" on *Coltrane*). Most of all, he swung harder than any other young pianist of the day, could truly hear the blues, and his playing had an extraordinary elegance of sound, phrasing, and a stretch of feeling (hear "Lonnie's Lament" on *Crescent*) that could encompass the noble and the incendiary.

Then Coltrane got Elvin Jones, who made the music cohere and swing with nearly peerless fury. Jones didn't play time, he voiced it. Expanding upon the innovations of Art Blakey, Kenny Clarke, Max Roach, Roy Haynes, and Philly Joe Jones, he began to hear the drum set as an ensemble in which time was orchestrated across the entire trap set. Jones's rhythmic tension perfectly complemented Coltrane, whose stacking of harmonies or scales often resulted in cones of phrasing that whirled like drum rolls, suggesting an expanded definition of percussive attack that can be heard perfectly as the tenor and drums mirror and echo each other on "Out of This World," from *Coltrane*.

Just as a pianist, or Coltrane himself, could weave together apparently unrelated chords that seemed to move outside the tonality but were inevitably resolved, Jones would stagger time all over the drum kit then resolve the rhythms at the end of four- or eight-bar sequences. Instead of conducting only a linear dialogue with the horn or the other players, Jones created a vertical approach, one that called for rhythms to appear simultaneously as notes do in chords. Each limb executed a moving part in an improvisational style that leaned, bent, and pulled time on different levels at the same moment, surrounding the group in the way big band brass and reed sections do. If one listens to Jones in that way, it isn't difficult to hear how his rhythmic complexity countered the harmonic simplicity that underlay many of the *modal* forms used by Coltrane.

Once Jimmy Garrison joined the quartet, the redefinition of swing took place with collective precision and refinement. His was a big tone and the force with which he plucked his notes expanded upon the percussive function the bass always had in jazz. He knew how to play the *bottom* and the ferocity of his spirit melded with that of Jones. Garrison was not taken in by the Scott LaFaro phenomenon; he was not about to slice the rump roast off the boom of the beat. Though he wasn't opposed to strumming his instrument, Garrison never forgot the *power* jazz bass is supposed to have (listen to him on the title track of *Impressions*, or "Miles' Mode" on *Coltrane*, either of which outswings almost anything else recorded during that period). As his remarkable time and sense of Negroid elegance show on *Crescent*, he could chug, he could lope, he could dance, he could chant, or he could *charge* in tempo. His ability to keep the time and change the texture, the angle, and the motion of the beat fitted so well with the piano and the drums that the collective phrasing of the rhythm and the form was given a fresh dimension of swing.

By bringing together the hardest-swinging rhythm section in jazz, Coltrane met the demands of his muse for a stretch of expression akin to Ben Webster. Like the older man, Coltrane mastered the timbral physics of his instrument, was an extraordinary balladeer and bluesman, and could rise to imposing levels of intensity. All of those inclinations are contained in *Impressions, Coltrane, Crescent,* and *A Love Supreme.* Each record contains at least one indelible classic, and *Crescent* provides a perfect opening for the new Coltrane listener. That album finds the quartet at a peak of expressive clarity, effortlessly remaking the blues, the ballad, 4/4, and the Spanish Tinge. Few ensembles have ever made such lasting music.

1987

Andrew Hill's
Alternative Avant-Garde

In 1963, Chicago's Andrew Hill began recording a series of albums for Blue Note that, in retrospect, provide perhaps the richest range and originality of any pianist then associated with the avant-garde. But Hill's avant-garde had nothing to do with that of those jazzmen who knew less about music than they did about the gullibility of their bohemian audience or those writers looking for something new to praise. *On Point of Departure*, probably his masterpiece, he absorbed sources as different, but as exacting in their musical systems, as blues bands and European concert composers. The pieces were neither derivative nor pretentious; only musicians as capable as Kenny Dorham, Joe Henderson, Eric Dolphy, Richard Davis, and Tony Williams could have performed them. The music avoids predictable structures, tempos, voicings, and effects, but it also swings, and maintains connections to the tradition its makers were reinterpreting rather than avoiding. Like the Monk Blue Notes of the late 1940s and those remarkable trio dates of Herbie Nichols in the 1950s, the best of Hill's work for that label was emotionally forthright and uncontrived in its surprises. But Hill, who appears at Sweet Basil October 29, temporarily left the jazz world in the early 1970s, when fusion was beginning to rear its electronic head.

Born in 1937, Hill points out that in Chicago, "before the music got separated," he could play a blues house, "sneak up on a gig with Gene Ammons, play accordion, or back up some rhythm and blues singers like the Flamingos. Then a musician was really getting his music across because there were bars on every corner and you couldn't go anywhere without hearing music. That's why people were so into music. Now they have commodities like ghetto blasters, but they don't have instruments and they don't hear the music. They have become consumers instead of listeners. A consumer buys what he's told to buy. A listener appreciates variety and individuality."

He was given lessons by Paul Hindemith between the ages of thirteen and fifteen, and at sixteen played the Graystone Ballroom in Detroit with Charlie Parker. "A friend of mine named Eddie Baker was taking lessons from William Russo. I took a few lessons with him, too. Then I sent a composition to Hindemith at Yale that allegedly had maturity beyond my years. When Hindemith came to Chicago, I went to see him and he showed me things about extended composition during the five times or so that I saw him over a two-year period."

The job with Parker was of signal importance because he got to hear the work of a genius at such an early stage of his own development as an improvisor and accompanist. At one point Parker told Hill: "When you get to be my age, a lot of people will be gone and the public won't know about the way things really were. Then, you will be the keeper of the flame." He also fondly recalls working a place called the Stage with Lester Young who "told me that he wouldn't live but a few years longer, but the younger musicians had the responsibility to keep their health and their minds together so that the truth can continue to live."

Hill moved to New York in the early 1960s, working with Roland Kirk. During a Joe Henderson record date, he was noticed by Alfred Lions of Blue Note, who offered the young pianist a contract. "I have heard a lot of bad things about Alfred Lions, but for me he functioned pretty much as a patron in the truest sense. He liked my approach and never got upset because I wanted to do many different things. Some people say that if I had concentrated on making one kind of music, I might have gotten over. Anyway, Alfred didn't try to do that with me. He even told me that some things I did that could have been hits weren't pushed because he thought it would hem me in. That's unusual for somebody who's only supposed to be interested in money."

During his Blue Note years, Hill matched the individuality of his piano style with the variety of his imagination as a composer. At the keyboard, he had personalized the sources of Monk, Tatum, and Powell, playing unusual phrase lengths, toying with dissonance for pathos, humor, and penetration, yet maintaining concern with melodic development. That same sense of compositional variation gave a sustained character to his albums, however different each of them was. His first was *Black Fire* with Joe Henderson, Richard Davis, and Roy Haynes; his second, *Judgement*, featured Bobby Hutcherson, Davis, and Elvin Jones; then came the *On Point of Departure* date. *Andrew!*, with John Gilmore, Davis, and Joe Chambers, brought a new sense of control to free playing. He also looked at percussion and ethnic influences on *Compulsion*, and worked in a quartet featuring two bassists on *Smokestack*. One of the most interesting was *Lift Every Voice*, where Hill augmented a jazz quintet with seven singers. Not long after that date in the spring of 1969, the decision to get out of New York's career struggle led him to the position of composer-in-residence at Colgate, where he also got a doctorate in composition.

During his time at Colgate from 1970 to 1972, Hill wrote experimental pieces for brass and reeds, gave individual piano lessons, and had his string works performed by the Syracuse Symphony. He also wrote an opera, *The Golden Spoon*, which he has been reworking over the years. "From going out and walking with the people, learning and listening to the way things arrive naturally, I was able to update myself perpetually. In *The Golden Spoon*, each character comes from a particular area of black music. So what I wrote comes from what I call 'the dictionary of black style.'"

From 1972 to 1975, he was part of the Smithsonian Institute's touring program, performing with his wife, Laverne, whom he considers not only an inspiration but provided superb advice and protection from the "negative aspects of the outside world." She would perform cabaret songs at the organ, then Hill would do an original piece of his music. As the program took him and his wife across the country, Hill was able to avail himself of the community orchestras and show bands in many of the little towns he toured.

In 1975, after his last Japanese tour, Hill moved to California, first to San Francisco, then Pittsburgh, about sixty miles away, in 1977. He and his wife still live there, and Hill has been playing piano in churches and concert halls over the last two years. His working schedule includes musical therapy in public schools and prisons such as Soledad, Vacaville, Susanville, and San Quentin. "I would truthfully say that I took alternative steps further than I did in the early '70s when I left New York. I think it is the responsibility of the artist to apply his talent to all the areas that apply to music, which is what I'm doing now."

His work in church music has clarified for him how jazz evolved from the rhythms and timbres heard in the voices of the choirs. "What those singers do with notes is inspiring because they make you realize how much color can be brought to the individual pitch. In my own music, the intervals and the tensions often create their own accents and I have always been aware that every song should have a rhythm of its own. But those things come from my learning music at the time that I did. Music has just recently become tonic-dominated from a harmonic perspective, but in the old days everybody was so individual that people were accustomed to variety. When individuality was king, the musician was treated like a sage simply because he had a different expression to reflect the range of the human texture of the time."

Hill believes that younger musicians are "taking the best from the avant-garde of the 1960s and bringing back the tradition of musicianship that used to excite me when I was coming up. They are also doing what Lester Young told me to do. By taking care of themselves and studying seriously, they are making sure that the truth will stay alive. The truth is what makes art important, because then it contains everything. When you limit yourself, you reduce the truth of your work and you give people less. I want to give as much as I can and I am thankful that I have been able to go my own way and develop my own alternatives."

1984

Rooster Ben: King of Romance
Ben Webster

During the late 1940s, Duke Ellington gave a college concert in which one segment featured Kansas City's Ben Webster as tenor saxophone soloist par excellence. The piece was an arrangement of "How High the Moon," which opened with an eight-bar up-tempo shout of brass and reed bebop figures intended to rattle. Then Webster, his tone a sensuous burr, entered and dissolved the tempo into a romantic flotation of a cappella swing, as surprising a break as any in the history of jazz (though Louis Armstrong had Johnny Dodds use the same dramatic de-escalation twenty years earlier). As the rhythm section joined him, Webster maintained the dream mood at a seductive tempo through which he shaped each note with such richly colored emotional characterization that the individual pitch had the effect of a song in itself. Next the tempo went up to a nice medium velocity and Webster stated the theme he had been so abstractly implying in belly rub rhythms, swells of assent rising from the band as he danced the melody along. Then the brass took a break that roared in a swift third tempo and Webster transformed his sound into a gravelly howl as determined as the controlled scorch of a great lover nearing the consummation of ardor. In fact those three tempos and the sultry coda that Webster performed, climaxing with a cry both raucous and sensual, seem not an onomatopoeia of the bare facts of sex but of lovemaking, from the tender to the mellow to the flaring and tempestuous. The difference is spiritual, and the tenor saxophonist knew it well.

By presenting Webster in a concerto arrangement that moved through three moods and tempos, Ellington provided as good an introduction to the art of Ben Webster as any novice listener would need. One heard the translucent tone so smooth and so powerful in every register, the crooner's skills that would decimate almost any actual singer; the boody-butt ease of absolute swing; and the giant killing power that never gave way to hysteria when Webster had to slash through a song on an express schedule. At that point, with his broad shoulders, the bags beginning beneath his pugnacious eyes, the handsomeness that seemed part Indian, and the reputation for being intolerant of jive (whether or not he was in his cups), Webster had completed an apprenticeship that made for one of the most lyrical and muscular styles in the history of jazz.

When Webster joined Ellington in 1940, he was thirty-one years old and had come a long ways from Kansas City and the distaste for the violin his family wanted him to play. He preferred the piano early on and performed in a honky-tonk style that perfectly mirrored one aspect of the latter-day Dodge that was Kansas City, where everything was wide open and fun was rarely corralled. Prohibition was ignored, hustlers and loose women were everywhere, people partied the night away, and there was such a large audience for music that it ranged from square-dance tunes to blues to jazz to hoity-toity society bands. Webster's great ambition at the time was to tickle the ivories in a stride style and he led one of his first bands from the keyboard, Rooster Ben and His Little Red Hens. He was playing piano in Amarillo, Texas in 1929 when Budd Johnson showed him scales on the saxophone, an instrument that began to entrance Webster. Saxophone-fascinated, but lacking a horn, Webster joined the Young Family, a traveling ensemble of parents and children who played musical instruments. Through the soon-to-loom innovator Lester Young, who was one of the children and five months Webster's junior, Rooster Ben fell for the tenor and was soon blowing like hell.

Near the end of 1932, Webster was already so good that he was recording with the Bennie Moten Orchestra, helping announce the new feeling of Kansas City swing, and flying over the instrument with brusque authority. Of that Webster, who was also to measure and develop his talent in many other bands, Rex Stewart wrote: "During his early period, he blew with unrestrained savagery, buzzing and growling through chord changes like a prehistoric monster challenging a foe." Webster played the instrument hard and with a heroic tone that Stewart says was the talk of the tenors when Rooster Ben arrived in New York, a big man whose eyes radiated the dark moods of a willing scrapper. In 1936, he recorded with Teddy Wilson and Billie Holiday, exhibiting a style that was part Coleman Hawkins and part Benny Carter tied together with traces of Chu Berry. But I think that Holiday's phrasing on "The Way You Look Tonight," where her voice arches itself up over the chunk-chunk-chunk-chunk of the rhythm guitar in lyrical phrases much like romantic smoke signals, struck Webster as he stood there listening just as Lester Young's gifts had seeped into the emerging saxophonist. Those two influences were not to surface in Rooster Ben's own work for a few years, and then they would be so transmogrified that their impact wasn't even noticed. (There were already Young-like rhythms in the last part of Webster's "Toby" improvisation in 1932.)

During his tenure with Ellington from 1940 to 1943, Webster established a role for the tenor in that most magnificent of jazz orchestras. Sculpting his emblematic passion through ballads and blues or serving as heavy artillery on stomping, swinging numbers, Webster's roar of triumph, terror, and rage celebrated existence, revealed the shocks of life and declaimed a bubbling disgust for all limitation. His performance on "Cotton Tail," "Congo Brava," "All Too Soon," and various others set such precedents that his successive replacements suffered the outrage of fans who couldn't get Rooster Ben's sound out of their ears and weren't above asking the other tenor players how dare they sit in Ben Webster's seat. Those fans relaxed when Webster rejoined Ellington from 1948 to 1949, and they calmed down a few years later when Paul Gonsalves began to develop his extension of Rooster Ben's approach.

In maturity, Webster crafted a style that embodied the rich stretch from the meditative to the violence inherent in blues, the whisper followed by the cry, the cry contrasted by a choked display of tenderness, and so on. But his greatest victory stemmed from a rejection of the European-derived idea of the virtuoso as a spokesman for velocity. Like Basie, Ellington, and Monk, he chose to strip his materials down to elemental Negro techniques. He became a virtuoso of nuance. In the process, Webster appropriated the entire vocabulary of Negro vocal and instrumental timbre into his saxophone. In a given performance, he could sound like the entire Ellington tonal arsenal compressed into a gold-plated, curved, and multi-keyed vessel of effortless expression. But there was a point larger than tonal variety as an end unto itself. Rooster Ben realized that the subtle to dramatic use of timbre could result in extensions of harmony and rhythm, even melody, a personalization of Ellington's idea that men with distinct sounds could make a chord as much an assemblage of colors as pitches. Webster not only reminded one of a wispy singer or a growling trombone or a cup-muted or plunger-muted trumpet, but his control of color also had the same melodic implications of timbre found in Lester Young, whose alternate fingerings could make a repeated single note successively sound like a different entity, given the lightness or the weight of it on the ear. Yet Webster took that control of texture beyond what Young, or anyone else, had done with it.

More than any other saxophonist in jazz, Rooster Ben rivaled the flexibility of the human voice and brought together a synthesis of phrasing rooted in Armstrong, Young, Holiday, Carter, Hodges, and Parker. His was a sense of rhythm as acute as that of Thelonious Monk; it disavowed prolixity in favor of the essences of delay, anticipation, and superbly placed accent, giving the individual phrase a feeling of suspense and victory.

However much he disliked the instrument when he was young, Webster later said of the violin that nothing could rival its sound for purity and sweetness. I think Webster was mistaken and that the irony of his contribution in that regard is that he was one of the central figures who made it clear that the solo and ensemble powers of the saxophone formed the American parallel to the function of strings in European music. Obviously Webster's concern with capturing the timbres of Negro speech, song, instrumental techniques, and the percussive rhythms of Negro dance were beyond the roles of the strings in Europe, but his clarity and variety of sound and subtle expression rival that of any instrumentalist and surpass the purity of all but the greatest players, regardless of idiom.

Though Webster had composing and arranging gifts that might have rivaled those of Benny Carter if he had chosen to focus on them, once Rooster Ben absorbed the work of his Ellington section-mate, Johnny Hodges, he settled for writing that never rose again to the height of the harmonized saxophone section in "Cotton Tail." He was content to become a drifter with a tenor.

Though he might tour with Jazz at the Philharmonic or sit in with Ellington, Webster moved around making beauty or railing through his horn at the shortcomings of the world when and where he felt like it. (In 1964, he moved to Europe, where he remained, working with pickup rhythm sections until his death nine years later.) In a sense, he telescoped his arranging skills through his own lines, riffs, and gestures, setting timbres against one another with such detail he could make a single performance sound as though it were the work of more than one horn player. Rooster Ben woodshedded a style of such inclusive expressiveness that he could follow a dramatic contrast in inflection with a dissolving note that went past pitch into pure air. It was sort of a toneless white noise, as much like the breath Armstrong let float past a sung note as it was a first cousin of brushes on a snare drum.

As the recorded work shows, he was invincible after a point. From 1943 until his death thirty years later, Webster made music as remarkable for its content as it was for its consistency. One could play a more innovative style than his or one could play something absolutely different from what Webster did, but it was impossible to sound *better* than Rooster Ben. Though the Ellington classics are rightfully made much of, I think there are a number of performances away from the Maestro that deserve attention. Though there are so many. I will only scoop out a few for this list. His overwhelming improvisation on "Funky Blues" (*Norman Granz Jam Sessions/The Charlie Parker Sides,* Verve) is a timelessly contemporary gathering of sandpaper tones that buzz forward in a superb cleanup feature to the work of Johnny Hodges, Charlie Parker, Benny Carter, and Flip Phillips. There is the peerless satisfaction and excruciation of his singing tenor on *Ballads* (Verve); the work with Billie Holiday on *Songs for Distingué Lovers* that might just settle a score with Lester Young; the nearly terrifying intensity of his "Fine and Mellow" work on the 1957 television show *The Sound of Jazz;* his own *King of the Tenors* (Verve), which includes astonishing versions of "Danny Boy" and "Tenderly"; the sessions with Coleman Hawkins and with all-star masters of his era that are in the two-record set, *Tenor Giants* (Verve); and the deftly expressive ballads and blues of *Soulville* (Verve).

But what impresses me most about Webster's continued dedication is his ability to create swing or cloudlike flotation even when held down by willing but unswinging European rhythm sections. Ten months before his death, Rooster Ben recorded *Did You Call?* Though the performances are slightly marred by the mannered piano of Tete Montoliu, Webster was in classic form. His expression was absolute. The precision of timbre, the variety of rhythmic ideas, the melodic gifts, the brusque to humorous swing, and the spiritual resonance of his lyricism were displayed to perfection. There, as ever, one is amazed that such a sound could come out of an instrument made of brass and sonically manipulated by breath pushing across a cane reed. The notes seem to radiate straight from the man and this is a man whose understanding of human desire and intimacy makes nearly every romantic lead of stage and screen seem like a beginner. I also like one of his last recordings from the year of his death, *My Man* (Inner City). Rooster Ben Webster, staring into the face of eternity, lets loose the lion's call of combat for all comers on "I Got Rhythm" especially. It is the sound of an uncrushable courage, the sort he probably found necessary to protect his devotion to the aesthetic revelations of romance.

1986

The Last of the Great Bandleaders
Sun Ra

Sun Ra is somewhere around seventy years old: The breadth and depth of musical experience he can bring to a performance make him the finest of the Chicago musicians associated with the vanguard of the last twenty-five years. Perhaps the reason he isn't properly appreciated is that his range of stylistic authority is nearly equaled by the number of things that can go wrong. When not the fault of inferior personnel, his problems can be attributed to an oceanic ego as capable of infinite, bombastic rage as it is of discipline, humor, dreaminess, and a buoyant, affectionate lyricism almost naïve in its translucency.

Unlike those contemporary musicians who are more masters of the self-promoting interview than of bandstand interplay, Sun Ra appears determined to simultaneously befuddle and beguile all who would speak to him. To that end, he talks a fluttering mumbo-jumbo that combines everything from astrology to ethnic nationalism and justifies his sequins, wigs, robes, and the outer-space showboat he brings to the stage. The upshot is a blazing comic mask that can illuminate or sear. Comedy is essential because Sun Ra is determined to preserve the performance styles and skills, from willfully amateurish to virtuosic, that he saw in the great days of theater shows, when bands had entourages that included singers, dancers, and comedy routines. His sense of humor frees an audience from the discomfort they might feel if Sun Ra's belief that he is a prophet sent here to save humankind were laid on too heavily, as it sometimes still is. His broad humor and ready self-parody also prove him the most traditional of vanguard musicians, and the least intimidated by European "respectability." From the homemade costumes to Sun Ra's waddling stutter-steps, his best performances deliver the Afro-American tradition with greater authority than any of the more celebrated Chicago avant-gardists; he is clearly the father of the AACM. His is discipline flavored with a sense of fun almost totally foreign to jazz since Monk, Rollins, and Mingus, and that element, as much as the spectacle, accounts for the cult following Sun Ra has developed since he brought his band to New York in 1961.

The early Chicago recordings of Sun Ra that are still available—*Sun Song* (Delmark DS–411) and *Sound of Joy* (Delmark DS–414), recorded in July of 1956 and November of 1957 respectively—show how well he learned his lessons from the masters and what he was in the process of putting together. Though his affection for Henderson and Ellington is well known, Sun Ra was as interested in exotic moods and tonal colors as he was in the short, contrapuntal themes, the driving syncopation, and the depth of texture brought to fruition by his predecessors. Expanding upon the Afro-Cuban techniques Gillespie introduced, Sun Ra added percussion, intervals, and phrasings that suggested the Middle and Far East, summoning to his palette a range not unlike the one Ellington developed to meet both the demands of show business and his own curiosity. But at the same time, as *Sound of Joy* shows, Sun Ra was busy adapting the rhythmic, textural, and harmonic language of Tadd Dameron. Such pieces as "El Is a Sound of Joy" and "Overtones of China," are closely related to Dameron's "Fountainbleau," while "Ankh" makes use of motifs from "Flossie Lou." On "Paradise," he sets the piano in a rolling percussive universe much like that which led to Ahmed Jamal's popularity, while "El Viktor" is a harmonically simple chant with lots of percussion, predicting the polyrhythmic washes with which Sun Ra would flood clubs and halls throughout the 1960s. And just as the music of both albums gives us an adventurous writer who well understands idiomatic colors, we also hear a band so disciplined it could deliver superb performances averaging four minutes.

After Sun Ra moved his band to New York, the balance between his talent, his mysticism, and his desire for success and attention took on new dimensions, with atmosphere and spectacle becoming as essential to his presentation as the compositions themselves. But as such late-1950s cutouts as *Super-Sonic Sounds*, *Angels and Demons at Play*, and *Fate in a Pleasant Mood* show, Sun Ra's ability to synthesize his love of tradition with his interest in electronic instruments, drums, and ethnic music could also lead to compositions that were rich in textural freshness and percussive timbres but might offer little more than atmosphere (those impressed with ethnic music tend to repress their own skills at melodic and harmonic development as they express fascination with systems new to them). The tendency to atmosphere and strident squeaking and honking dominated the more easily purchased 1960s recordings (an endless stream of cheaply made Sun Ra records, usually lacking personnel listings, are available on his own El Saturn label and sold at his performances) while the pageantry that was pre-saged in the middle 1950s, when his Chicago band wore white gloves, pur-ple blazers, and beanies topped by propellers, turned into a full-fledged avant-garde circus—glittering costumes, giant drums, lighting effects, films projected on the wall, singing, and dancing. More than any other musician of the period, Sun Ra had found a way to combine entertainment with the avant-garde and keep a large ensemble working, regardless of the constant turnover in personnel.

For my taste, his finest recordings from that period, 1966's *Nothing Is* (ESP–1045) and 1968's *Pictures of Infinity* (Black Lion BLP–30103), are live, and both benefit from the extraordinary swing and drive of Clifford Jarvis, the greatest drummer to have worked with the band. Though both records contain bleating performances that sound interchangeable, there are fine examples of what separates Sun Ra's men from the boys—his difficult charts (unfortunately, the band on *Pictures* destroys "Saturn," a brilliant synthesis of Hendersonia and bebop that can be heard correctly played on *Sound of Joy*) and his range of mood, not to mention the invaluable contribution of his tenor saxophonist, twenty-six-year Sun Ra veteran John Gilmore. Since then, the band has suffered from the quality of his players—sometimes good, but usually too mediocre to give the best renditions of the material Sun Ra chooses to play.

A recent release, like *Sunrise in Different Dimensions* (Hat Hut–2R17), recorded in 1980, finds the band woefully out of tune and botching the leader's arrangements, while 1978's *Lanquidity* (Philly Jazz PJ–666B) is pleas-ant but largely atmospheric. In person, however, things are moving back to the standards of his previous successes, for he has a drummer, Samurai (Eric Walker), who swings the band harder than anyone since Jarvis. At the Pub-lic Theater in 1981 and for the last two weekends at Jazzmania, Sun Ra ex-hibited both the old discipline and the pageantry in a package that was ir-resistible. Working with arrangements of Henderson and Ellington material, the band offered hot, snappy, and thrilling performances, with Gilmore's tenor solos and Marshall Allen's gorgeous magnificence on "Day Dream" standouts. Of course, there were "cosmic" homilies sandwiched be-tween performances, all of which gave his work the flavor of a backwoods church social and are probably the source of the stamina that has enabled him to continue his crusade for uniqueness with a science-fiction flavor. The upshot is that Sun Ra's self-celebration (nothing unusual for a home-made godhead) takes on a charm furthered by the great knowledge of deeply swinging grooves. After sending the band walking through the audience on their last night's finale at Jazzmania, Sun Ra brought Gilmore forward to improvise on "Christopher Columbus," with Samurai as he stood next to the tenor saxophonist shaking his bejeweled head. Unamplified and inspired, Gilmore's playing was put in a classic pocket by the drums. As Sun Ra strutted off, pushing Gilmore before him and turning to make faces at the audience, it was quite obvious that he is the last of the dedicated bandleaders and the only avant-gardist capable of holding together large ensembles of musical substance. Let us hope that he is properly recorded with first-class musicians before he goes to meet the masters, for there is still much light to be captured from Sun Ra.

1982

Don't Ask the Critics
Ask Wallace Roney's Peers

Those who hear the trumpeter Wallace Roney at Birdland in Manhattan this week will experience the art of one of the musicians most responsible for the jazz renaissance that took off in the early 1980s. They will also hear one of the best band leaders in the music, for Roney has found a personal way of fusing his three major influences on composition, arranging, and group playing—Miles Davis, John Coltrane, and Herbie Hancock, informed by the studying and the playing that he did with Ornette Coleman.

What one hears is a manipulation of the simple and the complex as well as a conception of improvising in which forms and approaches can be reordered on the spot, allowing the players to redefine melody, harmony, and rhythm with the kind of freedom that makes each performance suspenseful, thrilling, and unpredictable.

That should be expected of Roney, who was highly regarded by his peers long before he achieved public recognition. Born in Philadelphia in 1960, he grew up in a soulful household; his father's favorite musician was Miles Davis and his mother's was Thelonious Monk. So he always heard premier jazz improvising. He began studying music and trumpet at five. By his teens, he was attending Duke Ellington High School for the Performing Arts in Washington, and his name had a big star next to it in the underground of young musicians. In 1979, he won the *Down Beat* magazine award for best young jazz musician of the year.

But such early praise for Roney was not always shared by music critics. He was often dismissed as being little more than a clone of Miles Davis. It was the critics' way of saying that for Roney to base his work on that of a great musician is somehow a sin against the kind of contrivance often described as "cutting-edge." Yet the depth of his talent is something that other musicians have long recognized.

"I had first heard about Wallace Roney when I was in high school," said Wynton Marsalis. "People told me that there was someone serious who was from Washington. And when I first met him, I was astonished by how much music he knew and how much of it came through his horn when he was playing. He has maintained that level of seriousness throughout all of the years since then. This man has never been swayed, which is an achievement of very high integrity in this era."

I recall first hearing Roney in 1976 at Ali's Alley, the short-lived but hot club in SoHo owned by Rashied Ali, John Coltrane's last drummer. Roney, a shy, dark-skinned, and good-looking sixteen-year-old making his New York debut, sat in with the drummer Philly Joe Jones. As soon as Roney commenced to swing, the noise level in the club immediately dropped off, and those in the middle of conversations or laughing and joking turned their attention to the bandstand. People in the back room came out to hear that horn. There was plenty of Lee Morgan in that trumpet playing, and the passion for jazz was so thorough that the atmosphere inside the club was completely rearranged. At the end of the tune, the room took on a crazily jubilant mood, and the clapping wouldn't stop.

The saxophonist Greg Osby met Roney while they were both eighteen-year-old students at the Berklee School of Music in Boston. Osby says that even then Roney was impressing his fellow musicians and that that high regard has changed little since.

"What most people still don't know is that he is a very, very gifted musician," Osby said. "Not only does he have perfect pitch, but he has the supreme version of it. I've seen him outline entire arrangements without aid of his trumpet or a piano. Wallace also turned me on to the essentials of improvisational navigation. He detailed the finer points of melodious logic, how phrases related to one another and how the melody related to the chords that were implied."

Osby recalls Roney having once written out the chord changes to the standard "Cherokee" for him. "I still have a cassette of us playing that," Osby said. "He's playing piano and I'm playing saxophone. That's my first attempt at relating harmony to melodic output. I'll never forget that."

By the early eighties, Roney was a well-schooled trumpet player, fully aware of the tradition from Louis Armstrong forward. The bassist Peter Washington observed those qualities when he worked with Roney in Art Blakey and the Jazz Messengers.

"I'm still amazed at his knowledge of all aspects of jazz—brass, reeds, piano, bass, drums, arrangements, and everything else," Washington said. "He was always studying and trying to better his playing and his understanding of music on every level. His harmonic vocabulary is encyclopedic.

He can play out of any harmonic bag he wants to. The point he's at right now, he's just playing what he hears. He's completely free to do whatever he wants to do."

That encyclopedic knowledge and freedom are the result of working with a range of musicians that stretches from Jay McShann to Ornette Coleman and includes Philly Joe Jones, Cedar Walton, Wayne Shorter, Herbie Hancock, Ron Carter, Tony Williams, Elvin Jones, and Sonny Rollins, some of the most respected names in jazz. That bandstand experience explains why Miles Davis selected him to be a guest at Davis's 1991 Montreux concert, which was one of his last, and why he was invited to perform at the party for Coleman's seventieth birthday party earlier this year.

In the 1980s, jazz was considered passé, but Roney, like Marsalis, was at the forefront of the movement that reasserted the timeless vitality of the art. He was investigating the free melodic invention and harmonic juggling that were characteristic of Davis, Coltrane, Coleman, and Shorter—seemingly unfazed by the unflattering comparisons to Davis.

The results were clear to musicians like the saxophonist George Coleman. "You don't hear anybody else but Wallace who can handle that way-out chromatic stuff that Miles Davis was playing," he said. "Nobody else can hear what it is. To pick something like that, which nobody else has done, and play it with that kind of precision, you have to respect the originality of that."

The bassist Ron Carter, who worked in Davis's last great quintet and has shared many bandstands with Roney, further defends him against his critics: "Wallace seems to be the only trumpet player who understands how Miles did what he did. He didn't just imitate the order of the notes; he understands why they are in that order. Because he understands the concept way past the imitator stage, he's able to develop it to the next level of harmony, space, phrasing and achieve his own individuality. It's time people began to recognize that."

Washington maintains that Roney long ago developed "his own big, dark sound." It is also true that the influence of the trumpeter Don Cherry on Roney has never been appropriately noted. Overlooked is the fact that his playing expresses glee, pathos, sudden and unexpected emotions, as well as the noble gloom, sensuality, and humor passed down from Davis to Cherry.

What makes Roney most interesting at the moment, however, is the way in which he is working with his band, trying to define an ensemble approach in which each player can remake his or her part in reaction to what the featured performer is doing. Roney's music embodies the essence of jazz, both taking advantage of and building on the past. Like all superior jazz musicians, he grounds his music in swing, blues, ballads, and Afro-Hispanic rhythms. Even records as superbly realized as "The Wallace Roney Quintet" and "Village" do not capture the fire, nuance, and adventure of his public performances. So the best chance to experience the work of this artist is to sit in the audience and be taken to some fresh places.

2000

Duke Ellington:
Transcontinental Swing

Himself in Overture

Across all idioms and eras we can see that a daunting number of American artists fall apart or fail to realize their gifts completely, owing to dissipation, psychological problems, or career frustrations. In the wake of their youthful peaks others merely cease to be expansively creative, maintaining a style that might deepen but hardly extends its language. Still others, like Miles Davis, become so obsessed with novelty that they make fools of themselves for the last few decades of their lives. If those troubles don't apply, early deaths by self-destruction or because of bad luck do away with the rest.

Duke Ellington was none of those. A star by his early thirties, he sold millions of records; prevailed over the obstacles and setbacks of show business as successive trends rose to dominance then dissolved; and created masterpieces, short or long, in every decade until his death in 1974 at the age of seventy-five. Yet he is still seen by even those who think they know something about the American arts as no more than a smooth bandleading guy who seemed to be having far too good a time to be taken seriously. (The affected sullenness of the youth-culture star affirms that, from pop to the top, we consider the dour European posture a mark of the truly artistic.) The essence of the problem is that Ellington, a perpetually developing artist, was also a master of the bittersweet science of show business. The many ladies who literally and willingly laid themselves open before him, the infinitely bitchy demands of his prickly spirited musicians—including prudes, alcoholics, kleptomaniacs, drug addicts, gourmands, immigrants, intellectuals, and practical jokers—combined with the highly competitive intricacies of an entertainment night world that could write its name in blood as well as bright lights, were all unfairly matched against the blue-steel discipline that could shut everything out at will, allowing Ellington to compose somewhere between two and three thousand pieces of music before he joined the immortals.

Considering himself "the world's greatest listener," Ellington maintained such commanding touch with his craft and the culture of the world at large that his fifty years of development constitute what is perhaps the single most comprehensive evolution in all of

American art. Much of this has to do with something as American as the bandleading composer himself. Ellington was the greatest manipulator of blues form and blues feeling. He understood it as music and as mood. He knew that those who thought of the blues as merely a vehicle for primitive complaint had their drawers or brassieres on backward. The blues always knows its way around. It can stretch from the backwoods to the space shuttle, from wet blood on the floor of a dive to the neurotic confusion of a beautifully clothed woman in a penthouse overlooking the very best view of Manhattan. The blues, happy or sad or neither, plays no favorites.

In his stark to complicated uses of the blues we can see Ellington quite clearly. He struggles with forms and voices as successfully as Melville; satirizing the skin off of pomposity gives him the same pleasure it did Twain; he measures up to D. W. Griffith in his masterful use of the musical "close-up"—the solo feature within the cross-cutting antiphony and variously lighted tonal support of the big band; the surreal slapstick of certain pieces has the topsy-turvy spirit of Buster Keaton; there are numerous blue and moody parallels to the moments of tragic recognition that Hemingway delivers with a declarative lyricism; the dense intricacy of his tonal colors makes him part Faulkner; one hears a lilting combination of Bill Robinson and Fred Astaire whenever those percussive accents in brass flow through suave billows of Ellingtonian harmony; he is a twin of John Ford in his brilliant development of both his fundamental themes and his repertory team of players; the worldly melding of satire, gloom, and innovation is a fine match for his good friend Orson Welles; and, as the master bluesologist Albert Murray has observed, he is tuned in to Frank Lloyd Wright through his successful invention of a musical architecture that blends so perfectly with the shifting inner and outer landscapes of American life.

In Ellington, we hear the story of the Negro, maybe the most American of Americans. That story precedes the Pilgrims and the Revolutionary War and has proven epic enough to attract identification across color lines and national boundaries. For Ellington, that tale, if it goes on long enough, always moves toward some sort of romance. The guy who finds himself fighting dragons, communing with nature, dancing, mourning, celebrating, and stepping through fire to awaken that sleeping beauty is in for a big, fat surprise. If the initiator is a woman, a charismatic modern female who will be stopped by nothing, the facts remain the same. Both will discover that the blues, as Ellington said, is "the accompaniment to the world's greatest duet, a man and a woman going steady. And if neither one of them feels like singing 'em, the blues just vamps 'til ready!"

In order to tell us his epic tale of everything ending up in the arms of the blues, Ellington had to stay out there for over five decades, writing for every instrument in his band, from the clarinet to the baritone saxophone, from the trumpet to the trombone, for the string bass or the trap drums. He also penned show tunes for singers, worked on some unsuccessful musicals, did scores for film as well as for television, and kept himself afloat, no matter how many were capsized by the ill winds of the trade. Beneath those blue suede gloves were home-

made brass knuckles. Duke Ellington learned early on that his was a world both sweet and rough and that he had to be able to handle all extremes.

1. In the Magic of the Kitchen

In the same interests of self-preservation that keep magicians from ever revealing their tricks, Ellington enjoyed presenting himself as some sort of a velvet primitive not quite aware of just what he was doing, or as the kind of master chef who considered discussions of recipes no more enjoyable than sniffing stink bombs. He had no intention of letting the competition know how it was done. Ellington was well aware of the basic show business problem: An artist who was, in his words, "a number one himself," might someday find that he had been upstaged by an imitator, "a number two somebody else." But it was his systematic approach to sound, his willingness to build bracing or mysterious dissonances into his works, his curiosity about complementary and contrasting textures that gave his art so much depth.

Born April 29, 1899, in Washington, D.C., Edward Kennedy Ellington was, like many Negro jazz innovators, a favored child. He shared with Coleman Hawkins, Charlie Parker, Thelonious Monk, Miles Davis, and others a background in which he was pampered, tucked in, read to, and reared to believe in himself and his own opinions without reservation. Our simple-minded presumptions about color and consciousness frequently dupe us into missing the facts of these matters. The restrictions of race had nothing to do with how such artists saw themselves when accurate expression of their imaginations demanded that they innovate.

He got the nickname "Duke" because he liked fancy pants and was a charmer, ever quick with the kinds of aristocratic lines that pulled in women, and even made it easy for him to later fire musicians so gracefully that some described being asked to leave as having the feeling of either a compliment or an assignment of elevated duty. But Ellington didn't go in for social barriers and loved to hang out with anyone whose vitality or skill attracted him. Long after he had become a big success, the Duke might leave his Harlem apartment in silk robe, pajamas, and slippers to sit up all night in a little greasy spoon. While eating or smoking a cigarette and sipping coffee, he gave audience, listening to the stories of the commoner night owls and telling his own.

As were many young musicians of his youth, Ellington was bitten by the night creature of jazz. He was at first thrilled by the Harlem stride piano style he heard on James P. Johnson's 1917 recording of *Carolina*

Shout, which he learned by ear and played so well that a local reputation took off among Washington musicians. Since there were no formal ways to study this new music, he absorbed his art in the Washington and up-town New York streets during the innumerable jam sessions and the demonstrations where musicians argued technical points or discussed them. He had taken piano lessons as a child but his most important edu-cation included observing exchanges between trained musicians and un-trained players, each drawing something from the other. This is where Ellington initially sensed that music from both worlds could be fused, something that he worked at throughout his career. During those forma-tive years, when he was still making his New York way in the late 1920s, Ellington would sit with his drummer, Sonny Greer, way, way up in the balconies of concert halls and ponder the problems of emulating Euro-pean orchestral effects in the language of jazz and for the instruments at his disposal. Alone in his apartment, Ellington also studied the harmony books in Harlem that he forever pretended to have ignored because he was too busy bandleading.

The quality of his recognition was deep. Before long, Ellington figured out what would become the four most enduring elements of his art: 4/4 swing—fast, medium, and slow; the blues; the romantic ballad; and Afro-Hispanic rhythms. That quartet of fundamentals is reinterpreted over and over throughout the history of jazz innovation, from Louis Armstrong all the way to the most fruitful work of Ornette Coleman and John Coltrane. It was Ellington's substantial grasp of the essences of the idiom that allowed him to maintain such superb aesthetic focus at every point in his profes-sional life, no matter the trends and eras he evolved through.

In his 1943 *Black, Brown, and Beige*, a work of more than forty minutes in which all of his innovations had reached a culmination, Ellington built what was then the most adventurous long composition in jazz history. Be-ginning with a simple motive, as did Beethoven in his Fifth Symphony, he developed it into many different kinds of themes, lyric or propulsive. Ellington used or ignored conventional phrasing lengths, twisted the blues into and out of shape, wrote smooth or dissonant harmonies, and called upon many rhythmic modulations that moved from march beats to swing to jaunty Afro-Hispanic syncopations. It is a perfect example of why Ellington was the truest and most complete kind of innovator; he remade the fundamentals so thoroughly that they took on the freshness of an open sky while maintaining touch with the gutbucket earthiness heard in the best of the very earliest jazz.

Ellington achieved his ends through orchestrated instrumental techniques that were themselves about languages. Those ends were extensions and refinements of the vocal styles of blues and jazz singers. His often saying that he was no more than a primitive minstrel was usually taken as a joke. That was one of the many masks he wore when obliquely throwing historical daggers. In the 1960s he declined Charles Mingus's mischievous idea that they make an "avant-garde" record together by imitating the chaotic squeaking and honking of the day. Ellington said that there was no point in taking music back *that* far. Doubtless, he remembered exactly how it was before jazz became a music of casual virtuosity, back when so many musicians truly *couldn't* play, when they lacked the control of their instruments necessary to execute even the simplest passages. Yet Ellington never forgot the first time he heard just how great the sound of jazz could be, and that experience would inform his music forever.

In Washington, when Ellington was an easy-going and locally popular bandleader, he experienced an indelible epiphany upon hearing the cantankerous, pistol-packing New Orleans genius Sidney Bechet play "I'm Coming Virginia" in 1921. Ellington always referred to Bechet as "the great originator" and employed him for a brief period in New York during the middle 1920s. On Ellington's bandstand at the Kentucky Club, Bechet's soprano saxophone did nightly battle with the growling plunger trumpet of Bubber Miley, whose sound had turned Ellington away from the society music he was performing and convinced him that he "would never play sweet music again."

Bechet was a grand master of both the improvised blues line and a trickbag of vocal effects that he claimed made it possible for him to call his dog—Goola—with his horn. Miley's growl techniques formed a direct line to King Oliver, the New Orleans mentor of Louis Armstrong. What those two brought into Ellington's world never left it. His star alto saxophonist Johnny Hodges had been taught his way around the soprano by Bechet and was to keep the older man's melodic language and inflections within almost every phrase of his own alto style for his entire life, adding to that style a tone so original that it became one of the great instrumental colors of the century. Miley's plunger-muted influence—surely the most intriguing extension of the African talking drum in American music—spread through the entire brass section. The growl imitations and allusions to the Afro-American voice's timbres, inflections, and speech patterns were stable aspects of Ellington's palette.

The results on all fronts were frequently operatic within the terms of Ellington's idiom, bringing artistry to what could have easily been just comic, novelty effects. His brass and reed players delivered arias, performed duets. They wove their elevated, instrumental expansions of the Afro-American voice through compositions, assigning their fellow wind players the roles of choirs or tuned, jabbing percussion. Under the bandleader's direction, their efforts often disdainfully mocked the sentimental. One example is *The Mystery Song*, which not only contrasts empty-headed frivolity with a grotesque mood of fear and gloom, but was recorded in 1931—the same year, as Loren Schoenberg points out, that James Whale's *Frankenstein* opened in movie houses. As with opera, the enchanting sensuality of Ellington's many romantic ballads instigated true-life courtships from coast to coast, several realized within hearing distance of either the radio or the record player.

Yet it was the complex of sorrow and celebration, erotic ambition and romantic defeat—always fueling the deepest meanings of the blues—that gave Ellington his sense of tension and release in human terms. That blues sensibility also inspired him to the sustained development of his composing techniques, for it could be brought to any tempo. The timbres discovered in blues singing and blues playing could color any kind of piece, keeping it in touch with the street, with the heated boudoir beast of two backs, the sticky red leavings of violence, the pomp and rhythmic pride of the dance floor, and the plaintive lyricism made spiritual by emotion that has no specific point of reference other than its audible humanity.

One of the things that Ellington perfected as he enriched his expression is what I call "timbral harmony." I refer to Ellington's statement that when he heard a particular note, he always had to decide *whose* note it would be. That is to say that the very best jazz musicians in a brass or reed section have quite individual tones, even when they are playing perfectly in tune, something that was especially true of Ellington's musicians, whom he called a gathering of "tonal personalities." A given note in Ellington's three-trombone section could have at least as many different colors as players, and even more when the musicians were called upon to inflect pitches with emphasis on particular aspects of their already distinctive sounds. Such awareness on Ellington's part allowed him to change the sound of a given harmonic voicing by merely moving the players around to different positions in the chord—top, middle, bottom. The shifting might continue as the harmony progressed from chord to chord. A man might be asked to use any of a variety of personal colors—the airy or softer side of his sound, a weightier texture, the lush and sensual aspect, the more stringent dimension.

Further, the emotional and psychological riddles of the blues worked in the contrast between the melancholy or optimistic statement of the melody line and the nature of the surrounding orchestration or the rhythm itself. In the double consciousness of the blues, unhappy revelations might be stated over a jaunty rhythm (a perfect example is the powerhouse pulsation of Ellington's arrangement of the "St. Louis Blues," recorded at a 1940 dance in Fargo, South Dakota). Ellington also knew that the emotional turns of blues mood made possible the expression of intricate personality, or suggested the kind of expression he expanded upon and refined through the selection and the coaching of his players. Ben Webster could function as a Kansas City Siegfried-become-a-protean-tenor-saxophonist—innocent, romantic, erotic, combatively heroic—within the course of one performance, such as the multitempo 1948 arrangement of "How High the Moon." Johnny Hodges had a lyric voice capable of much flexibility. It could stretch from the spiritual pinnacle of "Come Sunday" to the glowing sensuality of *Warm Valley*; then, on Billy Strayhorn's *Half the Fun*, render the imperial flirtation of Shakespeare's Cleopatra on her barge or capture Romeo and Juliet's awe and yearning on Strayhorn's *The Star-Crossed Lovers*. As if that weren't enough, Hodges was ever able to croon the blues as majestically or as low down as Ellington wanted at almost any tempo. Ray Nance's trumpet or cornet, given specific timbral access through mutes, plungers, or his remarkably refined control of an open tone, could juggle the puckish, the plaintive, the buffoonish, the high-minded, and the translucently erotic. Consequently, the very selection of improvising soloists, and the order in which they performed a given piece, allowed for the musical, psychological, and emotional aspects of the performance to achieve variational development and operatic counterbalances in idiomatic terms.

Unlike literal singers, the members of the Ellington Orchestra also had the resources to emulate the dark or shining roles of strings, the timbres of wind instruments absent from the ensemble, the blunt syncopations of percussion, the rhythms of ballroom dancers, and various natural or technological phenomena when called upon—all in the service of an epic vision that brought as much detail to the general as to the specific. In the 1934 *Rude Interlude*, for instance, Ellington opens with the trombone quite confidently creating the effect of a French horn! The year before he produced the startling virtuoso display of *Daybreak Express*, one of the most perfect emulations of a train ever written. The 1946 *Happy-Go-Lucky Local* was so good that even the sometimes snooty British critic Max Harrison was inspired to write of it as "the supreme musical train piece, surpassing not only

Ellington's earlier *Lightning* and *Daybreak Express* but also the attempts of straight composers such as Villa-Lobos (*Little Train of the Caipira*) or even Honegger (*Pacific 231*)." In much later works, two clarinets shrewdly voiced within the overall sound of the ensemble achieve the weight and color of an oboe; the combination of two clarinets with either baritone saxophone or bass clarinet will create the illusion of a bassoon. In some pieces, a pair of tenor saxophones will play the same note together but their particularly distinctive tones will create a "chord" of timbre that sometimes seems like another—unrecognizable—instrument altogether. As baritone saxophonist Joe Temperley observes, Ellington would also have Harry Carney blow his baritone so strongly for certain effects that the overtones coming up off of the basic notes would add other "imaginary" notes to the orchestration.

Of course, Ellington himself often made mention of the fact that he had thought early on of being a painter. Then, as the story usually went, he would comment on how he had replaced the brush and the palette with brass, reeds, string bass, and percussion. The colors he was able to draw from his ensemble were matched in their remarkable range by the inventive uses he put them to, avoiding pure abstraction at nearly every turn. Almost every sound is connected to something particular in his experience or his mind—even the dimensions of a dream, a fantasy, a myth. There is always the magic of existence, however, which inevitably includes the mystery and the ambivalence. The sense of heartache and of complexity is countered by his affection for the emblematic moxie and charm felt in the rhythmic momentum of jazz swing. Rhythm was definitely part of his business. The endless combinations of piano chords and timbres in combination with plucked or bowed bass notes and the percussion ensemble of differently colored cymbals, bass drum, brushes, sticks, snare, and large and small tom-toms that the jazz drummer has at his disposal were used for beats that anchored or counterpointed or underlined Ellington's featured players. That triangular rhythm section of piano, bass, and drums also sparked, heckled, soothed, and lulled the improvisors it supported.

His orchestration and counterpoint were the result of how much he was taken by the polyphony of the New Orleans jazz bands he heard early in his career, with the cornet carrying the melody as obbligati were played above and below it by the clarinet and the trombone. Access to authenticity came directly. By hiring New Orleans men such as Bechet, clarinetist Barney Bigard, and bassist Wellman Braud, Ellington learned, in perfect detail, the specific techniques of the Crescent City style from musicians who had grown up at the source. Works such as Jelly Roll Morton's seminal

1926 *Black Bottom Stomp* taught Ellington tension and release lessons about thematic variety, modulation, changes of rhythm, and pulse that at first inspired progressively profound short pieces with fanfares, interludes, and so on—even though Ellington personally hated the braggadocious New Orleans Morton and was hardly mum about it. Years later and in uncharacteristic anger, he even made the ridiculous claim that he had heard schoolteachers play better piano than the marvelous "Mr. Jelly Lord," who credited himself with having invented jazz and contemptuously accused everyone else of stealing his stuff or not knowing how it was really done, which demoted their playing and their bands to positions below him.

It is highly possibly that Morton, who referred to New York musicians as "cockroaches," might have said something to the young Ellington that was so insulting he never forgot it. Perhaps Morton ribbed Ellington about his inarguable 1927 lifting of King Oliver's 1923 *Canal Street Blues* and calling it "Creole Love Call," a piece that remained in his repertoire, getting newer and newer arrangements, as did almost every piece that became popular. Still, Ellington, no matter his actual reasons for detesting Jelly Roll, from the diamond fillings of his teeth to the skin on the bottom of his feet, went on to use those Morton lessons for compositional techniques that were individualized and remained central to his sound. As with the unexpected coursings of human events, when Ellington's 1934 *Rude Interlude* appeared, trumpeter Rex Stewart wrote of how Morton stood out in front of Harlem's legendary Rhythm Club and defended the composition's unusual sound against such detractors as the mighty, hunchbacked drummer Chick Webb, whose ear for innovation was too small to pick up on that particular aspect of it, even from a musician whom he truly admired.

Ellington also took everything he could get from the instruction of bandleader and composer Will Marion Cook, who gave him informal lessons in composition one summer during the middle 1920s as they rode together in open-topped taxis through Central Park. Born in 1869 in Washington, D.C., and a graduate of Oberlin Conservatory who had studied the violin in Europe, Cook was highly regarded. He set down the violin after giving a Carnegie Hall performance in 1895 because of a New York review. The writer referred to him as "the world's greatest Negro violinist," something he considered a demeaning racial slur. Cook soon studied for a short period with Antonín Dvořák, then dedicated himself to inventing a Negro instrumental and vocal music based on the unique elements of the folk styles, religious and secular. It is far from improbable that Dvořák, who was so taken by indigenous American music, may well have helped Cook make his decision to build something from materials native to the feelings and rhythms of the nation.

Success dropped on him early. Paul Laurence Dunbar wrote the lyrics and Cook the music for the 1898 operetta, *Clorindy, or the Origin of the Cakewalk*, a Broadway hit. He traveled to Europe in 1919 with his Southern Syncopated Orchestra, which featured Sidney Bechet, whom Cook had heard in Chicago. So when young Ellington was in the company of Will Marion Cook, he was drawing technical knowledge from one who had been around the block a number of times. He may also have inherited Dvořák's vision as reinterpreted through Cook's belief that a Negro music, something original, was the greatest creative challenge facing an Afro-American musician. Ellington noted that he wasn't able to experiment fully with some of the things discussed with Cook until *Black, Brown, and Beige*, which premiered almost twenty years later.

Ellington also kept his ear on the playing and writing of the stride piano masters of Manhattan—James P. Johnson, Willie "The Lion" Smith, and Fats Waller. He listened closely to the Tin Pan Alley songs that sailed into the culture from behind the footlights of Broadway. The innovations that the writing of Don Redman, Horace Henderson, and Benny Carter brought to the jazz orchestra didn't fall on deaf ears either. Ellington heard everything that was going on around him and made so much of it that he, more than any other jazz musician, perpetually revealed how broad and rich were the possibilities of his art. Alone of the musicians of his generation, he was perfectly comfortable not only performing with the giants who created the fundamental languages of the music for their instruments during the 1920s and the 1930s—instrumentalists such as Armstrong, Bechet, tenor saxophonist Coleman Hawkins, alto saxophonists Benny Carter and Johnny Hodges—but was at ease playing with later innovators from the 1940s, 1950s, and 1960s, such as Charlie Parker, Dizzy Gillespie, Charles Mingus, Max Roach, and John Coltrane. Excepting Bechet, Carter, and Parker; he also made either intriguing or classic recordings with each of them.

In order to do what his creative appetite, his ambition, and his artistic demon asked of him, Ellington had to maintain an orchestra for composing purposes longer than anyone else—almost fifty years. The single precedent in the entire history of Western music was the orchestra Esterhazy provided for Haydn, which lasted twenty-nine years. The great difference, however, is that Ellington was artist and sponsor, using the royalties from his many hit recordings—and from the multitudinous recordings of his compositions by others—to meet his payroll, making it ever possible to hear new music as soon as he wrote it. That orchestra was, as Albert Murray observed in *The Hero and the Blues*, "booked for recitals in the great concert halls of the world, much the same as if it were a fifteen-piece innovation of the symphony orchestra—which in a sense it [was]."

That hand-picked orchestra was also an Ellingtonian version of the John Ford stock company, which used the images, voices, and cinematic talents of performers such as John Wayne, Henry Fonda, Maureen O'Hara, Victor McLaughlin, Donald Crisp, John Carradine, Ben Johnson, and other, lesser-known actors as often as possible. As with those actors, Ellington musicians like Johnny Hodges, Lawrence Brown, Ray Nance, Jimmy Hamilton, Harry Carney, and Paul Gonsalves did their best work in the bandleader's stock company. The contexts he provided for them were far more inventive, varied in mood, and challenging than anything they—or anybody else—could create to suit their talents so perfectly. As composer, arranger, coach, and rhythm section accompanist, Ellington was also the master screenwriter, director, lighting technician, dialect expert, head of wardrobe, set-designer, manipulator of special effects, and makeup man. While his legendary patience with his stars of sound was such that he could ignore a fistfight in a Hamburg hotel lobby between his son, Mercer, and a veteran band member, asking only if his suite was ready, Ellington could also explode, once ragefully slugging a drunkard to the floor because he had been embarrassing on stage one time too many. Yes, beyond extending, elaborating, and refining his themes and the talents of his players, he and John Ford had more than a bit in common.

2. Transcontinental Swing

One of the signal accomplishments of the music of Duke Ellington is its epic expression of American feeling. In evocation after evocation, Ellington proves that he knew in his very cells what William Carlos Williams meant when he observed in his classic *In the American Grain* that by truly exploring the specific an artist will achieve the universal. Ellington's music contains so many characteristics of the nation—its intricate dialogues between individuals and groups, its awesome and heartbreaking difficulties, as well as its skylines and landscapes, city or country. In a work like his three-part 1947 *Tonal Group*, we hear the stone, glass, and steel of industrial achievement summoned through brass, reeds, and rhythm section percussion; urban complexes remade into charm bracelets of sound, a mechanized society in which the technological thrust toward facelessness is met by a sense of transcendence through swing, the democratic pulsation in which responses to song and dance can bring individuality as well as community.

In Ellington's big city of music, one might stand enraptured by romance or share the communal sorrow of the blues; primp for some moment of prominent or private joy; ponder and thrill to the epic humanity ganged up in Harlem and usually happy about it; feel the torrid nostalgia for a period of early courtship; itch inside for recognition of some personal ideal; and experience the mutations of feeling that course through the soul with the swiftness of subway stations flitting at the eye as an express train speeds toward selected stops. Those passions coalesced into the bittersweet joy of modern life, the sense of style, and the throbbing vitality that syncopated its way onto the dance floor of the Savoy ballroom. That angle on style made Easter uptown on New York's Seventh Avenue a color-rich display of voluminous elegance. It also ran all the intricate way from pulpits to pitcher's mounds. In fox trot after fox trot, the aesthetic command of those sensibilities individuated the urban momentum of Ellington's music.

If the context was rural or Southern—as in a number of three-minute works, or the 1946 *Deep South Suite*, or his 1970 *New Orleans Suite*—Ellington supplied us with tones that told tales of down-home lore in earthy panoramas, detailing the distances from the sometimes blood-encrusted gutbucket to the ascendant melancholy of the singing in a country church. The music became pictorial, festive, and epic in another key of experience. One could witness the effects of home brew drunk from jars and so strong it was nicknamed "Jack Johnson"; hear the raucously dissonant, metallic percussion of the railroad rhythms that Albert Murray observed had so influenced the ground-beats of the blues; wonder at the hard labor done in the fields, the woods, and at plants; pass the school windows behind which high, high yellow to dark, dark teachers taught with missionary verve; see the old folks sitting and rocking on front porches; witness the visceral dignity of church services; walk in on the culinary splendor of picnics and family celebrations, those events at which you could taste and smell the things experts did with a slaughtered hog, knowing again the succulence of the greens and the sauces, the butter beans, the possum stew, the gumbo in myriad versions; the thin light-brown gravies and the gravies dark as chocolate cake and almost as thick as heavy syrup; those nose-twitching freshly baked apple, blueberry, and peach cobblers; the chicken made golden brown in a frying pan or off-the-bone tender in a pot of dumplings; view the startling richness of the sunrise and the fields of wild flowers, the trees so weighed down with foliage they were in danger of snapping into pieces; and meet, in ever greater detail, the black, brown, beige, and bone people whose suffering, whose celebration, and whose spiritual integrity formed beacons of tragic optimism for our culture. Those who spoke to the murky oracle of the abyss were answered with the hard blues, which they mutated into a love song or swung until the cows came home.

While his poetic miniatures were packed with aesthetic action, his suites usually focused on particular aspects of given places or musically depicted the variousness held together by a common subject. As noted earlier, many of the shorter pieces were fashioned by Ellington to capture his beloved Harlem, a bygone cultural jewel possessed of the pulsating light common only to golden ages. That now-mythic Harlem was not the piss-stained slum of those suicidal or smothered jungle bunnies found in the protest writings of James Baldwin. The Ellingtonian Harlem is what Ralph Ellison recalled as "an outpost of American optimism, a gathering place for the avant-garde in music, dance, and democratic interracial relationships; and, as the site and symbol of America's freewheeling sense of possibility, it was our homegrown version of Paris." In his own specific paean, *Harlem*, from 1950, Ellington wrote one of his finest longer works beginning with the plunger-muted statement of the title in two notes. There is then a tour through Harlem in montage, cutting from one tempo, mood, rhythm, and texture to another, always maintaining form through, as Wynton Marsalis notes, "its exploration of blues harmony." Near the end there is a marvelous rendition of a funeral that features a fine, fine example of Ellingtonian counterpoint.

It is quite easy to understand why there is such a rich body of composition in his canon dedicated to women, for there is no greater show business legend in the world of romance than Duke Ellington, whose appreciation and experience of the opposite sex inspired tales of almost mythic proportions. Tall, handsome, formerly an athlete, gifted with a grasp of gab that could mutate into magnetic honey, he quite easily drew women of all races, places, and classes to him. Those intimate experiences are symbolized in his fairy-tale jazz history, *A Drum Is a Woman*, which Ellington narrates. There, Madam Zajj—the dark enchantress, muse, and bitch-goddess of his art—says to Ellington: "Come with me to my emerald rock garden, just off the moon, where darkness is only a translucency, and the cellophane trees grow a mile high. Come climb with me to the top of my tree, where the fruit is ripe and the taste is like the sky. Star rubies are budding in my diamond-encrusted hothouse." In short works like *Sophisticated Lady; The Gal from Joe's,* and *Lady of the Lavender Mist*, and then in longer ones such as *The Tattooed Bride* and *Princess Blue*, the ardor of Ellington's musical women is complicated by his ability to make them emotionally and psychologically full-figured. The personalities of female Ellingtonia are combinations of grief and vivacity, insecurity and confidence, the childlike and the worldly, the pugnacious and the mystic, the down-home and the regal.

Because Ellington was also a man of the world at large, there was nothing of significant experiential import that he allowed to stop short of his bandstand. If it was human, if he saw it or heard about it, if he went there and felt the air, saw the colors, spoke with the people, ate their food, and got that instant feeling for replication a genius of his sort was prone to, it would end up in music. Ellington had been a local hero to the Washington of his musical youth and made his name working for gangsters in New York's Cotton Club, a segregated room off-limits to all but the most famous Negroes. It was an extended job that sometimes included being called down to the city morgue, where the police asked him to identify the corpse of someone who had been partying in the club the night before. In his memoir, *Music Is My Mistress*, it was made clear that whether or not he recognized the murdered man on the slab, Ellington always answered, "Hell, no," when asked if he knew him. It was impossible for him to be a naïf. Moreover, he performed solo piano in a big Harlem benefit for the Scottsboro Boys defense fund, keenly assessed the racial double standards of show business success, saw one of his musicians playing the tuba with the bones in his face periodically slipping out of place because he had been roughed up by gangsters, watched fellow musicians slowly dissolve in the acids of drink and drugs, and recognized the yearning for a fair shot that lay behind the eyes of so many, no matter their class, color, or religion. So his was an art boiled to early recognition in a crucible of glamour, racism, murder, and good, good times. The signal dissonances were perhaps acknowledgments of just how hard and cold the blues could get.

After first crossing the Atlantic in the early 1930s, Ellington and his band eventually toured Europe with the penetration of radio and television broadcasts, went on down to the Middle East and Africa, rode the air all the way to Japan, charmed them Down Under as far as the Outback, and crossed below the equator into South America. Over those forty years, Ellington learned that his versions of rhythm and tune were international languages and that those languages were capable of bringing whatever he knew of the human universe into any room in which he and his musicians were playing. Those foreign lands and societies were brought to the bandstand, sooner or later, their spirits wrestled or coaxed into melody, harmony, tonal colors, and rhythm. As Ellington told the writer Playthell Benjamin, he never composed music about other countries while in them. Only notes were made because he preferred to do his writing after returning to New York, which, for him, ensured the work maintaining an American identity rather than falling into imitation of a particular culture's musical surroundings. None of his efforts, however, stopped the blues from brewing.

3. Ellington and the Misunderstanding

Ellington's sense of artistry over long periods was revealed when he told his nephew Michael James: "It's not about this generation or that. The issue in art is *regeneration.*" That was his greatest achievement, but it led to the biggest problem he had once his accomplishments sent him to the top of his profession. By 1943, when Ellington premiered *Black, Brown, and Beige* to mixed reviews—some quite hostile—he had already produced far, far more great recorded works than any other jazz musician or bandleader. A decade earlier he had been celebrated in England as a major artist. But one of the photographs from a British hall finds the glamorously dressed Ellington bookcased by tall caricatures of the grinning, minstrel figures with banjos that had begun to appear in America a century earlier. The visual irony was that Ellington had become a hero among Negroes as well as unprejudiced whites for never, never sinking down into any kind of Tomming.* But as he became ever more adventurous back home, the minstrel reductions, the simplifications he gave no quarter to, took on another form in the criticism written by many who considered themselves supporters.

The misunderstanding that bedeviled Ellington to the end of his life and that has dominated the criticism written about him for many years is the idea that his greatest period was from 1940–1942. The ensemble he led during that period is now called the "Blanton-Webster Band" because it included the innovative bassist Jimmy Blanton and tenor saxophonist Ben Webster, both of whom were featured in such classics as *Jack the Bear, Sepia Panorama, Cotton Tail*, and *What Am I Here For?* The conventional complaint is that Ellington's later work either suffered from his reaching beyond the limits of his talent in extended works or that his music was less good because

---

*The way Ellington looks at the conventional buffoon Negro characters during his performance in the 1929 short film, *Black and Tan Fantasy*, gives a clear indication of what he thought about such things. In fact, his low-keyed performance, while no great shakes, is completely devoid of the exaggerations of silent film and an early example of the subtleties that developed with sound.

the quality of his ensemble never made it to that 1940–1942 level again. Those critics didn't realize that Ellingtonia is a mountain range, not a series of hills leading up to one mountain, which is followed by a descending line of smaller and smaller hills.

The collective way in which Ellington worked, crafting his writing with his musicians—who might even laugh at poorly written parts and throw them back at him—made experimentation an ongoing process that, given the individuals involved, guaranteed development. From the late 1920s onward, he also left open holes for improvisation or often encouraged a single clarinetist to invent counterlines against the written parts. In that way, he was much like the film directors who allow actors to change dialogue or the Hollywood makers of early silent comedies who arrived on the set with no more than a plot outline or a few situations that were then improvised into form. Yet the determining sensibility was always Ellington's, which is why the music maintained its identity through the many personnel changes, no matter how strong the personalities of his musicians might have been.

In 1939, Ellington had brought the marvelous composing talent of Billy Strayhorn into his organization. Strayhorn wrote *Take the A Train*, which became perhaps the most famous band theme of all time, and he collaborated with Ellington until his death in 1967, canceling all speculations about how he would do things once the Duke died. Strayhorn came to everyone's attention during the Blanton-Webster years in which the language Ellington had been adding to since the late 1920s reached a golden balance of composition, personnel, and musicianship. The new composer and arranger absorbed Ellington's language and wrote his own invincible works such as *Midriff, Passion Flower, Raincheck, Johnny Come Lately*, and *Chelsea Bridge*.

As his career went on beyond that 1940–1942 peak of creativity and personnel, Ellington composed more and more longer pieces, some alone, some in conjunction with Strayhorn. These works not only expressed his expanding vision but took on the vinyl fact of the long-playing, forty-minute record as a form itself, a space that could be used for the moods responsive to a central subject. While he grew by the decade, Ellington never failed to work on all that he had engaged before. To the very end, as examples such as the 1957 *Where Is the Music?* (over which the shadow of Bechet hovers) and the 1958 *Feetbone* prove, he was always capable of writing the immaculate small- and full-band compositions that were once demanded by the 78-RPM era, when discs held little more than three minutes on each side. Classic melodies inspired by women evolved. By the late

1940s a fifteen-minute masterpiece such as *The Tattooed Bride* is an updat-ing—in conception, not material—of *Clarinet Lament*, a miniature concerto for Barney Bigard from 1937. *The Tattooed Bride* opens with a tonally am-biguous overture and introduces its central motive during the piano and bass duet that recalls the ones with Blanton. There is then a snarling, romp-ing fast section, a lovely ballad of pure melody for clarinet, and an up-tempo concluding section that allows Jimmy Hamilton to display his ve-locity technique against a backdrop of reed writing that both winks at the rhythmic innovations of bebop while extending upon pieces like the 1927 *Hop Head*. Composer, conductor, and transcriber David Berger says of the magisterial *Princess Blue*, from 1958: "It has been really neglected and is one of Ellington's best pieces, incorporating, again, the blues. He's able to change textures and moods very smoothly. It's a seamless piece. It's one of the best examples of counterpoint in Ellington. Then there are the sonori-ties. It's really a marvelous piece. Genius on the loose. It has a regal feeling, which shows again just how broad the possibilities of the blues were in his hands." The piece is also a catalogue of allusions to earlier Ellington works such as "Creole Love Call"; *Just a-Sittin and a-Rockin; Never No Lament; Black, Brown, and Beige;* and *Transbluesency.*

Earlier "tonal portraits" of uptown New York—*Echoes of Harlem, Harmony in Harlem,* and *Harlem Speaks*—evolved into the aforementioned *Harlem* of 1950, which recalls "Bubber Miley" as it opens with a plunger-muted trum-pet "singing" the title in two notes. The explorations of Afro-Hispanic and exotic rhythms from all over the world heard in Blanton-Webster pieces such as "Conga Brava" and "The Flaming Sword," however classic, were ex-panded upon and excelled in the 1960s and 1970s with albums and suites such as *Afro-Bossa,* the *Far East Suite,* the *Latin American Suite, Afro-Eurasian Eclipse,* and the *Togo Brava Suite.*

The celebrated arrangements of popular materials such as *Three Little Words* and *Flamingo* weren't put on a lower timeless shelf, but the 1958 rein-ventions of American standards on *At the Bal Masque,* and the 1962 handling of French street and café songs for *A Midnight in Paris,* move on up to higher places, displaying the distinctions of the past in admixture with the exten-sions, elaborations, and refinements that experience made possible. Every aspect of arranging—harmony, counterpoint, rhythm, and timbre—is ma-nipulated with the substantially increased authority and depth we should expect of an older master. His joyously sardonic 1934 arrangement of the *Ebony Rhapsody,* based on *Hungarian Rhapsody,* is no preparation whatsoever for the *Nutcracker Suite* and the *Peer Gynt Suites* of 1960. The first selection of each suite—one swinging like mad, the other moving at the stately pace of a cloud—makes it obvious that one of the greatest ensembles in all of Western musical history is at work. The same experience of expanded powers is had when one compares Ellington's quite beautiful score for the 1935 film *Symphony in Black* with his writing for both the 1959 *Anatomy of a Murder* (which works and reworks three themes so well that writer and ex-jazz pianist Tom Piazza calls it "a vernacular American Symphony") and the 1961 *Paris Blues*. In the last, Ellington was able to make use of Louis Armstrong, who was a featured actor in the movie. The results were enduring. In the jam session sequence that produced *Battle Royale*, we hear one of Armstrong's most exciting late performances, his combative horn rising up over the charging band and making Gershwin's "I Got Rhythm" chord changes serve jazz once more. Armstrong's rhythms are still freely innovative, his sound is both darker and brighter, and he maintains a lyric choice of notes no matter how hot the proceedings get.

On *Jazz Party*, Ellington had done the same thing with *Dizzy Gillespie* early in 1959, coaxing participation from one of Armstrong's greatest songs in two of the album's four masterpieces (the others being the extended *Toot Suite* and *Fillie Trillie*, a jazz version of romantic comedy that boasts Johnny Hodges at his personal Bechet best, a parody of a striptease number, and a dialogue between Hodges and the puckish, Clark Terry-crafted, near-bop of the brass). One is a concerto for jazz horn, Gillespie the bop king whispering, bitching, and blasting his way through Strayhorn's *Upper Manhattan Medical Group*; the other a blues summation of things as they then were, *Hello, Little Girl*. The second masterwork also features the silvery, insinuating piano of Jimmy Jones and the Southwestern blues shouting of the magnificent Jimmy Rushing, who had come to national notice more than two decades earlier as part of the Count Basie band that revolutionized jazz swing. After Rushing's bitter, plaintive, and raging tale of romantic turmoil, there is an obvious splice that puts the overall performance into the arena of combined takes in films. We then hear an extraordinary improvisation from Gillespie, himself a revolutionary, clearly displaying his untouchable wares to the Ellington trumpet section with a virtuosity, a harmonic complexity, and a swinging rhythmic intricacy that must have left every one of those trumpeters gasping and trembling. The ending finds Rushing and Gillespie emoting in combination over a splendid saxophone riff, some mightily dissonant brass, and a gutbucket-bottom groove from the rhythm section. Just before Ornette Coleman and John Coltrane were to open the barn door for the anarchic honkers and squeakers of the sixties, Ellington showed that he was still the master chef capable of bringing together all that was inarguably good.

The uses of singers as far back as the 1927 "Creole Love Call" to imitate musical instruments, or the incorporation of the classical soprano Kay Davis in the 1946 *Transbluesency*, are brought to new levels of exploration and victory in the parts showcasing Margaret Tynes on the 1957 *A Drum Is a Woman* and the writing done for Alice Babs in the *Sacred Concerts* near the end of Ellington's life. While the 1958 version of *Black, Brown, and Beige* is largely a job of editing so incoherent that the form and development of the piece are butchered, it also includes Ellington's supreme liturgical achievement. Because she considered the Duke Ellington Orchestra "a sacred institution," the matchless Mahalia Jackson came to that recording date to sing "Come Sunday" and "The Twenty-Third Psalm." Then the tragic vocal majesty stretching all the way back to the most powerful spirituals and the twentieth-century achievement of a wholly original language for the idiomatic American dance and concert orchestra reached mutual apotheosis. In the liner notes, it is claimed that Jackson improvised the vocal line of "The Twenty-Third Psalm." That is more than doubtful, given the distance of the notes from anything the New Orleans high priestess of gospel normally sang. Ellington—or Strayhorn—wrote what is a decidedly modern composition, one so unbeholden in overall sound and effect that it may have created its own category.

One of the reasons that Ellington has been so misunderstood is that we Americans don't always know how to assess ongoing artistry outside of European concert music. We expect the finest concert musicians to ripen and deepen with middle age, but assume that jazz musicians will deteriorate once they leave the bristling province of youth. In fact, Ellington's greatest band was not the one of the 1940s but the one between 1956 and 1968, though he was still able to inspire strong performances from lesser musicians afterward. Beginning in the middle 1950s, what he got from Johnny Hodges, Paul Gonsalves, Harry Carney, Lawrence Brown, Ray Nance, Cootie Williams, Russell Procope, Jimmy Hamilton, and the others could only be achieved by men who had lived beyond forty or fifty. By then, the band members had played every note and register in every key for so long that they had the kinds of intimate and subtle relationships to the identities of their instruments that young players, however gifted, never possess. Their tonal colors could be even thicker or far more transparent, given the assignment. Their life experience brought increasing depths to the emotions they had lived through and had seen played out in the lives of those around them. They had watched children grow into adulthood, handsome

men and women lose their looks and shapes, friends and relatives die, innocent girls and boys become whores and ruthless hustlers, misfortune destroy, disfigure, or derange, and wars come and go; they had felt the shock
of assassinations; and they had witnessed myriad changes in society and
technology. The same was true of Ellington, who invented a piano style so
evolvingly creative that the line he improvises on Coltrane's *Big Nick* from
his 1962 album with the saxophonist could be transcribed and made into a
first-class jazz song. His range of touches and his ear for matching reed,
brass, and percussion timbres from the keyboard were equaled by an ability
to coax or drive or cushion a soloist that is unsurpassed in the music business.

Yet no amount of talent will forever hold out against the limitations of
life. Ellington faced his losses as certain great musicians left for good and
handled his grief when an irreplaceable man like Hodges died in 1970.
Standing up to all responsibilities, he remained in the sway of his muse and
continued to create masterpieces. Those who had overstated Strayhorn's
unarguable importance and believed that Ellington had become more and
more dependent on him for fresh ideas and new material must have been
shocked after 1967 when they listened to *The Little Purple Flower* (particularly
Part I), the *Goutelas Suite* (the whole of which is built upon the opening fanfare); the *Latin American Suite* (especially *The Sleeping Lady and the Giant Who
Watches over Her*); the finest sections of *Afro-Eurasian Eclipse*; the *Togo Brava
Suite*; and the best writing of his *Sacred Concerts*. No matter what happened
around him, Duke Ellington kept moving on up what seemed an infinite lad-
der of personal artistry. His sustained fecundity and the body of his work remain unequaled in American art. As he preferred his musicians to be, Ellington was a number one himself. Fortunately for the world of listeners and
musicians, he lived and died in terms of what he had declared in 1959:

> I don't want to feel obliged to play something with the same styling that
> we became identified with at some specific period. . . . I don't want anyone
> to challenge my right to sound completely mad, to screech like a wild
> man, to create the mauve melody of a simpering idiot, or to write a song
> that praises God. I only want what any other American artist wants—and
> that is freedom of expression and of communication with our audience.

1998

THOUGHTS

Martin's Tempo

This eulogy was delivered in April 1992 at a small memorial ceremony held in Virginia for the jazz and cultural critic Martin Williams, who had just left the living world and whose influence on my generation's writing about jazz was extremely large. Williams, who was born in Richmond, Virginia, in 1924, was one of the best who ever did it. He was always encouraging young writers to investigate the roots of jazz and had a rare grip on the value of artists across generations. Williams loved jazz as a unit and played no stylistic favorites because he hadn't been duped into believing that art "progresses." While Williams was quite aware of the essential Negro-American components of jazz, the material he wrote was pleasantly free of two tendencies in jazz writing—the ogling at noble savages and the reduction of music to aural sociology in rhythm and tune. Williams developed the skill to describe in clear language what constituted the art of jazz as he heard it. He was an editor who encouraged the writing of jazz books and was always working at something that helped document the art and expand respect for it, whether on college campuses or in the varied and important jazz work he did at the Smithsonian Institution. His critical interests extended across American art at large, and his last book, Hidden in Plain Sight, *was his attempt to step up next to John A. Kouwenhoven, who hit the longest balls on intellectual record. Martin Williams was one of those men whose passion, discipline, and intelligence helped define and give direction to the arena in which he worked. In every way, he was "made in America."*

An early law we all learn is that the velocity of destruction is much faster than the velocity of creation. We see this when a match is set to some paper or a wave does in a sand castle or some clumsiness results in a broken glass. All of the time that went into making those things, yet they are destroyed so quickly. We know, too, that no matter how boring the slowest days of our lives seemed, they were all on the express, not the milk train. The entire trip is over so soon. But what jazz has done, with its improvising attention to the details of memory, imagination, experience, passion, and design, is make the velocity of creation equal to that of destruction. No other art in our time, or perhaps in the history of Western performance, has done so much at such a superficially destructive speed.

I think that is why Martin Williams was so taken by jazz and why he dedicated his life to it and why he stood his watch through all those years when so few outside the community of the musicians themselves knew what it was. He understood the American miracle of the music and the wonder it brought to the arsenal of expression we use against the fall from consciousness to endless darkness that is the fate we all share. Martin knew that something had been added that could detail the passion of human life as it is given sense by aesthetic order. He bet his life on it and he tried to get as many others to bet theirs as he could. In that sense, Martin Williams was on a mission and one that few felt strong enough to join.

He was one who stood his ground against the Goliaths of contempt, of racism, of sloppiness, of disregard. He was dedicated and he was prickly, so knowing him could be inspirational one moment and similar to wrestling with a cactus at another. There was wit and sadness to the man, an affirmative grasp of the sensibility that enlivens the blues. In blues there is what I call tragic optimism, a vision that doesn't avoid the many shortcomings human beings are capable of but one that affirms in its very rhythm and its lyricism the bittersweet wonder of our lives. Perhaps that is what Martin meant when he described King Oliver's playing as containing "communal anguish." Of course, the idea of community is itself a form of affirmation, a recognition that we are all in this express drama of human existence, and a recognition of the fact that we can speak in some recognizable way of the wages and the elevations wrought by experience.

Martin Williams embraced it all. He wrote of television, of film, and of comic strips. Understanding the brutal pulse and the vitality of our culture, its fanciful conflation of folly and deep feeling, its irreverence, its hysteria, its unexplainable nobility, he became a high priest of perhaps that most invaluable human religion, the religion of integrity. In the process, Martin developed a language to describe the art of the invisible, which is music. He took it upon himself to learn what was necessary to render the feeling of jazz with the charismatic eloquence demanded of signal understanding. His was the way of dedication, and he would be moved by nothing other than the details of the meaning of the human heart in the motion of revelation we know as swing.

Like Thelonious Monk, whose work he loved so much, Martin was willing to stay out there, working often alone, creating small communities, and instructing by example. He was like no one any of us ever knew before and like no one we will ever meet. For a music so given to individuality, it is perfect that he was here. Martin, we will miss you, the tenderness of your spirit, your grit, and your vinegar. Your intellectual progeny may be small, but then, so was the stone that felled Goliath. You understood the velocity of that stone and knew it as one of creation. And in every encounter, you were willing to hand over a stone that had to move at the velocity of destruction in order to create the space against death that is the essence of human memory made eternal. You honored your time and you swung it and we will never deny all that you have done and all that you inspired. God bless you now, for you were surely blessed while you were alive.

1992

The Late, Late Blues
Jazz Modernism

This is an important book about jazz and twentieth-century art that arrives late, as do all important books about jazz. The American intellectual community has never been up to the challenge of the music, primarily because it has not been up to the challenge of the Negro, without whom no such music would exist, however many great to excellent to fine to mediocre to terrible white musicians, both Jewish and Christian, have found their identities within the art.

There has always been something about the Negro within the terms of American culture that shut down discussion or inquiry among intellectuals, unless the talk or the writing was condescending or the usually darker American was used as proof of how much bunk there was to all the crowing about the land of the free and the home of the brave. The Negro wearing the barbed-wire wreath of American racism around the neck and around or pushed into the genitals was preferred to any other. The idea that the Negro, like everybody else central to the shaping of Americana, could have produced cultural geniuses of all sorts was beyond consideration, especially if we might have to consider how well those geniuses defined the proposition of the nation itself—or, Lord help us, addressed the age.

In a forthcoming book, David Yaffe quotes what Ralph Ellison said in an appearance on a 1965 PBS show about jazz: "One of the most intriguing gaps in American cultural history sprang from the fact that jazz, one of the few American art forms, failed to attract the understanding of our intellectuals . . . the greater job of increasing our understanding is still to be done. A vacuum does exist in our understanding. It is a fact that, for all their important contributions to American culture, no Edmund Wilson, no T. S. Eliot, no Cowley or Kazin has offered us insights into the relationship between this most vital art and the broader aspects of American social life."

This is how it has been even though William Faulkner repeatedly made a case for addressing a difficult national reality and an equally expensive fantasy, both of them resulting from a most complicated interplay. That interplay crossed the lines of color and emerged as an American sensibility formed from opposites and from oppositions so charismatic that the old goddam dialectic achieved synthesis in the symbol of the mulatto or the Creole or the culture raised as much from black as from white, from Europe as from the American Indian, something our Mississippi genius made clear as the summer sun in *Go Down, Moses,* where he dropped this glittering bit of "science," as they used to accurately call insight in the streets:

> This Delta. *This land which man has deswamped and denuded and derivered in two generations so that white men can own plantations and commute every night to Memphis and black men can own plantations and ride in Jim Crow cars to Chicago to live in millionaire's mansions on Lakeshore Drive, where white men rent farms and live like niggers and niggers crop on shares and live like animals, where cotton is planted and grown man-tall in the very cracks of the sidewalks, and usury and mortgage and bankruptcy and measureless wealth, Chinese and African and Aryan and Jew, all breed and spawn together until no man has time to say which one is which nor cares . . .*

Faulkner clearly perceived that stretch, both human and ecological, from the backwoods of our nation to our cities and to our world of business, realizing something elemental to the soul, the culture, the economy, and the "many miscegenations" that haul us up from ethnic provincialism. Yet one could not expect people like Alfred Kazin, Lionel Trilling, Harold Rosenberg, and the rest of the gang called the New York Intellectuals to recognize the importance of the Negro when they had missed the importance of George Gershwin, Irving Berlin, and Harold Arlen, even though those guys were Jewish too, and, in common with said writers, had listened to tales of the old country and had heard Yiddish spouted around in the home and on the block. But, in the very deepest sense, they also found themselves out there in the streets, walking that American walk and, before long, talking that slang-heavy American talk.

Out there on those streets, Gershwin, Berlin, and Arlen inhaled Americana and, having good smellers of the sort always special to the gifted, followed the scent to Harlem—or some place like Harlem—and heard in the music the soul of the city, the transcontinental feeling of the blues that so successfully united the North and the South, which Faulkner summoned into literature by doing what Duke Ellington had done in *Black, Brown, and Beige,* the 1943 extended piece and "tone parallel to the history of the American Negro."

Faulkner was pushing us to perceive an epic that moves from the Mississippi Delta to the Jim Crow car to the mansion. Not only did those Jewish
musicians come to understand how that blues feeling has elasticity of reference and feeling; they also observed the dance beats that prodded Broadway choreographers in different directions. Such men saw the steps that
were invented in Darktown and nationalized by people like Vernon and
Irene Castle. They laughed their cakes off at the Negro humor and pan-
tomime that provided so many comedians, from Eddie Cantor to Jerry
Lewis to Rodney Dangerfield, with the foundations on which they built
their own personalities and reputations, sometimes beginning within the
minstrel convention of burnt cork.

Though Susan Sontag recently described herself as "a dancing fool," one
cannot imagine any of the other rightfully celebrated Jewish writers and
aesthetes going to the floor with anything other than two left feet, or seeing Louis Armstrong and knowing what he represented and who he was—
the Negro as world-class master of allusion, reconfiguration, transformation, and improvisation, the essences of jazz. Who could imagine any of
them kicking back to some Ellington and absorbing his layered upon layered fascination with the big city and the backwoods, or hearing Coleman
Hawkins make the tenor saxophone into a curved instrument through
which improvised and highly arpeggiated American opera was blown; or
facing the crack of doom and the idealism in the determined lyricism and
unprecedented virtuosity of Charlie Parker; or rising in feeling and thought
to the challenges laid down by Thelonious Monk as he remade the piano
into a metaphor for urban life as he knew it—romantic as soft rain, strong
and abrasive as concrete and steel, playful as a bouncing ball, isolated as a
single lit cigarette in all of Central Park?

These are truly American creators who could not have become the
forces that they were had their work not been preserved and replicated
within the terms of technology and the precision engineering that provided the same instruments for aspiring musicians and fans across the nation. Their ancestors had arrived in the holds of slave ships as the black
gold of labor cargo; they had been sold as chattel even more times than
they had been repeatedly sold out by the nation; they had taken the Christianity taught to them and removed from it an all-too pervasive sentimentality so that the tragic essence of the tale of Christ achieved the bottom-
less pain and the glory of transcendence central to its charisma. Though
they had been rebuked and scorned since early in the seventeenth century,
theirs too was the world of the recording and the radio broadcast, the

printing press and the motion picture, the steel mill and the railroad, the automobile and the cafeteria. They were not only Americans as pure as any others; they were also as modern as anybody else in the twentieth century because part of being modern was responding to life in a modern manner.

Inarguably, the Jewish and Christian intellectuals who missed all of that cannot be separated from the Negroes of the 1920s who considered themselves intellectuals and appreciators of the arts but had, for all of the talk about a "New Negro," no real understanding of what was taking place as those Southern Negroes—arrived from New Orleans and wherever else—brought to the big cities visions of jazz that would change the perception of musical possibility with group improvisation and redefine the instruments through fresh techniques bent on rivaling the vocal nuances of Negro blues singers.

That Alfred Appel Jr. is Jewish and in his late sixties and has written a most stirringly brilliant book proves that there is no excuse and there has never been an excuse for missing this phenomenon. In the wake of both Ralph Ellison and Albert Murray, Appel has created what is probably the best book about jazz as an art in the context of *all* modern art. It is a book quite different from those filled with the technical analysis of Gunther Schuller, who towers over all of his competitors, first because he can write and second because he is as capable of describing what makes a great musician wonderful in straight English as he is a frontiersman in his technical discoveries.

Appel cites and addresses a number of writers but makes nothing of either Ellison or Murray, which would seem incredibly egocentric if he had not revealed his peerless self-inflation on page two: "In matters pertaining to race and racial politics, my comparisons and unambiguous assertions should be stimulating if not definitive." Is that so? That Appel goes silent on Ellison's marvelous jazz essays and Murray's invaluable 1976 poetics of jazz, *Stomping the Blues*, puts him solidly in the tradition of white musicians and jazz writers who have used Negro models but remain mum about their sources. In reviewing this book for *The Nation*, David Yaffe charged Appel with rewriting an observation Ellison made about Armstrong, whose artistry the novelist described as Shakespearean in range and complexity. Even while trying to put a softening Harmon mute to the bell of my own horn, I would have to say that Appel most probably read *Notes of a Hanging Judge* and saw my own "Body and Soul" (1983) in which I compared Negro musicians with Renaissance creators in the visual arts and drew a connection between Picasso and Armstrong. I also recognize in his book things I have been saying in mass media about Fred Astaire for the past decade or so.

No matter: A man who thinks with the originality that he does can be forgiven, especially since *Jazz Modernism* is intended to be experienced as a work of artistic expression at the same time that it is supposed to be an assessment of some central jazz monarchs and empresses of style and invention. It is an autobiography of sensibility, as much about the author as the subject. Appel is asking the reader to see twentieth-century masters of painting and sculpture as he does. He is also asking his readers to hear the music in the way *he* does, accepting his translations of notes and *his* translations of vocal *interpretations*. The lyrics are sometimes too bad to be believed in a nation where too bad to be believed has such a track record that it is an assumed fact (that the writer also misquotes some of them is also interesting).

Appel has taken the liberties one would expect of an American who has studied the visual arts for many decades, taught literature for forty years, and also was on the scene listening to jazz. In the nightclub world of cigarettes and alcohol, concert circumstances were created because the rooms were too small and the tables too close for dancing. There Appel witnessed some of those signal things about the making of the music and the interplay among the musicians and with the audience that cannot be captured solely in the context of recordings, which remain the greatest available repository of jazz modernism.

What might be considered a unification theory in which the arts of the visible and the invisible are brought together amounts, like the late work of Andre Malraux, to the story of a mind and a heart that never exasperate each other. Like Malraux, Appel is concerned with triumph and the ways in which the private fate becomes public and, through aesthetic form, is relieved of its anonymity while speaking to and for all of those who are anonymous to the world but have in common with the world the troubles and the joys of human existence. Human existence, as we all know, is always accompanied by the mysteries and the clarifications of human passion. In the case of jazz, the Negro's troubles become metaphors for all troubles, just as the specific troubles of Homer's heroes, strapped to their tales by the conventions of the Greek pantheon, become metaphors for the troubles of us all.

Appel puts jazz in a broad context as he discusses recorded performances, advertisements, and the very labels of the recordings that now bring back an era as impressively as the artifacts of older times that preceded precision engineering. Photographs of jazz musicians, buildings, construction workers, dancers, and a number of others are well chosen and well placed, giving the visual side of the book an antiphonal role that both amplifies the text and challenges it. Appel does not miss the symbolic weight falling from the world of cartoons and slapstick as well as the denigrating humor warmed over from the days of the minstrel show. He is sometimes far too fanciful for this reader as he inserts racial meanings or caution in works that seem to me to be *only* recordings. Appel assumes some Armstrong love songs are low-key in order to keep from making white men angry. This seems a crock, particularly since they were recorded around the time Armstrong did his marvelous 1933 "Stardust," which is declamatory in its celebration and profoundly romantic in its suggestions, its dropped words, and its added ones, such as "baby low."

What particularly places Appel outside of the arena of most American intellectuals when it comes to Negro aesthetic matters is that he has not fallen for the repulsive limitations of the influential Frankfurt School as expounded by Theodor Adorno and Max Horkheimer, who had contempt for the United States and understood little about how American vernacular art functions or comes into being, and got even less right how the actual dialectic of American aesthetic enlightenment achieves synthesis through the imaginative transformation of the dull, the ugly, and the mindlessly or meretriciously conceived. That imaginative transformation provides us with an object of beauty that, when our culture is lucky, becomes popular enough to speak to and for our nation and the modern world itself. Cognizant of that process, Appel understands America as it is, not what some German somebody thinks it ought to be, especially if that somebody is too far removed from the horror, the beauty, the melodrama, the tragedy, the hopelessness, and the optimism of this nation. America is great because what it actually is so often triumphs over what it should never be; jazz, in the very faith it places on the improviser, is an art ruled by possibility, by the belief in the possible, not the conventions of the impossible.

Adorno and Horkheimer, Ted and Max, failed to understand that the team can function as something more than an extension of the power of the state and the rule of the owners, who produce constricting and debilitating products for the masses. They believed that the conventions of popular entertainment were beyond bending and that creativity was superseded by novelty, the manufactured blip of light on the screen that is sold as a three-dimensional thing. Even a genius like Orson Welles only underlined the power of the cliché to survive his decimation. When Appel writes of Armstrong or Fats Waller or Duke Ellington, he is fully aware of what the jazz artist learned: his arms were *not too short* to box with the commercial god of the cliché or the overstated. Appel understands that for such artists, inspired invention—either second by second on the spot or in the time it took to write either an original piece or a stupendous arrangement—provided an alternative to that expected thing everyone felt already cognizant of in terms of its expressive possibilities.

Armstrong rebukes all of Ted's and Max's theories about the meaninglessness of the individual in popular art and the subjugation of talent in the interest of a culture industry that teaches a public to hunger for an ongoing repetition in which every form uses a similar jargon that deceitfully stands in for expression and artistry. Armstrong refutes such baloney since he is one of those who helped create the true individual in popular art by proving that one's sensibility, however powerfully stylized, can so perfectly take aesthetic command of the present in the act of improvisation that the resulting substance and nuance prove themselves more than vaporous tricks by withstanding the repeated close reexaminations made possible by the recording. This was no small achievement. Played once on the wing, listened to thousands of times the world over, the best jazz fulfills one definition of the masterpiece: a work that cannot be exhausted.

The essence of it is that the improviser proves that the present can be as good as the past: We bring the past into the present to protect us from the abyss of the moment, which we should whenever possible. That is why the concert musician is more like the actor who takes a text from the past and makes it come alive in the present, giving it such vitality—if the actor is great—that those words arrive as if never said before, as if this is the spontaneous expression of emotions felt in the moment. The improviser, on the other hand, is bringing order to the present with material summoned in the present, profoundly turning around most of what we know about creation and destruction. Elsewhere I have pointed out that one of the first things we all learn is that destruction has a much faster velocity than construction. The broken glass, the burned piece of paper, the slaughtered lamb—each is destroyed more quickly than it is created. The best recent example is September 11, 2001. It took a long time to get those towers up, less than an hour for each of them to come crashing down. But what serious improvising posits in the magical world of the aesthetic dimension is the possibility that substantial creation can equal the velocity of destruction. The best jazz recordings break the story and make the case.

Ted and Max had no respect for the Negro or for America; otherwise they, like Appel, could have seen that every successful work of musical art achieved by a Negro was a victory over the assembly line vision of an ethnic group that is what we call the stereotype, the agency at the nub of what Ted and Max were talking about when attacking the culture industry as an instrument of state and business power, a reaffirmation of things as those in power assume they should be. To get right down to it: Every time a Negro, boring through the sentimentality and the corny rhythms of a popular ditty, asserted an individuality tangible to perception, a human opening had been blasted through the confines of minstrelsy and stereotypes, one big enough to release fresh air while allowing the audience a hole through which it could peep actual humanity. Such holes transform themselves and always provide the audience with mirrors in which it sees familiar humanity with unfamiliar faces. And since the stereotype is often an offshoot of superstition, another kind of enlightenment, a different kind of scientific revolution arrives as the human being transcends it and makes human recognition the only true form of progress.

Indisputable Dippermouth proof: Armstrong's individuality in public flight inspired white Charles Black to question the Negro's segregated "place" after a 1931 engagement in Austin, Texas. "What was 'the place' of such a man, and of the people from which he sprung?" Black asked himself. Twenty-three years later, in 1954, Black was on Thurgood Marshall's legal team that took down segregation before the Supreme Court.

It would have been too much to ask the New York intellectuals to appreciate the genius of men such as Armstrong and Ellington, for they would have had to think beyond their own conventions. American life would have had to be recognized as something other than a spittoon into which one hawked, following the lead of those revolutionists who celebrate the people for being too crudely pure to fall under the decadent sway of the upper class while hating them for having bad taste or for reminding them too much of their own families, who included few intellectuals among the dregs arriving at Ellis Island after traveling in steerage all the way across the Atlantic. These people came up through the public schools that the Negro legislators of the Reconstruction knew were essential to liberating those forced to exist outside of the world of reading and the world of the mind. Theirs was an aristocracy of readers who were pioneers bringing European visions into a savage land. Intellectual missionaries might have been a better term for them than the New York Intellectuals. One of their watchwords was: *Don't let anyone know that my peasant heritage is as real as my worn and faded library card.*

It is therefore all the more amazing that Appel was able to embrace the high achievements of modern art and writing—and all of the intellectual

frontiers that had to be crossed in order to introduce whole new perspectives. This was done while avoiding the condescending ideas that would have
rendered American vitality—and the context in which it arrived—incom-
prehensible. For this he should be celebrated, however wild his conclusions, however far removed some of his comparisons, and however absurd
some of his conclusions. He has done something quite well, for all of that.
His eyewitness reports are well told, as when he recalls Igor Stravinsky listening to Charlie Parker at Birdland one night in New York. He recognizes
the droll wit and satiric inclinations of Fats Waller though he makes heavy
reference to Eudora Welty's "Powerhouse," a story apparently about Waller.
It is a terribly square tale about darkies partying the night away in a Mississippi roadhouse. He tells us stories about drummers Big Sid Catlett, Jo
Jones, and Buddy Rich that have enormous gravity and atmosphere. All of
this arrives in a beautiful hail of reproduced paintings and photographs of
sculpture that even those who dislike the book will appreciate.

2004

Blues to Be Constitutional

*A Long Look at the Wild Wherefores of Our Democratic Lives As Symbolized in the Making of Rhythm and Tune**

Part I: Blue Rebellion Breakdown

I stand here not as a scholar of the Constitution but as a student of the human soul, which is what any writer with the ambition to capture the whys and wherefores of our lives must be. Before I have finished this talk, I hope to have examined the metaphor of the Constitution as it applies to a number of things in our society, and I hope also to have looked at a few of the elements that threaten not so much the democratic institutions of this country as much as they tend to lessen the morale necessary to work at the heroic expansion of this democracy into the unlit back streets and thickets of our civilization. I have chosen to be that ambitious. And in the process of expressing my ambition, I might kick off another version of a good number of the pitched intellectual battles I have had with people whom we continue to mistakenly describe by their color, since no one has ever seen anyone who is actually white or black, red or yellow, however close a few here or there might be. That level of imprecise identification in such a technologically advanced society is one of the ironies of our time and our place in the history of America and of the world.

As a writer, I find it ironic that I began working on these ideas in public at Harvard University in 1992, when I spoke on the thirty-seventh anniversary of the death of Charlie Parker, whose consciousness was swallowed by the grim reaper in Manhattan's Fifth Avenue Stanhope Hotel on March 12, 1955. It was nearly ten years after the performance of *Koko*—a

*Delivered on April 7, 1995, at Michigan State University, for The Symposium on Science, Reason, and Modern Democracy.

harmonic skullcracker built on the chords of "Cherokee"—had announced
Parker's ability to extend our expectations of jazz improvisation. Legend
lays it down that the virtuoso Kansas City alto saxophonist died while
laughing at an act on a television variety show, an electronic update of the
minstrel and vaudeville tradition Parker had so poorly fought against
throughout his career. A statistic of his own excesses, the innovative genius
had been nursed round the clock by not a Jewish princess but a Jewish
baroness, one who had driven North African ambulances during World
War II yet survived to so scandalize her Rothschild family that, so continues the legend, she was paid off to badly drive her Bentley and enthusiastically host her Negro jam sessions out of sight and out of earshot.

Parker is a man I have come to know quite well since I began working on
his biography in 1982. But Parker is most important to what I have to say
today because he represents both the achievement and the myth of jazz as
well as the trouble we Americans have deciding whether we will aspire to
the heroic individuality symbolized by Abraham Lincoln and Martin
Luther King, Jr., or sink down into the anarchic individuality represented
by Billy the Kid and the various bad boys our society has had crushes on
for over a century. However great his talent surely was, Parker was celebrated as much in the half light and the darkness of the night world for his
antics, his irresponsible behavior, his ability to embody what Arthur Rimbaud called "the love of sacrilege." He was a giant of a bluesman and a jazz
improviser of astounding gifts, but his position in the world and in the
overview this address seeks has much to do with the praise he received for
being an outlaw, a sort of praise that speaks directly to a number of our
dilemmas.

Since our actual preparation for becoming a democratic society was outside the law—dumping tea in Boston Harbor while disguised as Indians and
fomenting rebellion—since our moral assaults on the limitations of our
democracy were expressed in the illegal actions of the abolitionists who
worked the Underground Railroad and predicted the sorts of activities that
people of conscience would later replicate when spiriting Jews beyond the
death-camp clutches of the Nazis, it is not hard to understand why we have
such a high position in our pantheon for the bad boy. We love riotous outsiders as much as we once loved the sort of eloquence we no longer hear
from our politicians. And in our straining against the constraints of modern
civilization, we, like Charles Baudelaire and Rimbaud, have a love of symbolic violence.

That symbolic violence has two sides: one is rooted in a democratic assertion, an expression of the culture's vitality, a breaking away from European convention in pursuit of a social vision that eventually allowed for recognition and success beyond the limitations of family line and class; the other is a set of appetites focused on the exotic, bedeviled by a nostalgia for the mud, given to a love of sensationalism that completely hollows out a pretentious vulgarity. From the moment Americans joyously dumped that tea into Boston Harbor, we were in the process of rebelling against what was then a traditional denial of the colonized underdog's access to dialogue. But that Indian disguise also exhibited perhaps the first burst of what would evolve into the love of the ethnic mask as witnessed in burnt-cork stage presentations and the cinematic symbol of Al Jolson's jazz singer moving from Eastern European provincialism into the Negro rhythmic bustle of American popular art.

Since the rise of American nationalism that took off at an express tempo following the War of 1812, our art has as frequently reflected disdain as celebration. We love to make fun of the rules and prick those who think themselves superior for all the wrong reasons, especially since our democracy tells us that the little David of the common man can knock down the Goliath of wealth, unfairness, privilege. We believe the smart money can always be wrong. In the first third of the nineteenth century, the Yankee Brother Jonathan and the backwoodsman Davey Crockett often outwitted the stuffed shirt, as would the burnt-cork minstrel show figures who stood in for the rural whites endangered by the con men of the big city. Our art tends to pull for the underestimated and the outsider, perhaps because so many of us originate in groups and classes that were once outside the grand shindig of American civilization, noses pressed against the ballroom's huge windows. We have great faith in the possibility of the upset. There is no American who doesn't understand well the statement: "They said it couldn't be done, but we did it."

That dictum is basic to our national character and underlies the virtues of our society as much as it does the vulgar volleys against convention we presently find so worrisome in popular art. What we are now witnessing is a distorted version of our own understanding of the battle between the old and the new that is basic to an improvisational society such as ours, where policy is invented to redress previous shortcomings or to express attitudinal shifts. It is central to being an American that one doesn't necessarily believe that limitations will last very long, primarily because we have seen so many changes take place in everything from technology to the ongoing adjustments of policy. It is part of our history, from Eli Whitney, Thomas Edison, Henry Ford, and the Wright brothers in the machinery of modern life to Abraham Lincoln, Martin Luther King, and Sandra Day O'Connor in political influence and high national office.

But what we see as tendencies in our contemporary popular art is what has happened to the extension of identification with the outsider to a love of the scandalizing bad boy. This is a love that has evolved in our century from the silver screen gangster to MTV gangster rap, introducing a few other kinds of bad boys along the way. We have moved swiftly from the cardboard goody-goody to Cagney, to Humphrey Bogart, to Edgar G. Robinson, motorcycled forward to Marlon Brando and James Dean, hopped the racial fence to play out sadomasochistic rituals with Miles Davis, Malcolm X, and now Spike Lee, not leaving out all of the adolescent rock-and-roll intoxication our society guzzles to the point of hangovers left now by Prince or Madonna or Public Enemy. As Gregory Peck says: "The audience loves the bad guy because he will come up with a surprise."

Those surprises were first seen in our century in slapstick, with the many variations on the pie in the face of the society man and matron. That harmless disdain for smugness and pretension made us laugh when the superficially bad boy and comic figure, from Charlie Chaplin's Afro-balletic tramp to Eddie Murphy's *Beverly Hills Cop*, unleashed chaos at the pompous gathering. But Peck's observation says much about the dark glamour that surrounds the worst of rock and the lowest of rap, where the canonization of antisocial posturing and the obnoxious appropriation of the racial stereotype has been basic to rock criticism at least since the elevation of the Rolling Stones and Jimi Hendrix. As rock critic Gregory Sandow says: "It's all about the love of the outlaw. The outlaw is going against everything you want to fight in the society, he's doing all the things you would like to do and being the way you would like to be. He's beyond the pale of convention, and if he's black, it's even better."

Sandow's observation is corroborated when one reads the bulk of rock writers on the subject of rap, they who were so quick to shout down racists or fume about Jesse Helms and the 2 Live Crew obscenity trial, but are almost always willing to indulge their own appetites for contemporary coon shows, for the brute glamour of this racial replay—and affirmation—of "the love of sacrilege," of the extensions of Jolson's statement: "You ain't heard nothing yet." For these writers, and perhaps for the bulk of white rap fans, the surliest rap recordings and videos function as experiences somewhere between viewing the natives boiling the middle class in a pot of profanity and the thrill of gawking at a killer shark in an audio aquarium. For Negro rap fans we see another version of the love of the noble savage, the woolly-headed person from the street who can't be assimilated, who is safe from our American version of the temptation of the West.

All of those tendencies clearly express our young people's dissatisfaction with the shortcomings of our culture, but a dissatisfaction had on the cheap. In the world of the prematurely cynical, the bad boy reigns, for he represents a retreat into pouting anarchy. Of course, our kind of capitalism doggedly allows for almost any kind of successful career, even one that earns millions or television time or tenure selling defeatist visions, playing on or cultivating appetites for ersatz savagery, trumpeting segregation and substandard levels of scholarship on the campuses of our best universities. At the lowest and highest levels, say from Louis Farrakhan or from some professor of "victim studies," we hear all of the carping about the meaninglessness of American democracy, of the tainted moral character of the men who attended the Constitutional Convention and whipped the tragically optimistic fundamentals of our social contract into championship form.

Behind that carping, when what we discover is not merely opportunistic, we learn something quite distinct about the maudlin as it relates to the cynical. We come to understand that unearned cynicism, much more frequently than not, is no more than a brittle version of sentimentality. It is a failure of morale, a cowardly flight from the engagement that comes of understanding the elemental shortcomings of human existence as well as the founding fathers of this country did. Those given to no more than carping are unprepared to address the tragic optimism at the center of the metaphor that is the Constitution. They know nothing of heroic engagement, the engagement that would not allow one to misunderstand the singing of "We Shall Overcome" in the town square of Prague as Alexander Dubcek stood on a balcony looking into the faces he had been exiled from seeing in the flesh by the Communist party. It is an engagement that would not allow one to miss the meaning of the Red Chinese troops having to destroy a crudely built Statue of Liberty with even cruder means when the night was filled with the familiar violence of totalitarianism in Tiananmen Square. That engagement would recognize that the very success of our struggle to extend democracy has inspired the world, and much of that extending has been the result of the efforts of people at war with the social limitations that were so severely imposed upon Negro Americans.

One cannot speak of Negro culture in this country without speaking of the blues. The blues, which I shall soon talk about in detail, have much to do with the vision of the Constitution, primarily because you play the blues to *rid* yourself of the blues, just as the nature of our democracy allows us to remove the blues of government by using the government. The blues is a music about human will and human frailty, just as the brilliance of the Constitution is that it recognizes grand human possibility with the same clarity that it does human frailty, which is why I say it has a tragic base. Just as the blues assumes that any man or any woman can be unfaithful, the Constitution assumes that nothing is innately good, that nothing is lasting—nothing, that is, other than the perpetual danger of abused power. One might even say that the document looks upon power as essentially a dangerous thing that must never be allowed to go the way it would were it handled by the worst among us, many of whom remain unrecognized until given the chance to push their ideas upon the world. The very idea of the amendment brings into government the process of social redemption through policy. By redemption I mean that the Constitution recognizes that there may be times in the future when what we now think of as hard fact might be no more than a nationally accepted prejudice, one strong enough to influence and infect policy. So you use the government to rid yourself of the blues of government.

The Constitution is also a blues document because it takes a hard swinging position against the sentimentality residing in the idea of a divine right of kings. Sentimentality is excess and so is any conception of an inheritance connected to a sense of the chosen people. The Constitution moves against that overstatement with the same sort of definition Jesus had when his striking down the idea of a chosen people prefigured what we now think of as democracy, an open forum for entry that has nothing to do with any aspect of one's identity other than his or her humanity. I must make clear that I am not talking so much about religion here as I am about the idea that the availability of universal salvation is a precursor of the idea of universal access to fairness that underlies our democratic contract. Universal salvation means that no one's identity is static, that one need only repent and be born anew. That is what I meant earlier about social redemption: Every policy structured to correct previous shortcomings in the national sensibility that have led to prejudicial doctrines or unfair treatment is a form of governmental repentance. Once again, using the government to rid the blues of government.

Yet the Constitution, like the blues singer willing to publicly take apart his own shortcomings, perceives human beings as neither demons nor angels but some mysterious combination of both. That is why the revelations of scandal and abuse that rise and fall throughout our history, including our deeply human susceptibility to hypocrisy and corruption, prove out the accuracy of the Constitution. Every time we learn of something unfair that has happened to a so-called minority group, or even a majority group like American women, we perceive anew how well the framers prepared us to face the tar and feathers that our ideals are periodically dipped in—even if those framers might have been willing to tar-brush some ideals themselves! Every time there is any sort of scandal or we learn another terrible thing about some president or some hanky-panky in governmental contracts, we see more clearly how important freedom of the press is and how important it is for public figures to have to account for their actions. Ask Boss Tweed, ask Richard Nixon; both were felled by the press. The framers of this blues document could see it all and they knew that for a society to sustain any kind of vitality it had to be able to arrive at decisions through discourse that could stand up to the present or lighten the burdens wrought by the lowest aspects of the past.

In essence, then, the Constitution is a document that functions like the blues-based music of jazz: It values improvisation, the freedom to constantly reinterpret the meanings of our documents. It casts a cold eye on human beings and on the laws they make; it assumes that evil will not forever be allowed to pass by. And the fact that a good number of young Negro musicians are leading the movement that is revitalizing jazz suggests a strong future for this country. I find this true because of what it takes for young Negroes to break free of all the trends that overtake them, perhaps even more comprehensively than they do the rest of American youth. I find this true because Afro-American culture is essentially oral, and any oral culture is in danger of being dictated to by whomever has command of the microphone.

There is a large dream in the world of jazz and that dream is much richer than anything one will encounter in the ethnic sentimentality of Afrocentric propaganda. What those young jazz musicians symbolize is a freedom from the taste-making of mass media and an embracing of a vision that has much more to do with aesthetic satisfaction than the gold-rush culture of popular entertainment, where one takes the clichés of adolescent narcissism into the side of the mountain rather than a pickaxe, some pans, and a burro. These are young Americans who have not been suckers for the identity achieved through unearned cynical rebellion; they seek individuality through affirmation, which puts them at war with the silly attire and hairdos that descend directly from the rebel-without-a-cause vision of youth that Hollywood began selling adolescent Americans nearly forty years ago, when the antihero started to emerge. Less in awe of youth than of quality, those who would be jazz musicians would also be adults, not just shriek for adult privileges, then cry foul when the responsibilities are passed out. They have a healthy respect for the men and women who laid an astonishing tradition down. In their wit, their good grooming, their disdain for drugs, and their command of the down-home and the ambitious, they suggest that, though America may presently be down on one knee, the champ is about to rise and begin taking names.

But in order to get you to truly appreciate the direction these young musicians are taking, I should conclude this talk with a longish discussion of what the blues and jazz traditions offer us in the way of democratic metaphors, aesthetic actions closely related to the way in which our very society is organized.

Part II: Blues to Be There

Transition Riff on the Big Feeling

I am quite sure that jazz is the highest American musical form because it is the most comprehensive, possessing an epic frame of emotional and intellectual reference, sensual clarity, and spiritual radiance. But if it weren't for the blues, there would be no jazz as we know it, for blues first broke most clearly with the light and maudlin nature of popular music. Blues came up from this land around the turn of the century. We all know that blues seeped out of the Negro, but we should be aware of the fact that it also called backward into the central units of the national experience with such accuracy that it came to form the emotional basis of the most indelible secular American music. That is why it had such importance—not because it took wing on the breath, voice, and fingers of an embattled ethnic group, but because the feelings of the form came to magnetize everything from slavery to war to exploration to Indian fighting to natural disaster, from the woes of the soul lost in unhappy love to the mysteries, terrors, and celebrations of the life that stretched north from the backwoods to the steel and concrete monuments of the big city. It became, therefore, the aesthetic hymn of the culture, the twentieth-century music that spoke of and to modern experience in a way that no music of European or Third World origin ever has.

In a number of ways, the blues singer became the sound and the repository of the nation's myth and the nation's sense of tragic recognition. It was probably the sense of tragic recognition, given its pulsation by the dance rhythms of the music, that provided blues with the charisma that influenced so many other styles, from jazz to Tin Pan Alley to rock. In the music of the blues the listener was rescued from the sentimentality that so often threatens the soul of this culture, either overdoing the trivial or coating the significant with a hardening *and disfiguring syrup. Surely, the Negroes who first came to hear the blues weren't at all looking for anything sentimental, since the heritage of the work song and the spiritual had already brought them cheek to jowl with the burdens of experience, expectation, and fantasy. In the sweat- and ache-laden work song, the demanding duties of hard labor were met with rhythm, and that rhythm, which never failed to flex its pulse in the church, was the underlying factor that brought together the listeners, that allowed for physical responses in the dance halls and the juke joints where blues emerged as the music of folk professionals. Blues all night in guitar keys, the development of a common source of images, a midnight-hour atmosphere of everyday people out to rhythmically scratch their own—and somebody else's—itching, sensual essences.*

Yet there was always, as with any art given to the lyrical, a spiritual essence that referred as much to the desire for transcendence as it did to any particular tale of love and loss or love and celebration. In both cases, what was sometimes rightfully considered lewd could also constitute a sense of romantic completeness that was expressed with equal authority by men and women, that fact itself a motion toward women's liberation and the recognition of libidinous lore that transcended gender conventions. In fact, the first popular blues singers who rose to professional status were women such as Bessie Smith. And with the evolution of the blues singer into the jazz musician, an art came forward that was based in the rocky ground and the swamp mud of elemental experience while rising toward the stars with the intellectual determination of a sequoia. It was also symbolic, as had been the erotic wholeness basic to blues, of American democracy.

Part III: The Democratic Swing of American Life

In 1938, the great German novelist Thomas Mann, who had fled Nazism in his homeland, delivered a lecture from one end of America to another that was published as a small volume under the title *The Coming Victory of Democracy*. It is only sixty-five pages in length, and there are a few aspects of it that are now outdated, but the overall sense of the world and the observations Mann provides about democracy connect very strongly to the processes and the implications of jazz, which brings a fresh confluence of directness and nuance not only to the making of music but to the body of critical thought its very existence has challenged in vital ways that are peculiarly American.

The vision of jazz performance and the most fundamental aspects of its aesthetic are quite close to Mann's description of democratic thought: "We must define democracy as that form of government and of society which is inspired above every other with the feeling and consciousness of the dignity of man." The demands on and the respect for the individual in the jazz band put democracy into aesthetic action. Each performer must bring technical skill, imagination, and the ability to create coherent statements through improvised interplay with the rest of the musicians. That interplay takes its direction from the melodic, harmonic, rhythmic, and timbral elements of the piece being performed, and each player must have a remarkably strong sense of what constitutes the *making* of music as opposed to the *rendering* of music, which is what performers of European concert music do. The improvising jazz musician must work right in the heat and the pressure of the moment, giving form and order in a mobile environment, where choices must be constantly assessed and reacted to in one way or another. The success of jazz is a victory for democracy, and a symbol of the aesthetic dignity, which is finally spiritual, that performers can achieve and express as they go about inventing music and meeting the challenge of the moment.

Those challenges are so substantial that their literal and symbolic meanings are many, saying extraordinary things about our collective past as well as the dangers and the potential of the present. In fact, improvisational skill is such an imposing gift that the marvelously original Albert Murray has written in *The Hero and the Blues*: "Improvisation is the ultimate human (i.e., heroic) endowment." The very history of America's development bears this out, as does much of the history that preceded it. But perhaps no society so significant has emerged over the last five centuries that has made improvisation so basic to its sensibility. Even the conflict between Hernando Cortés and the Aztecs, for all its horrific dimensions, pivoted on the element of improvisation. As the French writer and critic Tzvetan Todorov observes in his startling *The Conquest of America*: "It is remarkable to see Cortés not only constantly practicing the art of adaption and improvisation, but also being aware of it and claiming it as the very principle of conduct: 'I shall always take care to add whatever seems to me most fitting, for the great size and diversity of the lands which are being discovered each day and the many new secrets which we have learned from the discoveries make it necessary that for new circumstances there be new considerations and decisions; should it appear in anything I now say or might say to your Majesty that I contradict what I have said in the past, Your Highness may be assured that it is because a new fact elicits a new opinion.'"

That quote sounds more than a little like an attitude foreshadowing the constitutional vision of amendments spoken of earlier, and it is also similar in tone and content to the way jazz musicians have explained how different nights, different moods, and different fellow musicians can bring about drastically dissimilar versions of the same songs. Part of the emotion of jazz results from the excitement and the satisfaction of making the most of the present, or what the technocrats now call "real time." Todorov follows that quote with an idea that is basic to the conception of improvising jazz: "Concern for coherence has yielded to concern for the truth of each particular action."

In jazz, however, *comprehension* of each particular action, the artistic truth of it, will bring from the better and more inspired players reactions resulting in overall coherence. And it is the achievement of coherence in the present that is the great performing contribution jazz has made to the art of this century.

1.

Just as American democracy, however periodically flawed in intent and realization, is a political, cultural, economic, and social rejection of the automated limitations of class and caste, jazz is an art in which improvisation declares an aesthetic rejection of the preconceptions that stifle individual and collective invention. But the very history of Afro-Americans has always been dominated by a symbolic war against the social and artistic assembly line, especially since stereotypes are actually forms of intellectual and emotional automation. In fact, slavery was a forerunner of the nation's social compartmentalization, especially the sort upheld by the pieties of stereotypes. Those stereotypes maintained that certain people came off an assembly line in nature and one needn't assume them capable of the endless possibilities of human revelation. They had a natural place, which was inferior, and they were sometimes to be pitied and guided, sometimes feared and controlled, but were never to be considered more than predictable primitives who functioned best in subservient positions.

The aesthetic revelation in the present that is so central to jazz improvisation repudiated such attitudes and rejected what Charlie Parker called "stereotyped changes." But long before the emergence of Parker, the level of virtuoso craftsmanship that evolved in the improvising world of jazz redefined both instrumental sound and technique in an ensemble where this idiomatic American music met all the criteria demanded of musical artistry. Even virtuosity took on a new meaning, a meaning steeped in unprecedented liberation. And it was no coincidence that this frontier of artistry came from Afro-Americans and eventually spoke to and for all. As this writer pointed out in an essay called "Body and Soul":

Given the attempts to depersonalize human beings on the plantation, or reduce them to the simplicity of animals, it is understandable that a belief in the dignity of the Negro and the joyous importance of the individual resulted in what is probably the century's most radical assault on Western musical convention. Jazzmen supplied a new perspective on time, a sense of how freedom and discipline could coexist within the demands of ensemble improvisation, where the moment was bulldogged, tied, and given shape. As with the Italian artists of the Renaissance, their art was collective and focused by a common body of themes, but for jazzmen, the human imagination in motion was the measure of all things.

The degree of freedom introduced into Western music by black Americans has touched some of the few truly good jazz writers deeply and has inspired in them ideas of substantial significance in twentieth-century aesthetics. Getting beyond the noble savage school that shapes the thinking of too many jazz critics of whatever hue or background, Martin Williams points out in his largely superb *The Jazz Tradition* that there has never been a music in the Western world that allowed for so much improvisation on the parts of so many, which raises telling issues. Williams articulates the depth and meaning of this improvisational freedom quite clearly when he writes:

In all its styles, jazz involves some degree of collective ensemble improvisation, and in this it differs from Western music even at those times in its history when improvisation was required. The high degree of individuality, together with the mutual respect and co-operation required in a jazz ensemble carry with them philosophical implications that are so exciting and far-reaching that one almost hesitates to contemplate them. It is as if jazz were saying to us that not only is far greater individuality possible to man than he has so far allowed himself, but that such individuality, far from being a threat to a co-operative social structure, can actually enhance society.

Williams also makes an observation that helps clarify the human *wholeness* jazz proposes through its bold performance conventions: "The Greeks, as José Ortegay Gasset has pointed out, made the mistake of assuming that since man is the unique thinking animal (or so they concluded him to be), his thinking function is his superior function. Man is at his best when he thinks. And traditionally, Western man has accepted this view of himself.

But to a jazz musician, thought and feeling, reflection and emotion, come together uniquely, and resolve in the act of doing." This artistically extends Mann's phrase "a new and modern relationship between mind and life" from *The Coming Victory of Democracy*. That new relationship in this context demands a cooperation between the brain and the body that is perhaps fresh to Western art, since the levels of perception, conception, and execution take place at such express velocities that they go far beyond what even the most sophisticated information about the consciousness is presently capable of assessing. These musicians hear what is played by their fellow performers, are inspired to inventions of their own, hold their places in the forms of the songs, and send tasks to their muscles that must be executed so swiftly that all functions of mind and body come together with intimidating speed. In the process, a bold and unprecedented radiance is brought to the performing ensemble. The music of jazz uniquely proves out Mann's dictum that "to come close to art means to come close to life, and if an appreciation of the dignity of man is the moral definition of democracy, then its psychological definition arises out of its determination to reconcile and combine knowledge and art, mind and life, thought and deed."

2.

Though the skills that make for jazz are the result of a musical evolution that probably began the moment African slaves started reordering music they heard from and were taught by the slave masters, this writer would again say that it is a dangerous simplification to hear jazz primarily as a music protesting the social conditions of Afro-Americans, even if its seminal inventors were often subjected to social limitations based upon race. That reduces the monumental human achievement of a sustained artistic vision that allows for the expression of every passion, from delicate affection to snarling rage at the very demons of life at large, those tragic elements that no amount of money, power, or social inclusion will hold at bay. If social problems in and of themselves were the only things that provoke the creation of great art, a century as bloody as ours would have inspired far more original and profound aesthetic achievement than it has. No, the miracle of this improvisational art is the fact that the techniques Africans arrived with evolved into *aesthetic conceptions* that reinvented every kind of American music they came in contact with, from folk to religious music to dance tunes, and finally achieved the order that is jazz, where all those aspects of American musical expression were brought together for a fresh synthesis.

That fresh synthesis was the product of a down-home aristocracy of men and women whose origins cut across class and caste, who might or might not have been able to read music, might or might not have used conventional technique, but who all had in common the ability *to make musical sense* during the act of playing. In no way did their rising to artistic prominence from the bottom, middle, or top of the social strata on the steam of their own individual talents and wills conflict with the collective concerns of the music. By doing so, they actually enhanced our understanding of the music's democratic richness, proving through their work what Mann meant when he said: "Real democracy, as we understand it, can never dispense with aristocratic attributes—if the word 'aristocratic' is used, not in the sense of birth or any sort of privilege, but in a spiritual sense." A jazz musician would probably say *soul*, knowing that those who possess the deepest spiritual connection to the music can come from anywhere and *have* often enough to affirm the merit system of aesthetic expression. It is actually the whole point of democracy itself: A society is best off and most in touch with the vital when it eliminates all irrational restrictions on talent, dedication, and skill.

No matter what class or sex or religion or race or shape or height, if you can cut the mustard, you should be up there playing or singing or having your compositions performed. You should, in fact, after all the practice and the discipline necessary to push your art into the air as a professional, be taking on the ultimate democratic challenge, which means bringing into the aesthetic arena the fundamentals of Constitutional discourse, checks and balances, policy, and the amendments in which you symbolically use government to rid yourself of the blues of government. When that challenge is met, children, we hear the lucidity rising into the air that is the bittersweet truth of the blues to be there—what Hernando Cortés predicted, what the framers put together, and what we, and our descendants, as all-American children of the Constitution, will continue to reinterpret until the end of our time in the quicksand of history.

1995

Body and Soul

I. The Last Day

During the day, Rome has the feeling of rot and revelation one experiences when in the private domain of a handsome old woman, where sweat, sex, cologne, rouge, yellowed notes and papers, bottled remedies with indecipherable labels, crumbling flowers, photographs that seem to have been taken in a brownish-gray mist, clothes stained with experience but never worn anymore, and the smells of countless meals have formed a heavy collective presence in the air. Its ruins are like the sagging and corded throatline of a beauty once too sensuous to be believed and now too soulful to be perfectly understood. Of course, nothing we worry about is old in the halls where the laws of nature were written, but in our human effort, with everything over so fast, a city like Rome seems very, very old.

On the last morning there, I decided to beat the summer sun to the punch. All of the notes, timbres, rhythms, and harmonies of the festival called Umbria Jazz, the feelings of awe and mystery, blood sacrifice and integrity that resonate from the cathedrals and museums of Perugia, Assisi, and Florence were moving from my memory to my spirit, and it was fully an hour-and-a-half before dawn. The forthcoming heat of the day was presaged by the quality of subtly repressed steam given to the morning air by the slight humidity. Two stars shone in apparent sympathy with the slow and gooey low notes of a brood of pigeons clustered somewhere up on the roof of our hotel, and outside in the street men were loading a white newspaper truck. From the distance of perhaps seventy feet, they seemed to be singing as they spoke in the sleep-laden, grumbling, dictatorial—even celebratory—Italian that makes so much of vowels that the most mundane order or response can sound like kindling for an aria. I thought again of how the flares and loops of Italian speech remind me of the sound and feeling of jazz, where the sensual weight, inflection, and rhythm of notes count for so much.

Within an hour I was on the street, intent on an early morning walk. After seven or eight blocks I turned, and nearly a mile away stood the Coliseum. As I walked toward it, part of the pleasure was watching the structure grow even larger and more distinctive as I grew closer. There had been a light rain sometime in the night and the wetness gave the Roman oval an evaporating sheen that seemed to fuse past and present, since the droplets that fell from one place or another made it appear freshly excavated and washed down. But mostly the Coliseum looked like a huge crown of chipped and perforated stone. Its circumference and height were less breathtaking than hypnotic, giving off an imagined hum of history much like that of a movie projector as my mind computed the emotion accumulated through a montage of associations, from Hollywood to the history book: decadents and gladiators, religious fanatics and lions. Of course, the greatest gladiator of our age came from Kentucky and attempted to immortalize his Olympic victory in 1960 with some pool-hall doggerel—"How Cassius Took Rome"—at a press conference held on the newly painted red-white-and-blue steps of his home in Louisville, where his father broke out with a patriotic song in his best Russ Columbo imitation.

II. On the Way

In the winter of 1982, I had been invited to Umbria Jazz by Alberto Alberti, an alternately melancholy and exuberant ex-soccer player who books the bands. He described Perugia as a charming medieval town in the hills, and guaranteed me that I would love it and the music and the people. I thought he might be right, but I also figured that there would be much more to write about than fine jazz playing, since I could do that in New York. That section of the world, stretching from the Greco-Roman era to the Renaissance, had inspired in me a repository of images: Poseidon hanging out down Africa way, enjoying fast women of river hips who baptized him nightly; the tugs of literal war between the Greeks and the Carthaginians for control of Sicily; Hannibal; the genetic footprints of boots in the boudoir that left an olive complexion and a twisted wooliness to the hair of certain Italians; and the Renaissance paintings in which the solemn black king is right there in the manger at the beginning of Christianity. No doubt about it: I would go.

The flight itself was quite swinging, given its complement of Negro jazz musicians. For all their ego and sometimes crippling pursuit of hipness, they bring with them a down-home quality that personifies the best the race has yet produced. Among them I know again the barbershops and the pool halls, the big family dinners and the counterpoint of whist and domino games, the back porches and the locker rooms, the street corners and the church parking lots where I had learned so much while tested against the gruff friendship and gallows wit that have come, sometimes as slowly as the proverbial molasses in January, all the way from those slave cabins where the partying and the singing went on late into the night, puzzling old Thomas Jefferson, who knew his human property had to meet their mules and their labors in the dawn morning, to grunt and sweat until dusk. Standing at the back of the plane, swapping tales and jokes as the jet's windows opened to darkness on the left side and light on the right, I thought of how the old people had always said, "Justice may not have delivered our mail yet, but we still had a lot of goddam fun along the way—and raised as much sand as the alligator did when the pond went dry! You can believe *that*."

III. Perugia

We arrived in Rome and took a bus to Perugia, the headquarters of Umbria Jazz, traveling north on roads that passed between hills that supported both simple tiled houses and, now and again, castles embodying the will to security and civilization that resulted in armaments as well as the quarrying and dragging of the stone up that terrain. From those heights, the citizenry fought for sovereignty from invaders and rival provinces or, much later, against the control of the church. Perugia, whose history stretches back to the Etruscan age, is at the pinnacle of an especially steep group of hills, now partially surrounded by walls that provided the Romans with models of unscalable protection. Because of its very long past, Perugia, like all of Italy, is so steeped in a complex range of human time that it pulls together the superficial incongruity of the historical periods that create its atmosphere—the ancient walls, the misty and green and faded-orange landscapes already familiar from Renaissance paintings, the churches, the town squares, the sloping stone streets, the small cars designed to get through them, the motorcycles, the buses whose wide turns barely miss the walls and pedestrians, the opera house, the sidewalk cafes in which the culture of the city slowly sizzles, and the clothes that look a season or two ahead in elegance and verve of style.

IV. Hannibal Ad Portas

Later, on the train to Florence: Out that window, where Italians are presently sunbathing, had come Hannibal, fighting at Lake Trasimene in 217 BC, utilizing the beginnings of tank warfare, his Negro mahouts on elephants, the pachyderms girded for battle, their voluminous bellowing in the Alpine air behind them, their tusks and tonnage ready for the Roman legions that would be whipped to their knees and crushed. The survivors of slain Flaminius's decimated army fled throughout Etruria and Umbria, some hiding within the walls of Perugia; Perugia that was to send doomed volunteers to the terrifying Roman defeat at Cannae, where Empire seemed at end, and Perugia that was to furnish wood and grain for Scipio's fleet, helping to bang the gong on the big Punic dream of victory within the bastion of the boot, since Hannibal—great, wily, eloquent, and treacherous Hannibal—after seventeen years of fighting, would return to an invaded Carthage, sue for peace, be refused by a bitter Scipio, and face his multi-tongued army's destruction at Zama, elephants and all.

V. Umbria Jazz

Umbria Jazz wasn't like any other festival I had attended because it included jazz clinics, films, and concerts for audiences that sometimes had better ears than I expect even in New York. Those ears were also evident in the Italian tenor players I heard in the clinic, many of whom startled me with more soulful sounds than the canned Coltrane you hear so often in New York. Somewhere down the steep stone streets and around this corner and that, passing through the cool shadows of buildings that date back to the Middle Ages, the classes were held in an edifice that bore the inscription "Charlie Parker School of Jazz," an insignia that bespoke a conquest much different than the Roman seal of "Augusta Perugia." Dan Morgenstern of Rutgers University was brought over to lecture on jazz history, while tenor saxophonist Paul Jeffrey headed a faculty of musicians who ranged from their early twenties to their fifties— trumpeter Terence Blanchard, alto saxophonist Frank Strozier, pianist Harold Mabern, guitarist Kevin Eubanks, bassist David Eubanks, and drummer Jimmy Cobb. Jeffrey, a repository of jazz facts and lore and a model of patience and inspiration, said of the students: "They want to know about the soul part, about phrasing, time, and sound. Soul. They come looking for that." Mabern taught with the fervor of a deacon assigned a recalcitrant Sunday school class and had similar observations. "The reason cats come over here and have a good time is that they hear the truth. These people want the best they can get. They don't let this skin scare them into some other stuff. They want the real deal."

Carlo Pagnotta's plan for the festival included David Chertok's jazz films, music in the piazzas, in the tent—Teatro Tenda—twenty minutes away, and a concluding performance in Narni, an hour from Perugia. Other than the excessive treble from the sound crew, who botched the first few concerts in the tent, there were no problems, unless one considered some well-deserved booing and cat-calling problems. But it had not always been that way. When Pagnotta began producing concerts with the cooperation and financing of local government in 1973, many of the young people who came treated the performances like rock-and-roll happenings polluted with radical stances. Music with melody, harmony, and instrumental control was considered the art of repression and the symbol of the enslavement of black people, while the opportunists of the "avant-garde" were celebrated as the voices of freedom. The concerts moved from town to town with the unruly young people following them, and things became so bad that the owners of local shops began to board up their windows and doors when the festival arrived. But in 1978, Pagnotta pared down the traveling aspects of the festival, adding a resident American group every night at Il Panino, a club at the end of a twisting street that descends and descends, testing the mettle of those who drink too much and try to walk home. Professor Germano Marri, an old friend of Pagnotta, was elected president of Umbria that same year. With his handsome seriousness and idiomatic wit, Marri appears to represent a communism as distinct from that of Russia and its totalitarian satellites as his superb suits are from their bad tailoring. Perhaps because aesthetic quality is so thick in the air and ambience of Perugia, Marri and his staff appreciate the human complexity that has eluded almost all socialist creation. The communist organization ARCI puts together the concerts in conjunction with Perugina Chocolate and Al Italia Airlines, and allows the music to exist free of avant-garde fashion. Perhaps they know it makes more sense for the new order to spread public joy than to risk the bitterness and stoic paranoia that pervade *The Book of Laughter and Forgetting* and *Man of Iron*. But this is in keeping with the history of Italian art, which provides strong proof that variety and divergence of taste are what have made the country and the culture what it is.

VI. Dear Old Southland

In the warm afternoon light of the courtyard of the Hotel La Rosetta, over meals served under big umbrellas by waiters in white coats, Italy, as unfamiliar and foreign as it was, recalled the best in the American South. But in the streets, people seemed to float or sit in a meditative silence, or fashion their own angles on an effortless aristocracy shaped equally of confidence, curiosity, and sympathy, all of which could explode into lucid laughter or the metallic chatter of argument. The disdain for excessive activity during the hottest part of the day meant that Perugia's streets were nearly empty from one in the afternoon until four, when the shops opened up and the people filled the outdoor cafes, drinking mineral water or coffee or beer or wine, often mulling over ice cream, then strolling or stretching. I was convinced of the parallels when I found out that what we call hanging out is known there as *dolce fan niente*——sweet time for nothing. As Albert Murray was to say when I asked him about Italy later, "Long before there were Southerners in the USA, there were Southerners in Italy, and it also meant a certain climate, a certain hospitality, a certain musicality in the language, and sometimes even a certain kind of violence and tendency to vendetta. In the more learned circles, the European vision of the Southerner is much like that of anyone who understands our South: The feeling created is that of an easeful relationship to culture and a spontaneity that says, deep down—the point of learning how to cook all this food and talk this way and wear these fine clothes is to have a good goddam time, man!"

In that atmosphere, usually in the courtyard or the hotel's bar, the moody and attractive George Coleman, who has the demeanor of a powerful Memphis deacon, would move from mournful aloofness to earthly humor, from impassive sullenness to buoyancy, carrying his ex-fullback bulk in a relaxed march, his arms swinging almost straight up and down, his long elegant fingers ever ready to throttle from the tenor saxophone virtuoso passages that manifested the loneliness of many years of discipline. In residence at Il Panino with the wonderful Ronnie Matthews Trio, Coleman was to play every night as he always does, giving everything he had, working mightily for his money and not backing up until he'd forced roars and loud applause from the audience. He is clearly one of the lords of his instrument, but, above all, he is a house-rocker.

VII. Tunes in a Tent

Rocking a house is not the same as rocking a tent, and that is what was expected of the players the first few nights. The procession of events began at lunch, after which many of the musicians, observers, and listeners would go to see Chertok's films in Teatro Pavone, the opera house with painted ceilings, gold-leaf railings, five tiers of boxes, and an atmosphere reminiscent of the finest American movie palaces. The splendidly photogenic faces and forms of artists like Louis Armstrong and Duke Ellington, Lester Young and Charlie Parker, Jo Jones and Thelonious Monk, recalled Kenneth Clarke's description of the men in a Masaccio: "They have the air of contained vitality and confidence that one often sees in the founding fathers of a civilization." After Chertok's films, an American band would play in the opera house, followed later on by an Italian group heard in the open air of a piazza. Then there was dinner and the choice of a bus ride to the tent concert or an American group in a piazza. I always went to the tent.

The bus ride was brief and there was an excitement to riding downhill, passing the foreign signs and shops while lolling back in the pleasant air of Umbrian summer as it flowed in through the windows, and seeing the lights thicken on the right as we neared the blue-striped tent patterned with Union Jacks. We leaned to the left as the bus wheeled around the tent in a big arc and let us all out at a gate near the artists' trailers. There was also a small tent where you could buy beer and snacks. Given the history of Umbria Jazz, if one bought a beer in a can or a bottle, it had to be transferred to a paper cup in case the buyer got riled during the performance and decided to throw the container at the stage. Everywhere were fans, including families with small children in tow, all surveyed by a number of good-looking, young Italian men in splendid khaki uniforms, carabiniere serving the years of their mandatory military terms. There is something attractively civilized about young policemen who can represent authority with neatness, confidence, pleasant manners, and a physical strength reserved for lawbreakers, not the victims of their own boredom or problems with aggression. I thought that if the law ever became important again in America, the draft could supply an antidote to the fatigue and cynicism of the understaffed and overworked police, who would be provided with a constant influx of young fresh blood. There would be enough police to have them strolling beats again. If the uniforms were as fine as those in Italy, the cop might even become a heartthrob for the ladies, a role young men have always found attractive.

In the tent there was playing both excellent and deplorable, while in the late-night jam sessions in the sweatbox of Il Panino, the music was alternately blistering and romantic. This was made clear on the first evening, when the Italian audience showed its taste by booing the grotesque flute playing of Herbie Mann, though they applauded Freddie Hubbard, whose mixture of Clifford Brown and Clark Terry has resulted in a sound now as golden and streaked with red as a ripe peach. Hubbard was inventive with Mann's terrible rock band, but he got what he needed later that evening when he sat in with the group at Il Panino, building motives from the line of *Rhythm-a-Ning*, shaping harmonic charges prickling with dissonance, and firing staccato punctuations that now and again gave way to smears that arced through the air like big, bright fish. George Coleman sustained the excitement with his style of perpetual substitutions—note-laden arpeggios as slippery as beaded curtains of polished stone dipped in boiling oil—while the rhythm section of pianist Ronnie Matthews, bassist Walter Booker, and drummer Hugh Walker coalesced into a mighty engine of harmony and percussion. It had been a long night, but I left Il Panino rekindled and ready for the next day, greatly satisfied by the dragon blasts of inspired artistry I had heard in that boiling club down that long and winding street.

VIII. Were You There?

Italy is a land of many masters, and it would have been provincial not to take advantage of what was available on walks or at the National Gallery of Umbria right there in Perugia, or at the Cathedral of St. Francis in Assisi, less than an hour away by bus. On a morning when I had decided to explore the city or travel someplace near, I would be out on foot, feeling the uneven stone of many of the streets as the people seeped from their homes and the sounds of footfalls, rustling clothes, and voices replaced the silence. As I made my way to the Assisi bus past the farmers wheeling their produce into Perugia, I saw a Gypsy boy with a concertina and a frazzled cat on a chain. For some reason, he reminded me less of a kid imitating an Italian organ grinder than of the street preachers of my youth who used to stand at the bus stops, chanting the promises of damnation for most and salvation for the rest each time one of the big yellow and green vehicles would stop and release passengers.

After taking a bus down from Perugia into a valley, then through flatlands backdropped by low hills, where little farms were pressed together as closely as possible, going on through small towns with their second-story windows covered by wooden shutters that kept out the day's early heat, ascending again on roads that rolled and weaved until arriving in Assisi, only to see the Cathedral of St. Francis at the highest part of the city, I experienced the calm such places must have provided for their congregations as soon as I entered the huge church, felt its easy coolness, and began to concentrate on the craft and the emotional radiation of its painted walls. And though there are still those who think that the Negro, like Caliban or the gigantic Moor in Bernini's *Fountain of the Four Rivers* in Rome, should recoil in bitterness, disgust, and alienation at the abundance of those works that document a star-bumping plateau of Western Civilization, I felt that the painted walls were as familiar in feeling and function as the religious and secular music I had heard as a child in church and at home. People are exalted by a great religious painting hung in a gallery in much the same way they are by a superb recording of Mahalia Jackson.

Whether in biblical tales or annals of the suffering of the saints, perhaps the most important religious vision projected through the Italian plastic arts is its sense of moral responsibility. It can cost your life, or tear your heart, but it can also separate you from savages. They understood the costs in blood and also, as one sees in Donatello's *The Sacrifice of Isaac* in Florence, the costs in overwhelming anguish. Oh, yes, I had encountered that sense of life in those Negro churches, where the deacons stood before us, big men humming and singing in their soaked white shirts and dark suits, where the choir would enter from the rear in their swishing robes and so fill the room with mighty song that the roof seemed in danger of loosening and blowing away, where the tales and dreams of the Bible became almost three-dimensional as the worshippers rose to an impersonal oneness with what they expressed, preaching or crying or singing of the rumblings and the ruthlessness—and the *rightness!*—in the bosom of this old world.

Just as biblical lore had provided a comprehensive range of human situations for the painter, the sculptor, and the architect, Christianity had proven a perfect conduit for the movement from the vital though superstition-ridden world of Africa into the accumulated complexity of theme and ethics inherent in the biblical stories, an accumulated complexity that stood them well in the society of successive riddles that is America. Not only did the body of reinterpreted Old Testament beliefs born in rebellion against the Roman Empire speak to the slaves, but they sometimes fought to give voice themselves, reenacting the sedition of their forebears in Rome. I recalled how I had been told in Texas that, since old evil master didn't want his chattel property practicing religion, the slaves would wet down the walls of the cabins at night and gather many buckets and bowls and basins of water to also absorb the sound so that they could preach and pray in secret, separating themselves from the savages who owned the big house and the beasts of the fields.

In much the same way the Italian painters made their religious figures look Italian rather than Middle Eastern or even Negroid in features, facial expression, and dress as they personalized the lessons of Alexandria and Constantinople, the Negro slaves modified the stiff hymns to fit sensibilities that demanded richer conceptions of melody, percussion, and call-and-response. By adding an Afro-American dimension to religious material that remained Protestant, they made music that would provide an essential model for secular Negro musicians in the same way the mastery of perspective is essential to secular Renaissance painting. And eventually the sermons of the most imaginative ministers evolved into a poetry that functioned as an oral equivalent of Dante, who brought to the vernacular literature of Italian Christianity what Homer had to the mythology of Greece. A perfect example is this selection from a sermon Zora Neale Hurston took down in Florida in 1929:

> *I heard the whistle of the damnation train*
> *Dat pulled out from the Garden of Eden loaded wid cargo goin to hell*
> *Ran at break-neck speed all de way thru de law*
> *All de way thru de prophetic age*
> *All de way thru de reign of kings and judges*
> *Plowed her way thru de Jordan*
> *And on her way to Calvary when she blew for de switch*
> *Jesus stood out on her track like a rough-backed mountain*
> *And she threw her cow-catcher in*
> *His side and His blood ditched de train.*
> *He died for our sins.*
> *Wounded in the house of his friends.*

In short, a metaphoric and epic sense developed that proved perfectly compatible with how Vincent Sheean described the sweep of the spirituals Marion Anderson selected after sailing through Bach and Schubert in Salzburg in 1935: "At the end . . . there was no applause at all—a silence instinctive, natural, and intense, so that you were afraid to breathe. What Anderson had done was something outside the limits of classical or romantic music: She frightened us with the conception, in musical terms, of course, but outside the normal limits, of a mighty suffering." Had Sheean heard Anderson in the Cathedral of St. Francis, I believe he would have found himself surrounded by visual expression of the same sort.

IX. Uplift and Frustration

The feelings left after the last notes on the second and third nights fused uplift and frustration. V.S.O.P. II, under the leadership of pianist Herbie Hancock, also featured bassist Ron Carter, drummer Tony Williams, trumpeter Wynton Marsalis, and saxophonist Branford Marsalis. Except for Williams, who proved a great drummer can sound as insensitive as a four-year-old, the group performed with invention, fire, and dazzling taste. Wynton Marsalis played shocking pedal notes at fast tempos; Branford Marsalis was never less than a split second behind Hancock's often complex chords, spelling them out as he twisted and bent them; Hancock pulled his unique timbre out of the instrument and spaced his ideas with dramatic effectiveness; while Carter inspired and supported as he crafted bass parts and rhythms of such drive that they almost made up for the drummer's incessant banging. On the third night, the Rutgers University Saxophone Ensemble under the direction of Paul Jeffrey was a casualty of the sound crew: Guest soloist George Coleman was either distorted or inaudible, Jeffrey's orchestrations of Coltrane improvisations were so muddily amplified that they might as well have been written in unison, and only the extraordinary piano and drums of Harold Mabern and Jimmy Cobb could be heard throughout, with the good bass beat of David Eubanks appearing and disappearing. Protests resulted in vast improvements the next evening and, after Richie Cole's aggressively mediocre set, Sphere—tenor saxophonist Charlie Rouse, pianist Kenny Barron, bassist Buster Williams, and drummer Ben Riley—displayed distinct arrangements that primed the ear for their improvised command of the subtleties of inflection, color, and rhythm. From the first note, the chill on the patina of the evening air lifted and the huge tent felt intimate. It was one of the best performances I have heard all year.

X. The Religion of Glory: Cakewalking Babies

The new religion, as I have called the love of glory
. . . a thing of this world, founded as it is on human esteem.
—**Bernard Berenson,**
The Italian Painters of the Renaissance

When I considered how the development of Afro-American music telescoped the evolution of Italian art, I had no difficulty seeing slavery and segregation as American versions of the Dark Ages, or recognizing how the soaring self-assertion and mocking false faces of the parades and social clubs of New Orleans provided the local musicians with a Renaissance sense of carnival. After all, Berenson says, "[t]he moment people stopped looking fixedly toward heaven, their eyes fell upon earth, and they began to see much on its surface that was pleasant. Their own faces and figures must have struck them as surprisedly interesting. . . . The more people were imbued with the new spirit, the more they loved pageants. The pageant was an outlet for many of the dominant passions of the time . . . above all [the] love of feeling . . . alive." Given the attempts to depersonalize human beings on the plantation, or reduce them to the simplicity of animals, it is understandable that a belief in the dignity of the Negro and the joyous importance of the individual resulted in what is probably the century's most radical assault on Western musical convention. Jazzmen supplied a new perspective on time, a sense of how freedom and discipline could coexist within the demands of ensemble improvisation, where the moment was bulldogged, tied, and given shape. As with the Italian artists of the Renaissance, their art was collective and focused by a common body of themes, but for jazzmen, the human imagination in motion was the measure of all things.

As I thought of turn-of-the-century New Orleans, the Crescent City with its street songs and its opera houses, with the visual stretch of Afro-Americans from bone to beige to brown to black, with its Negroes dressed as Indians or parodying the Mardi Gras in their own Zulu Ball, with the bands riding on wagons and battling for the affection of the listeners, with the grief of the music on the way to the bone orchard and the zest of its celebration on the way back, the frescoes reminded me of the aural palimpsests of the old 78 RPM recordings with the red or blue-black labels that my mother had saved, those fragile discs that carried the hissing documentation of blues divas and jazzmen on their worn surfaces, from which the music struggled through the haze of primitive engineering. Just as Kenneth Clarke observed that the Italian Renaissance contributed its ideas in visual terms rather than reasoned argument or speculation, the same can be said about jazz, since its thoughts about American life arrived not in the philosophical text but in the well-picked note on moment's notice and the physical response of dance. You can tell that those people believed in an African-derived sense of infinite plasticity that lent to the bending and drastic rearranging of songs, just as they believed in the molten democracy of the *groove*, when a band catches its stride and every decision made by

every individual not only carries his stamp but makes for a collective statement that transcends the particular. You can hear their frothing exuberance
as they recognize that they can control the formless rush of the present and
paint their faces on its canvas.

XI. Dizzy Atmosphere

It was the next night and the last night of tunes in the tent, and Dizzy
Gillespie looked less handsome than angry. He had been loudly booed
after kicking off his performance with two dull would-be funk numbers. I
was told later: "In Italy, we feel if a musician is great, he should be great. In
America, it may be necessary for Miles Davis or Sonny Rollins to play
rock-and-roll—or perhaps it is less painful to act young than wise. Here we
feel sad or angry when a great man will abandon wisdom for ignorance.
The more polite would say innocence. Why should they travel this far to
put on a silly mask?"

The booing was to the good: Gillespie, who had been sulking on the
piano bench, rose and roared forth with a succession of improvisations of
such savage invention it must have been somewhat difficult to be Jon Faddis standing there next to him, knowing the only thing you could add that
night was higher notes. The old master feinted, ducked, and worked out
phenomenal accents that italicized the abstractions within his long phrases,
proving that when angered, a sore-headed bear will rise to beat the band.
Trombonist Curtis Fuller was exquisite and guitarist Ed Cherry worked
some pulsive variations on the voicings of McCoy Tyner. Everyone left that
evening aware that they had witnessed a master in matchless form.

XII. Renaissance in Red Beans and Rice

You cannot have a Renaissance without a Giotto di Bondone. He stripped
away what Clark calls the "decorative jumble" of images that made the medieval school both highly stylized and emblematic, offering in its place the
weight and the sacrifice, the disappointment and the exaltation of human
beings concurring and conflicting. In a sense, he discovered the individual
in the pageant and, sometimes with the aid of bas-relief halos, pushed the
force and substance of experience right at us, settling for neither mush nor
surrender. Berenson points out that all of his lines are functional, that they
are defined by movement, that he charged trivial objects with a power that
not only transformed them but ignited the consciousness of the viewer.

In his own way, Louis Armstrong did the same. He discovered that his powers of imagination could stand alone, with the clarinet and the trombone of the conventional New Orleans band silenced, no longer needed to express the intricate and subtle musicality provided by the multilinear antiphonal style. His monumental ideas swelled a fresh world above his accompanying improvisers. In Armstrong's work there is a new kind of confidence that had never existed in Western music, an aural proof that man can master time through improvisation, that contemplation and action needn't be at odds. A quantum leap of control heralded a new relationship between the artistic consciousness and the body that has yet to inspire what could be a new school of brain research. Armstrong found that he could hear a chord, digest it, decide what to play, tell his lips, lungs, and fingers what to do, and express his individuality within the mobile ensemble as rhythms, harmonies, timbres, and phrases flew forward around him. He had mastered what A. E. Hotchner calls "the ability to assimilate simultaneous occurrences."

Unlike Giotto, Armstrong had immediate impact. He became a hero of epic proportions to fellow musicians. One remembers first hearing him sound like an archangel from a riverboat, another touching him just as he was going on stage and feeling an electric shock. Yet another recalls him taking the measure of a challenge at a cornet supper in Harlem and standing the listeners on their chairs, tables, and plates as he played notes that were like hot, silver solder splashing across the roof that supports the heavens. In his sexuality and the daredevil displacements of his abstractions, Armstrong is more in spirit with Picasso, but his position in an Afro-American Renaissance is inarguable. He delivered a virtuosity fresh from the frontier of his imagination, giving the trumpet an expressive power it never had. Armstrong brought a purer sound to the instrument's upper register, playing high notes that were functional rather than decorative, and his strings of eighth notes invariably delivered with a triplet feeling lifted the horn from a vocal, shouting riff style to a standard-bearer of melody interwoven with virtuoso rhythms. And it is clear that in the spirit of Giotto, Armstrong ignited the consciousness of his listeners by charging often uninteresting songs with artistic power, spontaneously transforming them through both an editing and embellishing process. When you hear Armstrong at his finest, he is like the Negro acrobat in the Roman sculpture, calmly balanced on the head of the crocodile of the moment. Berenson says that what a major artist does is show that human beings can cope with the complexities of life—and who could deny that in the face of Armstrong's greatest improvisations?

XIII. Blues for Julius III

The final night of Umbria Jazz in Perugia, before the festival's actual conclusion in the mountain town of Narni, took place at Piazza IV. A bandstand had been set up next to the Great Fountain, which dates from 1275, and in front of the Cathedral of St. Lawrence, where a bronze statue of Julius III sat facing the back of the stage and the eyes of the assembled masses. In a way, the feeling of festival that had been building all week was now swelling in the streets with the people. There were African students in small clusters, Americans who were there studying Italian, Europeans on vacation, but, most of all, Italians, from the very young to the older women with calf muscles built from walking the inclines of the stone streets. There were no costumes and no streamers, yet the air felt full of colors and thick with the moisture of dance.

Before joining the dinner group, I listened to some of Ray Mantilla's "Space Station," as it started the people near the bandstand dancing to the rushes and thumps of its Afro-Hispanic rhythms. Especially entrancing was the orchestral use of the traps by Joe Chambers, whose spare musicality gave the impression of a pianist playing timbres and multiple rhythms instead of lines and chords. Next, in the summer air, Jackie McLean played with a passion as scarlet as a fall maple and notes as bright and golden as an October birch. In the spirit of the Pagliacci lyricism of Charlie Parker, McLean's sound was as brutish in timbre as it was plaintive and prideful. But his tone could also glow when he swung on the hard New York blues, or floated his ballad notes on the stream of flesh and memory. He had the urgency, power, and presence of a grand master. Yes, he was in fine form, skittering his lines across the chords set by vibist Bobby Hutcherson, whose music rushed forth or lulled in the air like hankty and piss-elegant chimes. Billy Higgins balanced both instruments on his ride cymbal and buffed them with his stripped-down snare accents, now and again using his toms and bass drum like nearly inaudible thunder. Bassist Herbie Lewis had the heavy and dark effect of a tonal percussionist. A very hot stage was set for the Umbria Jazz All-Stars.

It was late when the All-Stars took the stand, bringing with them the lore of many a dancehall, night club, jam session, and party rich with fine women, handsome men, whiskey, whist, coon can, dominoes, and the smells of down-home food steaming in the pots. On the front line were the Texas tenors: Arnett Cobb, who stands on his metal crutches and shapes each saxophone note like an individual bellows crafted to build heroic fire; Illinois Jacquet, a barrelhouse bull on wheels roaring into red capes; and Buddy Tate, who can rattle the pulpit of the bandstand with his sensuous renditions of blues-toned scripture. There was Al Grey, a master of the plunger who sometimes plays as though coaxing bulbous notes into his trombone rather, than pushing them out. The rhythm section of pianist John Lewis, bassist Eddie Jones, and drummer Gus Johnson strung and loosened the bow of the beat with wit and encouragement. Then there was Scott Hamilton, less a seasoned star than a young man still in search of himself, wavering back and forth between recitations of Lester Young and Tate. But on song after song, with the rhythm section simmering and steaming under them, the veterans tore away everything that stood in the path of celebration, creating a pulsation that could be answered only with dance. And dance they did engender, especially with the inevitable en-core—"Flying Home"—lifting the crowd with the bells of their horns into a massive articulation of unsentimental happiness. As green Julius III gave his blessing and the medieval Great Fountain bubbled over a democratic series of reliefs spanning local politics, Christianity, astrology, history, edu-cation, Roman origins, and the most popular fables of Aesop, I heard the sound of American democracy become an international phenomenon and thought that if Hannibal had these kinds of troops, he would have easily taken the Roman Empire. With a song.

XIV. Bird of Paradise

The next day I went to the National Gallery of Umbria, again watching the figures slowly change from dark-eyed and dark-skinned to Northern Ital-ian. When I got to Piero della Francesca's polytych, it was like an explo-sion. Even though he was working with the new level of virtuosity that full-blown control of perspective allowed, della Francesca carried everything with him—the gold leaf and steepled frame and the sacrificial themes. There was an arrogance to his lyricism, especially in the perfectly measured distances and details of the section depicting the annunciation, but there was also the aloof idealism most confident virtuosi have in common. He used "no specialized expression of feeling," as Berenson observed, and the effect at first is one of coldness. Thomas Craven describes his figures as "masked in sullen gravity . . . their attitudes majestic and defiant." But what actually is taking place is a protest against the limitations of painting and an expression of unruffled confidence in the command of detail, a mastery that can concentrate on subtlety and overall effect rather than a conventional display of emotional states. That may account for the absolute stillness an-other writer sees in his figures.

In two cases, della Francesca's version of what Clarke calls "the new pessimism" rivals—or exceeds—Giorgione's *Col Tempo*, where a withered beauty stares with the remorse of age at the viewer. In della Francesca's *The Flagellation of Christ*, we see a whipping in the background while a group of well-dressed men converse about other business in the foreground, presaging the modern theme of public indifference to personal pain and degradation. On the right side of *The Death of Adam*, he comments on the loss of Eden. An old man who had once been vibrant and handsome now sits feebly on the ground as his wife stands behind him, equally aged and with her flaccid dugs drooping and uncovered, a dead-pan comment on the Renaissance ideal of physical beauty that no paintings of fine faces and figures—or prayer—will diminish.

As I examined della Francesca's work, his absolute stillness and his rejection of conventional expression reminded me of Charlie Parker. Parker brought a fierce and fresh virtuosity to the saxophone, protesting its limitations, and discarded the vibrato many considered necessary for the expression of deep feeling in the work of his predecessors. He depended on the voluminous details of his loquacious melody notes, his high-handed harmonic sophistication, and the seemingly impossible gradations of attack he brought to rhythms that themselves seemed beyond enunciation. Like that of the Italian painter, Parker's work brims with sullen gravity, majesty, and defiance; it is an art possessed by an idealism that says that only in the transcendence of the difficult can we know the intricate riches and terrors of the human soul. Both the painter and the saxophonist created continuity and contrast through echoing and near-echoing. The painter used figures and faces as motifs while varying features and skin tones, hair color and texture, dress and body position; the result is a series of geometrical calls and responses from one end of a painting to the other. In Parker's best work, he constantly reshapes phrases and rhythms, extending them, leaving something out here, adding something there, or compressing what he has previously played into a swinging board from which he bounces into more elaborate linear variations. Parker also left nothing behind, revolutionizing every detail of the jazz tradition. Parker became a colossus of human consciousness who could process and act upon material with a meticulous lyricism at any tempo. In his finest improvisations, you hear an imagination given the wide dimension of genius, running up a hill potted and mined with obstacles, but delivering its melodies with a sometimes strident confidence in their imperishability.

XV. Not Until Narni

Traveling from Perugia, we crossed frightening gorges and saw the terrain become steeper until we arrived at a gas station and had to switch to buses small enough to get through a gate and up the narrow road to our destination. Narni is made almost completely of stone, with arches that cast shadows and lead into the descending side streets or into buildings that crest the city on the other side of the square where the concert was held. A big bandstand had been set up in front of a large fountain and, though the music was more than an hour away because of a power failure, Italians of all ages had begun to gather around the stage and were staring at us with overt curiosity and pleasure as we made for the bars or the little stand beyond an imposing Roman arch where sandwiches and beer were sold.

I found myself wandering through the city and its backstreets, imagining the time when the clop of shod hooves and the rattling of wagons had filled the air, when word of Giuseppe Garibaldi's triumphs arrived, when the problems of putting in telephone service and electric lights and plumbing had been met with wires and fenced-in generators and the sewers full of turning pipes. Then I wondered if the first jazz notes had arrived by phonograph or radio. Narni had the look and feel of a place where modern life was but another loop on a very long tape of time. As I had been told by an Italian named Maurice Cohen: "In Italy, you can stand in the middle of your past and feel the present and dream about the future. You know that what is adaptive is what is lasting and that the key to Italian civilization, what some mistake for exceptional friendliness, is a confidence in the fact that though you might be influenced, you won't be consumed. You will merely take what is good and make it Italian. After all, the spaghetti first came from China with Marco Polo, but the Chinese did not make *pasta*. Italians did. Merchants came from all over the world to Florence, but Italians invented banking. And so it goes. That is our way and that is our safety." (I later found out that Cohen had been born in France.)

By the time I returned, the klieg lights were on, an Italian television crew was at work documenting the event, the square was filled with many people either standing or sitting on the ground, and in the houses that surrounded the square were families seated and crowded in their second-floor windows or old women leaning on sills with their elbows. A big band from Rome had finished their set and I was soon to wish they would kidnap American tenor saxophonist Bob Berg and teach him to cook. Even with the same rhythm section that had so perfectly supported George Coleman and Freddie Hubbard, Berg managed to never swing a note, only bluster through the tunes with the aimless intensity of a fly caught between a closed window and a screen. The staff Paul Jeffrey put together played quite well until monitor problems led to tempo waverings even stable swingers like Harold Mabern and Jimmy Cobb couldn't set right. There were also early conflicts between Mabern's thick voicings and the obbligatos of Kevin Eubanks until the guitarist let Mabern have it and made his statements with good lines in his features. Frank Strozier invented bittersweet alto saxophone melodies, built tension with circular breathing, and delivered his ideas with rhythms both fluid and bumptious. Terence Blanchard, always a poignant player, surged through the trumpet with big intervallic leaps and an almost impersonal sense of heartbreak interwoven with desire that stung the audience, while Jeffrey, caught in the memory of the Umbria All-Stars, reached in the bucket and swung the bell off of the tenor. I admire Woody Herman's refusal to sit down and moulder away, but his Young Herd concluded the concert with more precision than passion and swung about as hard as a buried log of teakwood, while the leader's singing was an unpleasant memento of minstrelsy.

It was after two in the morning and the streets were still filled with listeners who seemed reluctant to turn in, especially the old women in the second-floor windows, who were apparently determined to watch everything dismantled and packed before they called it a night. As for us, we were all taken to a banquet on the elevated patio of a hotel in Turni, where the staff showered Pagnotta with champagne and I stared at some of the most beautiful women I had ever seen in my life. By the time we returned to Perugia, it was almost dawn but I was still lit up and ready for the train ride to Florence, all the jazz notes behind me but the memory of an extraordinary people and their thirst for festival still in the front of my mind.

XVI. Firenze

One of the first things that impressed me in Florence was the army of well-dressed men and women on motor scooters shooting down the streets, their double-breasted summer suits, their striped dresses and sheer stockings, their briefcases and purses in place as they rounded corners or deftly moved between cars. There was also the sunlight that would smooth itself across the sky and loom in its seemingly imperishable weight just beyond the city's many shaded spaces; the cypress trees and the hills where Michelangelo designed the snaking fortifications; the huge cathedrals that maintain their grandeur in an almost ancient skyline dominated by tile the color of dried red mud; the infinity of shops with everything available from custom-made shoes to the most remarkable suits and dresses, wallets, purses, and scarves; the street market near the Duomo that the sellers would build each morning from poles and rectangles of plywood or formica; the horse-drawn carriages in which you could travel near the Ufizzi; the squadrons of pigeons that would light near the Fountain of Neptune, hustle a few bread scraps, and march in place behind the platoons of Japanese tourists, who faced the labor of lugging around their many cameras, packages, and guide books with determination and explosive smiles. The smallest sandwich stand might provide a simple but delicious snack, a glass of mineral water, and the parting choice of forty-two imported beers. It was hard not to be impressed.

But I met a small, dark man from a town in Calabria who had been living in Florence for twenty years. He gave an impression of the city that was less hostile than sarcastic and indicative of the hometown pride you consistently encounter in Italy. He felt that the Florentines were very closed and unfriendly because they thought they were "too civilized." Yet they made more grammatical mistakes than anybody, he went on to say, and suggested that when Frederick II conquered Sicily and opened schools in which Italian was taught, he may have inspired Dante to write in the language: "The Florentines cannot say it is not so. Like all of us, they do not know. But I will bet you they have *never heard* of Frederick II."

I mentioned that I had been surprised by how softly people spoke during dinner the previous night—when I joined some Americans and we began laughing and joking, the people at the other tables kept staring at us. "On the bus," he smirked, "where people should be talking and enjoying themselves, you would think they are whispering inside themselves in church. They do not like the loud."

It would be silly to come to Florence where they do not like the loud and not join those who line up in the morning outside the Gallery of the Tribune to see *Prisoners* and *David*, standing huge and lighted by the sun beneath the cupola at the end of the room, its musculature and the stare of the eyes familiar as the remembered images of the greatest boxers. Kenneth Clarke says that the look of the head "involves a contempt for convenience and a sacrifice of all those pleasures that contribute to what we call civilized life. It is the enemy of happiness." Looking at it, I could not help but think of Muhammad Ali, fresh from the attrition and the tuning of the training camp, coming up the aisle to face Sonny Liston, the Goliath of the boxing ring; or Ali standing in his sullen poignance as he recited with charming bravado one of his rhymed predictions of how he would fell the big ugly bear from Philadelphia or going to his locker room after his victory and suffering through the ice-covered and blackening cummerbund of bruises left by the bear's body punches.

There is also an air of gloom surrounding *David* because we know, as Michelangelo must have, how he was torn down by temptation and megalomania. There is perhaps no story of forbidden love quite so great and heartbreaking as the tragedy David enters when struck by the wonders of Bathsheba's lush and naked body bathing in the morning light. Though he knows from firsthand experience the power and wrath of his God, David will still commit adultery, thus spitting upon the laws he is bound to uphold, then further corrupt his powers as king by eventually using them to design what was perhaps the first example of bureaucratic murder as he moved to rid himself of Bathsheba's husband, Uriah the Hittite. Next he must face the whirlwind of incest and fratricide among his children that culminates when Absalom, groomed in princely privilege as favorite son, rises to try and smite down his father. When I think of David moaning the name of his slain and seditious son, finally aware that even the chosen and the most gifted have no guarantees against the wages of obsession, I also think of Ali: his ego and addiction to celebration, his victory over the second Goliath of George Foreman in the humid bush of Zaire and the almost mythological grandeur of his third fight with Joe Frazier in Manila, then his desire for one last dance in the light of international praise and awe shaping in him a belief in magic that helped result in the once-quick tongue now battling ruefully—at the pace of a child reading his first schoolbook— to enunciate a simple sentence. Even so, just as we know that *David* is at the edge of a journey to a pinnacle from which he will fall, dragged in the dirt by his lust, we will always also know that there were moments when Ali, expanding our expectations of a heavyweight's grace, courage, and cunning, won and made it New Year's Eve all over the world.

The Duomo nearly overcomes the visitor through the grandeur of its collective art and design. I was most surprised by the black, gray, white, salmon, brown, and plum patterns of its marble floor. In an apparent attempt to simultaneously prove the glory of mathematic precision and illustrate the perfect construction of the universe, a series of rhyming geometrical images on either side of the huge church reveals the contemporary painting that begins with Piet Mondrian's *Broadway Boogie Woogie* as little more than contrived decoration.

But the Florentine sensibility also encompasses the Medici chapels, where the gargoyle narcissism of the room honoring the Medici princes makes technical mastery revolting. Its overdone green, gray, plumb, red, and apricot marble has the garishness associated with drag balls and expresses not the resonance of a culture but its hollowness. By contrast, there is the consonant poetry of the white and green marble Michelangelo used to design the New Sacristy under the same roof, diminished only by the predictive science fiction of the female figures who are dangerously close to transsexuals, with their male thighs, muscular bodies, and tacked-on breasts.

I will never forget how many times I circled Michelangelo's unfinished *Pietà* in the museum behind the Duomo, fascinated by the possibilities for style it suggested. Its mix of the finished and the unfinished gives the impression of an intersection between realism and expressionism, between living flesh, dead flesh, and the spirit. For me, the big figure that hovers over the expired Christ seems to be death lifting his body beyond the equally spiritual figure of Mary, who is lost in lamentation for her son. I floated back much faster than I could have by plane and much further, all the way to a street not far from my old home in Los Angeles and into the living room where a wake was being held, with food and liquor everywhere, with men and women in dark clothes, and was memory-listening to a mother talking about how she had been with her dead son in the chapel for the last time as he lay in state, his body waiting for the ritual next morning that would take him to the burying ground. "I took Oran's hand and put it in mine, just like I did when he would get sick and ask me to rub his arms. The hand was cold but it wasn't stiff and it felt like it always did. The only difference was the fingertips had turned blue." She looked up, her face the color of mustard with a subtle undertone of beige, worn with grief and surely knowing what Mary had known.

XVII. Roma

On that last morning in Rome, I stood before the Coliseum, relaxing into the thought of how much of my own experience had been clarified by exposure to foreign forms. It had been a steaming afternoon the day before when I arrived, bedding down in a hotel near the train station, in a section popular with the vacationing Arab middle class. A cab ride had taken me around the ancient city, which combined past and present even more startlingly than the others. Rome is both sad with the knowledge of the mystery of fate and vital with the awareness of how clearly human passions can speak through the ages, whether from the Egyptian obelisks that shoot up toward the sun or the ruins and fountains that detail the carcasses of empire and the glory of invention.

Because it was summer, many of the residents were vacationing and avoiding tourists, but there were still plenty of Italians at work who never gave the impression of oppressive boredom you become accustomed to in New York. One feels the presence of time with a special intensity here because the drive that brought those obelisks back from Egypt and pushed up the Pantheon or the Vatican or the Coliseum or the many fountains seems almost tangible. There is also a glow of confidence that comes from having survived monsters from antiquity to Mussolini, who used to speak from that balcony there. At the same time, there is the silt and the brown dust that has accumulated from the exhaust of automobiles and mutes the surfaces of streets and buildings with the gloom of the modern age. But perhaps that gloom has been overstated by pessimists who ignore the modes of redress and the reduction of degradation and squalor that have come in the wake of the Magna Carta and the Continental Congress. After all is said and done, the world has a richer human image of itself now despite its problems, but the way those Italians carry themselves is not so much an assertion of hope as of the ironic continuity that a long history provides.

On my only evening there, I saw a tall and darkly attractive group of African women walking in line as the Italians covered the streets on the way to shop or eat. One was especially striking, with brilliant black eyes, a long neck circled by the lines that are often seen by Africans as marks of beauty, and a long red dress that billowed and stopped just short of her ankles. She reminded me of the bas-reliefs at the Tazza D'Oro coffee shop where an African woman is depicted showering Rome with coffee beans, but not of a brace of Brooklyn ersatz Africans I had met in Florence, with their hair looking like sooted mops, their noses run through by rings, their bodies reeking the overwrought oils sold with incense in New York, and their attire the tacky and misbegotten emulation of an Africa that exists only in the minds of romantic primitivists rather than the continent that may someday rise to shake the world with its natural resources as Hannibal shook Rome with his elephants.

As I looked at those African women, I wondered if the descendants of slaves owned by fellow Africans would ever influence the world in the way those who were brought to America had. I knew then that slavery in America was as much ironic luck as it was enormous misfortune, since what U.S.

slaves had endured made for a culture in which celebration was a form of protest that remade social, aesthetic, and athletic conventions. We are indeed fortunate to live in a period when we can see changes that began when the first slaves ran away from the plantation or learned to play the fiddle or sing hymns or read. Of course, that was only the beginning. E. Franklin Frazier once observed that certain field slaves, never having seen the master and the mistress work, thought freedom meant preening and kicking back behind mint juleps. It is pretty clear that too many African regimes haven't understood that a well-oiled and functioning infrastructure that marshals and markets all resources must precede the underhanded luxuries of success. The attempts to leap-frog directly to corruption have cost their economies dearly but, given the history of France since the Revolution, there is no need to count them out prematurely. Africans will probably learn their lessons the hard way, as others have, and then push more chairs to the big table of world power.

XVIII. Precious Lord

On the returning flight, I struck up conversation with a group of Negro pilgrims from Florida who had just been to the holy land, where they had walked in Jerusalem just like John. I had noticed them almost as soon as the plane took off, for they sat together and exuded a familiar combination of sobriety, wit, and warmth as they listened to one another, joked, or mused. The men all wore dark or gray suits with vests and the women either pantsuits or straight and simple dresses, their occasional diamond rings shining below knuckles and above their liver-colored nail polish. As I had first looked at them, recalling the heat of the churches and the steam of the sermons, I was reminded of the old saying: "Our race is like a flower garden, everything from lily-white to blue-black." When an Afro-American painter masters mixing all the colors necessary to capture such a range of skin tones, the painting of figures might be revitalized.

The pilgrims were still excited by what they had seen in Jerusalem and were comparing emotional reactions to the religious art of Rome. One woman said that there was a lot wrong with the way Catholics practiced the religion, but that their paintings and the sculpture told the truth. "They knew how a mother feels when her child is in pain and she can't do nothing about it," she observed. Their pastor said, "[i]f I had somebody like that Michelangelo to paint my church, a man that inspired, we couldn't stay in there. We would need a bigger place. They would feel the truth vibrating through that paint. Yes, sir, when you stand in that Vatican, you can't help but feel the glory behind everything."

The preacher's words brought me back to the Coliseum, where I'd remembered how the Christians who had been meat for the lions began the protests that led to the fall of the Roman Empire after it converted to Christianity and could no longer justify chattel labor. I then recalled the Civil Rights Movement, when an empire of segregation and lynch law had been torn asunder by those radicalized pastors and their nonviolent troops cracking the pillars of a temple to injustice with their bodies while singing reworked old spirituals that stung with political messages and threats to the redneck kingdom of violence. Then I saw again Mahalia Jackson painting an aural portrait of the suffering of the Southern saints as she sang "Precious Lord, Take My Hand" at Martin Luther King's funeral, her image projected by a television set, a wet handkerchief in her hand, her hair thick and dark above her head, the dress frilled and white, and her body trembling with the passage of each note. For some strange reason as I walked near the ruins of the Senate, it came to me how radio waves and phonograph recordings had beamed the disembodied songbird of jazz into the ears of many virgins, giving birth to an international body of listeners who had been transformed in some vital way by that annunciation. At that moment, it was easy to see that the melancholy I have often felt when staring at the sealed-up palace of bebop innovation that was Minton's Playhouse in Harlem, or the stripped-away testaments to the nightlife of Kansas City, is a melancholy unfounded. The human point is not that something has decayed, but that when the times and the spirits were right, men and women met their challenges, and their efforts rose as brightly as the sun did on that last Roman morning.

1983

BATTLE ROYAL

JazzTimes Columns:
Introduction

Included here are a number of columns from what became a controversial tenure at *JazzTimes*. I had been chased by its publisher, Glenn Sabin, for a number of years. He had offered me a column at the magazine, which I always turned down. I did this because I did not believe that there was an editorial interest in an independent opinion that did not coincide with the lock-step thinking that there was no definition that could be applied to jazz, that there was no characteristic sound to the music, that all someone had to do to be considered a jazz musician was to say that he was a jazz musician, and so on. Sabin said that this was not true and that if I came into the magazine and did a monthly column I would have the absolute freedom to make any arguments that I wished.

Well, that is not quite how it went. My column became a target for exceptional hostility and finally led the *JazzTimes* editor to fire me by e-mail, which was not only insulting but highly unprofessional. Many thought that I was fired because I had attacked the darling of the jazz establishment, the trumpeter Dave Douglas, about whom I wrote a column entitled "Putting the White Man in Charge." It was conveniently considered racist even though the article praised the saxophonist Joe Lovano, whom I think I may have been the first to single out years ago for his high level of excellence as an improvisor when I wrote an article for the *Village Voice* about big band master drummer Mel Lewis.

That was to no avail because the biggest trouble with what I said was the fact that I had, once again, called into question the way things were done and why they were done. But, after all, I am not the only one who has noticed the racial politics of the jazz critical establishment. When the very fine drummer Matt Wilson received the Jazz Journalist award for best drummer of the year from the Jazz Journalists Association a few seasons back, he looked right into that sea of satisfied nerds and said almost these exact words: "There's something wrong with this picture. I appreciate getting this award but Elvin Jones is still alive and so is Roy Haynes, as two examples. How do I rate this?" Wilson knew how he got the award and why he got it. His mirror told him every day. He just happens to be an honest man.

In that respect, Wilson reminds me most of Dan Morgenstern, a jazz writer of absolute integrity, who has an unsentimental affection for the music and the artists who make it. His collection, *Living with Jazz*, is proof of what distinguishes him. Yet even a writer as inarguably talented and insightful as Whitney Balliet can get caught up in the racial politics of the day. After having failed to be disturbed by all-white repertory jazz bands or repertory bands that included no more than a few Negroes, he could suddenly become color conscious, count the number of white players in some Lincoln Center concerts, and accuse Wynton Marsalis of prejudice against white musicians. Affirmative Action at its worst—the numbers game—turned pale! As Gideon Feldstein, who played baritone in the Lincoln Center Jazz Orchestra, said, "Why don't these guys ever ask any of the white musicians who have played in the band what they think? They haven't talked to me or Joe Temperley, who has been here from when the band was started, or Ryan Kaiser, or Ted Nash or any of the white musicians who have played." Feldstein did not understand that facts were less important than "proving" that a black musician with "too much power" might exclude white musicians solely on the basis of color. That turned out to be one of those conceptions, like most conspiracy theories, that is invincible to facts. Another Lincoln Center enemy was a highly visible writer of substantial intellectual acumen who constantly tried everything he could to destroy the program because, obviously, his hatred of the trumpeter started to fester when he was so disturbed by the dressing down that Marsalis gave him in the Middle East. According to the bartender who witnessed the aftermath, this conflict in aesthetic opinion led to repeated orders of Jack Daniels lifted with a trembling hand by the writer. Hmm.

Actually, none of this is very surprising from the bulk of jazz journalists because hardly any of the men who write about jazz can be considered intellectuals or very knowledgeable about aesthetics. They tend to know little about the arts at large and do not really understand much about what really makes jazz unique. Almost always very square and painfully insecure in the presence of musicians, they tend to defend themselves with their recordings and their memories of obscure trivia. Unlike Ted Panken and Russ Musto, they are rarely seen in a jazz club, which all of the staffs who work the best of the rooms joke about. Most of them are glorified fans and are, unfortunately, very susceptible to the same kinds of ideological troubles that dominate our college campuses on which political correctness and victim studies have made it veritably impossible to be hired if one does not submit to the most simple-minded ideas of the unquestioned ideologues who dominate ethnic, feminist, and homosexual studies.

Consequently, the real trouble with my columns, as far as I can tell, was that I had been systematically dismantling the clichés that pass for thought in the jazz world. Beyond that, *JazzTimes* had no real interest in providing space to a voice very different from the collective mind of the jazz establishment, where there is nothing even close to actual aesthetic disagreement. This section includes another dismantling: that of LeRoi Jones, whom I lost respect for many years ago, not only as a jazz writer but as any kind of writer on any subject. I see his racial hysteria as the kind of thing that the jazz establishment is often responding to but refuses to admit. If one wants to see what Jones wrote in an exchange about jazz criticism that took place at a conference sponsored by the Smithsonian Institution in 1990, his dreadful ideas in full can be found in a little book called *New Perspectives on Jazz*. Along with my slicing up the corpse of the fallen king and would-be Negro leader, I believe this selection of columns offers the opinion that there definitely is something we can call jazz, and it is not simply determined by color or improvisation or using jazz instrumentation. It is an art. It has always been an art. Attempting to define that, as opposed to creating a racial stir, was the real problem that I caused.

The Jazz Tradition Is
Not Innovation

I came of age in the 1960s and was accustomed then to a higher level of artistic discussion about jazz than we presently expect. When thinkers such as Gunther Schuller, Don Heckman, Martin Williams, George Russell, Richard B. Hadlock, Nat Hentoff, Charles Mingus, Dan Morgenstern, Bill Mathieu, Bill Russo, and others wrote about the traditions of jazz or about individual players or movements, or put their two cents into the whirlwind of controversy that dominated the air after Ornette Coleman opened at the Five Spot in November of 1959, they did so with more than a casual understanding of the music. Whether or not they were musicians, and whether or not one agreed with everything that those guys concluded, they came to the art with a great sense of what made it valuable and unique in the first place. They knew that jazz was not European concert music in disguise, that it was not African music, and that it was not merely improvised music. Those writers knew that jazz was not anything other than what it was, regardless of how many ways it had been played between the time Louis Armstrong left New Orleans to join King Oliver in Chicago in 1922 and Ornette Coleman packed up his plastic alto saxophone and headed out of Los Angeles for Manhattan.

This does not seem to be very true to me today. Now, critics maintain a perpetual pursuit of novelty, of something that might become the writers famous for "discovering." There is little measured thinking about what is going on and little respect for those who are not bent on "innovation." We even have to endure imbecilic statements like "the tradition of jazz is innovation." This means absolutely nothing since the vast majority of musicians at any time in history and in any idiom are not innovators themselves—even if they are among the first to embrace fresh vocabularies.

During the 1940s, the innovators were Charlie Parker, Dizzy Gillespie, Fats Navarro, Miles Davis, Lee Konitz, Warne Marsh, Bud Powell, Thelonious Monk, Lennie Tristano, Oscar Pettiford, Ray Brown, Kenny Clarke, Max

Roach, Roy Haynes, and Art Blakey. Should everyone else of their generation have stopped playing, or should they have made the most that they could of what attracted them to the things they heard in those musicians? The answer is rather obvious, isn't it?

Innovators are no more—and no less—than individuals whose individuality demands dramatic reinterpretations of the present language, so much so that they add fresh choices to the community and to their idiom. They do not necessarily "advance" the music.

Adding is plenty. Is John Coltrane more advanced than Sonny Rollins or Charlie Parker or Lester Young or Coleman Hawkins? Hardly. He added some choices that they didn't, which is true of each of them as well. But a musician could ignore all of those players and put together a combination of Eddie "Lockjaw" Davis, Charlie Rouse, Paul Gonsalves, and Dewey Redman for something that would be highly individual as well, though it might not result in an entire school of thinking—that is proven by those four players themselves. Who is more of an individual than Davis or Rouse or Gonsalves or Redman?

Beyond the question of innovation, there is the absurd issue of what the music should be called and what gives it identity. Perhaps the most naïve are those who use Duke Ellington's discomfort with categories to justify their preferred idea that jazz should elude definition. They seem to think that Ellington himself had no idea what jazz was or that he was absolutely serious about his "beyond category" pronouncements.

Sure, he was serious, but not in the way that they think he was.

Ellington's music, whether secular or sacred, almost always addressed the irrefutable jazz fundamentals that have maintained themselves from generation to generation: 4/4 swing, blues, the meditative ballad, and the Spanish tinge. So it should be obvious that when he was attacking the reductive impact of categories, he was actually addressing the problem that anyone had in the arena of artistic respect when described as a jazz musician. After all, Ellington was born in 1899 and grew up when jazz was considered—in far too many circles—whorehouse music and was associated with the nightlife criminal types who came to power during the twenties, earning their slimy livings through the sale of illegal booze, prostitution, and gambling. Ellington, therefore, was dealing with academic, aesthetic, social, and racial prejudice. All the while, he was writing and playing jazz and leading a band of jazz musicians—jazz, and jazz alone.

January 2002

The Negro Aesthetic of Jazz

Jazz has always been a hybrid. A mix of African, European, Caribbean, and Afro-Hispanic elements. But the distinct results of that mix, which distinguished jazz as one of the new arts of the twentieth century, are now under assault by those who would love to make jazz no more than an "improvised music" free of definition. They would like to remove those elements that are essential to jazz and that came from the Negro. Troublesome person, that Negro.

Through the creation of blues and swing, the Negro discovered two invaluable things. With the blues, a fresh melodic could be framed within a short form of three chords that added a new feeling to Western music and inspired endless variations. In swing it was a unique way of phrasing that provided an equally singular pulsation. These two innovations were neither African nor European nor Asian nor Australian nor Latin nor South American; they were Negro-American.

Through the grand seer, Louis Armstrong, swinging and playing the blues moved to the high ground. After Armstrong straightened everyone out and indisputably pointed the way, there was a hierarchy in jazz, and that hierarchy was inarguably Negroid, so much so that many assumed Negro genius came from the skin and the blood, not from the mind. That is why one white musician brought a recording of the white New Orleans Rhythm Kings to Bix Beiderbecke and excitedly told him that they sounded "like real niggers." Ah, so. The issue was one of aesthetic skill, not color, not blood.

That white musician understood exactly what every black concert musician realized upon truly meeting the criteria of instrumental or vocal performance. At some point, perhaps even at the start, Leontyne Price learned that being black and from Laurel, Mississippi, did not shut her off from the art of Schubert, Wagner, or Puccini, no matter how far their European social worlds were from hers, in terms of history and geography. Nor did Price's becoming a master change those works she sang into German-Negro or Italian-Negro vocal art. They remained German and Italian and European, but were obviously available to anyone who could meet the measure of the music.

Hierarchy has always given Americans trouble. We believe that records are made to be broken, or to be broken free of, which is why, along with that pesky skin color, the Negroid elements central to jazz were rebelled against as soon as possible. Martin Williams, the late, great jazz critic and himself a white Southerner, told me once that there used to be a group of white jazz musicians who would say, when there were only white guys around, "Louis Armstrong and those people had a nice little primitive thing going, but we really didn't have what we now call jazz until Jack Teagarden, Bix, Trumbauer, and their gang gave it some sophistication. Bix is the one who introduced introspection to jazz. Without him you would have no Lester Young and no Miles Davis."

In such instances, Beiderbecke ceases to be a great musician and becomes a pawn in the ongoing attempt to deny the blues its primary identity as Negro-developed, introspective music, which is about coming to understand oneself and the world through contemplation. To recognize that would be to recognize the possibility of the Negro having a mind and one that could conceive an aesthetic overview that distinguished the music as a whole. Troublesome person, that Negro—especially one with an aesthetic.

The most recent version of the movement to neutralize the Negro aesthetic was made clear to me by a European twenty-five years ago. He told me that someday we would all embrace the idea of a great jazz drummer like Ed Blackwell improvising with Asian Indians, North Africans, South Americans, Europeans, and so on, each playing in the language of his culture on instruments from his homeland. "This, to me, is the jazz of the future," he said.

It sounded like the United Nations in an instrumental session to me, not the jazz that is more than improvisation alone, not the jazz that always engages 4/4 swing, blues, the romantic to meditative ballad, and Afro-Hispanic rhythm as core aesthetic elements. If these people from all over the world want to truly play with jazz masters such as Blackwell and be considered jazz musicians, they have to learn how to play the blues, how to swing, how to play through chord progressions—just as Leontyne Price had to meet the essential refinements of the music to set free the talents that made her famous.

Jazz is an art, not a subjective phenomenon. Negroes in America, through extraordinary imagination and new instrumental techniques, provided a worldwide forum for the expression of the woes and the wonders of human life. Look like what you look like, come from wherever you come from, be either sex and any religion, but understand that blues and that swing are there for you too—if you want to play jazz.

October 2002

Coltrane Derailed

With McCoy Tyner, Jimmy Garrison, and Elvin Jones, John Coltrane found new ways to swing, play blues and ballads, and use Afro-Latin grooves—the essential elements of jazz. But there are persistent questions buried deep in the John Coltrane mythos, ones that are hidden in the background of the discussion of his music because few professionals want to say publicly what they really think of him and the albums he made in the summer and fall of 1965 with augmented personnel—*Kulu Se Mama*, *Ascension*, *Om*, and *Meditations*—and the post-Classic Quartet LPs he made up until the end.

Before McCoy Tyner left the band in late 1965—unable to deal with the many squeakers, howlers, shriekers, and honkers his boss invited onto the bandstand—he asked Coltrane what he was doing. But the pianist could get no answer in musical terms, something that had not happened before. When Red Garland asked Coltrane if he truly believed in what he was doing—leading "the new thing"—the saxophonist said only that if he stopped he would abandon all of those who had followed him. Many then and now believe Coltrane's apprentices followed him into an artistic abyss.

Though he filled the It Club in Los Angeles in 1965, when Coltrane returned the following year with Pharaoh Sanders, Alice Coltrane, Jimmy Garrison, and Rashied Ali, there were three people in the room the night I heard him. Sanders says that they never talked about music and never rehearsed, but he feels that Coltrane was interested in experimenting with the saxophone because, being such a relatively new instrument, it had not been fully explored. Perhaps. But there are also rumors about hallucinogenic drugs, which intensify narcissism and spiritual fantasies.

Whatever the case, by 1966 Coltrane was not only having troubles in clubs, sometimes being fired on opening night, he could also empty an entire park, which, as Rashied Ali recalls, he did in Chicago. During that performance and others witnessed in New York, Coltrane put down the

saxophone and started shouting, yodeling, and screaming through the microphone while beating on his chest. The saxophonist told Ali that he
couldn't think of anything else to play on his horn so he tried that.

What could have led one of the intellectual giants of jazz—one of the
great bluesmen, one of the most original swingers and a master of the ballad—into an arena so emotionally narrow and so far removed from his
roots and his accomplishments? While *Interstellar Space*, the 1967 duets session with Ali, are models of their kind, and Coltrane's melody statements
are often majestic, the other post–mid-1965 recordings, whether studio or
live, are largely one-dimensional and do not vaguely compare to what
Coltrane accomplished with his Classic Quartet.

What Coltrane's late music does prove, however, is that he might well
have been caught up in the "hysteria of the times," as Cecil Taylor once
wrote of him. During that period of the 1960s, everything traditional was
under fire, from politics to ethnic identity, for both rational and irrational
reasons. It is not impossible to believe that Coltrane was attracted to the
romantic fantasies about Africa that black nationalists attempted to impose
on both Negroes at large and Negro artists. This was when Negroes sought
what should now be recognized as a laughable version of "authenticity"
that never assessed jazz itself with any actual depth.

In fact, much black nationalism was really about enormous self-hatred
and contempt for Negro-American culture. Its vision misled certain black
people into denying the depth of the indelibly rich domestic influences
black and white people had had on each other, regardless of all that had
been wrought by slavery and segregation. The greatest of John Coltrane's
music reflects that confluence of races and influences.

A country Negro from North Carolina, Coltrane was as much an heir to
all that Bach and his descendants gave the world as he was to the blues. He
was an heir to all that Negroes had done with the saxophone and what he
admired in Stan Getz. None of Coltrane's music, early or late, ever sounded
like African music because his classic band didn't play on one and three,
which Africans do, and because—until the end—they swung, which
Africans do not—nor does anybody else unaffected by that distinctly
Negro-American contribution to phrasing. (For those who persist in calling
jazz African music I ask but one question: Where in Africa is there anything that resembles the arpeggiated harmonic grandeur of Art Tatum or
Coleman Hawkins?)

Coltrane may have been on the way back from the abyss, however, before he died in 1967 at age forty. Rashied Ali remembers playing with Coltrane and Jimmy Garrison in a "straightahead" trio session recorded in Japan, interpreting standard songs. Near the end, Coltrane was calling McCoy Tyner and talking of how much he missed the old band. He even said to one saxophonist close to him that he was about to try and put the Classic Quartet back together. Perhaps Coltrane wanted to feel again all of the fresh beauty and swinging power that he had turned his back on.

September 2002

Jazz Criticism and
Its Effect on the Art Form

When I received a copy of the preceding paper, it appeared to have been written in one sitting, its very sloppiness symbolic of the lack of aesthetic seriousness so obvious in its content. In an effort to reduce the artistry of jazz to no more than political pulp, LeRoi Jones* has simplified the complexity of inspiration, invention, adaption, and context to a battlefield on which black victims war against a conspiracy of racist corporate heads and white jazz writers. Clearly, any analysis of Negro-American history that ignores racism as an enduring element would be naïve. But what Lincoln Kirstein called a "lazy bravado" (to describe what we have now come to expect from tenured Marxist revolutionaries) so dominates Jones's thesis that the grandeur of an internationally influential music has been reduced to either the cries of the victimized or the anthems of a homemade, far-left square dance. Jones further convolutes his largely hysterical argument by describing jazz as a latter-day variation on possession-oriented African religion, as well as an expressive protest against the conventions of Western art and the economics of capitalism. Only LeRoi Jones could try to strap such a lightweight saddle to the galloping horse of jazz and expect us to miss the fact that all he largely has to offer is a mouthful of dust.

But what we must address here, and what Jones clearly avoids as often as possible, is factual information that will provide us with a better understanding of the art itself and the strengths as well as the shortcomings of jazz criticism. It is quite true that spirit worship and possession were central to the music of the Africans brought into the Western Hemisphere as slaves. It is equally true that the drums were usually suppressed when it was learned that they could send messages. Yet it is also true that in the North-

---

*Throughout his paper, Stanley Crouch chose to refer to Amiri Baraka by his original name, LeRoi Jones.

east during the colonial era, slaves were allowed to celebrate holidays playing drums and performing African dances, as Eileen Southern documents in
The Music of Black Americans. She also makes it clear that as early as the late
eighteenth century, Negroes were influencing popular dance rhythms with
qualities that became universally popular. But those black people who
played fiddles during bondage or as free citizens were the result of a social
crucible that produced perhaps the most influential synthesis of Western
and non-Western ideas since the indelible impact of the Moors on Spanish
and southern European cultures. They were a new people—some mixed
with European blood, some with that of the American Indian, some with
Hispanic tributaries in their family lines. Above all, the raw impositions of
slavery ironically liberated them from the tribal enmities and religious conflicts that still bedevil contemporary Africa, allowing for a richly distinctive
Negro-American sensibility of remarkable national consequence.

What they maintained of their African heritage is far more important to
this discussion and to American culture than what they were forbidden to
perpetuate, what they lost, or what they forgot. What existed within the
ritual confinements of polytheistic African cultures and has been dubbed
"an affinity for distortion" was transformed into what I call *a sense of infinite
plasticity*. In Africa, this sense of plasticity has been observed in the stretching of necks with rings, the extending of lips with wooden plates, the filing
of teeth, the elasticizing of slit earlobes so that they could hold large
wooden discs, and so on. The plasticity of stylization in African singing allowed for a scope that included falsetto, whistles, tongue-clicking, shouts,
plaintive to joyous slurs, growls, and enormous changes of register, rhythm,
timbre, accent, and intensity. That the shifts of meter, tempo, and accent in
African drumming reflect this sense of plasticity almost goes without saying, as should any observation about dancing that demands independent
coordination of the head, shoulders, arms, trunk, and legs. As any contemporary visual artist knows, African masks are also given to plastic distortion,
with their multiple heads, huge eyes, angularity, intricate rhythms, and the
near-collision of materials—beads, stone, mud, wood, straw, metal, animal
skins, blood.

This disposition, this sense of plasticity or "affinity for distortion," had
an impact on professional Negro musicians at the same time that it was
functioning in a folk context. As we also learn from Southern's *The Music of
Black Americans*, by 1818 the immensely popular Frank Johnson's Colored
Band was observed "distorting a simple, and beautiful song, into a reel, a jig,

or country dance." In other words, Johnson, who was a resident of Philadelphia, was rhythmically rearranging the familiar in a surprising fashion, setting a precedent for what we would later hear from jazz musicians such as
Roy Eldridge, who in 1938 followed the slow rendition of "Body and Soul"
with a classic, up-tempo improvisation. Johnson also predicted the popularity of the golden era of Negro jazz bands that played for dances across
America. Johnson led marching bands up and down the East Coast, even as
far south as Richmond, Virginia, where one planter wrote of his ensemble,
"who ever heard better dance music than this?" In 1838, eighty-one years
before Ernest Ansermet was stunned by Sidney Bechet's improvisations
with Will Marion Cook's Southern Syncopated Orchestra during a European tour in 1919, Johnson made old England quite merry as he traveled,
putting his Negro-American rhythms on listeners and receiving a silver
bugle for his efforts when he played a Buckingham Palace command performance for Queen Victoria.

Between Frank Johnson and the jazz improvisation that was brought to
revolutionary fruition by Louis Armstrong, the folk source of the Negro
spiritual introduced a sense of profound joy and tragedy, an emotional
bloom of maturity that evolved into the bittersweet power of the blues,
that least sentimental of American vocal musics. Somewhere between the
spiritual and the blues arrived ragtime, a popular dance music that extended
the precedents set by Frank Johnson's Colored Band. As Roger Pryor
Dodge observed in *Harpsichords and Jazz Trumpets* in 1934:

> Ragtime, we now perceive, was the rhythmical twist the negro gave to the
> early American dance tune. Here, the different instruments were finding
> their place in the musical pattern and already daring to add their own
> peculiar instrumental qualities. But—suddenly, the whole breadth of
> melodic and harmonic difference between the *folk-tune* stuff Ragtime was
> made out of, and the Chant stuff the racial Blues were made out of,
> touched something very deep in the negro. He found himself going way
> beyond anything he had done so far. For he had now incorporated his
> own melodic Blues within his own syncopated dance rhythms and mirac-
> ulously created a new music—a new music which moved him so emotion-
> ally that Jazz bands sprang up like mushrooms all around him. The Blues,
> retrogressed hymn, secular spiritual, had fathered itself by way of the clar-
> inet, trumpet, trombone, banjo, drums and piano into a rebirth, and chris-
> tened itself JAZZ!

Dodge's writing presented the richest ideas in early jazz criticism be-cause he heard the art within a serious context, understanding that impro-visation wasn't the incredibly new thing many thought it to be, pointing out that "[i]f we turn to the musical literature of the seventeenth and eigh-teenth centuries we find that no two artists were supposed to play identical variations and ornaments on the same piece; on the contrary, the artist was expected extemporaneously to fill in rests, ornament the whole notes and rhythmically break up chords. The basic melody, as in Jazz, was considered common property. If the player exactly imitated somebody else or faith-fully followed the written composition of another composer, he was a stu-dent, not a professional." As a dancer, Dodge wasn't put off by the fact that jazz was performed for a dancing public. Still describing the seventeenth- and eighteenth-century European context, he went on to say:

At that time one listened first, as one does now in Jazz, for the melody, then recognized the variations as such and drew intense enjoyment from the musical talent familiarly inspired. Instead of waiting months for a show piece to be composed and then interpreted (our modern academic procedure), then, in one evening, you could hear a thousand beautiful pieces, as you can now in Jazz. Instead of going to a dance hall to hear Armstrong, in earlier times you might have gone to church and heard Frescobaldi; or danced all night to Haydn's orchestra; or attended a salon and listened to Handel accompany a violinist—with his extemporaneous variations so matter of course; or sneaked in on one of Bach's little evenings at home, when to prove his theory of the well-tempered clavier he would improvise in every key, not a stunt improvisation in the manner of someone else, but preludes and fugues probably vastly superior to his famous notated ones.

Dodge then made a point that is perhaps even more important today than it was half a century ago, given the irrefutably dull ways in which students tend to play the transcriptions learned in most jazz teaching situations:

Academicians of today can improvise in the styles of various old schools but the result is commonplace, not only because the fact of improvising in a school that is out of date, but because such an urge is precious and weak in itself, limiting the improvisor to forms he has already seen in print. Even in contemporary modern music, the working out is so intellectual that the extempore act does not give the modernist time to concoct anything he himself would consider significant.

I would strongly disagree with the idea that certain jazz schools might now be considered out of date: Classic languages have been developed since Dodge's era that can inspire young improvisors to find their own identities, just as developing artists with a variety of schools to choose from within a given idiom have always done, given the intrinsic merit of the styles that inspire. Yet the contemporary problem of the academic is as real as the fact of death, whether it is the young musician who sounds more like a recording than an improvisor or the pretentious composer so in awe of twentieth-century concert music that we are asked to suffer through third-rate Stravinsky, Schoenberg, Bartók, Messiaen, Stockhausen, and even the leftovers from the minimalist school—the last imitation especially surprising in face of the fact that the repeated melodic or rhythmic kernel known as the riff was a Kansas City dance-band building block fifty years ago!

What Dodge contributed in that essay, and in a later attack on the many critical pieces of one sort or another that had appeared by the time he wrote "Consider the Critics" in 1939, was the sense that jazz was at once a decidedly Western music but one that had developed its own instrumental, rhythmic, and harmonic styles. Dodge was limited largely to what he and many others called the "hot" style that grew to fruition by the middle 1920s; he was incapable of hearing the refinements that Ellington was making in a decidedly avant-garde way, just as he missed the point of bebop. But it is not the role of a critic to know everything or to be right at every instance. The job is to illuminate, and illumination is the true art of criticism. Dodge recognized the dangers of pretension, and he was smart enough to know that once techniques that were initially considered bizarre become part of a recognizable tradition, it is rank foolishness to pursue only the bizarre when there are true accomplishments from which to build new ideas. "The whole confused attitude towards Modern Art," he wrote in *Consider the Critics*, ". . . hung on one hook, and still hangs on it to a degree, that shock must prevail, that it is only from him who shocks that we may expect Modern Art!"

Yet when Dodge wrote *Harpsichords and Jazz Trumpets*, his discussion of the piano's potential was perhaps the most far-reaching of any jazz criticism written before the middle of the 1950s. Thelonious Monk was seventeen years old when Dodge laid out a vision of the piano in jazz that had yet to emerge:

Owing to the conspicuous commonplaces of our virtuosi, the negro pianist only too easily slips into the fluid superficialities of a Liszt cadenza. This tendency of the negro to imitate the florid piano music of the 19th century which he hears all around him, has kept the piano backward in finding its own jazz medium. It takes a very developed musical sense to improvise significantly on the piano, a talent for thinking in more than one voice. The counterpoint that Jazz instruments achieve [in the] ensemble is possible to a certain extent on the piano alone, but this takes a degree of development Jazz has not yet reached. The best piano solos so far, in my opinion, are the melodic "breaks" imitating [the] trumpet and trombone. Lately the pianist has found some biting chords, and felt a new desire to break up melody, not only rhythmically as inspired by the drum, but rhythmically as a percussion instrument fundamentally inspired by its own peculiar harmonic percussion. This, perhaps, will lead him to contribute something no other musician has.

That is what I consider first-class jazz writing, because its insight into the future style of Thelonious Monk was based upon the specifics of the idiom itself, rather than on an attempt to make it sound more European by reducing the aesthetic elements that made the music such a singular phenomenon in the first place.

What was wrong in 1939, when Dodge took on the abundance of flimsy ideas about the music, is still wrong. This problem, of course, is not exclusive to jazz. Like most American criticism, jazz writing is either too academic to communicate with any people other than professionals, or it is so inept in its enthusiasm or so cowardly in its willingness to submit to fashion that it has failed to gain jazz the respect among intelligent people necessary for its support as more than a popular art.

Unlike the European improvisation that Dodge described, jazz is primarily a performance art that takes place in an ensemble context of collective improvisation. Until the middle 1960s, the music's basic vocabulary had to be redefined in a functional sense by every generation that could be considered innovative. Adventurous musicians had to redefine the blues, four/four swing (fast, medium, and slow), the ballad, and the Afro-Hispanic or "Latin" rhythm that Jelly Roll Morton suggested when he used the term "the Spanish tinge." Those were technical requirements that had been in place at least since 1940, the result of a continual wrestling with the problem of form, perhaps initiated by Buddy Bolden in New Orleans near the turn of the century.

I think that those technical requirements demand that the jazz writer know how to illuminate a given performance in terms sufficiently specific to let the reader in on aesthetic thrills or to warn the layman against ineptitude or fraud. These are the functions of all intelligent criticism. And however much people such as LeRoi Jones are obsessed with content over form, claiming that formal attention is some version of Western imperialism dressed in aesthetic armor, what made Louis Armstrong and every other important jazz musician so significant to the music of this century was much more than feeling or a susceptibility to uncontrolled trance; it was the ability to create logical music on the wing, responding both to the structure at hand and to the invention of his fellow players. Only the catatonic are incapable of feeling, but what separates the artist from others is more than the nature of his or her passion; it is the skill that allows an interior human feeling to move all the way out into the world as an objective artifact, replete with the synthesis of technical mastery and expression that makes for all living, as opposed to academic, art.

So it is the illumination of the life, the vitality of the art, that is the fundamental issue. Taste and opinion are always individual—or should be—and every writer will prefer certain styles, instrumentalists, singers, and composers over others. What is essential, however, is integrity, an integrity based upon as clear a perception of the identity of the art as possible. Though there have almost always been debates over the racial components of jazz, it is obviously an Afro-American form, meaning that the irreplaceable force at the center of its identity has been the musical imagination of the Negro. But this fact does not imply that white musicians, listeners, and critics have no place in the making or the evaluation of the idiom. Its Afro-American essence isn't nullified by whites, anymore than Jessye Norman's singing of Schubert or Leontyne Price's renditions of Puccini neutralize the German and Italian origins of those musics. Yet when I once heard Woody Herman say to Edwin Newman that jazz was initially the black man's music but white musicians made it universal, I wondered what the response would have been had a Negro performer of European concert music claimed that the idiom was originally the white man's music but black concert artists had made it universal!

Human meaning and human value are what make an idiom universal, nothing else. Specific stylistic elements are the things that create individual, idiomatic identity, and style is inevitably a code for the perception of human life and human meaning in a particular context. When Leontyne Price performs *Tosca*, what we observe is that Italian opera is so inclusive that a Negro from Laurel, Mississippi, can meet its requirements and express her own artistic identity as well.

Parallel truths are witnessed when we hear a white American play good jazz, or when we listen to a Gypsy named Django Reinhardt light up the guitar with such authority on his recordings that we can understand why Duke Ellington, who took a backseat to no one in terms of ethnic pride, chose Reinhardt as his special guest for performances with the greatest idiomatic orchestra in the history of jazz. Consequently, to recognize the core component of the Negro when we discuss jazz is not to pander to genetic theories or to the superficial impositions of lightweight political theories; it is to recognize cultural facts too well documented to argue. America obviously has much to do with it, since no comparable so-called minority of African extraction has produced as internationally influential a body of artists, performers, athletes, entertainers, and even political visionaries as the United States. As Albert Murray observes in his extraordinary *Stomping the Blues*: "The synthesis of European and African musical elements in the West Indies, the Caribbean, and in continental Latin America produced calypso, rhumba, the tango, the conga, mambo, and so on, but not the blues and not ragtime, and not that extension, elaboration, and refinement of blues-break riffing and improvisation which came to be known as jazz." And no Africans in the history of the modern world have come to mean what Louis Armstrong and Duke Ellington symbolize in this century. Were it merely a matter of genetics, or even oppression, this would not be the case.

Armstrong, who is to jazz improvisation what the Wright Brothers were to aerodynamics, and Ellington, who is to jazz orchestration what D. W. Griffith was to the grammar of cinema, represent freedom, eloquence, discipline, lyricism, sexuality, joy, tragedy, ambivalence, and transcendent elegance as aesthetically expressed through jazz. They were the products of a culture so peculiar and so penetrating that it inspired converts far beyond the distinctions of skin tone. Though I fundamentally disagree with the conclusions that Martin Williams arrived at about the comparative quality of the Fletcher Henderson and Benny Goodman orchestras in a 1984 essay entitled "Just Asking," Williams raises some questions that are unavoidable when considering the influence of jazz and the quality of jazz criticism. As a white man near sixty who has been writing extremely well about jazz for at least thirty years, Williams asks questions about Goodman and about Mick Jagger. For the purpose of this discussion, I will only cite what he asks about Goodman, then quote his final questions about the success of both:

Putting it in terms of my generation: why would it be that a young man growing up in Chicago in the teens of this century, the son of Russian Jewish immigrant parents, would want to learn to play the clarinet like a colored Creole from New Orleans named Jimmie Noone? Why would the act of doing that be so meaningful to him? And having done that, why would he then want to form an orchestra that played like that of an American mulatto from Georgia named Fletcher Henderson? And stake his career in music on doing that? And after that, why would the world make him a celebrity and one of the most famous musicians of the century?

Of course there is the question of why mass audiences seemed to want to hear Goodman over Henderson and Jagger over Muddy Waters. But it can't be blamed on Goodman that more people wanted to hear him than wanted to hear Chick Webb, or on Jagger that more people attended him than John Lee Hooker.

My question here is what drew Benny and Mick to make such music in the first place, and such large audiences to want to hear it at all? Both men obviously express something deeply, abidingly important to their followers. What is it?

Why do we all, at whatever level, find such meaning in the musical culture of Afro-Americans? Why has their music so triumphed throughout the world? We invoke it to get through our adolescence and most of us keep it, one way or another, central in our lives.

Those are the kinds of questions only a critic with integrity would ask, questions only a person committed to the high seriousness necessary to inform, challenge, and stimulate would publicly contemplate. One aspect of what Williams poses takes in the human level that is inextricably woven into the experience of artistic inspiration and communication, the other encompasses the relationship of race to American economic success. On one level, I think that the appeal of jazz has been its daring, its charming cockiness, its projection of individual human value as expressed in a collective context. There is also what I consider a double consciousness very different from the one described by Du Bois. What I refer to is the expression of sorrow or melancholy in a melodic line that is contrasted by a jaunty or exuberant rhythm, that combination of grace and intensity we know as swing. In jazz, sorrow rhythmically transforms itself into joy, which is perhaps the point of the music: joy earned or arrived at through performance, through creation.

That affirmative underpinning of swing has always been explicitly or implicitly connected to dance, but the appeal of Afro-American rhythm is much older than jazz, even older than the emergence of Frank Johnson's Colored Band. Joseph Marks, in *America Learns to Dance*, quotes an observer who was startled in 1789 when he saw some undergraduates at Princeton "dancing up and down the entry as a Negro played upon a violin with twenty students hallooing and tearing about." Since dancing is so important to every culture in some form or another, it is understandable that the group that we see inventing so many of the steps and so much of the music that goes with them would penetrate so deeply into the consciousness of the society. Beyond that, there is the fact that in the United States the technological elements that make for the modern age were developing in tandem with the complexity of social evolution that took place when the issue of democracy had to meet the multiracial components of American culture.

There is another fact that cannot be ignored in this discussion. Ours is a century in which percussion and polyrhythm are fundamental to its identity, in which the machinery of the age and the activities of the people parallel the multilinear densities and rhythms of the very rain forest that could easily have been the inspiration for Africa's drum choirs, with their broad sense of sound and their involvement with perpetual rhythmic motion. The celebratory rhythm of swing became a new kind of lyricism, a feeling that gave the drums a fundamental position in an art music that didn't disavow dance, a role in which set and improvised syncopation took on a fresh fluency. The result was that Negro-Americans put the Western world on two and four, asserting a conception of time that created an uproar when Stravinsky emulated the accents of a ragtime band in his *Rite of Spring*. As Wynton Marsalis points out, "Stravinsky turned European music over with a backbeat. Check it out. What they thought was weird and primitive was just a Negro beat on the bass drum."

I would also submit that cinematic cross-cutting is not only percussive but antiphonal, a visual call and response as indispensable to modern imagery as it has always been to Negro field hollers, church music, and jazz improvisation. Further, I would say that the close-up parallels the jazz solo, the featured voice. In fact, Fred Astaire, perhaps the most famous and successful American dancer of the century, became a screen star by often using the Negro pedal percussion of tap dance and performing most of his numbers to Tin Pan Alley songs such as "Top Hat" that could not have arrived without the inspiration of Negro melody and phrasing. And considering that James Reese Europe collaborated with Vernon and Irene Castle, writing the music for the dances they popularized and inventing the fox-trot and the turkey trot, we can see with clarity a line easily traceable back to 1789, when those Princeton students began to shake their cakes to the intoxicating music of the Negro. Combine all those elements with the Negro-American vision of infinite plasticity as expressed in the democratic ensemble of the jazz band, and I believe that you have the answer to Williams's question about the overwhelming appeal of Afro-American musical culture.

The subject of white success over that of black is grating and sobering, sometimes depressing, but the fact that soars above all those inequities is that the lasting aesthetic achievements of black musicians haven't been lessened by the taste of the public. The thrill one experiences in listening to the recordings Count Basie's band made when it came roaring out of Kansas City to redefine swing and elevate the thrust and depth of the rhythm section isn't minimized by the differences in Basie's and Goodman's paychecks. What we can actually draw great comfort from is an incredible victory for dedication, knowing that Negro musicians, regardless of what could have been discouraging career obstacles, continued to create splendid music that has withstood, as all true art does, the inexorable passage of time.

We can explain the public preference for Goodman by simply citing racism. We could further that by noting that the sexual energy that always curls and pulsates somewhere inside dance was more easily accepted, matinee-idol style, when the music that provoked those movements was played by white bands. We needn't even agree with Freud to use his area of speculation as an acknowledgment of the truth that sexuality is far from simple; nor, at this point, do we have to pretend that the sexual access of and to Negro men has not inspired much of the violence at the most furious end of racist practices. Discrimination always maintains a who's who in the boudoir. That, perhaps, explains why Caucasians playing Afro-American styles have often been more popular than the artistic merits of their own works would objectively indicate.

As far as the Mick Jaggers, Cyndi Laupers, and Bruce Springsteens are concerned, unlike LeRoi Jones, I'm not particularly interested in the careers of pop stars, nor do I care about black recording labels such as Motown that showed no affinity for jazz. Even the question of racism seems no more the point, especially since a rail-tailed Negro named Michael Jackson sold more copies of a single album than any singer or instrumentalist in recorded history; or a blind Negro named Stevie Wonder has earned more dollars than the most popular composers and instrumentalists in both jazz and European concert music; or a horse-faced Negro from the South named Lionel Richie pulls down millions for songs that contain so little melodic, harmonic, and rhythmic character that even the most imaginative jazz musicians haven't tried to use them as bridges to a larger audience in the way they could when the best of Tin Pan Alley was in flower.

What I am concerned about, and what I see as the task facing the serious writer about jazz, is how the literature on the music might help create a following for the art in this country that would parallel the listening public that European concert music has. I say "in this country" because jazz musicians do very well outside this country—the best ones, the journeymen, the mediocre, and even the fakes. But in the United States, since jazz is no longer the popular music it was fifty years ago, the problem is getting its aesthetic richness appreciated by all who consider themselves sophisticated and civilized. Again, unlike European concert music, the idiom hasn't inspired the support of wealthy patrons (black or white), the erection of concert halls, or quality explanation in the most prestigious musical institutions across the country. This is where the battle for jazz writing really lies—not in the arena of popular music. Our era is characterized by a lack of interest in variation and by a love of repetition that dominates the sound of popular music, making it much harder for the jazz musician to achieve the attention of the listener. Ironically, the appetite for mindless trance-states that LeRoi Jones celebrates can best be witnessed in the world's discos. Perhaps this is why some people say that Hitler was the first rock star; his message inspired the masses of Germany to turn their backs on the complex demands of modern life in favor of brutish primitivism. As André Hodeir wrote in *Toward Jazz*, "the crowd's need to be convinced is the nose by which it is most easily led. The millions of addlepates who cheered Hitler on the eve of World War were expressing and sharing an absolute conviction; many of them died before they could realize that their enthusiasm reflected nothing more than abysmal feeblemindedness."

So the jazz writer has a big job, a task that demands illuminating an idiom dominated by adult passion in an era overshadowed by an international appetite for adolescent obsessiveness. Living in a world where adults too frequently look upon teenagers as sages, we must know we are no longer in a jazz age; the music that first took virtuoso flight on the wings of Louis Armstrong's imagination dispensed with sentimentality, spoke as directly and as ambivalently about adult sexuality as *Ulysses*, and allowed for the perpetual rejuvenation of material through the process of improvisation. It is the art of grown men and grown women, which was part of its appeal and part of its attraction to the young musicians who were bitten by the night creature of jazz. In order to serve this idiom, we must speak of it with the insights expected of adults, not some one-dimensional fervor for a beat, not some savage attraction to frothing intensity that fails to express the bittersweet stretch of human feeling, and not some political theory that reduces a long march of heroic achievement to checkers on a board of supposed scientific materialism.

At this point, after many years of avant-garde frauds and sellouts to the rock-and-roll god of fusion, we are lucky to see a growing number of young musicians, most of them black, who are committing themselves to jazz. Wynton Marsalis has been an extraordinary catalyst in this resurgence of interest among young musicians in jazz, but he is only an indication of what is now taking place. Every few months, another young man or woman, black or white, arrives in New York expressing the ambition to swing and to meet the artistic standards set by the music's greatest practitioners. This is something that all of us who believe in jazz must be grateful for, because the vast majority of those who were considered avant-garde twenty years ago represented the first generation in the history of the art who were incapable of meeting the technical standards set by their predecessors. Unlike Charlie Parker, who could play with anyone, or John Coltrane, who so mastered his tradition that even Johnny Hodges admired his work on the recording Coltrane made with Duke Ellington, these supposed avant-garde players arrogantly described their narrow skills as expressive of stylistic advances. But history and aesthetic standards are now manhandling the bulk of them, though others still escape under the cover of arguments bootlegged from the world of cultural anthropology, where relative value is trumpeted as a shield against racism.

To achieve the respect for the idiom that it deserves, the jazz writer must accurately perceive real mastery as opposed to rhetorical compensations for incompetence, and should know the difference between thorough contributions to jazz and the submissions to pop trends or the pretensions to European avant-gardism that shape the work of those talented but misled musicians incapable of inventing fresh directions within the parameters of the jazz tradition. In considering the attempt to make something of value out of the mire Miles Davis pushed jazz into, we should remember what Roger Pryor Dodge wrote of the premiere of *Rhapsody in Blue*:

February 12 now stood for two births, that of Abraham Lincoln and the *Rhapsody in Blue*. Critics, whose business was sharp musical observation, succumbed to the reasoning that something vital must have occurred since a concert crowd roared. Even those sympathetic to Gershwin's bathos, but trained enough to recognize and comment upon the inept handling of the completely familiar concerto form, followed the line of least resistance.

And as far as those who claim to be working at the frontiers of the art are concerned, we should be aware of what Hodeir wrote of Thelonious Monk in 1959: "Monk's solution, though related in some ways to the formal conceptions of serious modern music, is not indebted, for its guiding principles, to any school of music, past or present, which is foreign to jazz; this, I feel, is essential." Regardless of what quarrels one might have with certain other ideas of Hodeir's, he hit the appropriate after-beat in the perpetual rhythm of dialogue between this art and its commentary. If we examine what is presented as innovative, it is our responsibility to also understand what Hodeir meant when he wrote in the same essay: "Ten years of mediocre row music have taught us that discontinuity can, at times, be no more than an alibi for incoherence." Alibis can never stand in for the truths of artistic beauty, and if we are to spread the word on jazz with any authority, we must know the difference between them.

September 1986

Jazz's Own Sweet Time

Jazz drumming has no precedent in music history. It is an original way of putting together and playing drums and cymbals, which introduced a new kind of virtuosity demanding independent coordination of all four limbs. The swinging time jazz drummers keep—whether 4/4 or not—is profound because that pulsation arrives as part of the only Western fine-art music given to melody, harmony, and counterpoint in which the statement of the very meter itself, however syncopated, is a lively and thoughtful aesthetic aspect of the music.

Today there is a stereotyped idea of swing as a very narrow thing, but the fluidity of jazz time is exactly the reverse. This has misled some to believe that jazz time is metronomic. Jazz time is almost never metronomic.

Unlike the metronome, which rigidly ticks and tocks its way, jazz drumming keeps the tempo and functions as part of the highly nuanced antiphony among the players that helps define and determine the quality of the improvising. Time is played and played with. It speaks and is spoken to. Further, as any close listener knows, when a musician suddenly rises with what Ron Carter calls "the strongest beat," that person will take over the feeling of the rhythm, and the others will go in that direction. That is part of the freedom and the power of jazz.

Anthony Braxton once said to me that Connie Kay "had fifty ways to play 4/4." While I am not sure that fifty is an accurate number, the last time I heard Kay with the Modern Jazz Quartet, at the Carlyle Hotel, he approached 4/4 time from so many different angles, mixing shuffle grooves, gospel beats, and something from the Caribbean. He did all of this while playing with so much control that the unmiked piano, vibraphone, and bass were perfectly audible throughout. I have rarely heard such virtuosity.

Some young drummers are so unaware of what their predecessors have achieved that they will contemptuously dismiss playing time as "holding the listener's hand," when the question of how many swinging ways one can play time, or how many swinging grooves one can bring off, or how many swinging tempos one can play never comes up. Such young drummers think that there is a great achievement to ignoring all of that and playing percussive coloration, "like a symphony drummer," as one bassist described a controversial "free" drummer to me almost forty years ago. (Yes, people have been playing like that for forty years. Ask Sunny Murray.)

Percussive coloration—timbre, reverberation, and register—is a basic element of altering jazz time. Strokes on drums tend to have little ring; they are there and gone. With a cymbal, the stroke is the beginning of the sound, which means that the key to the ride cymbal is making that ring swing. A beat played on a closed sock cymbal is a different beat when played on an open sock—or, as Tony Williams so cleverly realized, a triplet figure played by Elvin Jones on his snare drum had a very different effect when executed on a cymbal heavy with reverberation. As for something like "white noise"—of the hissing, pitchless sort heard in electronic music—the brushes handle that, creating purely modern timbres while swinging or, as masters of ballad drumming show, singing.

The super-swinging quality of invention Al Foster brings to his understanding of these issues is audible in the varied pings as well as burrs or metallic slurs and smears he imposes on his cymbal sound through highly sophisticated touches. This approach pulls more than one tonal quality from each of his drums which might be struck anywhere from the center to the rim. On Latin tunes, Foster might use a different version of that groove *every* chorus. I believe this is an innovation.

Compared to such achievements and the kinds of drama and overall effects they bring to jazz drumming, merely playing percussive coloration might be interesting—even forty years later—but it is more than a bit "neo-conservative" when one realizes that such approaches to percussion have been in concert music since Edgard Varèse wrote "Ionisation" nearly eighty years ago.

If one were to do, as one superb example, what Herlin Riley does during "Gagaku" on Wynton Marsalis's *Jump Start and Jazz* (Columbia, 1996) and bring such highly unusual rhythms into the world of swinging, we would hear something fresh that—finally—builds upon the conceptions Tony Williams brought to the Blue Note avant-garde of the 1960s. That, however, would demand actual aesthetic thought, something we witness little of in an era when "advanced" almost always means either imitating European concert music or going ethnic and "inclusive."

November 2002

Putting the White Man in Charge

Because Negroes invented jazz, and because the very best players have so often been Negroes, the art has always been a junction for color trouble in the world of evaluation and promotion. By the end of the 1920s, Duke Ellington was trying to get his buddies to call their art "Negro music," possibly because Paul Whiteman had been dubbed "The King of Jazz." Variations on this phenomenon have risen and fallen throughout the history of the art.

Since the 1960s, however, certain Negroes who *cannot* play will claim to be of aesthetic significance on the basis of sociology and some irrelevant ancestral connection to Africa—which provided only *part* of the mix that became jazz. That had an ironic impact because we are now back to the Paul Whiteman phenomenon, as if all of those white people who had to put up with black nonsense now have their chance to express their rage. This time white musicians who *can* play are too frequently elevated far beyond their abilities in order to allow white writers to make themselves feel more comfortable about being in the role of evaluating an art from which they feel substantially alienated. Now, having long been devoted to creating an establishment based on "rebellion," or what Rimbaud called the "love of sacrilege," they have achieved a moment long desired: Now certain kinds of white men can focus their rebellion on the Negro. Oh, happy day.

In his essential *Blues Up and Down*, Tom Piazza pulled the covers off of these men when he wrote: "Many jazz reviewers—especially among the generation that grew up in the 1960s and '70s—suffer from intense inferiority feelings in front of the musicians they write about. This results in a vacillation between an exaggerated hero-worship of musicians and an exaggerated sense of betrayal when the musicians don't meet their needs." Piazza surely knew what he was talking about, especially since he was a white man who had been among these jazz writers *when nobody dark was around*, which allowed him to understand them and their various insecurities and their various resentments close up.

232

In Francis Davis's *Like Young: Jazz, Pop, Youth and Middle Age*, one can get a good deal of insight into Piazza's thesis. It is a classic of its kind. Davis unintentionally makes it clear that he is intimidated by Negroes and also quite jealous of them. The intimidation arrives because of the troubles and the fun he imagines Negroes having when he is not around. The resentment flares if these Negroes have *any* power to define themselves and what they are doing or if they have reputations independent of Davis's permission or if they cannot be conventionally condescended to from the abolitionist's perspective that so many jazz writers have in common. Their job, they believe, is to speak up for the exotic Negro or use that Negro as a weapon against their own middle-class backgrounds or make that Negro into a symbol of their desire to do something bold, wild, and outside of convention. Even being in the *presence* of such stuff will do, since Davis points out that rap now allows the young white person to come in contact with the Negro most removed from the white world, which used to be the role of jazz. Is that so? Since the rap Negro is nothing more, at his most "street," than a theatrical version of Zip Coon, a character from the minstrel shows, how is he removed from the white world? Every Negro inferior to a middlebrow white man like Davis fits comfortably in the white world, where black refinement is never expected or is dismissed as pompous.

Disturbed by the way things have gone over the last couple of decades, Davis's answer to his Negro problem is to create an alternative order of significance. He sees, as do so many of these men, jazz that is based on swing and blues as the enemy and, therefore, lifts up someone like, say, Dave Douglas, as an antidote to too much authority from the dark side of the tracks. Douglas, a graduate of Exeter and a dropout from the New Jersey upper-middle class, is the perfect white man to lead the music "forward." Unlike these misled uptown Negroes who spend too much time messing around with stuff like the blues and swinging, Downtown Dave brings truly new stuff into jazz, like Balkan folk material that surely predates the twentieth century in which blues and jazz were born.

There is nothing wrong with Douglas, who can play what he can play and who should continue to do whatever he wants to do, but there is something pernicious about Davis and all of those other white guys who want so badly to put white men—American and European—in charge and put Negroes in the background. Douglas, whom I have heard since he worked as a sideman years ago with Vincent Herring, is far from being a bad musician, but he also knows that he should keep as much distance as possible between himself and trumpet players like Wallace Roney, Terence Blanchard, and Nicholas Payton, to name but three, any one of whom on any kind of material—chordal, nonchordal, modal, free, whatever—would turn him into a puddle on the bandstand. Unlike the great white players of the past, such as Jack Teagarden, Bobby Hackett, Benny Goodman, Stan Getz, Lee Konitz—or, now, Joe Lovano—Douglas will never be seen standing up next to black masters of the idiom. The white critical establishment couldn't help him then.

But the deepest part of this is that it, finally, is not so much about color as it is about the destruction of the Negro aesthetic, which is why Negroes like Don Byron and Mark Turner are embraced. They accept an imposed aesthetic of "pushing the envelope" in ways that have nothing to do with blues and swing. Above all, they help these writers to bring things disguised as bulls into the middle-class china shops in which these critics themselves were born.

April 2003

Piano Prodigy

What is actually going on out in the jazz world is very different from what one usually reads about in jazz magazines or what one would conclude from taking critics' polls seriously. There are musicians out here who not only can play but who have continued to develop their skills outside of the praises of the critical establishment, whose words of admiration are usually reserved for those musicians who claim to be moving the music "forward" but who are never heard of outside of their small circles (primarily because they don't impress other musicians who can actually play).

One ignored example of a consummate jazz musician is Eric Reed, who—with the exceptions of Bill Charlap and Brad Mehldau at their very best—can easily outplay all other piano players under forty. Neither Mehldau nor Charlap can walk past him either; it's just that all three, for now, are in a circle reserved for the most formidable.

One needn't be hostile toward any of the younger so-called avant-garde pianists to notice why Reed is superior to all of them. After all, these supposed avant-gardists are never caught swinging, but they will annex hip-hop rhythms, use electronic gimmicks, and be celebrated for "keeping jazz alive." Reed's superiority is technical, emotional, and aesthetic: He has far greater command of the keyboard and of the pedals as well as the touches and nuances which make him a first-class jazz pianist.

Listen to how soulful and free of clichés he can be on some blues (hear his "Blues Five Spot" on *Manhattan Melodies*), or how well he can hear his way through very complex harmonies, or the size of the sound he can get out of his *fingers*—not by banging the instrument with his arms. In the "Jazz Composer Portraits" series that he produced for Columbia University, Reed has made it clear that he is not only quite an individual but also a charming bandleader and arranger.

At Columbia, I heard Reed give two concerts. One featured the music of Billy Strayhorn; the other the music of Eric Dolphy. Each was well rehearsed, and the musicians did not come on the bandstand looking as though they were rehearsing in somebody's garage or basement (which is surely the influence of rock, that screw-you conception of looking like an unmade bed.)

At the Strayhorn concert, after his arrangements sufficiently featured fine players such as Frank Wess and Lew Soloff on other numbers, Reed took a very long solo on "Blues in Orbit." He was absolutely splendid. The improvisation was built on a few motives that were tried in every register, using the whole keyboard. The motives which began as trills, built to a couple of notes, which then became entire phrases. The phrases evolved into complete, thematic choruses, each phrased in one sweep of twelve bars, wrung out in marvelously controlled varieties of timbre. An improvised masterpiece.

When playing the Dolphy music, which is *extremely* hard, Reed managed to still swing, swing, swing. He outplayed everyone, too, which was no simple task since he used Marcus Printup, Greg Osby, James Carter, and the marvelous Steve Nelson, the lone vibraphonist between Bobby Hutcherson and Stefon Harris.

Gifted with perfect pitch and soaked in the soul source of Negro church music (his late father was a minister), Reed came to the public's attention on Wynton Marsalis's *In This House, on This Morning*. In that band's broad context, Reed came to master the sweep of jazz piano, from New Orleans to the present. For an example of Reed's imagination, listen to his feature on "Brake's Sake" on *Standard Time, Vol. 4: Marsalis Plays Monk*.

Or check him out on Marsalis's *Live at the Village Vanguard*. Reed's humorously "out" invention on "Uptown Ruler" contains a startling twenty-four-bar run of sustained thematic and rhythmic complexity that *addresses the time*, starting at 6:39 into the piece and not ending until 7:04. Then there's "Pedro's Getaway," where—like Wynton Kelly on "Blue 'n' Boogie" from Wes Montgomery's *Full House*—Reed starts smoking on the first beat!

Reed has also learned, from Monk and Ellington, how to creatively accompany the rhythm section, as if he is playing an arrangement, which means, among other things, laying out chords with a melodic direction, inventing riffs, contrasting piano registers with those of the featured player, and moving around in the time so that harmony arrives with the ultimate amount of drama as well as subtlety.

I once saw grand master Tommy Flanagan at a Javon Jackson gig on which Reed was the pianist. Usually much less than loquacious, Flanagan stayed all night and raved ecstatically about the younger pianist. Peter

Washington, who worked with Flanagan for fifteen years and was playing bass that night with Jackson, commented on how well Reed could handle the time and the exciting clarity of his ideas and execution.

If you get a chance to hear Eric Reed, don't miss your moment. Some changes will be made, some serious rhythmic invention will take place, some deep soul will be displayed, and some real jazz will be heard.

May 2003

DETOURS AHEAD

On the Corner

The Sellout of Miles Davis

The contemporary Miles Davis, when one hears his music or watches him perform, deserves the description that Nietzsche gave of Wagner, "the greatest example of self-violation in the history of art." Davis made much fine music for the first half of his professional life, and represented for many the uncompromising Afro-American artist contemptuous of Uncle Tom, but he has fallen from grace—and been celebrated for it. As usual, the fall from grace has been a form of success. Desperate to maintain his position at the forefront of modern music, to sustain his financial position, to be admired for the hipness of his purported innovations, Davis turned butt to the beautiful in order to genuflect before the commercial.

Once given to exquisite dress, Davis now comes on the bandstand draped in the expensive bad taste of rock 'n' roll. He walks about the stage, touches foreheads with the saxophonist as they play a duet, bends over and remains in that ridiculous position for long stretches as he blows at the floor, invites his white female percussionist to come, midriff bare, down a ramp and do a jungle-movie dance as she accompanies herself with a talking drum, sticks out his tongue at his photographers, leads the din of electronic clichés with arm signals, and trumpets the many facets of his own force with amplification that blurts forth a sound so decadent that it can no longer disguise the shriveling of its maker's soul.

Beyond the terrible performances and the terrible recordings, Davis has also become the most remarkable licker of monied boots in the music business, willing now to pimp himself as he once pimped women when he was a drug addict. He can be seen on television talking about the greatness of Prince, or claiming (in his new autobiography, *Miles*) that the Minneapolis vulgarian and borderline drag queen "can be the new Duke Ellington of our time if he just keeps at it." Once nicknamed Inky for his dark complexion, Davis now hides behind the murky fluid of his octopus fear of being old hat, and claims that he is now only doing what he has always done—move ahead, take the music forward, submit to the personal curse that is his need for change, the same need that brought him to New York from St. Louis in 1944, in search of Charlie Parker.

Before he was intimidated into mining the fool's gold of rock 'n' roll, Davis's achievement was large and complex, as a trumpet player and an improvisor. Though he was never of the order of Armstrong, Young, Parker, or Monk, the sound that came to identify him was as original as any in the history of jazz. His technical limitations were never as great as commonly assumed, except when he was strung out on drugs and didn't practice. By January 1949, when he recorded "Overtime" with Dizzy Gillespie and Fats Navarro, he was taking a backseat to nobody in execution. By May 1949, when he traveled to France and was recorded in performance, he was muscling his way across the horn in molten homage to Navarro and Gillespie, the two leading technicians of the bebop era; he was three weeks short of his twenty-third birthday and already had benefitted from big band experience with Billy Eckstine and Gillespie, already had stood next to Charlie Parker night after night on bandstands and in studios.

The conventional idea that Davis discovered that he couldn't play like Gillespie, and proceeded to develop a style of stark, hesitant, even blushing lyricism that provided a contrast to Parker's flood of virtuosic inventions, is only partly true; a methodical musician, Davis systematically worked through the things that were of interest to him. Eventually he personalized the levels of declamation, nuance, melodic fury, and pathos that are heard, for example, in Parker's "Bird of Paradise." But first he examined Gillespie's fleet approach and harmonic intricacy, which shaped the dominant approach to bebop trumpet. From Gillespie, he learned bebop harmony and was also encouraged to use the keyboard to solve problems; he even took from Gillespie an aspect of timbral piquancy that settled beneath the surface of his sound. But Davis rejected the basic nature of Gillespie's tone, which few found as rich or as attractive as the idiomatic achievements of the Negroid brass vocabulary that had preceded the innovations of bebop. Davis grasped the musical power that comes of having a sound that is itself a musical expression.

He moved in the direction of a refined and raw understanding of tonal manipulation based in the blues. His early problems with pitch demanded that he focus first on the quality, the weight, and the accuracy of his sound. Once he established control over his tone, Davis's work began to reflect his affection for the resources of color and nuance heard in Armstrong, Freddy Webster, Harry Edison, Buck Clayton, Rex Stewart, Navarro, Dud Bascomb, and Ray Nance. But his extraordinary discipline led him to strip everything away, striving for a sound that was direct in its clarity, almost pristine in its removal from the world of Negro trumpet tone. On that clean slate, Davis later added dramatic timbres and attacks.

Next Davis chose to work out a style that was superficially simple, that was rarely given to upper-register explosions or to the rhythmic disruptions that the boppers had built upon the droll games that Lester Young played with the beat. On his first recording as a leader in May 1947, Davis already had the dark, warm sensuousness that he later extended and refined. By using Charlie Parker on tenor, rather than on his customary alto, Davis got a richer texture, the sort of thickness that he favored in his later quintets; and a number of writers have heard premonitions of the tonal concerns, the phrasings, and the moods of "The Birth of the Cool," the highly celebrated but essentially lightweight nonet sessions that Davis steered a few years later.

But the essential influence on Davis's first recordings as a leader was still Parker. The saxophonist's 1946 recording of his "Yardbird Suite" with Davis as a sideman shows precisely the ease that characterizes the playing and the writing of the trumpeter's own session, especially "Half Nelson" and "Milestones." On that first date, Davis not only plays quite well himself, but uses the mood of the material to inspire Parker to reach for an emotional projection that the saxophonist rarely called upon. Davis resides comfortably in the middle register as he improvises through the difficult harmonies of his compositions, sailing and swinging in almost seamless legato eighth notes on "Little Willie Leaps" and inventing a meticulous thematic improvisation on "Half Nelson." Harmonically his notes say bebop, and he works toward the layered sound that has a top, a middle, and a bottom, all the while understating a thoroughly felt joy as he nearly swings the ink off his tail.

Equally important were a number of other recording dates under Parker's leadership. There are examples in the ballad sessions of the winter of 1947 of the softer approach to sound and ensemble, as when Parker plays delicate and soaring obligatos behind Davis on "Embraceable You," "Out of Nowhere," and "My Old Flame." Even earlier, as the flutist and composer James Newton points out, the contrapuntal Parker writing of "A-Leu-Cha" and "Chasing the Bird" brought to bebop qualities that Davis's "cool" nonet explored. By "Marmaduke" in 1948, Davis is much closer to the almost purely melodic style of quiet but calling intensity that became an important aspect of his musical signature.

Then came "The Birth of the Cool." Davis's nonet of 1948–1950 played little in public and recorded only enough to fill an album, but it largely inspired what became known as "cool" or "West Coast" jazz, a light-sounding music, low-keyed and smooth, that disavowed the Afro-American approach to sound and rhythm. This style had little to do with blues and almost nothing to do with swing. That Davis, one of the most original improvisors, a man with a great feeling for blues, a swinger almost of the first magnitude, should have put "cool" in motion is telling. Indeed, it is the first, premonitory example of his dual position in jazz.

Heard now, the nonet recordings seem little more than primers for television writing. What the recordings show us, though, is that Davis, like many other jazzmen, was not above the academic temptation of Western music. Davis turns out to have been overly impressed by the lessons he received at Juilliard when he arrived in New York in 1944. The pursuit of a soft sound, the uses of polyphony that were far from idiomatic, the nearly coy understatement, the lines that had little internal propulsion: All amount to another failed attempt to marry jazz to European devices. The overstated attribution of value to these recordings led the critical establishment to miss Ellington's *The Tattooed Bride*, which was the high point of jazz composition of the late 1940s. Then, as now, jazz critics seemed unable to determine the difference between a popular but insignificant trend and a fresh contribution to the art.

Davis began making his truest contributions as a leader in the 1950s. The Prestige recordings from 1951 to 1956 have been reissued in a single package, and it constitutes one of the richest bodies of work in small-group jazz. One hears Davis consolidating influences, superbly cross-weaving improvisational styles and instrumental approaches, in his own playing and in that of the musicians he brought together. The quintet included John Coltrane and a rhythm section that was nearly as important to jazz of the fifties as Basie's was to that of the thirties.

In the early fifties, inspired by Monk, Armstrong, Young, and Holiday, Davis learned to strip away everything not essentially musical. He maintained the harmonic sophistication of the bebop school, but picked only the most telling notes for the construction of his melodic lines. He recognized that the smooth swing of Basie and the territory bands used pulsations that, for all their flirtations with the beat, were never jerky. In this work Davis sublimely combined the unsentimental detailings of tone, emotion, and attack of the blues; the joy and the surprise of Armstrong and Young that melodically rose up over the tempo and meter of ensembles in the thirties; and the idealistic but earthy sensuousness of the romantic balladeer.

One of the more interesting things about Davis during these years is that he brought together musicians with varied tastes in sound. As early as 1946, when he recorded "Yardbird Suite" and "Ornithology" with Parker, the smooth, vibratoless sound of Parker was contrasted by the heavier Coleman Hawkins-derived tone of Lucky Thompson's tenor. Davis himself had worked with Hawkins, and used tenor players rooted in Hawkins's work (such as Thompson and Sonny Rollins) until he hired Coltrane. But his alto choices were always Parker derived, such as Jackie McLean and Davey Schildkraut. Just as he was interested in bringing together the essences of blues-based trumpet and ensemble swing with the lessons of the bebop movement, Davis also seemed to want to fuse the tones of those different schools in his ensembles.

Thus, in 1951, he brought McLean and Rollins together for a sextet recording, the instrumentation foreshadowing the six-piece group he later led with Cannonball Adderley and Coltrane. Davis played with confidence on the blues, gave poignance to the ballads, and swung with very individual articulation on McLean's "Dig." But perhaps the high point of the session was Rollins's tenor on "It's Only a Paper Moon," where his gruff and ghostly sound reached startling levels of lyricism and fresh phrasing. For the next three years he was playing marvelously, with J. J. Johnson, Jackie McLean, Jimmy Heath, Horace Silver, Gil Coggins, Percy Heath, Kenny Clarke, and Art Blakey on Blue Note Records. And in 1954, Davis reached one of his first peaks as a bandleader and a player. In March, he recorded a version of "Old Devil Moon" that had an arranged and recurring vamp that anticipated the sound of the Coltrane rhythm section of the 1960s.

In April he brought together trombonist J. J. Johnson, tenor saxophonist Lucky Thompson, pianist Horace Silver, bassist Percy Heath, and drummer Kenny Clarke. According to Silver, Thompson had written arrangements that didn't come off, and they did two blues numbers, a fast and a slow blues, "Walkin' " and "Blue and Boogie," to avoid a failed day in the studio. The results were signal achievements. The weight of the ensemble sound is perfectly balanced and darkened, Davis's and Johnson's broad brass tones melding in unison with Thompson's thick, breathy tenor; Silver's percussive attack and the ideal mesh of Heath's bass notes with Clarke's cymbals and drums form perhaps Davis's first great rhythm section. On the swift "Blue and Boogie," the trumpeter moves over the horn with grace and pride, his last two choruses a response to the emerging challenge of Clifford Brown.

In December, Davis used Heath and Clarke again, but instead of horns he brought Monk's piano and Milt Jackson's vibes. The overtones of Davis's trumpet and the ringing of Jackson's metal keys achieved another superior texture (this one foreshadowed the electric piano on *Filles de Kilimanjaro*, the trumpeter's last important jazz record some fourteen years away); Davis's abstraction of the melody of "The Man I Love" reached back in conception, but not in execution, to Parker's classic transformation of "Embraceable You." Because of the trumpeter's problems with Monk's style—contrapuntal, icily voiced, given as much to ongoing improvised arrangement as to chordal statement—Davis asked the pianist to "stroll," or lay out, during his improvisations. The musical effect is systematically wonderful, however much Monk was irritated. Monk's improvisations are easily the highest expressions of originality and profundity in all of the Prestige sessions.

They are also the peak of piano playing on any Miles Davis recording. Monk brings a motivic brilliance, a command of inflection and timbre, and an idealistic lyricism that are unexpected in their purity. His playing is as far from European convention as bottleneck guitar work. His melodic response to Davis on "The Man I Love" is startling. And on "Swing Spring," Davis pulls off what must be one of his best spontaneous decisions. Featured first with just bass (Percy Heath) and drums (Kenny Clarke), he jumps back in after Jackson has finished his improvisation and Monk is about to play. Monk stops immediately, and Davis plays again with Heath and Clarke, choosing to use a patented Monk phrase for his last chorus. He builds upon it and finishes. Monk then picks up the phrase and invents one of his most masterful recorded performances. It is, quite simply, one of the high points of jazz.

As Davis developed into the next phase of his bandleading and his improvising, he continued to expand on blues, pop songs, Kansas City swing, and the conceptions he personalized from Parker, Monk, and Ahmad Jamal, whose 1955 arrangement of Morton Gould's "Pavanne" provided the structure for Davis's 1959 "So What" and the melody for Coltrane's 1961 "Impressions." When he formed his great quintet in 1955, with Coltrane, pianist Red Garland, bassist Paul Chambers, and drummer Philly Joe Jones, Davis not only improvised marvelously eight times out of ten, but also wrote particularly imaginative arrangements. Much of the praise that this quintet has received is deserved. It was a unit that had invincible swing at any tempo, that utilized the possibilities of group color with consistent intelligence, that stoked fire as ably as it crooned. No small part of Davis's achievement was his rhythm section, an ongoing, spontaneously self-orchestrating unit of piano, bass, and drums that delineated the forms of the tunes, responded to the improvisation of the featured horns, loosened and tightened the beat, and swung with an almost peerlessly precise attention to color and the varied possibilities of harmonic-percussive drama. Still, what made this band so wonderful was Davis's breadth of emotional expression. His sensibility drew on the entire sweep of jazz feeling, from the playful to the tender to the pugnacious to the aloof to the gutbucket-greasy and the idealistically lyrical.

When he moved to Columbia Records in 1957 and *'Round About Midnight* was released with the same musicians, Davis was on the verge of becoming a star, a large influence, a matinee idol, and a man destined to sink down in a way no one—himself least of all—could have imagined. Columbia Records, with its distribution and promotion networks, its record club, the air play its products received, and the ink it could generate outside the jazz press, started the most significant leg of Davis's march to celebrity. The trumpeter soon saw his performances and his recordings become emblems of taste in contemporary art.

With Nat Cole and Sidney Poitier, moreover, Davis became part of an expanding vision of American glamour in which dark-hued Negroes were admitted into precincts of romance and elegance that had previously been almost the exclusive province of light-skinned Afro-Americans like Billy Eckstine. As Betty Carter observed of Davis's matinee-idol appeal, "Miles wasn't a power trumpet player, he was a stylist. He had a soft, melodic approach that made him very popular with women. Women really liked him the way they liked Dexter Gordon, Gene Ammons, Ben Webster, Johnny Hodges, and all of those guys who knew how to play things that had some sweetness in them."

Davis also benefited from a shift in audience taste that harked back to the popularity of the glowering, sullen, even contemptuous nineteenth-century minstrel characters known as Jasper Jack and Zip Coon, who sassed and sometimes assaulted the plantation white folks. Davis's bandstand attitude originated in the bebop generation's rejection of Armstrong's mugging and joking, in a trend of aggression that opened part of the way to what became blaxploitation ten years later (and now causes whites who confuse their own masochism with sensitivity to celebrate Spike Lee). The result was superbly described by Ralph Ellison:

> ... a grim comedy of racial manners; with the musicians employing a calculated surliness and rudeness, treating the audience very much as many white merchants in poor Negro neighborhoods treat their customers, and the white audiences were shocked at first but learned quickly to accept such treatment as evidence of "artistic" temperament. Then comes a comic reversal. Today the white audience expects the rudeness as part of the entertainment.

A story about Davis from this period may be apocryphal, but it has poetic truth. It has been related that one night a European woman approached Davis at the bar in Birdland to tell him that she loved his music,
that she bought all his records, even though they were quite expensive in
her country. Davis is said to have replied, "So fucking what, bitch?" As the
stunned woman walked away, the musician with Davis said, "Miles, you really are an evil little black sonofabitch, aren't you?" And the trumpeter
replied, "Now the bitch will buy *two* of every one of my records. When you
have stock in Con Edison and make all the money I make, you have to act
the way people expect you to act—they want me to be their evil nigger,
and that's what I'm ready to be."

These first developments in ugliness aside, Davis's achievement in those
years was genuine. It drew not only on the detailed idiomatic thought of his
own musical conceptions, but also on his interaction with his musicians. Just as
Davis had been deeply impressed by the spare side of Monk's decidedly Afro-
American approach to instrumental technique, and by Monk's immaculate
sense of thematic variation, so Coltrane, when he left Davis to work with
Monk in the summer of 1957, was inspired to push beyond his superior bebop
art; Monk remade Coltrane substantially, and even the sixteenth-note rhythms
that the saxophonist worked on until the end of his career were introduced by
the pianist's formidable *Trinkle Tinkle*. Thus, when Coltrane returned to Davis's
band in 1958, he brought materials that elevated the intellect, the surprise, and
the fire of the group. In fact, as the 1960 Stockholm recording shows, the saxophonist was blowing the trumpeter off his own bandstand.

But Davis understood how to use Coltrane. By now he was fully his own
man. The album *Milestones* shows how well he understood that a jazz
recording should emulate a strong forty-minute set in a nightclub. Though
the under-recorded piano greatly reduces the power of what is quite
mighty swing, the recital shows just how much of a bopper Davis still was,
and how strongly he believed in the blues as an organizing tool for the
overall sound of a recording. Four of the six pieces are blues numbers; each
is approached differently, utilizing varied tempos, big-band effects, saxophone exchanges of entire choruses, drum breaks, harmonization, unisons,
antiphony. With the title work, moreover, Davis began his exploration of
modal materials—limited harmonic structures that relied on scales—and
pointed toward *Kind of Blue*, perhaps his most influential album and certainly
one of his finest achievements.

In the interest of accuracy, however, it is important to recognize that
Davis's publicity, and the cult that has grown up around him, inflated his work

out of proportion. As a trumpeter, Davis was constantly challenged by Clifford Brown, who died, at the age of twenty-five, in an automobile accident in 1956. By 1953 Brown was being hailed as "the new Dizzy." His extraordinary technique, his large sound, his unlimited swing, and his heroic combination of melancholy and grandeur brought an Armstrong-like bravura to the bebop trumpet. Brown's recordings show that he possessed qualities of beauty that Davis would never equal. Had Brown lived, Davis would have had to deal with another force of unarguable potency. It is the influence of Brown, not Davis, that has dominated the instrument, from Donald Byrd and Lee Morgan through Freddie Hubbard and Booker Little, and now Wynton Marsalis.

Other strengths of Davis's have been overstated too. His idea of the small group was, finally, no more sophisticated than John Lewis's, Charles Mingus's, or Horace Silver's, and he was rarely as imaginative in his arrangements. Though his fame grew, he had yet to explore the kinds of metric innovations that obsessed Max Roach. And as the Dizzy Gillespie–Sonny Rollins–Sonny Stitt sessions of December 1957 reveal, especially in the playing of Rollins and Gillespie on "Wheatleigh Hall" and of all three on "The Eternal Triangle," the Davis group on *Milestones* was far from the last word in swing or fire.

As for formal innovations, both George Russell and Mingus examined modal forms before Davis, and each made use of pianist Bill Evans (who became important to the next stage of Davis's development). Rollins's *Freedom Suite*, from the summer of 1958, exhibits a much more provocative and successful conception of group rhythm and extended form than anything Davis had produced. (What Rollins did with tenor saxophone, bass, and drums has still to receive the critical recognition it deserves.) And compare Davis's much-lauded improvisation on "Sid's Ahead" from *Milestones* of 1958 with Louis Armstrong's "Wild Man Blues" of 1957: You will hear a vast difference in subtlety, nuance, melodic order, and swing. As fine a player as he had become, Davis could not even approximate Armstrong's authority.

Still, of all the trumpet players who came to power during and after the first shock waves of Parker's innovations, Davis seemed the one who would eventually come the closest to Armstrong's emotional gravity. As he proved with his eerie, isolated, and mournful playing for the score of the murder thriller *Escalator to the Scaffold*, and in the better moments of his collaborations with the arranger Gil Evans (*Miles Ahead, Porgy and Bess, Sketches of Spain*), he had a talent for a transfixing musical logic and a scalding melancholy. It is true that those albums with Evans also reveal that Davis could be taken in by pastel versions of European colors (they are given what value they have in these sessions by the Afro-American dimensions that were never far from Davis's embouchure, breath, fingering); if Davis's trumpet voice is removed, in fact, a good number of Evans's arrangements sound like high-level television music. But these infirmities pale before the triumphant way that Davis summoned a range of idiomatic devices far richer in color and in conception than those of any of his fellow beboppers.

In the liner notes of *Porgy and Bess*, Davis noted a movement in jazz away from harmonic complexity toward simpler structures that emphasized melodic invention. In early 1959—the watershed year in which Ellington recorded *Jazz Party*; Coleman, *The Shape of Jazz to Come*; Coltrane, *Giant Steps*; Monk, *Orchestra at Town Hall*; and Mingus, *Blues and Roots* and *Ah Um*—Davis made *Kind of Blue*. Here the modal movement reached a pinnacle, precisely because Davis understood that blues should be the foundation of any important innovation in jazz. The record, which uses his sextet with Coltrane, Cannonball Adderley, and Bill Evans, has the feeling of a suite. It is dominated by the trumpeter's compositions. (On one piece where straight-out swing was called for, Davis used Wynton Kelly instead of Evans; but on the softer pieces the things that Evans had learned from Debussy, George Russell, and Mingus issued in voicings of simple materials with intricate details.) The set realized all of the possibilities of cool jazz without sinking into the vacuous, the effete, and the pretentious.

By 1960, Coltrane and Adderley had left to lead their own bands, and Davis began to cope with a jazz scene of expanding technical and emotional means. Davis's playing continued to grow in power and intensity, but for all his success he was no longer the center of the discussion. The centers, instead, were Coltrane and Ornette Coleman, who were inspiring charlatans as well as serious musicians. It seemed possible that the crown would slip from Davis's head, that he might be relegated to the neglect experienced by many of the older masters. Former Davis sidemen—Coltrane, Silver, Blakey, Adderley, Rollins—were leading the most imposing small bands of the day. Musicians he had been associated with, such as Monk and Mingus, were either refining, or adding to, the art, especially to its formal scope. In terms of pure bebop, Gillespie's quintet with James Moody was playing extraordinarily well, as was the Modern Jazz Quartet, with its lyrical use of percussion and harmony instruments. When his second great rhythm section of Wynton Kelly, Paul Chambers, and Jimmy Cobb left him in 1963, Davis had to rebuild for what became his last great period.

He soon found the musicians who provided the foundation for his final creative years. With *Seven Steps to Heaven*, Davis introduced George Coleman on tenor, another of the fine tenor players who had followed Coltrane into the band, and the rhythm section of Herbie Hancock, Ron Carter, and Tony Williams, the force that was to shape the orchestration and the propulsion of his next phase. The band with Coleman made its finest music in concert performances, released as *Four* and *My Funny Valentine*. Wynton Marsalis has noted that on the many fast numbers of *Four*, Davis produced unorthodox phrases that are technically challenging and demand unique fingerings. *My Funny Valentine*, by contrast, and particularly the title tune, captured Davis in a moment of heroic intimacy that he rarely reached again.

When Wayne Shorter joined him in the fall of 1964, Davis had what has been considered his best group since the *Milestones* ensemble. In January 1965 the band recorded *E.S.P.*, and the music still sounds fresh. The trumpeter was in superb form, able to execute quickstep swing at fleet tempi with volatile penetration, to put the weight of his sound on mood pieces, to rear his way up through the blues with a fusion of bittersweet joy and what Martin Williams termed "communal anguish." The rhythm section played with a looseness that pivots off Williams's cymbal splashes and un-clinched rhythms, Carter walking some of the most impressive bass lines of the day, and Hancock developing his own version of the impressionism that Evans was making popular.

Shortly afterward, Davis went into the hospital for surgery and didn't return to work until late in the year, when he recorded *Live at the Plugged Nickel* in Chicago. At the Plugged Nickel, he and his musicians were staring right in the face of the period's avant-garde, spontaneously changing tempi and meters, playing common or uncommon notes over the harmonies, pulling in harsh timbres, all the while in a repertoire that was roughly the same as the trumpeter had been using for a decade. Again, as with *My Funny Valentine*, the pieces were remade. Shorter was in such startling form that his improvisations remained influential through the 1980s. Davis himself seemed to be having trouble with his instrument; his authority on *E.S.P.* is rarely heard. His "Stella by Starlight," however, with its masterful touches of brass color, is one of his supreme late efforts: It swells with intimacy, voices an elevated bitterness that seems to argue with the human condition, then rises to a victorious swing.

The remainder of Davis's studio recordings with that band drew on the chromaticism of Warne Marsh and Lennie Tristano, who influenced Shorter and Hancock—and, to the surprise of almost all concerned, on popular dance music, on rhythm and blues, and on rock 'n' roll. Though the albums vary in quality, though they sometimes lack definitive swing or co-hesive fire, even the weaker ones have at least a couple of first-rate performances. The range of ideas heard from the rhythm section put it in line with the best of the day, and Shorter wrote many fine compositions, especially on *Nefertiti*. But the clues to Davis's course were in his own pieces, in "Stuff" and in much of the work for *Filles de Kilimanjaro*. His extended "Country Son," which features perhaps Shorter's finest studio improvisation with Davis, revealed that he was capable of a flirtation with pop rhythms. He was headed, in fact, in the direction of Motown, the English bands, and the black rock of Sly Stone and Jimi Hendrix.

"Mademoiselle Mabry," on *Filles*, is a brilliant example of Davis's ability to elevate pop material. An innovation in jazz rhythm, it is an appropriation and an extension of Hendrix's "The Wind Cries Mary," and proof of what Davis might have done had he kept control of his popular sources, rather than succumbed to them. The borrowing was in perfect keeping with the tradition begun by Armstrong's alchemical way with banal popular songs. In fact, what Davis does with popular influences throughout this recording shows off his sophistication and his ability to transform yet another universe of music in his own image.

That Davis was able to initiate what became known as fusion, or jazz rock, and with it to inspire musicians as different as Hancock, Rollins, Hubbard, and Coleman, shows what a powerful position he had in the minds of Afro-American jazzmen. Jimmy Heath described his position this way:

> Miles led the way for a lot of people because he was one of the ones who got through. He had the fine clothes, the expensive cars, the big house, all the magazine articles and the pretty girls chasing him. He seemed like he was on top of *everything*. Then you had all of this rock getting all of the press and it was like Elvis Presley all over again. Miles stepped out here and decided he was going to get himself some of that money and a lot of musicians followed his lead. It was like if Miles had led the pack for so long they didn't know how to stop following him, even if the music wasn't any good.

And then came the fall. Beginning with the 1969 *In a Silent Way*, Davis's sound was mostly lost among electronic instruments, inside a long, maudlin piece of droning wallpaper music. A year later, with *Bitches Brew*, Davis was firmly on the path of the sellout. It sold more than any other Davis album, and fully launched jazz-rock with its multiple keyboards, electronic guitars, static beats, and clutter. Davis's music became progressively trendy and dismal, as did his attire; at one point in the early 1970s, with his wraparound dark glasses and his puffed shoulders, the erstwhile master of cool looked like an extra from a science fiction B movie. He was soon proclaiming that there were no Negroes other than Sonny Rollins who could play the saxophone, and that musicians like Ornette Coleman and Mingus needed to listen to Motown, which was "where it was at." Many hoped that this would be only a phase, but the phase has lasted twenty years. In his abject surrender to popular trends, Davis sank the lowest in 1985 in *You're Under Arrest,* on which one hears what is supposed to be the sound of cocaine snorting. His albums of recent years— *Tutu, Siesta, Amandla,* and the overblown fusion piece that fills two records on *Aura*—prove beyond any doubt that he has lost all interest in music of quality.

As usual, where Davis led, many followed. His pernicious effect on the music scene since he went rapaciously commercial reveals a great deal about the perdurability of Zip Coon and Jasper Jack in the worlds of jazz and rock, in the worlds of jazz and rock criticism, in Afro-American culture itself. The cult of ethnic authenticity often mistakes the lowest common denominator for an ideal. It begets a self-image that has succumbed to a nostalgia for the mud. What we get is the bugaboo blues of the noble savage, the surly and dangerous Negro who will have nothing to do with bourgeois conventions. (This kind of Negro has long supplied the ammunition for the war that many jazz and rock critics have waged against their own middle-class backgrounds.)

Davis's corruption occurred at about the time that the "Oreo" innuendo became an instrument with which formerly rejected street Negroes and thugs began to intimidate, and often manipulate, middle-class Afro-Americans in search of their roots, and of a "real" black culture. In this climate, obnoxious, vulgar, and antisocial behavior has been confused with black authenticity. This has led to blaxploitation in politics, in higher education, and in art—to Eldridge Cleaver, Huey Newton, and the Black Panthers; to black students at San Francisco State demanding that pimps be recruited to teach psychology classes; to the least inventive and most offensive work of Richard Pryor and Eddie Murphy; to the angry cartoonish coons of Spike Lee; and the flat, misogynist, gutter verse of Ice-T and racist rap groups like Public Enemy.

Davis provides many unwitting insights into such phenomena in his autobiography, *Miles,* written with Quincy Troupe. His is, at least in part, the story of a jet-black Little Lord Fauntleroy attracted to the glamour and the fast life of the jazz world during the period when heroin was as important to the identity of the bebop generation as LSD was to the youth culture of the late 1960s. The book draws a number of interesting portraits—of Dexter Gordon, of Sugar Ray Robinson, of Philly Joe Jones—but it is overwhelmingly an outburst of inarticulateness, of profanity, of error, of self-inflation, and of parasitic paraphrasing of material from Jack Chambers's

Milestones. Would Simon and Schuster publish such a book, without sending the manuscript to any number of experts for evaluations and corrections, if it were written by a white man? Perhaps the editors assumed that since Quincy Troupe is a *Negro*, he should know.

Davis's book is divided against itself. His sensitive and lyrical recollections of experience are constantly overwhelmed by his street corner poses. The trumpeter's desire to be perceived as the hippest of the hip has destroyed his powers of communication. This is particularly unfortunate, since his story falls far outside the clichés of jazz and racial lore. His father was a successful dentist and a gentleman farmer who reared his children to have a high sense of self-worth. Davis recalls riding horses and living on a three-hundred-acre estate; there was a cook and a maid. It was a world as full of sophistication as it was of superstition, as full of privilege as prejudice.

Davis tells of what he heard about the St. Louis Riot of 1917, of his father's looking with a shotgun for the man who called his son a nigger, of a preference Negro bands had for light-skinned musicians that blocked a young friend of his from working with Jimmy Lunceford, of the way women started throwing themselves at him as he grew into his late teens. His involvement with music is well described, as are the personalities of many musicians he grew up with, some of whom fell by the wayside. There are powerful evocations of certain aspects of the times: of how drugs took over the lives of musicians, of the difficulties musicians had negotiating the territory between the cult world of bebop and the more general kind of success enjoyed by Ellington. And some of what is probably Troupe's best writing has nothing to do with music; the brief section on Sugar Ray Robinson sheds unexpected light on the influence of boxing on Davis's playing. If one listens to Davis's jabbing, suspenseful, aggressive improvisation on "Walkin'" from the 1961 *Black Hawk* recording, one hears not only Monk, but also, we can now say, Robinson:

> Sugar Ray Robinson would put an opponent in four or five traps during every round in the first two or three rounds, just to see how his opponent would react. Ray would be reaching, and he would stay just out of reach so he could measure you to knock you out, and you didn't even know what was happening until, BANG! you found yourself counting stars. Then, on somebody else, he might hit him hard in his side—BANG!—after he made him miss a couple of jabs. He might do that in the first round. Then he'd tee-off on the sucker upside his head after hitting him eight or nine more times hard in the ribs, then back to the head. So by the fourth or fifth round, the sucker don't know what Ray's going to do to him next.

Once our memoirist gets to New York, however, the book begins to lose itself in contradictions and obscenities. On one page Davis will say that Parker was "teaching me a lot about music—chords and that shit—that I would go play on the piano" when he went to Juilliard, and then a few pages later that "Bird didn't teach me much as far as music goes." Davis claims that he became the musical director of Parker's group, but Max Roach, who was also in the band, vehemently disputes the claim. (It is proof, he says, that the trumpeter has "become senile.") Davis recalls being taken to Minton's in Harlem for the great jam sessions by Fats Navarro, whom many considered second only to Gillespie, but then says, "I would tell him shit—technical shit—about the trumpet." Jimmy Heath has a rather different memory of what Davis did or did not learn from Navarro: "Fats ate Miles up every night. Miles couldn't outswing him, he couldn't outpower him, he couldn't outsweet him, he couldn't do anything except take that whipping on *every* tune."

On things racial, it's impossible to figure out from this book what Davis really felt. "I could learn more in one session at Minton's than it would take me two years to learn at Juilliard. At Juilliard, after it was all over, all I was going to know was a bunch of white styles: nothing new." But only one page later he says:

> I couldn't believe that all of them guys like Bird, Prez, Bean, all them cats wouldn't go to museums or libraries and borrow those musical scores so they could check out what was happening. I would go to the library and borrow scores by all those great composers, like Stravinsky, Alban Berg, Prokofiev. I wanted to see what was going on in all of music. Knowledge is freedom and ignorance is slavery, and I just couldn't believe someone could be that close to freedom and not take advantage of all the shit that they can. I have never understood why black people didn't take advantage of all the shit that they can.

Of the interracial couples that he saw in the clubs on 52nd Street, Davis observes:

> A lot of white people, though, didn't like what was going on on 52nd Street. . . . They thought that they were being invaded by niggers from Harlem, so there was a lot of racial tension around bebop. Black men were going with fine, rich white bitches. They were all over those niggers out in public and the niggers were clean as a motherfucker and talking all kind of hip shit. So you know a lot of white people, especially white men, didn't like this new shit.

And then, explaining why he didn't want to do an interview for *Playboy*, he declares, "All they have are blond women with big tits and flat asses or no asses. So who the fuck wants to see that all the time? Black guys like big asses, you know, and we like to kiss on the mouth and white women don't have no mouths to kiss on."

Davis's treatment of women is disgusting. He details the way he destroyed the career of his first wife, Frances Taylor, who was a dancer, and later, claiming that black women are too bossy, he cites Taylor as an example of the way a good colored woman ought to be. He volunteers tales of slapping Cicely Tyson around, though she was probably responsible for his not dying from a binge of cocaine that spanned nearly six years.

The cavalier way that Davis imputes drug use to black musician after black musician is no less objectionable. (He claims repeatedly that the white jazz press didn't start paying attention to white guys being junkies until Stan Getz was arrested, but Leonard Feather has shown that in fact white musicians got the bulk of the attention for using drugs.) And the morality of the trumpeter's memory is oddly selective. About a woman who helped him during his time as a drug addict, Davis says, "I was seeing this same rich white girl who I'd met in St. Louis; she had come to New York to check me out. Let's call her 'Alice,' because she's still alive and I don't want to cause her trouble; plus she's married." And the customers of a white call girl were "very important men—white men mostly—whose names I won't mention." It seems that militant Inky respects the privacy of those mouthless, gluteus minimus white women and those white Johns more than he does the dignity of his fellow musicians, some of whom were his very close friends.

One of the most disturbing things about *Miles* is its debt to Jack Chambers's *Milestones*, a critical biography written in two parts between 1983 and 1985 and now available in one volume from Quill. Pages 160–161 of *Miles*, for example, look alarmingly like pages 166–167 of *Milestones*. (There is even a cavalier reference to Chambers as "some writer.") Davis and Troupe:

> Bird had an exclusive contract with Mercury (I think he had left Verve by then), so he had to use a pseudonym on record. Bird had given up shooting heroin because since Red Rodney had been busted and sent back to prison at Lexington, Bird thought the police were watching him. In place of his normal big doses of heroin, now he was drinking an enormous amount of alcohol.

Chambers:

> . . . the man behind the pseudonym was Charlie Parker. Parker was under some pressure, not only because he had an exclusive contract with Mercury, but also because the trumpeter in his band, Red Rodney, had been arrested and committed to the federal prison in Lexington. Parker believed that he was being watched by narcotics agents, according to Ross Russell, and he had given up narcotics for the time being and was consuming large quantities of alcohol instead.

Much of the material used in *Milestones* and again in *Miles* comes from interviews done over the years. Troupe denies using any of it, then says that "the man can quote himself," then blames the publisher for "messing up" by omitting a discography and a bibliography, and by not checking facts.

But the important point, finally, is that *Miles* paints the picture of an often gloomy monster. It is full of stories that take the reader down into the sewers of Davis's musical, emotional, and chemical decline. Once the rage at his cruelty and his self-inflation has passed, we are left aghast at a man of monumental insecurity who, for all his protests about white power and prejudice, is often controlled by his fear of it, or of any other significant power. (One example of many: Davis asserts that he never listens to white music critics, and blames many of the woes of the music business on them, but then he admits that once they had him worried that he sounded inferior to Chet Baker, who was his imitator.) Obsessed with remaining young, and therefore willing to follow any trend in pop music, Davis is now a surly sellout who wants his success to seem like a heroic battle against the white world.

To that end, this former master of musical articulation often reduces himself to an inarticulate man. Davis has worn the mask of the street corner for too long; he thinks, like Pryor and Murphy and Lee, that his invective gives him authenticity. Gone is the elegant and exigent Afro-American authenticity of the likes of Ellington, at ease in the alleys as well as in the palace, replaced by youth culture vulgarity that vandalizes the sweep and substance of Afro-American life. The fall of Davis reflects perhaps the essential failure of contemporary Negro culture: its mock-democratic idea that the elite, too, should like it down in the gutter. Aristocracies of culture, however, come not from the acceptance of limitations, but from the struggle with them, as a group or an individual, from within or without.

1986

THE WAY IT WAS,
THE WAY IT IS

Come Sunday

Duke Ellington, Mahalia Jackson

How big does a person have to grow, down in this part of the country, before he's going to stand up and say, "Let us stop treating men, women, and children with such cruelty just because they're colored?"

—Mahalia Jackson

In the second week of February, 1958, Duke Ellington brought the great gospel singer Mahalia Jackson into a Hollywood studio and recorded one of the masterpieces of the twentieth century, a somber yet elevating religious ballad called "Come Sunday." No doubt about that. The way Ellington and Jackson sounded together has yet to be equaled in the world of jazz, because we have not since had such a great jazz orchestra and we have not heard again a voice of such spiritual breadth and depth. Their meeting was a pinnacle for the music of New Orleans. The Crescent City is where Jackson was born, having left at sixteen for Chicago, where she would soon be noticed for singing with stirringly individuated passion, volume, and rhythm. We can always hear what was made of that New Orleans music at the hands of the peerless Ellington, whose art was so thoroughly shaped by the influences of Sidney Bechet, Louis Armstrong, King Oliver, and Jelly Roll Morton. But the music that Mahalia Jackson made with Duke Ellington was, above all else, created in recognition of a reckoning. It was created during a tumultuous moment in the history of this nation, at a time when a social wrong that should have been taken care of about eighty years earlier was no longer going to be accepted by those upon whom it had been imposed. It is in this distinct context that what those two superior artists brought off together should be understood. Such awareness neither increases nor decreases their artistry, but it surely deepens our understanding.

In 1958, America had not yet descended to the low place where it now resides, caught in commercialized sexual desperation and hungering for something of spiritual value that cannot be reduced to a spotted trend or packaged like dead sardines in oil. There was still serious religious music in that year, and Mahalia Jackson was its most shining symbol. Within her marvelous brown being, the entire heritage of the religious music from slavery and the spiritual music that came after bondage was given communicative residence of a special kind. She was a woman of large beauty and regal presence. Her voice was humbling because it was absolutely pure in its impersonality, which meant that it sounded unlike personal expression or autobiography or belief. She possessed the quality that all great religious singers must have—the ability to give the impression that they are not telling you what they believe or what happened to them somewhere in the world at some time, no, but what was always true in every time and in every place.

That was the source of the purity in her sound, and that purity was also an instrument of innovation because she and the composer Thomas A. Dorsey took the traditional spiritual—or plantation song of worship—and created an extension called gospel. With her huge and compelling voice, so accurate in pitch and so perfectly developed for the expression of nuance, the singer from New Orleans had, with a succession of recordings and public performances, made a world for her art and had remained beyond reproach. To hear her was to have a transcendent spiritual experience that was not beyond criticism but was surely beyond bloodless commentary because, in the world of God, people need to sing something or play something or just listen.

Jackson had built up quite a career by the time she met Ellington in the studio after arriving by train in Los Angeles at Union Station, which has a floor plan in the shape of a cross and an exterior that is a hybrid of Spanish Mission, Moorish, and art deco styles, clearly a stylistic mixture of old and new that now seems a first cousin of jazz and gospel music. She had appeared on concert stages across the nation and in Europe, had been heard and seen on radio and television, and had proven in person to be one of the most impressive performing artists on the face of the earth. Jackson had neither dreamed of nor expected any of that. Her wishes were spiritual, but the technology of her time had made it possible for her to sell millions of records and for her voice to be heard in far more homes and ears than she could ever have imagined. It had all been an unprecedented surprise.

By 1958, she was revered by her listeners for making unspoken conditions of feeling audible and exalting. The full-figured diva from New Orleans, who had done scullery work, picked plantation cotton, and studied how to "do" Negro hair in Chicago, certainly was treated by the Negro Red Caps who carried her luggage and then the waiters and porters on the train from Chicago to Los Angeles with the special respect reserved for Negro nobility. She was one of those who had earned aristocratic status through their deeds and, therefore, had proven the truth of the democratic ideal. Her meals had to be given that special touch and her quarters made especially comfortable and each of her wishes attended to with the eloquent passion of *service*, as opposed to servitude. She may well have been asked for autographs and, however used to it, might have almost felt overwhelmed by the fuss they made of satisfying her every desire. But that was how people of her level of achievement were handled, and they, far more often than not, proved themselves true aristocrats by the grace with which they received the very best that someone could offer them.

But at that time, there was trouble in the land. It had been building in the four years since Senator Joseph McCarthy had been brought down through the instrument of television by Edward R. Murrow and censured by the Senate. The abuse of power and the danger of lies in high places were made clear, and the sting of that public recognition of such abuse was national. McCarthy had been proven to be a demagogue. The senator from Wisconsin had sensed that the country was in the mood for demagoguery and he had made the most of it. McCarthy had lied, he had exaggerated, he had created the kind of public paranoia that almost always grants more power to those who say they are protecting society, and he did his best to make the committee gavel sound like the crack of doom. We can say from this distance that Senator McCarthy, in the wake of a world war against the very obvious evils of European totalitarianism, was in the process of bringing American democracy as close to that very evil as he possibly could— though we can never be sure whether or not McCarthy was fully aware of everything that he was doing when he claimed to know the location of Communist spies here, there, and everywhere. But the most important fact of the matter is that unchallenged lying in high places is antithetical to democracy and its effects are nothing less than evil. In the wake of the McCarthy years, and the understandable obsession with freedom of speech and censorship, something that was to reshape the entire United States had already jumped off.

That something had been renewing itself since the end of the Civil War and had most recently drawn an enormous amount of fresh wind from the 1954 Supreme Court decision *Brown v. The Board of Education*. Led by the remarkable Thurgood Marshall, an NAACP legal team had argued against school segregation before the nation's highest court and had won. So in that same year that McCarthy fell, the unchallenged consistency of the lying at the center of segregation and racism took a serious hit. Goliath was down on one knee. The destruction of segregation at large was the next job. Both those genteel whites and redneck crackers residing below the Mason-Dixon Line were about to learn that there were native-born citizens who had an interest in living in the United States and, thank you very much, having their constitutional rights as well. A new storm in the sky that would later be called the Civil Rights Movement was in motion.

By 1958, young men and women were shattering and battering and challenging Southern racist conventions at every opportunity. It was not so much that Negroes had *finally* had enough; they had *always* had enough. The bigoted white man had always been a serious pain. The only difference at that point was that communities that had been largely independent—usually with some version of their own schools, churches, and businesses—were making use of their secular and religious resources for organization, for support, and for the numbers necessary to have their way and tear the house of segregation down.

Duke Ellington, who was ever attentive to the troubles and triumphs of his people, had in mind what seems to have been a complexly supportive message to those who were in the midst of that Southern battle. It was a message in music that spoke with an understanding of slavery, of tenant farming, of exclusion, of segregation, and of the heroic gratitude for merely living that is at the center of the bittersweet joy of jazz and of Negro culture at large. Ellington had no doubt about whom he needed to project that spiritual missive, to nail its notes upon the air of the world. There was just the one. He and she had been talking about doing some music together for years, and now, when he reached her by phone, the answer was an unqualified yes (though she actually hoped her deeply admired Ellington would not try to take her out of her spiritual world). He gave her the dates and sent her some music with no words, just notes.

Ellington had decided to reach back to January of 1943 for the music that he would adapt for the recording. It was from his single piece of symphonic jazz, *Black, Brown and Beige*, which had premiered in New York at Carnegie Hall. Ellington called the piece "a tone parallel to the history of the American Negro." It was nearly an hour in length and traced the Negro from slavery through the end of the Civil War and then into the North. The long work contained extraordinary invention in melodic, harmonic, and rhythmic terms. There was protean, uplifting zest, as well as

sumptuous, romantic, and prayerful lyricism—every aspect counterpointed by the ambivalence that went with living in America and the unfinished business that was still at hand. Part of its singular charisma came
from the way in which Ellington made use of all kinds of black American
music, from field chants and marches to very urbane and seductive
melodies. It was all personal, and every bar drew upon Ellington's massive
compendium of remembered experience—his many gigs in small clubs
where pistols might be drawn and fired; the greasy, after-hours piano battles where he learned his trade; the Harlem clubs owned by murderous
gangsters; the uptown Negro days and nights of great parades, style, dancing, inimitable food, and brave, wistful dreams; the Savoy Ballroom, where
his band took on the best of the day as they played for couples in love or
looking for love or for some hot and sensuous affirmation barely con-
cealed behind a silent mating call; and every college he worked in, black
or white, from coast to coast, not to mention all of the private, the very
private, and the very, very private parties. The music told a story that
began in the plantation fields of the South and ended in a penthouse on
Sugar Hill in Harlem, with plenty of Negro life between those extremes.
It was the most ambitious jazz piece of its time and remains a formidable
achievement. Yet, as he was to learn over and over, Ellington's work was
beyond the ears of the critical establishment, which largely hated it and
said, essentially, that the boy needed to stay in his own backyard and not
attempt to go beyond his own talents or the depths of his idiom.

Ellington was deeply hurt by the rejection of his work and chose never
to pursue the symphonic form again, even so imaginatively remade for his
own purposes. *Black, Brown and Beige* was never performed in its entirety after
that, though he presented excerpts from it in his concerts. Along with his
shorter pieces, he continued to write long works—which he usually called
"suites," whether they were or not—but none of *Black, Brown and Beige's*
length or of its expanded ambition. Though Ellington's hero-worshipping
supporters deny that his musical horizons were so stunted by his detractors, I don't think there can be any other explanation for his artistic behavior after that fateful night in January 1943.

Nearly four years after the Supreme Court's monumental decision of
May 17, 1954, Ellington had conceived of something that was, as he knew,
unexpected. Why not redo his extended work and focus its development
on "Come Sunday," with Mahalia Jackson, delivering what would amount
to a prayer in support of the movement that Ellington and Jackson and
every member of his band had been a part of since their first day on earth?

It could work. The band was in *very* good shape since it had fired up the Newport Jazz Festival in 1956 and shot Ellington back up to the top of his profession after a low time in the valley of the business. They had been strutting, usually without barbecue, roaring with fury when it was necessary, and laying it on with finesse when there was just no other way to do it. It wouldn't bother them—as if anything ever did. They had been around the world, had traveled by every possible means, had blown all kinds of stuff in everybody's faces—gangsters one night, society types the next, high school boys and girls falling in love the night after that. They had been to the mountain top and they had been treated like slop. You couldn't tell them anything.

You couldn't tell Duke Ellington anything, either. He had been through it all, experiencing elevation and humiliation, something that was hard to avoid if one traveled the entire United States, east to west, north to south. During the era of segregation, an entirely different pattern of travel arrangements had to be made, one in which people learned that separate but equal was surely separate but very rarely—if ever—equal. In Ellington's case, it was much the same as it was for all bands once they traveled by bus behind the Cotton Curtain and knew themselves to be where the enemy regime was in full power. When they could find no lodgings, they had to stay at the homes of local Negroes, who might well supply them with meals much better than one could get any place other than the finest hotels. Or they might find themselves in the local whorehouse, sleeping downstairs while Ellington spent the night upstairs, with the girls. The Negroes who attended their dances down South were separated by ropes or, as was often the case, waited until the white folks were done and then hit the floor. If there were no Southern dance halls, Ellington and his band would play tobacco barns, where country Negroes and their girls showed up, some nearly reverent, others stooped or made gangly by too much of that moonshine. Everything could be all right or it could be far from all right. Even in the 1950s, long after Ellington had been an internationally respected artist, trumpeter Clark Terry was told a harrowing story by other band members after he joined the organization. When the band was in Carbondale, Illinois, a gangster shot into the floor during a tirade that ended with his cutting Ellington's tie off just below the knot and demanding that he dance for him. The road could be wonderful, it could be awful. That was how it was and anybody who says anything different is lying.

So by the time Ellington got Mahalia Jackson in his musical circle, he had many things on his mind and there had been some horrific things happening

down South of late; they lay in the air like the sweet stench that follows battle and had to be in both Ellington's and Jackson's thoughts. For one, in the
summer of 1955, Emmett Till, while visiting from Chicago, had been murdered in Mississippi for getting fresh with a white woman (what would that
constitute now?). The casket at his funeral in Chicago was open, and his
hideously unrecognizable corpse was viewed by thousands because Till's
mother wanted the world to know what those rednecks had done to her boy.
As for those gallant men who considered murder not too much but just
enough to protect the soft pink purity of Southern womanhood, they sold
the details of how they killed the boy to a magazine after their acquittal on
September 23, 1955. That murder roared through black America, waking
those who had slept through the malignant evils of racist violence and the
toy courts of the South. Till's mother said of the tragedy: "Two months ago I
had a nice apartment in Chicago. I had a good job. I had a son. When something happened to the Negroes in the South, I said, 'That's their business, not
mine.' Now I know how wrong I was. The murder of my son has shown me
that what happens to any of us, anywhere in the world, had better be the
business of us all."

It was the business of the music that Duke Ellington intended to make
with Mahalia Jackson but he had to figure out a way to elegantly walk over
the eggshells of her extreme religious beliefs and her refusal to ever sing
any blues. She was adamant about that. That is where Ellington's genius for
adjustment came in. He was still smarting from the critics' rejection of
Black, Brown and Beige when he premiered it fifteen years earlier, but he had
figured out a way to ram at least some of it down their throats and make
them like it. Most importantly, he had figured out how to create a piece of
music focused on the American Negro that would culminate in the appearance of Mahalia Jackson. It would be his statement on racial matters and on
the inevitability of victory over segregation.

What he had in mind was not propaganda but a fully artistic statement
about things as they actually were at the time. But in order to make the
music work for Mahalia Jackson, and to keep her from feeling aesthetically
abused, he had to streamline his marvelous composition so that it did not
take in that much of the city or tell too much of the tale of the people on
Sugar Hill—not *everything*, anyway. In the original concluding section, a
waltz eventually gave way to a slow, symbolic coupling that would not do
at this time. Ellington would keep only the heraldic opening movement,
with slight adjustments, and shape it into three parts, or tracks, that formed
an overall ABA structure, the first introducing or alluding to all of the

themes but focusing on the South; the second introducing the contrast between religious gravity and blues; the third introducing a picture of the
Negro in the world of Harlem, where such an astonishing culture of limit-
less style and groove had been created. What Ellington now conceived of
as the first part was perfect, because it told the story of slavery and was also
possessed of a feeling of determination and of struggle, both emotions un-
dergirded by a melancholic longing and a high-mindedness. In the second
track, we hear the first of the two themes that Jackson will sing, "Come
Sunday," contrasted with some rowdy blues. With track three, an extraordinary variation on the first track, Ellington set up the New Orleans priestess with a big, proud, mocking fanfare of roaring, stomping city music,
which was also vitally urbane, meditative, even lonely, yet maintained
awareness of its spiritual roots (represented, again, by the trombone statement of "Come Sunday" near the end of the track). It was symbolic of how
much things had changed as Southern Negroes, formerly sure-enough
hicks, became city dwellers well adjusted to the pace of their environment
and ready for more opportunities to present themselves. The work song,
the spiritual, and the blues—separately, in counterpoint, or intertwined—
went the furthest and the deepest. They were all there. That was side one.

In the days of the long-playing record, with about twenty minutes on
each side, Ellington decided to make the first side instrumental and the
second side, opening with "Come Sunday," two vocals separated by a violin feature for Ray Nance. It was a shrewd decision, because those who
had no use for jazz or who had no use for such sophisticated jazz composition could just turn the record over, looking for their Mahalia, and be
knocked to their knees. Now the original fifty-seven-minute work had
been trimmed to thirty-six minutes and was, for all practical purposes, a
different piece of music with vastly different ends in mind. With no pronouncements, Ellington wanted the world to hear how deep his commit-
ment was to Negro history and culture. He also wanted everyone to know
how strongly he felt about racial justice and how deeply he believed in the
necessary support of God.

Writer Patricia Willard, who was then doing public relations for
Ellington and had been given the assignment of making sure that everything was all right with his guest singer, recalls that Ellington and Jackson
had suites across the hall from each other at the Watkins Hotel near
Adams and Western Avenue. Some of the band may have been at the
Watkins Hotel and others might have been scattered around Los Angeles
because, as Willard remembers, "[t]hey may not have been welcome in

Hollywood just yet. They soon would be but, at that time, they may not have been." Willard also recalls that Jackson did not take her assignment lightly. "Mahalia was in such awe of Duke Ellington. She was nervous because this man was one of her idols and she wanted to be good enough. She was very humble."

The session took place at Radio Recording Studios in Hollywood. Mahalia Jackson knew her music when she arrived in Los Angeles and was to learn the lyrics either before going to the studio or at the session itself. Ellington made her the star of the sessions that she attended so that she would focus only on what she was going to do and he would use his musicians solely in an accompanying or obbligato role. He would record the other material after she was done. She didn't need to hear the other music; all she needed was to give her soul over to the notes that were there for her to fill up with the light that was in her voice.

"The thing about 'Come Sunday,'" says Wynton Marsalis, "is that it brings together a lot of different American music. It alludes to many different forms, first the pentatonic sound of the Spiritual and the fiddle ballad, then the I-IV progression that is central to the blues, then the movement to the relative minor, which was done a lot in fiddle tunes as well as American popular songs. The use of the augmented V chord, which is always evocative of the blues, and when it precedes a dominant II chord, connects us to the sound of 'Mood Indigo.' It also has, in the final turnaround, the type of triadic inversions that we find in almost all Afro-American church music. And the AABA form is the classic form of the American popular song. So what it all adds up to is a summary of a number of American things, including that allusion to Ellington himself, to 'Mood Indigo.' But then, why should he leave himself out? There's nothing more American than Duke Ellington."

Though the words have been dismissed as banal, even by so great a writer as Ralph Ellison, I have to disagree with all detractors because, from the very opening, it all becomes clear what Ellington had in his thoughts and there is hardly a more straightforward way to say what he wanted to say. This deeply private man enjoyed the freedom of being absolutely explicit. He also knew that if there was anyone on the earth who could give the meaning the majesty with which he felt it, he now had that person in the studio, standing there in all her heavy down-home beauty. The melancholic gentility on her face was characteristic of those who knew both the universal weights of life and the specific burdens of color, but that knowledge had been given an added strength by the blessing that is the capacity for the expression of unlimited purity. It was the disarming authority that Mahalia Jackson gave him in spades as she made even clearer the obvious emotion Ellington had put in his lyrics.

> *Lord, dear Lord of love*
> *God almighty*
> *God above*
> *Please look down*
> *And see my people through*

> *Lord, dear Lord of love*
> *God almighty*
> *God above*
> *Please look down*
> *And see my people through*

Knowing the troubles and the dangers facing the Negro people, whether in political situations or not, Ellington was offering a prayer that these people, who had been so abused on every level, who had been disappointed so often, be looked out for, taken care of, and gotten through what was surely the bloody and sacrificial road that lay ahead.

Next there was a cosmic sense of order and recognition of the fact that always stood up above all others: No matter how much darkness there was, no matter how black and unlit the night might be, all of it would pass, and light, of every sort, was a forthcoming *fact*. The great Jackson, as much aware of that fact as Ellington himself, let those words and notes loose with so much confidence that they needed no overstatement to achieve a convincing state. The idea is a simple one, but the way she sings the words that are the nouns and what she does with the adjectives and the verbs creates the wonder and the inevitability that only our most special singers have within their power.

> *I believe the sun and moon*
> *Will shine up in the sky*
> *When the day is gray I know it's clouds passing by*

Out there in the struggle that is not about color but is about the nature of living, discord and turmoil arrive and lie like rings of thorns inside the mind that needs those thorns removed and their wounds, if not healed, at least attended to with what results in the experience of that stranger called comfort. The Negro, even when it was illegal, learned that there was a God who lived somewhere above all that the world had to offer or used to oppress, above bondage or sheer bad luck, and that He could be met on Sunday, with nothing more than belief, which was the ticket that allowed entrance into something called peace. If no other day, Sunday was there, waiting. With her expansive and intimate lyricism, Jackson again makes each word, each image, and each state that is referred to, both earthly and unbound, some mixture of opposites made true by the clarity of her emotion.

He'll give peace and comfort
To every troubled mind
Come Sunday, O come Sunday
That's the day

The fatigue that arrives with abuse is always the servant of defeatist feeling. The tiredness that is experienced as the weight of all wrong seems never to lighten, the blows that strike the soul arrive as if from a tireless machine, and the universe appears, for all purposes, to have become an infinite and deaf ear, capable of hearing nothing—not whining or wishing or praying. A man as private as Ellington, who said his prayers every night and who must have often felt nearly overwhelmed by the complex of artistic personalities, deadlines, and the treacherous dictates of show business, had learned to lean up against something that was as invincible as it was invisible, as quirky as all get-out but, finally, right there when it was needed. At Newport, just eighteen months earlier, the great spirit of God, appearing in the flesh as a blonde overtaken by the swing of his band and the searing blues tenor saxophone of Paul Gonsalves, had pulled Ellington up from the dregs into which his career had fallen. Incapable of sitting still, this all-American sandy-haired heifer jumped up and started dancing with so much liberated soul that she sparked the crowd to near-hysteria and gave Ellington's career another wind strong enough for the bandleader to capture the cover of *Time* magazine. So Ellington knew—yes, he did—that there was always that resource out there, effortless and infinite, capable of reversing fortune or defining it. That was as true to him as the facts of spring and should be understood together. Jackson, who had lived for so many years in the world of prayer, which could take place anywhere and at any time, and who also looked upon life as a great gift beyond all suffering and all want, again connects two things that seem outside of logic with the lyric power of her diction, her time, and the control of her voice's timbre.

Often we'll feel weary but He knows our every care
Go to Him in secret He will hear your every prayer
Lilies of the valley they neither toil nor spin
And flowers bloom and spring time birdies sing

The importance of *knowing* that one can be heard by the highest of high authorities has to be repeated, because that is a central message of the song. If all else has been exhausted and has exhausted you in the process, you may have to get down on your knees in private, or in the secrecy of your mind, and ask for what you truly need. Jackson reiterates that with an empathetic sincerity, the sound of having been there, too, giving the words *secret* and *prayer* a feeling of safety as well as a lilting tenderness in the way she lifts up off the note and pushes in more depth at the same time.

Often we'll feel weary but He knows our every care
Go to Him in secret He will hear your every prayer

Finally, Ellington is talking about the South, where the Negro worked from "can't see in the morning to can't see at night." Those sore muscles, those calluses, that aching back, those tired feet meant almost nothing when Sunday arrived and it was possible to dream into the face of God, to think about a future different from the hard present. Something like transcendence could happen then and give the kind of strength not only to get through a difficult life but to support those who would risk their lives trying to change things from the way they were to another way altogether. Jackson, having known what it felt like to pick plantation cotton during the week and to feel liberated on Sunday, sings the final words with the illuminated recognition that is not a flight from the world, as so many would have it, but a stepping into a deeper understanding of the meaning of freedom.

Up from dawn 'til sunset
Man work hard all day
Come Sunday, O come Sunday
That's the day

She then hums a chorus, the language gone and the music delivered with a voice that is beyond words but that amplifies all of the feelings that they were written to express. At this point, Jackson becomes the mother of us all, those hums arriving on Sunday morning accompanying the smells of breakfast in preparation; she becomes the mother at the bedside of the sick; she reminds us, through her ascendant tenderness, of the reverential empathy that underlies all of the dreams and the facts of civilization. There it was. Ellington had had his way and had made a masterpiece with the aid of an artist of unparalleled quality, one of the geniuses of feeling that America has been so lucky to produce. Her second song, "The Twenty-Third Psalm," is also a masterpiece, and it perfectly concludes the recording with a foreboding solemnity that constitutes tragic recognition of great danger yet assumes ultimate salvation. But we will not discuss that right now. We will end by letting Jimmy Woode, who played bass on the date, tell us about the effect Jackson had. "At one point, Duke decided to turn out the lights and have Mahalia sing 'Come Sunday' a cappella. Now, as you know, the band at the time was full of alcoholics, knuckleheads, dope shooters, kleptomaniacs, gamblers, and just about any kind of person you would meet in a band. They were all there. These men had been through it and they had been around. They were, you might say, rough customers. So we're all standing or sitting in the dark listening to that wonderful and incomparable sound of Mahalia Jackson, who was just singing her heart out. Beautiful beyond belief. And don't you know that when those lights came back on, there was not a man among that wild bunch who did not have a very, very obvious tear in his eye."

2004

The Presence Is Always the Point

Within five years of having arrived in New York from California in September 1975, I had the good luck of being able to assess the Manhattan jazz scene from three perspectives—as a drummer; as the booker of a jazz club, the Tin Palace on the Bowery; and as a writer of jazz criticism for the *Village Voice*. When I got to town, Duke Ellington had been dead for over a year, Louis Armstrong had been gone for five, and jazz itself was widely rumored to be on its way out, but the music that had evolved in so many directions during the lives of those two greatest of all jazz musicians. It had such vitality and presence that thinking back to how it was in those days now seems almost a dream of the way it should have been.

There were still so many fine players of so many different instruments that they created an enormous fugue of individual personalities, interpretations, techniques, and tonal colors. Though they were sometimes demoralized by the position that jazz had been forced into by a largely disinterested media and the notion that actual jazz playing had become a thing of the past, these artists pushed their music into the face of the present with the kind of transcendent coherence that not only improved the quality of their art but bettered the world through what they gave to and inspired in other human beings.

These were, as McCoy Tyner says, "special people." At this point, so many of them are gone that one could start asking if it had all been a dream, a collective wish agreed upon and supported by doctored photographs and unreal images delivered through film and television. Hardly. As with so many of the miracles of American life, those men and women did walk this earth, did take to bandstands and stand at bars and joke in dressing rooms and talk on the telephone and have rehearsals and travel the world, providing the human presence of jazz.

If you were in New York and were able to see and hear jazz for yourself, birth, affirmation, reaffirmation, decline, and death were right there to be had as experiences that would never leave your sensibility. If you lived at 2

East Second Street and felt like walking a couple of blocks west, you could step into Studio Rivbea, the avant-garde stronghold, where it might sound as though the world was ending that very night and where nobody sounded better than its owner, the avant-garde tenor saxophonist Sam Rivers, lean, high brown, and given to nearly knocking his knees together once his music got in complete touch with his nervous system. Or you could walk over to the Cookery at Eighth Street and University Place, where the rediscovered Alberta Hunter, who had been a star in the twenties, and who dressed like a lumberjack during the day, might be singing in a wonderful evening dress, while Barney Josephson, the man responsible for integrating downtown clubs in the thirties, sat and listened, his hair white, his body thin, his glasses held in place on his nose by thick black frames. Were Jo Jones in the house to lead the way, a trip to Gregory's might be necessary, where drummer Sonny Greer, alto saxophonist Russell Procope—both over sixty-five—and pianist Brooks Kerr, nearly blind but youthful and full of drive, were working. Greer and Procope could summon up the sound, or at least the memory, of the entire Ellington band, while Kerr had the whole of jazz piano from the turn of the century to 1940 at his fingertips.

From Gregory's, Jones might take me with him to hear Roy Eldridge at Ryan's in midtown. A small man, like so many jazz giants, Eldridge, with his white hair and mustache, his brown skin and the spirited gait of one who could have been a fast and vicious boxer with class once upon a time, was almost always good for at least one streak of fury through the chords, building, note upon note, a bonfire of intensity, loosing a pugnacious growl from the bell of his horn like the sound of a lion telling the world that he was not about to give up lording it over the jungle that was his bandstand.

Whether talking with his buddies from the good old days or orating about the nature of the world with his clipped enunciation, Jo Jones himself was never less than imperial in his baldness. He seemed indomitable standing there with his newspaper in his pocket, his long johns on if it was winter, his brandy bottle in his coat, a knife hidden somewhere as a testament to his understanding of the nightlife and proof that he was, as he loved to declaim, "a thug." But if one caught him in the aesthetic slaughterhouse that was the West End, a little club across the street from Columbia University way up on Broadway, his position in the hierarchy of the drums was quite evident—the touch, the power, the exultation, the pain, the finesse. It was all still there.

If you went to a concert at New York University presented by Jack Kleinsinger's "Highlights in Jazz," you might witness a miracle of assembly.

One after another—at someone else's show—Eubie Blake, Sam Wooding, Earl Hines, and Claude Hopkins sat down to the piano and played alone. Blake was then the oldest man of jazz and told a story of how he had learned a particular seventh chord from a cook when he was just a kid, then illustrated with an original piece from that time. Earl Hines (whom Jo Jones called "Toupee Willie") spoke of how he had been playing the ivory off the keys in Pittsburgh one night when Blake—in racoon overcoat, derby, and tuxedo, with cigar and carrying a cane to give more aristocracy to his stroll—warned the younger man that, as much music as he was playing, if "I come back through here and find you in this town I'll wrap this cane around your head." Hopkins, who had led a big band in the thirties, played a soft and beautiful something in which all of the notes and all of the chords sounded as though they were made of feathers and silk.

Part of the reason that a number of jazz musicians were disheartened in those days was that the battle for the future of the music was taking place against a threat that now seems never to have been there at all. The threat had come from a direction so unexpected that when it was first detected around 1970, no one could quite believe what they were starting to see. Major players were abdicating, abandoning jazz in favor of the fusion phenomenon. And the man who showed them the way was Miles Davis himself.

For some, like this one writing, who can still recall how Miles's band with George Coleman, Herbie Hancock, Ron Carter, and Tony Williams looked at an after-hours show sometime in 1964 at the Adams West Theater in Los Angeles, it seemed inconceivable. Then, four grown men had come onstage in dark suits followed by what appeared to be a little boy in a yellow suit with brown shoes who sat down behind the drums. This was the same kid who had been standing next to Ron Carter before the show, drinking a soda and giving off the ready-to-go feeling that adolescents always have. Davis was backstage, having a good time because the trio that came on before him was swinging and he was playing at conducting the band, moving as if in the boxing ring, snapping out his fists in approval, which meant more to those men up there than any kind of review or fat-salaried contract ever could. This little black giant was enjoying them. They had been accepted by one of the masters. His ruffling nickname was "Inky," and he had a house full of night creatures, hustlers and their women mostly—pimps, gamblers, numbers runners, drug dealers, sellers of hot clothes, and females who knew things about men that very few of their sex would want to find out. These were raucous people, given to loud talk and big laughs, too much cologne and too much perfume, their own debased ideas of aristocracy and a kind of distancing that could become intimate through violent confrontations if the wrong word was said or the bitterness resulting from an old grudge forced itself into bloodletting action. But when Miles Davis came onstage, every one of those denizens of the shadows got quiet, each aware that if something out of line took place, the little splendidly dressed prince might turn around and head for the door, no amount of imploring strong enough to bring him back. The genial Inky of backstage was gone when he walked out of the wings. The stern Davis face, a combination of anger and anguish, was in place, and the trumpeter began with a ballad, putting a mood into the air with his tone that seemed to draw something quite gentle out of even these street women, perhaps memories, perhaps dreams. A mist of romance took over and transformed this filled movie theater to a hoop of emotion surrounding the bandstand. Tony Williams, the little boy on the drums, touched them and swiped his cymbals and a sound we had never heard before went out into the theater. When they moved from the ballad tempo into a lightly sailing straight 4/4, a spiritual cheer went up every time the audience felt safe enough to applaud. That was when Miles Davis was at the top of his form, sharp as a tack, clean as a white fish, hipper-seeming and more confident than a man whom God had personally guaranteed would be going to heaven when his time came. That musicianship and that ritual then seemed invincible, but Davis proved that it was not and that we can never assume that there is a straight course, even for the greatest among us. Anyone can fall and nearly bring the building down on the way to the dirt.

Given his prominence and power, it is easy to understand how seriously many musicians took Davis when he claimed that his demon for adventure was pushing him "forward" toward fusion. As the bassist Jaymie Merritt said to me one night, "When genius is involved, you have to listen closely." What Davis did in his new guise and with his electronic guile helped set the new trend. Wayne Shorter, one of the most gifted composers and players of his generation, went into Weather Report, which began as a collective many musicians found interesting, but eventually evolved into Joe Zawinul's band, leaving more and more jazz elements behind. Tony Williams led a rock-influenced group called Lifetime, featuring British guitarist John McLaughlin, which seemed intent mostly on setting new levels of volume.

At least for a bit, Herbie Hancock seemed as if he was going to hold up high the flag of jazz truly remaking itself. The Swahili name of his band, Mwandishi, reflected the ethnic pretensions of the time, but that group—

with Buster Williams, Billy Hart, Eddie Henderson, Benny Maupin, and Julian Priester—was one of the great ones of that era and perhaps of any. No one had ever heard anything like it, and there were times when no one in the audience seemed to breathe from the first note to the last. The harmonies and the blends of the front line, the shifts in and out of different tempos and rhythms, as well as its sense of adventure, gave the Hancock Sextet that performance glow only the most compelling ensembles have. Had it lasted, a strong alternative to what became known as fusion would have been out there to inspire others to hold on. But Hancock also eventually submitted to the call of the wild cash register, got to the crossroads, and began sinking down.

Jazz was in the process of being redefined as merely a form of instrumental pop music. While the mixture of jazz and rock did create something that had not existed before, it also introduced instruments and beats that had nothing to do with swing, the propulsive essence of jazz phrasing. That jazz is a music built on adult emotion while rock is focused on adolescent passion created another problem for jazz musicians who tried fusion. They could never get to that teenage feeling of ardent ineptitude and resentment of sophisticated authority because they were not inept and their music was as sophisticated as any performing art that had evolved in the Western world.

But despite everything, evidence began to accumulate even during those dispiriting years that the music could remain true to itself and prosper. In October of 1976, on a very rainy evening in midtown Manhattan where the jazz impresario and pianist George Wein had a nightclub called Storyville, the bebop master Dexter Gordon found himself back in The Apple again. He had been living across the big water since 1962. Long since forgotten was his identity as a founding father of the approach that had so much to do with how Sonny Rollins and John Coltrane played the horn early in their careers. Or so it seemed before that night. The weather would have been prohibitive in most towns, but the house was packed and the saxophonist was obviously touched that people were so interested in hearing him that they weren't going to be stopped by rain.

Gordon immediately let everyone know that it was worth the wait and the wet. Standing in a cloud of charm at the microphone, his deep voice containing the essence of masculinity and whimsy as well as oblique, ironic humor, the long tall one introduced tunes and sometimes recited a portion of the lyrics of a ballad he and his men were about to perform. He held the saxophone as easily as he might stroke his chin and made the air of the room submit to him, blowing his horn with the magisterial confidence one would expect of a bebop master. At the same time, Gordon didn't seem to be playing bebop. As with any of the masters, the style was secondary to his expression. On that night, the stir began that would not only revitalize Gordon's career but reveal the power and the aesthetic scale of an art that this tenor saxophonist embodied for a moment so radiant it was indispensable.

A few months later Gordon was leading his band at the Village Vanguard for an in-person recording. The Vanguard was packed with musicians and lay listeners night after night, and he was on the way to a level of celebrity that greatly helped turn things around. If we look at it outside of how the business world reacted to it, we might think that the stardom that fell upon Dexter Gordon was some form of magic. It was not. Gordon had one of those unpredictable aces in the hole—Bruce Lundvall, a jazz fan and the president of Columbia Records. Had Clive Davis, the former president—who had fired Ornette Coleman, Keith Jarrett, Bill Evans, and Charles Mingus from the label in one day—still been at the wheel, the course of jazz would surely have been different. Lundvall loved the music and was the only president of a major record label willing to put money behind jazz artists. Tall and always superbly attired, Lundvall was the sole record executive of such high station who often went to clubs or to concerts to listen to his artists. If he signed them, he liked them. If he liked them, he went to hear them.

Gordon's reemergence and all the attention he got due to Columbia's marketing campaign soon sparked interest in straight-ahead swinging jazz and inspired the return of other expatriates. Johnny Griffin, the little giant who had such a fat tone and could play so lickety-split that he seemed actually to grow taller as he blew, came home to play again. Back in the kitchen during his breaks, or at the bar drinking red wine, he would talk of how he, Thelonious Monk, Elmo Hope, and Bud Powell would walk miles through the night on the way to Hope's house far up in the Bronx. Along the way, Powell might suddenly run up to some big guy and slap his face, which meant that Monk, Hope, and Griffin then had to keep this fellow from turning the great genius into mashed potatoes.

With his handlebar mustache and stoic eyes, Art Farmer, visiting from his home in Vienna, was the soul of poise and yearning lyricism. He always seemed somewhere else while on the bandstand, somewhere in the middle of a dream that might be extended as Clifford Jordan, the big, brown-skinned Negro from Chicago who often played tenor saxophone alongside him, unwove his many melancholies. One of Jordan's most remarkable nights came when he played with Harry Edison at Condon's after having been diagnosed with terminal cancer earlier in the day. Featured on "I Should Care," the big saxophonist didn't unburden himself or dirty his music with self-pity. In his own style, he played as Ben Webster might have, announcing that the melody of the life he had lived with both its sweet and bitter harmonies, was all of a lyrical piece, a gift that allowed one to croon or howl or snarl at the moon of a dream as long as there was the strength to do it.

Domestic exiles came home, too, some of them from the temporary sanctuary they had found in academe. All the drummers were there at the Village Vanguard when Max Roach returned to action and taught them, once again, that he was the master, playing with a poetic command of his instrument that has never been equaled, even as he so completely absorbed the free, timeless drumming style that the avant-gardist Rashied Ali, both moping and admiring, said: "Well, Max is playing free now. I guess I'll just go home and get my little rubber practice pad and wait for him to get another ten years older."

Roach would go on to perform in duet with Cecil Taylor, to perform with his percussion ensemble M'Boom and with the World Saxophone Quartet at the Cathedral of Saint John the Divine, to do multimedia solo concerts, to create a double quartet—his own pianoless group with a string quartet—and to polish his crown every way he could. But on one of the saddest nights of his life, Roach sat like a kid in Seventh Avenue South, a room now gone, as Jo Jones, who had by then depreciated to being no more than a thin drunk muttering to himself, took over the bandstand and went through a routine that seemed, as Ellington family member Michael James says, "part of the King Lear period."

Trumpeter Woody Shaw's evolution into a bandleader and an individual influence on horn players was very important to the morale of the music in those days because, with Miles Davis and Freddie Hubbard both mired in fusion, there was nobody out there who was making sense of what had happened in the early sixties. On many nights, in his full power, Shaw played as if each note was a finger in the dike holding back the deluge of commercialism.

There was a way that he went into his stuff. In the Vanguard's no-longer-functioning kitchen, which doubled as a dressing room, he could be cursing someone out or talking about the harmony Charlie Parker played on "Bird at St. Nick's" or recalling some adventure he had had when young and an apprentice member of Horace Silver's or Max Roach's or Art Blakey's band. Then, when it was time to hit, Shaw, who was legally blind but had memorized his way to the bandstand, would walk out of the kitchen, up the narrow hallway into the room, turn right past the front door, make another right behind the chairs, take the couple of steps into the gallery rather casually, move between the tables, and walk out on the stage where he performed a few tai chi moves before playing. This took only a minute or so, and Shaw then commenced to play, almost always something fiery as an opener. If you were close enough, you could see that he had the determined look of a snake about to strike, made even more intense by the vast human intelligence and fire he brought to the music.

Then there was the terrible end. Shaw had been strung out for years. He didn't look good and he was surely blind because I passed him a couple of times, not saying anything since the sight of a man as great as he was looking a few steps from homeless was depressing. Once when I did say something, he turned to me and there, behind the edgy, embittered, and anxious look of those desirous of some dope, were those eyes and that intelligence. I remembered then how much of a jazz musician he was and how, even when he was most successful and winning jazz polls that were thought to have been rigged by his management, Woody would finish off a job at the Vanguard and ride somewhere into Harlem or the Bronx or Brooklyn to sit in with unknown guys he heard were trying to play something.

On a tragic night when Max Roach was at the Vanguard, the drummer arranged for a private car to bring Shaw to hear the band. While Roach was on the bandstand, Shaw got the driver to take him into Brooklyn. The driver had been given instructions not to take Shaw anywhere, but the trumpeter, who could be very aggressive, had apparently convinced him that Max had changed his mind. The next morning Woody either slipped or stumbled down the stairs at a subway station and ended up so near the track that the incoming train cut off his right arm. Max called me after going to see him in the hospital. There Shaw was, he said, his head shaved and a long dark line of stitches down the middle, lying still with his arm shorn away, in a coma from which he would never recover. The sorrow in Max's voice carried the grief he had felt many times for special people who had been removed from the world too early.

In June of 1975, Cecil Taylor, too, came back to New York and performed at the Five Spot. Taylor had never had much of an audience, nor has his music ever been much of an influence on jazz, but that summer Gary Giddins in the *Village Voice* and Robert Palmer in the *New York Times* wrote about Taylor's return as a major event and the club was packed night after night. Audiences, enjoying it or not, sat before the unrelenting fury of Taylor's music, which had created its own category, one in which a vocabulary predominantly influenced by twentieth-century European music was delivered as though the piano was an enemy that had to be beaten into submission by the small brown-skinned man with the knitted cap who took off his glasses before starting and did not stop for an hour or more. The sheer velocity of his articulation, the size of his sound, and the parallel obsession with grandeur and all that either blocked or denied it, made the emotion Taylor projected reflect not so much a jazz feeling as that of a Beethoven without lyricism. Big statements and triumphant pounding delivered with unequaled physical strength arrived as though they could go on forever. Then, never acknowledging the audience, Taylor put his glasses back on and left the stage for the dressing room. There, far more educated and intellectually engaged than 99 percent of jazz musicians, he might be gleeful, full of wit, given to extraordinary leaps of association. Or he might be almost glum. Or, quite easily, he might break into a contemptuous rage leveled at bigotry and critical incompetence, describing the European concert world's aversion to black musicians, the similarities and distances between African dance and ballet, which he loved equally, the historical racial hiring policies that were why he hated the New York Yankees and the Boston Celtics. Taylor knew plenty about plenty. Therefore, whatever he was, and whatever he was playing, those who had heard it knew that he was the only one on the earth who could meet—or even wanted to meet—the challenges he had set for himself. The sheer intelligence of the man, genius actually, gave him a special color in any light, particularly because he had brought together intellectual thought with athletic prowess. While what he played had little to do with jazz, it was still a massive achievement on a human level.

That September, the Art Ensemble of Chicago worked at the same club for two weeks, awakening Manhattan to what would become a migration of Midwestern musicians who were members of the Association for the Advancement of Creative Musicians (AACM). They did little of the one-dimensional screeching and honking that characterized the music John Coltrane's talent sank under the burden of embracing in his last years. As Muhal Richard Abrams, one of the AACM's founders often said, they were not interested in playing a style, they wanted to play music.

That was evident at the Five Spot. There on the bandstand were saxophonist Roscoe Mitchell in street clothes, trumpeter Lester Bowie in a white lab coat, saxophonist Joseph Jarman, bassist Malachi Favors, and drummer Don Moye in face paint and African getups. Mitchell and Jarman seemed to have been largely influenced by Ornette Coleman, but Bowie's style owed much to Don Ellis. Ellis had embraced the whole of jazz trumpet, not just what had happened since 1945. His own recordings, such as *New Ideas* and *Essence*, his work on George Russell's *The Outer View*, and his *Down Beat* article, in which he called the New Orleans veteran Red Allen the most avant-garde trumpet player in New York, all make it clear that Ellis had been there first, by a decade. Don Cherry, the greatest mind and heart of all the avant-garde trumpet players, could not have done what Ellis did even if he wanted to, since his command of the horn never went far enough. Bowie was not the trumpet player that Ellis was, either—far from it—but he could play the instrument, which immediately separated him from the one-trick blats and squeals of purported avant-garde trumpet players. New York seemed to be waiting for him and for the Art Ensemble itself.

They had arrived in New York that fall on a big (and old) school bus. Though given to breaking down, it had room for the band, all the saxophones Mitchell and Jarman doubled on, and all the percussion instruments—the "little instruments" that any band member might pick up and use in performance as well as the astonishing array of African instruments at Don Moye's command. Moye had made himself as much a virtuoso at his African battery as any symphonic percussionist surrounded by his array of kettle drums, bells, and xylophones. With Favors and Moye back there, the Art Ensemble could stoke up any kind of ethnic black groove, any kind of beat associated with Afro-American music, while the compositions they played could be as simple as street rhymes or executed with tight, well-rehearsed up-tempo ensemble playing.

It was during that period that Air, featuring saxophonist and flutist Henry Threadgill, bassist Fred Hopkins, and drummer Steve McCall—all of them also AACM members—moved to New York from Chicago. At the time, while living above the Tin Palace, playing drums with my loftmate David Murray, and after a Hamiet Bluiett big band concert we held upstairs drew so many people and got so loud that the police came and told us we were making too much noise, I started booking Sunday-afternoon bands that played for the door. That series presented a lot of musicians new to Manhattan, almost all of them associated with what was considered the vanguard of the time.

On the Sunday afternoon that Air debuted in New York, everybody knew that this was a very special band. Most of the music was written by

Threadgill, who went on to form a septet that almost blew the windows out of the Tin Palace.

Musicians who hadn't been heard in New York for a while also came to play at the Tin Palace, like the alto and soprano saxophonist Gary Bartz, who had spent a lot of time messing around in fusion but made it clear that he was one of the great men of his horn. Musicians came to enjoy working that club so much that they started playing an extra fourth set, beginning at two a.m., which meant that the club crowded up again and one might see Dexter Gordon or Art Blakey or Cecil Taylor or Ornette Coleman or Max Roach in there as Clifford Jordan, Barry Harris, Walter Booker, and Vernell Fournier performed opposite Dewey Redman, Freddie Simmons, Mark Helias, and Eddie Moore, who was so black and huge I used to joke with him that Dewey must have mailed a cargo plane ticket to San Francisco so he could fly east in comfort.

Sometimes, as happened during the eighties, a spirit can take over and people will get busy on every level. These were the years when one young musician after another came to New York and seemed intent on doing only one thing—learning how to play jazz while fully aware that it was not the kind of art in which anything lucrative was guaranteed. People such as Wynton Marsalis, Wallace Roney, Geri Allen, Greg Osby, Rene Rosnes, Cyrus Chestnut, Lewis Nash, Peter Washington, Kenny Washington, Bob Hurst, Reginald Veal, Herlin Riley, Russell Malone, James Williams, Mulgrew Miller, Benny Green, Cassandra Wilson, Vanessa Rubin, Cindy Blackman, Teri Lynne Carrington, Jackie Terrason, Leon Parker, Javon Jackson, Kenny Garrett, Tony Reedus, Jeff Watts, Marvin Smitty Smith, and still more younger players kept leaving home for The Big Apple, surging up out of the ground, as if the music had its own will to live.

The renaissance of jazz in the eighties was fostered as much by Art Blakey as by anybody else. One Sunday in the middle of the decade there was a Father's Day celebration for Blakey at the Apollo. The theater was filled, and backstage, as the drummer Roy Haynes said: "It looked like some kind of an African king's place." Blakey had many children, grown and toddling, as well as girlfriends, wives, and numbers of musicians who had played in his training school for the art, The Jazz Messengers. He had been the sacrificial hero who played and played, night after night, while those fledglings stumbled over themselves until they began to swing with enough confidence to take off and begin their own bands. Sitting in the audience that afternoon was the singer Betty Carter, who was now doing exactly the same thing that Blakey had done for years—bringing young musicians into her band and putting them through the rigorous tasks necessary to learn how to swing and to play in many different tempos, from extremely slow to as fast as possible.

They had some help. The reissue boom that had been spearheaded by Orrin Keepnews at Fantasy Records, classic material handsomely packaged and with good liner notes, provided young players with recorded examples of high-quality music that had been unavailable for years. This meant that, perhaps for the very first time, jazz musicians were truly learning how to play in styles that stretched back to the beginnings of the music.

More encouragement came from the stage of Cooper Union, where Abraham Lincoln once spoke. There, the American Jazz Orchestra, conceived by Gary Giddins, gave splendid performances of classic jazz under the leadership of John Lewis. As Loren Schoenberg, who took over after Lewis left, once explained during an especially powerful concert of Ellington music, the repertory movement offered plenty of options. Music could be performed as faithfully to the original recordings as possible, or new improvisations in the styles of the period could be allowed, or different arrangements of a given piece could be brought together, another take on the idea of variations on a theme. The point was that jazz did not have to lose bodies of great music just because those who once played it were no longer in the world.

As the jazz spirit started to rise higher and higher, fine bands came into existence. One of the best was Old and New Dreams, featuring Don Cherry, Dewey Redman, Charlie Haden, and Ed Blackwell, which played a repertoire dominated by the music of Ornette Coleman, and made it clear every night how very different what Coleman had introduced into jazz was from the bulk of the music played by those usually said to be in the jazz vanguard. They swung, they were melody makers, and the whole tradition of jazz flowed through their playing exactly as it did from the best of the musicians who had come forward since the bebop movement of the forties.

There was also the return of the prodigals. Tony Williams began to lead a wonderful band with trumpeter Wallace Roney, saxophonist Billy Pierce, pianist Mulgrew Miller, and—in succession—bassists Charnette Moffett, Bob Hurst, and Ira Coleman. At the Vanguard one night a few weeks after Art Blakey died in 1990, Williams could be heard mixing into his playing signal things that had touched him when he was a kid. Some Max Roach for a bit, then Philly Joe Jones, then Roy Haynes, Elvin Jones, Kenny Clarke—almost an autobiography of his own beginnings. By playing so much less loudly than when he was struggling to blast his way into the fusion world, Williams made the power of his entire conception audible, which included writing that defined him as the most complete drummerleader of any period. All of the music on that bandstand was his—every note, chord, arrangement. The result was a very serious extension of what the Miles Davis Quintet had been doing in the sixties, the drummer's most glorious period of recognition. No, this didn't mean Williams had gone backwards, as too many of the intellectual clubfeet of jazz writing would automatically assume. By setting aside his apparent dreams of pop stardom, Williams had reached through the recent musical dark ages to a period of illumination, brought forward a flame, and was piling fresh logs on it. At forty-six, Williams was doing what all masters do once they accept the richness of their own perceptions: They come to embody every element of what initially attracted them to music and to their instruments. Williams sometimes jacked himself up chorus by chorus into the sort of swing no young drummer, however gifted, could lay down. For the first time I heard the weight in his sound that only comes of emotion and substantial experience.

But of all the prodigals, the one who returned to the highest point of glory may have been Freddie Hubbard. In almost biblical fashion, the trumpeter had a revelation when he was nearly shocked to death as he was warming up backstage for an outdoor concert and the wire to an electronic gadget he had attached to his trumpet was pulled through some water. Once the fusion ruse was behind him, Hubbard eventually worked at the Blue Note, the largest and best-paying jazz club in the city, the one responsible for presenting people such as Sarah Vaughan, the Modern Jazz Quartet, Oscar Peterson, Billy Eckstine, and Joe Williams in the kind of setting jazz listeners never thought they would experience again.

There, Hubbard did the richest trumpet improvising of the time. Almost gone were the memories of the platform shoes and plaid pants of his fusion days. Handsome and looking more and more like Louis Armstrong, Hubbard now wore exquisitely cut suits, beautiful shirts, and silk ties, and he played with all the accumulated luminosity of a man who has been at his horn for over forty years. His time feeling, which was as witty as it was mock-pugnacious, his melody lines, and his harmonic personalization of what he learned from Coltrane and Rollins were at a point of imposing effortlessness. He was also the ox of his instrument, given to unflagging strength and projection, a clarion authority that recalled Armstrong as much as his looks did. One night he picked up the flugelhorn and did a version of "Blue Moon" that included a long, long introduction, a rhythmic rebuilding of the theme, and chorus after chorus of extemporaneous purity, motifs varying from the pinnacle of the horn's reach to the bottom, smears that transformed themselves into melody, harmonic choices that were so surprising they accented themselves, and a longing that heroically emphasized the first word of the tune's title and led his listeners back to the beginnings of the music.

In the end, that this kind of power continues to exhibit itself is far more important than the regret that the music is not appreciated to the degree jazz lovers would like to see. When you get down to it, no matter the style, no matter what anyone says about it, the point is what happened when those musicians were standing there in the flesh, shaping, sweating, and emoting. They displayed the wonders of an extraordinary art through their own talents and their collective victories. If there was truly a paean to the presence of jazz, it was the way they were and what they did.

2000

Live at the Village Vanguard
Wynton Marsalis

Band stands in jazz clubs are altars of swing and there is no more famous altar than the one in the Village Vanguard, which is the oldest jazz club in the world and the one in which the most swing has been dispensed. The Vanguard is a basement that one enters by walking down the stairs. It is on Seventh Avenue in Greenwich Village, which means that there is always something going on outside the club. There might be a tourist bus full of Japanese loaded down with cameras and stepping onto the sidewalk as though they are now in the presence of a very special American temple, which they are. Any imaginable kind of person, dressed any kind of way, might be ambling north or south on Seventh Avenue and stop in front of the club to say that he or she remembered when some you-know-who was playing down there, back in the day. Somebody this same person knew who's now dead worked there and got him or her in, either through the front door or the back door. A listener old as the hills could recall when Harry Lim, the Javanese lover of swing music, used to organize jam sessions at the Vanguard in the forties, which established masters and a genius named Dizzy Gillespie attended, instruments at the ready. Another who worked in radio and now lives in Japan could tell you of how he came upon John Coltrane and Red Garland having a conversation near the stairs at the back of the club about the sexual rites of wolves, with Coltrane speculating hilariously on the erotic psychology of the male wolf. Or who could forget, as Elvin Jones once said, how Thelonious Monk had such a large presence that he could sit near the end of the bar late at night when the club was nearly empty and fill up the entire space? Or the apocryphal night that Max Roach and Charles Mingus, bent on rattling Ornette Coleman (who was playing his saxophone with only bass and drums), devised a plan at a bar across the street. Roach loudly came in pretending to have lost his mind and began banging on the piano and asking why it wasn't being used, then Mingus, dressed in black from head to toe, came down the stairs, picked Roach up and put him across his shoulder, turned to look at the audience, and left. Those are some of the things that make the club what it is and place it within the realm of myth, where Americans of all colors and people from many countries have gathered either to play or to listen or to do both and hang out laughing and reminiscing about the bad times and the good times.

On an unsuspecting night, a customer might be accosted by an atrocious and rightfully unemployed drummer who promotes himself endlessly, trying to force a tape of his one recording on whomever lacks the intuitive smarts to give him no more than a nod and a brush off. For a few years he was banished from standing in front of the club because he began—out of nowhere—collecting admissions as people waited to get in and made off with the bucks. At present, like so much of what makes New York exactly the thing that it is, he is back now and again.

On a good night, lined up outside with others ready to get a healthy dose of Americana in rhythm and tune, one feels the emotion of being among very special people. These are jazz people, no matter where on this earth they might come from. These are people who listen beyond the commercial arenas and beyond the drum machines and the overland patching together of bits that have transformed the making of pop recordings into something much more like movies than the art of jazz, in which the refined skills of interacting musicians construct the art on the moment. But those people in that Vanguard line with you out there, the ones who will come if it's hot or cold or raining or snowing, they are people who want to hear some musicians get up on that bandstand and perform. They want to witness that interplay in which the present is taken over and the glow of life given form seeps into or sears its way through the air. Such people, down in the deeper parts of their souls, seek the experience of becoming better versions of themselves.

Jazz people know swing is what they're after. Why? Because swing, as one musician observed, is the sound of support and welcome and recognition. So those listeners want to be in on that number, that improvised occasion when the entire room—everything on the bandstand and off the bandstand—becomes one force defined by swing. I'm talking about when swing becomes both invisible and solid. Then all that falls within hearing distance starts swinging and becomes that swing. That, for those of you who don't know, is the highest aspect of the performance relationship between the jazz musician and the jazz listener and the jazz place. In that relationship, the willing listener hears something both extremely sophisticated and, at its best, no more than a note away from an equally greasy condition. That combination of high-minded expression and the gutbucket funk of the blues—the sweet stink of love and the filth of the rot ever encroaching on existence—is what makes a jazz moment particular in its feeling. The feeling of jazz, finally, is something adult, not adolescent. Listeners either aspire to that grand condition of the grown-up or, as with those who are there already, they wish no more than reaffirmation swung so hard or crooned in jazz time with so much charisma that the wounds, the toil, and the heartbreak become no more than spiritual seasoning. That's why jazz people have a different look to them, no matter their point of origin; they are seekers and veterans of sophisticated feeling.

The Village Vanguard, so steeped in those moments and those far, far more than a thousand nights of magical tale-telling, is the perfect place to get the full weight of jazz laid on you. One of the reasons is that the sound up on that bandstand and out in that room has no equals, just as the club has no dressing room, only a kitchen where musicians and their friends hang out and talk before or between or after shows. There used to be food served but that's over. Now all you can get is a drink and a place to sit. Some of the people who used to work the door but are now gone gave the place a reputation for demanding money for abuse. Audiences endured them because of where they were and who was playing there.

The late Max Gordon (1903–1989) started the whole thing in the middle thirties and was there almost every night, even when he was in his eighties and tumbled down the entire length of the stairs, only to sit at a table near the door until closing, his overcoat still on, his face not exactly dazed but at a distance in its demeanor from everyone and everything in the room. A tough old bird as they used to say. He was some character, that Gordon, short, full of brine and vinegar, an Eastern European Jew who grew up in Oregon, had a prominent forehead and smoked bad cigars because, as he said, "I'm a cheap sonofabitch."

Gordon sometimes was seated in the very back of the club under a WPA painting of a nude, where he drank champagne with a pretty girl on either side of him, patting them occasionally and referring to each of the fillies as dollink. Sometimes he sat in the kitchen at his desk across from the stove that was no longer used for anything and told stories of the Depression or of how one famous singer who hustled hot furs in his club during an engagement removed an entire full-length mink from a very small bag and handed it to her driver, who made the sale. He could tell you about Miles Davis, the haughty emperor of resentment, and all of his girls, famous and not famous, some so beautiful one's eyes had to be overhauled after looking at them. There was John Coltrane, a quiet man whose enormous, sustained intensity eventually gave way to endless hysteria on the bandstand and sovereign gloom during the breaks. Blowing some of his last songs, Coleman Hawkins, in full gray beard as death leaned on him, filled his tenor saxophone and the room and would, every so often, stop after he played a phrase he liked and laugh as though he were at home alone, not working in front of an audience. Thelonious Monk, always tardy and sometimes coming down the steps in heavy collisions of shoe leather and concrete, not even removing his coat and going straight to the piano, once explained to Gordon that he was late for work because the downtown subway train he got on started going backwards! Old man Gordon had the entire Count Basie band in the Vanguard for one night. There was the time that Louis Armstrong came in and every light became brighter, even the glint on the instruments took on more power, and that man, the king of jazz, talked to everyone as though he had known them since the day he was born, now and again telling remarkably bawdy stories. Duke Ellington, the grandest expression of ongoing genius in jazz, sat in a corner and listened intently then gave the waitress a fat tip before floating up the stairs like a very expensive cologne so out of the ordinary that it had never had a name. The little club owner brought them all in there at one time or another, if they were great or not so great, if they performed or if they only listened, or didn't seem to listen as they joked around in the kitchen or in the hallway behind the bar and near the bathroom while somebody else was up on the bandstand playing as if heaven and earth depended on every note. So when you saw Max Gordon, he carried the spirit of jazz inside him as a facilitator, a patron, and a witness, just as he shuffled along in his running shoes one night carrying a pile of bucks in both hands to his desk, growling, "Ah, money. I hate this shit."

The trumpeter's manager, Ed Arrendell, part of the young, feisty, and adventurous crew that distinguished the bandleader's artistic, social, and business situation, made the first deal with Gordon in 1983. Then, Wynton Marsalis began bringing his septet into the Village Vanguard, after first moseying down the stairs during the earlier eighties and sitting in with trumpeters like Clark Terry, Woody Shaw, and Jon Faddis. In that more than special room, the young man, his band, and their music were swirled round by the spirits of a place where legend was made and sustained. He was himself something of a legend at even so early an age because Marsalis had very quickly become a force much more formidable than any would have assumed when he arrived in Manhattan twenty years ago, a talent from New Orleans whom musicians such as Buster Williams were telling everybody about after they heard him in his hometown. "There's a boy down in New Orleans who's going to upset everybody when he comes to New York," Buster said.

What Marsalis became went far beyond what anyone thought was in the offing, even those most impressed by his enfant terrible stage. As Woody Shaw told Maxine Gordon: "He's going to go beyond all of us, not just on the horn but in the music. He's going to take it some place else. I can hear it." Shaw was right. His impact was to go far beyond the level upon which he could play his horn at eighteen years old. Easily the most totally gifted trumpeter to arrive since 1960, he was described in the middle eighties by Ron Carter as the best player to have appeared in the last fifteen years. That was because, by 1970, things were beginning to go bad for jazz. The phenomenon of fusion was on the build and it was debunking swing, in all its magnificent variety, through static rock and funk beats, electric pianos, and bass guitars. At the same time, so-called avant-garde jazz of the sort distinctly separate from the swinging version that Ornette Coleman brought to New York in 1959 had dispensed with jazz rhythm altogether. Major figures in jazz either sold out to pop trends or abdicated, while those with serious integrity continued to swing in contexts of increasing obscurity. Those given to premature autopsies were sure that, this time, jazz was on its death bed. So when Marsalis moved north to New York in 1979, things looked fairly grim for jazz because, in terms of aesthetic troops, younger musicians didn't seem to have much interest in the true identity of the art.

Marsalis changed that situation dramatically. By example, through recruitment, teaching, and his own accomplishments, he became, as Betty Carter said, "the fate of the music. I believe he arrived here to bring the music back." As the youngster developed and his vision clarified, he went on to become both the Dizzy Gillespie and the Duke Ellington of his generation. He created a new plane of technique and rhythmic complexity for his instrument as Gillespie had and went on to compose perhaps the most wide-ranging and impressive body of music since the death of Ellington. Like Gillespie, the swing-struck lad from the land of red beans and rice also possessed the missionary zeal to gather and encourage other musicians. He would talk them into coming to New York and help them maintain morale once they got here. This Gillespie redux was given to showing these young musicians many technical things and, as his own comprehension deepened,

Marsalis urged them to learn the entire language of the music, not just the superficial sound of it. The four major drummers of their generation are Kenny Washington, Lewis Nash, Jeff Watts, and Herlin Riley; half of them, Watts and Riley, came to power in Marsalis's band. Pianists Kenny Kirkland, Marcus Roberts, Stephen Scott, Cyrus Chestnut, Eric Reed, and Farid Barron have come through there. Alto saxophonist Wes Anderson, tenor saxophonists Don Braden, Todd Williams, James Carter, Walter Blanding, and Victor Goines have been in that band of his. Bassists Charnette Moffett, Lonnie Plaxico, Bob Hurst, Reginald Veal, and Ben Wolf have had to handle their register in the rhythm section. Not a lightweight list. For the premiere performance, the recording, and the road tour of Marsalis's Pulitzer Prize-winning *Blood on the Fields*, the Lincoln Center Jazz Orchestra was dominated by personnel brought from across the country whom the composer had encountered in master classes he had given when some of them were little more than children.

That level of engagement with music and musicians never gave in and maintains itself to this second. While such devotion was expected of Art Blakey and Betty Carter, it was surprising from young Marsalis, whose home was always filled with young musicians talking about music or going to the piano or practicing; some sleeping in the bathtub of his first apartment, others calling from places like Detroit to learn certain harmonic sequences and the sounds of particular chords, which he played for them over the telephone. Like a contemporary Ellington, he turned his back on the ragamuffin minstrelsy of the fusion period and his sartorial example got most musicians out of coming on bandstands ragged up as though they were rehearsing in somebody's funky basement or were dressing the part to get a job with a rock band.

While the technical expansions of his art, the reiteration of virtuosity, and the reassertion of bandstand elegance were not met happily by the critical establishment, that made no difference to an international audience of listeners, who knew almost immediately that something special was afoot. Besides, those listeners did something that few jazz writers do: They went out to hear music and stuck around, listening throughout the night whenever possible. Sometimes these listeners traveled to the Vanguard from as far away as Minnesota in order to hear Marsalis and his players, or they went every year from Detroit to Washington, D.C., when he was doing engagements at Blues Alley as Christmas and the New Year approached.

Celebration was the name of the game and every night had a festive quality to it because the sound of welcome and of support, the essential feelings of jazz, were in the air. Marsalis recalls that when Herlin Riley joined the hand, that the deep connection to the humanity of New Orleans started to assert itself in the way all of the musicians dealt with each other. This gave the music itself the same kind of quality one experienced when a New Orleans girl gave a party for the band one night on New York's Upper West Side and the food, the music, and the human interplay made one realize that the warmth and style Louis Armstrong always remembered so fondly were still firmly in place. That warmth and style were extended by the audiences. The listeners were often well-dressed and classy, the guys good looking and the women sometimes fine enough to redefine fine. Audiences packed the clubs and were lined up outside the Vanguard until two or three 'o clock in the morning, thrilled to get in and given to joyous shouting, whistling, and clapping as the music lifted up. These kinds of reactions were much deeper than the promotional power of a record company, which cannot sustain the audience of someone whom the listeners don't like. If record companies could make audiences do whatever they wanted them to do, there would be much more profit because anybody foisted on the public could remain a star over the years instead of, in regular fashion, becoming just another lucrative flash in the pan, here yesterday, gone today, sometimes rich, almost always forgotten.

As the breadth, substance, and depth of Marsalis's work makes clear, he will be remembered long after his most irrational detractors are forgotten. Gifted enough to conquer both jazz and European concert music, going to the top in both idioms—an achievement that has no precedent—he has also chosen to play jazz itself, not a style of jazz, which means that he has had to develop authority in approaches that range from New Orleans to the best work of Ornette Coleman and John Coltrane as well as the Miles Davis Quintet featuring Wayne Shorter, Herbie Hancock, Ron Carter, and Tony Williams. The upshot is that Marsalis the bandleader and composer, like Charles Mingus, John Lewis, George Russell, and Horace Silver at their finest, became fascinated with the challenge of breaking out of conventional forms while maintaining the strengths and subtleties of the blues, of swing, and of the counterpoint that arrived from New Orleans, not Europe.

In order to thoroughly address the weight of the music, Marsalis had to turn his back on the car-dealer mentality that dominates so much of jazz discussion in magazines. The people given to this mentality, all willing to promote the sale of anything eccentric, whether it drives well or not, are part of a jazz car-dealership clan that has a thirty-five-year intellectual tradition of crumbling under innovation the word, not innovation the fact.

While the car dealers were looking the other way, Marsalis applied his talent with such originality that he became, album by album and public performance by public performance, the most important innovator to arrive in jazz since the middle sixties. He rethought the playing of his instrument, the harmony, the rhythm, and the nature of composition with such expanding authority across layerings of reinvented style that his output now seems beyond the capabilities of one person.

Those achievements are, in fact, beyond a single individual. Art historian Kenneth Clark could have been writing about Marsalis when, in *What Is a Masterpiece?*, he discussed two aspects of a transcendent work, describing them as a confluence of memories and emotions forming a single idea, and a power of recreating traditional forms so that they become expressive of the artist's epoch and yet keep a relationship with the past. This instinctive feeling of tradition is not the result of conservatism, but is due to the fact that, in Lethaby's familiar words, slightly adapted, a masterpiece should not be "one man thick, but many men thick."

Marsalis himself points out that none of what he has achieved would have been possible without a whole heap of gracious instruction in the musical specifics of various styles, not nebulous rhetoric. Those specifics were presented to him both on the bandstand and in conversation with musicians such as Danny Barker, Lionel Hampton, Sweets Edison, Roy Eldridge, Joe Wilder, Dizzy Gillespie, Clark Terry, Walter Davis, Jr., Charlie Rouse, Jimmy Heath, Frank Foster, John Lewis, Art Blakey, Elvin Jones, Barry Harris, Ron Carter, Herbie Hancock, Wayne Shorter, Tony Williams, Ornette Coleman, Ed Blackwell, James Black, and of course, his father, Ellis Marsalis, the legendary New Orleans jazz teacher and smoking piano player.

Coming in contact with those musicians and many others, Marsalis was able to see clearly the size of the art he had chosen. He came to understand the scope of the music, beginning with his horn. From close study of recordings and from discussions with other trumpeters, he digested a vocabulary that might now be the broadest in the history of jazz trumpet. In that sense, the actual magnitude of Louis Armstrong was a revelation in terms of tone, melody, rhythm, and giving a form to improvisation. Marsalis was so thorough in what he learned that, in the dressing room of the now-defunct New York club Lush Life, he took Don Cherry's pocket trumpet and began playing improvisations the older musician had created on Ornette Coleman's *The Shape of Jazz To Come*. Everything that Marsalis took seriously, each thing that had added to the expressive palette of the music, contained what Kenneth Clark pinpointed when he wrote: "Effective revolutions depend on convincing details."

The maturing power of those effective details is what has made the career of Marsalis such a surprising voyage. In the middle eighties, when he began reinventing New Orleans music on *Black Codes*, the bass line of the title track came from the Crescent City street theme, "Hey Pockee Way." With that recording, pianist Anthony Wonsey says: "He changed jazz. It was some new stuff, no matter what anybody says. But they know. We all listened to that. It was something different, different from Miles, Wayne, Herbie, from everybody. He set a new direction and everybody was listening to it." Alto saxophonist Jon Gordon observes that "[f]rom *Black Codes* forward, Wynton obviously became one of the greatest arrangers for small groups in the history of Jazz. Anybody with ears can hear that. His writing for his small groups is just incredible."

Those reinventions continued through his reduction of his band from a quintet with his brother Branford to a quartet featuring Marcus Roberts, which rewrote the book on avant-garde trumpet, piano, and rhythmic complexity on *Live at Blues Alley*. In the quintet with Todd Williams, Marsalis continued to explore his favorite area, the blues, the high point of that band captured on the remarkably structured recording, *Uptown Ruler*. His sextet with Wes Anderson produced the marvelous *Levee Low Moan*, followed by *The Majesty of the Blues*, which first laid down the broad aesthetic scope that Marsalis has continued to develop. The depth of the connection to the soul sources of the music are quite evident on the "Uptown Ruler," included on this Vanguard set, where the chanting and singing move us into the life of the night and the sensuality that underlies the proud intelligence.

Marsalis has—since the Classical Jazz series that was conceived by Alina Bloomgarden began at Lincoln Center in 1988—been artistic director of what later became Jazz at Lincoln Center in 1991, the most important jazz program in the world. His programming choices and the amount of preparation have resulted in dozens upon dozens of superb performances, featuring, as examples of the sweep of the personnel, trumpeters from Doc Cheatham, Sweets Edison, Dizzy Gillespie, and Art Farmer to Don Cherry, Wallace Roney, Nicholas Payton, and Roy Hargrove. Under an expanding staff, the program has become, since 1994, the first full-fledged jazz constituent at a major American arts complex, standing equal with ballet, opera, film, and theater. There are commissions, lectures, film programs, master classes, national and international tours, concerts for young people, and a national big band competition. Starting in 1989 as the Classical Jazz Orchestra, The Lincoln Center Jazz Orchestra is now ten years old and, as proven on *Big Train* and *Sweet Release/Ghost Story* from this massive release of Marsalis music, it has become the best orchestra of its kind on the planet. Without Marsalis, none of this would have been possible.

Bassist Peter Washington, who is but thirty-five and has played on more than two hundred albums, says of Marsalis: "No one can deny that he has brought much more respect to jazz as an art. Anybody out here can feel the difference. Wynton is responsible for a new level of respect, here and around the world. He also has a phenomenal work ethic. He keeps developing and working at his craft and writing long pieces, when he wants to, that make plenty of musical sense. The backlash against him is proof of how much good he has done out here. If he wasn't so good for the music nobody would care about him."

These recordings, all seven of them, provide a mythical seven nights at the Village Vanguard, since no band works there Monday through Sunday and since the personnel switches back and forth between bands with Todd Williams and Marcus Roberts as opposed to Victor Goines and Eric Reed. But that is all part of what makes this such an imposing set of performances. One can see that this band, with either personnel, was one of the greatest not only of its time but of all jazz time. As "Pedro's Getaway" lets you know, the swing, the precision, the fire, and the originality of the music is often overwhelming. Much of this has to do with Marsalis himself, whose opening version of "Cherokee" changes the record book as far as his horn is concerned and whose playing on "Black Codes," "Uptown Ruler," and "Jig's Jig," as but three examples, makes it clear, yet again, that he is the king of avant-garde trumpet firmly rooted in jazz, blues, and swing. Marsalis has pointed out before that his quite detailed familiarity with the European avant-garde language from his own performances of it in orchestras under the baton of men like Gunther Schuller determines his unwillingness to write or improvise what is called jazz but sounds like second-rate imitations of twentieth-century European music. The swelling fire with which he executes a number of the passages in those mightily adventurous improvisations recalls Roy Eldridge realigned for another time. His ballads speak for themselves. In fact, the extended "Embraceable You" sets forth new plans of lyric majesty and rhythmic intricacy.

Then there is the playing of the band itself. Both rhythm sections have very original ways of accompanying the featured improvisors, with Riley weaving together New Orleans street beats and his own inventive version of the jazz language; Veal, in his introductions to "Down Home with Homey" and "In the Sweet Embrace of Life"—not to mention the stuff he whips out on track after track in the rhythm section—makes it inarguable that he is not only the great power bassist of his era but the one with the most unique set of syncopations and ideas used to create swinging counterpoint. Ben Wolfe, by the way, is not even vaguely playing around either, always attacking the bass with his own drive and sense of counterpoint. That counterpoint is worked at variously by perhaps the two most impressive piano players of the last decade-and-a-half, Marcus Roberts and Eric Reed, each of whom invents with rhythmic daring and originality of the sort that takes up the slack and expands upon the improvised, orchestral arrangement from the piano in the rhythm section that Ellington, Monk, Lewis, and Silver brought to such profound authority. As—to just pick two—his features on "Down Home with Homey" and "Pedro's Getaway" underline, Wes Anderson is the main man on his instrument in his generation, the alto player slept on the longest but the one who keeps lighting up the music with ever-higher stacks of flaming logs. Williams and Goines are equally impressive and Wycliffe Gordon is acknowledged among musicians as the young master of what he does with that trombone. In all, these are the kinds of musicians who make audiences jump and shout, which they did nightly at the Village Vanguard. There were no houses more awed than those who sat there as the first section of "Citi Movement" was played, exhibiting a kind of ensemble virtuosity that, given the length of the performance, sets another standard for group playing. Oh, yeah.

If you weren't there, you missed some of the champion jazz playing of any era. But you have this document in your hands. It will take you back to a mythical place and a mythical time, one filled with hot and sweet music, people packed in like sardines, and women who made solid all of the metaphors in the most beautiful and lyric moments of the invisible activity on the bandstand. What can you say? I guess no more than Marsalis himself often says when he hears a strong performance: "It was swinging. It started off swinging. It kept swinging, and those who heard it will remember it."

1999

Epilogue

Nothing in art ever really leaves unless every last bit of it is lost, like the very great bulk of Sophocles's plays. In the world of jazz improvisation, each performance becomes no more and no less than life impressing its prints upon the invisible glass of our experience. It is there as long as we can remember it, or it is insufficiently served by even the best recording equipment, which can capture the tracks of the sly mongoose or the big bear of jazz in motion . . . but will never be able to pull in its *presence*. Everyone who has ever seen a great athlete in person knows this because they become aware of the fact that virtually perfect camera placements and the finest crews cannot give the television or film viewer the dimension, the power, the grace, and the speed of the moment. In person a great tennis player or a great pitcher or a great boxer might be bigger than the average person and might display a level of authority at points of competition that would not be as stunning on the television or the movie screen. The sheer speed and power of a pitch or a hit in baseball cannot be captured on film, nor can the sound of leather gloves pounding against flesh, or the game of giants that is basketball because, on television, they all seem to be normally sized since they are not playing with men of average height. That is why the viewer can be startled at the end of a game when a player is interviewed by a sportscaster whose head is a long distance from seeming, like his interviewee, to scrape the roof of the heavens.

The meaning of the present can be made available, but the *force* never can. In jazz, as in any performing art, the aesthetic existence of a statement arriving in the present is reserved only for those who were there; the rest, however wonderful, amounts to no more than leftovers. After having heard James Earl Jones on stage, I knew I would never have any idea what Richard Burton sounded like in a theater, where it is said that he had one of the most powerful stage whispers ever summoned. A woman I know who sang with Pavarotti remembered that his sound filled up so much space on stage that she could not hear herself and had to assume, through the muscle memory of her body, that the notes were coming out! Paul Bley says that information in jazz is passed on only on the bandstand and that one cannot get close enough to understand it, even if sitting in the first row with one foot on the stage. "That's still not close enough. You have to be *in* the sound because that's where the deepest information is passed on to you."

We can rant and rave against such an icy truth as the closed arena of the present and the indelible fact of presence, or we can attempt to take seriously Malraux's belief that art is a protest against man's fate: decay, dissolution, and death. What Malraux said was interesting, and some would believe that the enduring quality of art can be captured by that statement. I am not one of them. I believe that art is about only one thing: the pervasiveness of the present, since no past and no future ever makes itself felt. As a Wallace Shawn character says of the past and the future, "Where are they right now? Where are they? I mean they're not here and, God knows, they're not anywhere else."

I agree because it seems to me that art is about always, which is the story of the present, its beginning and its end, neither of which ever takes place because the present continually gives way to another version of itself: the ocean of the moment forever becoming another moment. Only material, from stone to flesh, shows wear; the present never does. As for art as a form of warfare: Only a mad German like Nietzsche or a French writer given to self-promotion, little fibs, great lies, and sometimes even greater thoughts, would put art in the position of attack, which is what rebellion is about, the shaking up of the order, even the Malrauvian order of rapid and inevitable destruction. I believe that art is not about shaking up the order or any form of resistance anymore than breathing is a form of rebellion against suffocation. Art is about presenting the order ever more accurately. Those who are shaken up are only experiencing a reaction, which is very different from the statement of always that art never fails to make when it accomplishes the effusive or Spartan state of the real, which can be based on the truth or exist in a world of total fantasy.

I did not think about much heavy-duty stuff when I last heard Francesco Cafiso, who might inspire many thoughts as one listens to him. But I did feel the myth of jazz reborn in his form because Cafiso has the ability to take command of the present and ride it like a young man ready to give direction to a wild and tireless stallion. Cafiso is from Sicily and is only seventeen but can play with much more authority than many men two or three times his age. He is the sort of wunderkind who can only be ignored at a time like this, when the critical establishment is so averse to jazz that it resents nothing more than a real jazz musician, even a white one as far removed from the geographical roots as Sicily. Someone too naïve to understand the real nature of intellectual conventions in jazz would have thought that the desire to constantly place someone white at the head of the pack would have influenced them in Cafiso's favor. That he is European would seem to fit in with the desire of those writers who say that nothing of importance is coming from America these days. Not in this case. Cafiso sounds too good and he sounds too much like a jazz musician because he has an affinity for the feeling of jazz. Yet he has been ignored by virtually all concerned. Perhaps strange, perhaps not.

I was first told about him by Wynton Marsalis, who heard the youngblood at fourteen and was so stunned by Cafiso's abilities that the adolescent saxophonist was hired to go on tour with the Lincoln Center Jazz Orchestra that summer in Europe. I did not take seriously what I heard from Marsalis, Wes Anderson, or any of those raving about his ability to play at such a young age. Yeah, right, thought I. After all, unlike Marsalis and his crew, I had heard Tony Williams within his first year of joining Miles Davis. So how was I going to be impressed by some Italian kid whom many thought was a Pagannini of the jazz saxophone? Still, I paid attention because I had first been told about Marsalis from Buster Williams and first about Wes Anderson from Marsalis. Oh, yeah: I knew how those two subjects of enthusiasm had turned out.

So I heard Cafiso when he first came to New York at fifteen, but had a much better time joking with Carlo Pagnotta of the Umbria Jazz Festival. Yes, he could play, but he reminded me too much of Phil Woods, whom I had never enjoyed much outside of the 1963 recording with Thelonious Monk's expanded group, playing Hal Overton's arrangements and showing a deft ability to turn Frankie Dunlop's drum responses into melodic developments. Now I don't think I heard Cafiso on a night when his talent caught fire. All I heard was his remarkable muscle memory and his unexpected relaxation. I did not hear what had been described to me as a special kind of genius.

He was playing downstairs at the Au Bar on 58th Street between Park and Madison. The place was laid out like a big living room and there was a gaggle of Italian musicians who played some kind of a burlesque of jazz. The intent was more comical than musical. There was a loud circus quality to their show and plenty of mugging in an Italian style. After his set, Cafiso

had to play with them and I dismissed the kid as no more than an uninspired whippersnapper whom Marsalis and the rest had been overly impressed by because he was so young and was interested in the instrumental
challenges of jazz rather than the pop clichés of the day. I left neither
elated nor disillusioned, just indifferent. At fifteen, the teenager who had
apple cheeks and looked like a short cherub with a saxophone, produced
music that was analogous to just another well-made wooden nickel that was
still too thick to make it through the aesthetic slot.

At seventeen, still looking more the short boy than the short man, he
had matured a great deal, which is not unusual in jazz, where so much
seems to happen almost literally overnight. It was the summer of 2005 and
there he was on the bandstand of Dizzy's Coca-Cola room, playing in front
of the backdrop of Columbus Circle with pianist David Hazeltine, bassist
David Williams, and drummer Joe Farnsworth, all New York musicians beyond journeymen. The first thing that made itself obvious was how big and
soulful a tone Cafiso had, then how clear his intonation was, and finally the
startling quality with which he articulated his notes. One couldn't miss his
command of time, which was flawless. He had no trouble with the harmony of the songs and he played with a decided melodic direction in
which the motives of the tunes were pared down and embroidered with
high skill and deep emotion. Hmmm. I went back with a couple of musicians whom I was sure would verbally smack him around if he failed to impress them. Both were startled because neither had ever heard anyone that
age play that well. One of them had even heard the superior natural talent
of Stan Getz, who had perfect pitch and was a giant killer early in his career back during his time in the saxophone section of Woody Herman's
band. He thought the kid might be better than Getz was as a kid.

Those musicians I took with me were white guys who were never easily
impressed. What struck me was a black piano player who is always out of
sorts when *anyone* gets attention because he feels that he has never gotten
his due, nor have his hometown friends, each of whom is actually a great
musician or close enough to be handed a cigar. The piano player was
grousing about Cafiso and comparing him unfavorably to a buddy who
played the alto back home but never had the backing that would have
given him a boost in his career. That talk stopped as soon as Cafiso began
moving on "Cherokee," the bebop anthem that preceded "Giant Steps" as a
harmonically forbidding tune that should, by all means, be avoided by the
unskilled. Cafiso's saxophone became an aural hot knife that treated the harmony like a stick of butter. Glowering but his eyes lighting up, the piano

player said: "I give it up to him on "Cherokee." Yeah, he can play, but I wasn't impressed before this." Then he was silent, obviously marveling at what he heard though unwilling to say anything more because nothing would have been as negative as he might have liked it to be and because he is, for all of his bitterness, an honest man who loves nothing more than to hear a fine musician play brilliantly or help an upcoming one learn something.

The next set was even more impressive because Cafiso played "Misterioso" with a blues fury so pure that the rattling authority of it spooked the rhythm section into doubling up the speed in order to avoid that very slow desert of a tempo in which the young Italian screamed and shouted the blues. His lyrical squalling was delivered with such dominion that one could only wonder at where his affinity for the blues came from, since it is quite possible that no one has ever heard a European play the blues quite the way that he does. Cafiso was clarifying one fact that is always true about art: The national and biographical details are never more than secondary to talent and sensibility. He played the mood indigo that goes beyond sorrow to a state of consciousness wallowing in the simple greasy fact that human frailty, in every way, is always the basic truth of our tale. Always.

The perpetual present, this time masquerading in the perishable container of memory, made a number of moves in the spring and summer of 2005. Those days were as they always are because musicians whom you have heard over many years or have begun to hear recently in performance with familiar personalities provide Proustian associations because many bandstands and rooms and conversations can be recalled either the moment you see one of them or as you listen to or watch them throughout a night, speaking if you are both in the mood and bringing one another up to date.

Larry Willis is a black bear of a man I have been joking with over the years, especially having fun with the idea that a marriage to a woman from the Emerald Isle made him a *true* black Irishman. We had those kinds of exchanges that are part talk and part guffaw because some people in the jazz world rarely speak of serious things and know, as did Louis Armstrong, that joy is as serious a proposition as any in the world.

When I heard pianist Larry Willis with saxophonist Gary Bartz, trombonist Steve Davis, bassist Buster Williams, and drummer Billy Drummond, so much music and so many New York nights came back to me, evenings gone by and peaks of swing that are forever embedded in the mind and the spirit.

I first heard black Larry on a recording with the Creole-looking giant of the alto saxophone we know as Jackie McLean. The record was called *Right Now* and I liked that black spasm then. I met him and sat next to this dark fellow on a plane flight to Florida, where he was to play a gig with Nat Adderley. Willis was intelligent and somewhat condescending at first but, as the plane made its way through the clouds and we got down further and further into our experiences and our opinions, we began to laugh loudly and put some glasses of champagne through a disappearing act.

Willis, as many did during the eighties, spoke of Wynton Kelley with high regard and said that he admired his groove more than he did the beat of anyone else. At the concert, Willis sat inside the time and swung by turning the beat into a blue thermostat capable of raising and lowering the heat instead of measuring it, like a thermometer.

Some years later, but still back a while, Gary Bartz was paired with Willis at Bradley's for one of those engagements that became so special it seemed a form of luck. Bartz had first come to my attention back in the dark ages of Los Angeles, when I purchased a recording on which he played "It Don't Mean a Thing" with Rashied Ali laying down an extremely loose and fast 4/4 that seemed at the time to contradict his position as the only free drummer who had ever worked with John Coltrane. Following that, I saw Bartz appearing to be waiting for instructions in a line of black men on the cover of a Pharaoh Sanders recording named *Summun, Bukmun, Umyum*. One of the men photographed was the doomed Woody Shaw, who is paying so little attention to the man taking the picture that he could be in Da Vinci's "The Last Supper." The photograph was taken in front of the fountain at Lincoln Center, with the crest of the photograph almost filled up by the Metropolitan Opera House in the background. The title song is nothing much other than a bunch of drums and improvisations that remain static, but "Let Us Go into the House of the Lord" from the 122nd Psalm is a strong example of the gestural side of the Coltrane legacy. The simplicity of the melody and the harmony make every interval and motion of a chord an event. The pace is flotational and effective somehow. Everything moves very slowly and is filled with tremolos, sleigh bells, arco bass, and uncomplicated statements.

By the time he got to Bradley's, Bartz had become none of the prodigals who had spent—or wasted—time trying to become rich or famous or something in the world of fusion and jazz rock, which he entered after leaving the Miles Davis Band—a clearinghouse for information on selling out. He began his comeback at the Tin Palace, growing stronger by the

night and making it clear to everyone in attendance that, for whatever reason, he had chosen to play a Coltrane repertoire at Bradley's and everyone
was surprised by what he did with it.

First of all, Bartz was able to get the depth of majesty in his tone that has
escaped all impressed by Coltrane other than his son, Ravi, whom I witnessed performing *Crescent* in a duet with his mother one night about ten
years ago. On that night, the younger Coltrane exhibited such a clarion
grasp of the sound of his father that it was far beyond an imitation; it was
a summoning replete with absolute integrity and such melting lyricism that
Alice Coltrane appeared to be on the verge of weeping as she accompanied
her son at the piano. She might have never heard that quality of sound
since the death of her husband. But Bartz was right there; his tone took on
the aural substance of "the clarified butter" that Coltrane and Pharoah
Sanders refer to when reciting a variation on a passage from *The Bhagavad-
Gita* in the opening of the recording *Om*. Bartz made his music with a broad
and lofty tone that was entirely personal. It was also devoid of conventions
such as a pretentiously soppy vibrato and, further, his improvising did not
contain the meaningless trills that have so often stopped the development
of the music by substituting an effect for an idea.

The melodic imagination of Bartz's dissonantly sophisticated playing
and the luminous shadowing and extending of his ideas that characterized
Willis's accompaniment made those nights even more outstanding. That
accompaniment was so much more in the nature of a duet, about which
Bartz said: "What I like about Larry is that when we get to playing, if I do
something kind of out there with the harmony, Larry will respond by upping the ante in a very musical way that is *with* you instead of *competing* but
also says, 'Okay, I heard you, but what can you do with this—*bam?*' I like
that. When somebody who knows what he's doing drops a lug in the harmony, that's actually better than all right. It keeps you from falling asleep
into a lullaby of licks, but—and here's the important part—it *stays* musical
instead of feeling like two muscleheads trying to out-lift each other with
some big, dumb weights. Music can be about many things, but it can't be
true music and be about lifting weights."

To hear Bartz fill up the club with his dark and vibrant tone as he expressed the sublime recognition of Coltrane's "Wise One" in both his reading of the theme and his improvisation was to experience what amounted
to a summation of the great saxophonist's contribution at its finest. The
Coltrane material became a point of inspiration, not a technical reference
for the recitation of a great musician's ideas that had become clichés

through repetition. The originality of Bartz's playing humbled both musicians and lay listeners. It wasn't magic in that it changed any of the ups and downs of the night life, but the message was so clear that the people who heard it knew what was shaping itself in the air. They had been there for the arrival of the branding iron of art, which left its mark on the moment the way hot metal identifies each one of the herd by leaving the personal symbol of the owner irrevocably burned into its hide.

In Willis's band at the Jazz Standard, Bartz played with the ongoing freshness and pursuit of linear illumination that continues to distinguish his playing while Steve Davis, always an understated player, used his trombone in the way that Grachan Moncur III once did, seeming to want the sort of music that Miles Davis and Monk made. Davis sought to make inverted clarion statements that asked the listeners to come on in and do some work by following the musical logic instead of waiting for familiar licks to which each audience member could react like a trained seal that had been hurled a *very* dead fish. Willis inclined himself in the direction of Herbie Hancock, using many of the chords we associate with the unsteady master, but inventing his own melodies and propelling his inventions with an understanding of the beat stabilized by his love of Wynton Kelley.

Willis was playing in a way that went back to the conception of the grandest of the old masters to arrive after 1940: Thelonious Monk. Working from an imposing command of that conception with his own material, Willis made the bass of Buster Williams and the drums of Billy Drummond *part* of what he was improvising as opposed to using the bass and drums like a rhythm section floor upon which one only pays attention to where his feet come down and lift up. Willis not only played with Williams and Drummond, he left unpredictable spaces for them to interject ideas that became clear elements of an overall thematic, harmonic, and rhythmic development. When his amplified bass is in balance with the band as opposed to the same volume as the piano, Williams is always a marvel of lower-register understanding in that each note and each rhythm fills out an area of the sound and supports, challenges, inspires, or moves along in complete sympathy with the big feeling that gives swing its most fearsome and calibrated presence.

It has become informative to listen to Drummond, whom I dismissed as no more than an unswinging echo of Tony Williams when he first came to New York about twenty years ago. Wrong you were: Drummond, due to his seriousness and his depth of thought, has developed into an individual who can use styles and the quality of different rhythms as parts of a palette of jazz time in which the front, the middle, or the back of the beat can be emphasized as the architectural designs of a unique complex of sound. Those independently coordinated orchestrations of drums and cymbals might make use of, at different points, the kind of triplets we have heard from Elvin Jones or Art Blakey or Roy Haynes or Tony Williams. Those triplets, rolls, and syncopations are organized in an ebb and flow of structure that never loses the form of the tune and gives them thematic unity resulting from the kind of highly refined intelligence that Max Roach introduced to jazz drumming. Drummond does all of this without aping the authors of his references or the designs of grand master Roach. Quite an achievement.

Looking at Buster Williams always takes me back to a number of places because I have seen him play with so many different people, though a few stand out and will never be forgotten: Betty Carter, Sweets Edison and Lockjaw Davis, Sphere, John Hicks, and his own bands. In 1966 or 1967, at a Los Angeles club on Arlington Avenue, I and members of the acting troupe working at Studio Watts under the direction of Jayne Cortez would go there to hear Carter. She was young then and looking good from all sides and all angles. The Detroit chanteuse carried herself as if there was nothing important that she could do with her attitude toward life other than sing. Standing there behind the mike with her feet apart and those superbly big legs quite prominent, the viciously tempestuous design of her dorsal side so obvious when she was in profile, this woman hypnotically glazed the eyes of a guy in our group who couldn't speak because each of her notes zippered his lips more firmly. This young man wasn't interested in any kind of art but came around the workshop because he was after one of two extremely fine middle-class girls who were sisters and lived in some Watts projects under the command of a mother whose heart seemed made of *House and Garden* magazines tightly wrapped in plastic covers. I don't think the young man knew what art was until he heard Betty Carter, and I am sure he had never experienced the miracle of precisely expressive improvisation in swinging time until he witnessed brown Betty in duet with Buster Williams during "Blue Moon" when Tommy Flanagan and Joe Harris dropped out, leaving the two of them out there to fill up all that space for a few choruses of give and take.

With no place to hide, the singer, always as delicate as the whiff of a rose petal and as game as an heroic pugilist, came perfectly alive inside of the music, assured in the correctness of her style by the cunning assents of Buster Williams. He went right to it with her. The bandstand was soggy with swing. Carter and Williams proved what Thelonious Monk meant when he said of closely aligned improvising: "Two is one." I think Betty Carter was there once a week for about a month, and so were we. We were never let down. It was strictly personal. It was always new. It was always swinging. It was always the essence of always.

That same feeling arrived whenever the collective band known as Sphere worked at the Village Vanguard, boasting Charlie Rouse on tenor, Kenny Barron (always a shocking blast furnace of swing and creativity) on piano, the bass of Buster Williams, and Ben Riley's drums. Most of their repertoire was the music of Monk, and everyone played extremely well, but the highlight on those evenings when I caught them came forth as Rouse made his way through an original he called "Pumpkin's Delight." After jogging the room along in a medium-tempo sweatsuit, the swing began to slowly lower in volume as the saxophone expressed itself while moving backwards through a field of dynamics that became unexplainably stronger as the sound of the band took on a descending quality of volume, something like the long goodbye defined by a sonic fadeout that says all there is to say in a lyrical whisper decaying toward the dissolution of silence. Everyone felt that.

Sweets Edison and Lockjaw Davis used Buster when they were working at Fat Tuesday's twenty years ago, and George Coleman, according to Harold Mabern, had left the room shaking his head because he was mystified by what Lockjaw was playing, even though Coleman is a flesh-and-blood thesaurus of harmony. With their processed hair and their suits, perhaps some alligator shoes, and rings with big hustler's gems in place, each of those men represented places known for granting degrees in house rocking, stomp-down smoking, and proof that one knew how to blow the blues away. Sweets was from Kansas City by way of Ohio and Lockjaw was from Harlem by way of Harlem. They were welcome in every place in the country or the world where some blues, some ballad crooning, and some swing were never considered less than passports to the good part of the night.

I always remember an evening in the middle sixties at Shelley's Manne Hole in Hollywood. Miles Davis waved Sweets up to his bandstand, where the shiny-haired veteran in a tan windbreaker borrowed the far more famous trumpeter's green horn, stood behind the piano at the back of the bandstand and let loose with such a blues blast that Tony Williams snapped his head around so fast he appeared to nearly break his neck at the surprise that tone put on him. A descendant of Louis Armstrong, Edison knew how to line his quarter notes up in the beat. Sweets lifted up the thrust of the swing as he played some blues so serious and natural that Miles Davis had a shockingly ecstatic look on his face, which probably surprised only those who didn't realize how much he loved to hear great jazz in *any* style at that time.

As Lockjaw howled and purred through his tenor twenty years later at Fat Tuesdays's, or played fall-away swift passages that never seemed to settle in the right place but always appeared to do the job, Buster Williams looked on with awe as he laid down his bass lines, saying to me at the end of the night: "When I'm listening to Jaws I never have *any* idea what he's thinking. He's a mystery man, but he sure can swing. We all know *that*. But those strange *notes*, where do they come from?" Whatever it was and wherever it began, Lockjaw seemed at ease in the mystery of his style. Hair glistening and laid just so, he always ended up with his scotch and milk at the bar, surveying the room, gesturing to the bartender in a way that got his ring twinkling. There, with one foot up, Lockjaw Davis had the amused look of a man who was sure that he was in charge and equally sure that everyone else knew it.

When Buster Williams leads his own band, I especially enjoy the version with Stefon Harris on vibraphone, Geri Allen on piano, and drummer Lenny White, whose return to jazz from the aesthetic death valley of fusion was one of the best decisions of the 1980s. With Williams, White provided swing from the mountaintops of rhythm raised up in the music by Elvin Jones and Tony Williams. White could even be heard providing a substantial innovation that no one seems to have noticed yet. While performing Monk's "Epistrophy" and keeping the time, White orchestrated and played the tune's rhythms *as part of the form*. He used his snare, tom, and bass drum figures as if he was walking the chords of a bass line. The upshot was that if some people had come in after the head was played, they could have told what the tune was by listening to the drum accompaniment! It was that clear.

I first heard Stefon Harris sit in with trumpeter Nicholas Payton at Iridium, where he seemed to have played about twenty choruses that didn't seem to build but showed abundant enthusiasm, something that didn't bother Payton because he said that the only way that anyone learns *how* to play is by *playing*. Payton was right and should have known since he had begun his career as a highly intelligent fat boy from New Orleans who looked much like Louis Armstrong and was always over at Wynton Marsalis's house the way Terence Blanchard had been before him. He was absorbing everything that he could and the word was out that he was

going to be an important jazz voice in his own right, which became clear
in two circumstances. One was when he helped bring a rare drive to the
thick counterpoint of King Oliver's music when he was chosen to play
second cornet with Marsalis at a Lincoln Center concert; the other was
when he tried to stomp Roy Hargrove's guts out during an evening of
trumpet battles in which he and the Texas trumpet player whom Marsalis
had discovered in Dallas were teamed. Payton, with a much bigger sound
and a far more refined arsenal of harmony and rhythm, was doing what
he intended until they were concluding a long series of exchanges and
Hargrove suddenly joined him in unison to play a riff that not only drew
a roar from the crowd but supplied a moment in which unexpected camaraderie said much more about the meaning of jazz than the stings of
brutal combat.

In Williams's band, Stefon Harris's solos had come a long way. They
weren't necessarily any shorter than they were when I first heard him with
Payton, but they were so much better shaped. This meant that Harris used
the themes much more craftily and made use of the jolting, the dissonances
that the vibraphone provides most individually because of the sound of the
hard metal keys and the impact made possible by smashing hard colors
from them and letting the ring of the instrument raise them into an auditory cloud that hangs over the ensemble like a prickly mist that becomes a
gauze of harmonic smoke as it decays into silence. Harris also made the
most of the springing, aggressive, or sympathetically suggestive chords of
Geri Allen, who always played as if she had an appointment with the gallows at the end of the set. Allen never missed a turn or a quirky syncopation from the full-tilt swing of Williams and White, having learned the
great lesson of jazz playing, which is incorporating the environment into
the sweep of your statement while in motion, much like an amoebic form
that changes shape and content as it consumes everything with which it
comes into contact.

With players of this level, the responses are not always immediate. That
would be corny, much like choosing to play tip when they play dip, or scat,
when they say slat. In the most intelligent players, the material might be
held onto and used at another place in the song, as I once heard Kirk Lightsey do at the keyboard when at work in Bradley's with vibraphonist Steve
Nelson. Nelson's horn-rim glasses, goatee, casual dress, and subdued car-
riage always make him look like one of those all-day-walking and lean Los
Angeles Negroes who used to move in reserved ballet steps as they sold
pharmaceutical products door to door; but, as he lifts and lowers his shoul-

ders as the music enters him, Nelson plays his instrument like Vulcan, using his mallets to shoot thunderbolts through the metal sky of keys before him. Nelson quoted "They All Laughed" at one point, which Lightsey only partially echoed but returned to throughout his own feature, using it as a refrain and a satiric comment on the lyrics of the song they were playing.

Williams will do the same thing, reiterating interesting things he has heard from the featured player when they return to the same place in the song where they were first introduced. If, say the ideas come in the first sixteen, or the bridge of a song, he will build on them in the same part of the form if they are especially potent and, thereby, make the improvisation part of the structure of the performance. White uses a parallel technique with rhythms, reiterating those that struck him but varying where he will play them on his kit—one of the cymbals, the snare, across the toms, strongly or lightly pushed out of the bass drum, or broken up into commentary across a variety of the drums and cymbals, making clear the registers and timbres that give orchestral possibilities to the drum set. Such playing always made it a necessity to be at the Vanguard at least one evening of any run of the Buster Williams Quartet.

In the 1980s, it was an event, as it still is, to hear Ornette Coleman perform in public because Coleman had a set price for himself that he considered commensurate with his position in music, or that he felt was fair for his efforts and would allow him to pay his musicians what he thought they deserved. I think this concert was the last one for a very long time in which one could hear Coleman in an acoustic context, though the presence of James Blood Ulmer on electric guitar and the amplified bass of Buster Williams begged the question. When he did create the electric maze called "Prime Time," it was prefigured by Coleman going to hear Miles Davis, who was stumbling around in platform shoes on the bandstand, after which he was heard to say that *they* would never get *him* to wear high-heeled shoes. Not long afterward, in his very large loft in SoHo at 131 Prince Street, the stubborn Texas innovator was heard clopping his way to answer the door. His take on fusion was not far away.

One of the most revealing performances of "Prime Time" took place at a theater on 11th Street near Third Avenue. The house was packed with white people, as was usually the case, regardless of the jazz style, making it clear once more that, had it not been for white listeners, promoters, and scholars, jazz would have faded from the world and, perhaps, returned to the limited phenomenon it was before leaving New Orleans. Think about that.

While his audience was waiting for Coleman and his electric guitars and electric basses and two sets of drums, the famous clip of Charlie Parker and Dizzy Gillespie on television in 1952 was shown. The din of conversations stopped immediately. Everyone there appeared to know that they were seeing Charlie Parker speak in his aloof stage manner. Parker showed a disdain for the familiarity with which columnist Earl Wilson attempted to put them in the expected minstrel place that the Kansas City innovator had resisted throughout his short career. His ultimate reply, as the alto saxophonist leaned into "Hot House," was a jagged barbed-wire streak of melody that ended with a screaming riff. One could see that Gillespie, always capable of clowning, transformed into the flame-throwing intellectual once the music opened for him. He was serious then and his powers were monumental. Here were the twin fountainheads of the style that had taken the battle to the enemy of contempt and entertainment, which far too often asking for the sacrifice to the blue cannibal god of dissipation that swallowed Parker within three years after his only television appearance (though legend has it that he is somewhere in the miles of footage from a Jerry Lewis telethon).

I had heard Coleman in San Francisco during the early seventies when he was playing in San Francisco at the Keystone Corner with Ulmer, bassist David Williams, and Billy Higgins. Coleman was playing in a way that his ensemble didn't seem to completely understand because he was not thinking of himself as a soloist with a background but wanted everyone in the foreground, playing together. It was Coleman's continuation of New Orleans ensemble improvising. Though Ulmer and Williams played well, they didn't seem to step forward in the way that Coleman seemed to want them to, which meant that they responded to him as a guitar and a bass would accompanying someone.

Now and then, Coleman would step back and let one or the other of them come to the fore while he stood and listened. When inspired, he would begin playing again, but each of them thought he was concluding the guitar or bass feature and fell back into an accompanying role. It may have been frustrating to Coleman but it was still more than slightly exciting. Coleman was always the master of free improvisation and can make his melodic inventions work from wherever he ends up. It does not mean that there are no mistakes, but that mistakes can be remade into ideas, something that expands upon that moment I witnessed in 1964 at the Monterey Festival, when Monk incorporated the rhythm of a plane flying over into the music, or had first heard on *Eric Dolphy at the Five Spot* when Richard Davis pulled the syncopation of a glass being knocked over on a table into his bass feature. (As remarkably as he played at the Keystone, what I remember most about Billy Higgins during that engagement was a point when he changed shirts backstage and the perpetual reminder of his former life as a heroin addict slapped the onlooker in the face. His upper body was covered with endless scars of many different shapes but almost every one formed a depression in his skin as if he had been gouged over and over in a torturing action that removed small bits of skin. Here, in all his pride and good humor, was a brownish-gold version of Ray Bradbury's *Illustrated Man*. I also understood then why Higgins had such large hands: I had begun to notice such disproportion years before when I saw some addicts around the corner from my mother's home shoot up between their thumbs and index fingers and watched their hands swell as the dope went its way. In some cases, they never went down. Grotesque scarification and mitts for hands, the blues two different ways.)

Coleman can create melodic variations from wherever he ends up in the music. This means that if he misfingers and is thrown a distance from his intended note, he can continue from where he is, even if the note results in a modulation that takes him into another key. This also has rhythmic implications of a profound nature. We always hear notes that we didn't expect, sounding as if they are accented. If one plays a series of certain intervals, then breaks the sequence but uses *exactly the same attack*, the *surprise* creates what I can an illusory accent. This, of course, is something quite common to written composition, but it has equally dramatic impact in improvisation and Ornette Coleman is a grand master of that kind of music drama.

At Avery Fisher Hall, there were plenty of anxious Coleman listeners about ten years after he had played the Keystone, but no one had any idea what they would hear because there was always the idea that Coleman would suddenly surprise or shock everyone with some newly conceived idea about writing or playing. So expectation was heavy in the air and it got a bit more intense as the musicians walked onto stage. It was an unusually large ensemble for the innovator. There were drummers Higgins and Blackwell, bassist Buster Williams, tenor saxophonist Dewey Redman, trumpeter Don Cherry, guitarist James "Blood" Ulmer, and Coleman himself, a small man who often seems either burdened or apprehensive.

Of course, there was no tuning up, since Coleman does not really believe in the conventions of sharp or flat, both of which he hears as no more than colors to be used in his melody lines at the command of his ear. What rose into aural bas-relief was Coleman's confident lyricism and the free motion of his ideas, which never were determined by anything other than the logic of his line—not the key, the meter, the tempo, the mood. Modulation is an important word in Coleman's musical vocabulary and means that every element can shift and that the phrasing can arrive in a musical version of Williams Carlos Williams's "variable foot," which writer Debra Rae Cohen observed many years ago in the *Village Voice*. Coleman's phrasing is governed by meter only as long as it doesn't block the inspiration central to the statement. He also plays his notes in whatever tempo he hears and feels them, sometimes extending Armstrong's soaring fermatas and large triplets that could dramatically suggest another tempo. In 1954, on both takes of "The Man I Love," Monk rearranged everyone's mind on the Miles Davis All Stars date by reinterpreting syncopation in terms of tempo. Davis himself appropriated that freedom and can clearly be heard making use of it on "Solea" from *Sketches of Spain.* In Coleman's playing, that expanded redefinition of syncopation brings the surprising effects of altered velocities but makes one aware of the fact that some emotions have their own tempos. All of this makes Coleman the most important leader in the avant-garde of jazz because of his unerring connection to the blues feeling, which seeps through his tone like rain through a window screen, putting the wet surface of new life on everything inside.

The most exciting moment in the Avery Fisher concert was the last piece on which everyone played alone in succession before stating a theme and diving into a collective invention that had the cutting fury of bobcats in a bag, but evolved into the new quality of compassion that Coleman reintroduced to jazz, updating the collective sound of New Orleans to include everything that had happened since—the big bands, the joyous swinging of the blues that came out of Kansas City, the unpredictable phrasing lengths of Lester Young, the phenomenal apotheosis of joy and despair that was Charlie Parker, and all of the best thoughts and feelings that came in his wake. In his *Free Jazz* recording from December of 1960, Coleman brought a fresh level of empathy to improvising. His vision was that the purpose of jazz playing was to *help* everyone in the environment achieve what they were trying to do or make the very best thing that you could of what they were doing. Self-expression through empathy. It is still a very high goal and is rarely achieved on the scale that Coleman's music proposed, but the essence of it, as proven by Billy Higgins, applies to every style.

Dewey Redman recalls that when he was a member of Coleman's quartet and they were on a tour of Europe in 1971, bebop maestro Sonny Stitt was playing with The Giants of Jazz and had a dressing room right next to Coleman's. Stitt walked past Coleman and said nothing to him and so did Dexter Gordon, who went next door to see his old buddy. They were laughing the laugh that distinguishes all of those who made it through the long travail and have in common the memories of the dead, the mad, the broken, and the imprisoned. With bebop came the sense of life that was somewhat like the rebellion that Baudelaire and his crew asserted in the world of French art, when being dandies and refined men also meant embracing varieties of decadence and self-destruction in order to put up resistance against satisfying the expectations of the middle class. As Negroes for the most part, the beboppers went away from minstrelsy but embraced another version of it that was being hip or, at the time, "hep." Behind all of the dope, the same-sex unions, the leopard coats, and the contrivances of slang, there was a high-mindedness that one could hear in songs like "Half Nelson."

All of those memories were filling the air of the dressing room next to Coleman's and coming through the wall when Redman went over to see what Gordon and Stitt were talking about. "I thought I might learn something since these were two masters. They were drinking and talking and Dexter was showing Stitt a fingering that worked for the upper register of the tenor saxophone when suddenly we heard Charlie Parker. Everybody looked. It was like a ghost in the house. I think it was 'Little Willie Leaps.' Pure Charlie Parker. Everybody got quiet. The talk was over. After about five minutes it stopped, and I left. Coleman had this little smile on his face and he was putting his horn in the case. I didn't say anything to him and he didn't say anything to me. On the other side, it was still quiet. Then Dexter came over and grabbed Ornette's hand and said, 'Ornette, you really sound good. Good evening.' He left and Sonny Stitt came over and did the same thing, shook Coleman's hand and told him how good he sounded. I fell out. I couldn't stop laughing."

At the Tin Palace, Redman got his chance to do something similar when his quartet was booked opposite the Clifford Jordan-Barry Harris Quartet. Jordan and Harris represented bebop at its highest level of refinement, both having learned how to hear through the harmony with sometimes spectacularly melodic results arriving in that eighth-note-triplet pattern of phrasing that was central to Charlie Parker's rhythm. Redman, while capable of the many noises and screams that characterized the most limited version of the avant-garde, was really about the long line that had come to him through Lester Young, under which the swing of the blues was imperative to what Albert Murray calls "the velocity of celebration."

Jordan and Harris also represented the social evolution of jazz in New York and most of the country. There was no longer any interest in the black community, so the musicians either lived or did most of their playing on jobs downtown. Harlem had become no more than an uptown memory. Jordan was a handsome hero who had come through the bands of Horace Silver, J. J. Johnson, and Max Roach, which meant that he was as aware of alternate structures, multiple tempos, demanding harmonic underpinnings, and complex rhythms as anyone in New York, meaning he could play through his bebop repertoire with a very high level of sophistication and a sense of abandon that never sacrificed the thematic source to chaos.

Highly respected, Jordan used a cane before he got the hip replacement that corrected a worsening condition brought about by a horse having fallen on him when he was a kid. He was big man whose repaired step had a sweep that included a bounce that constituted a light exclamation point of style and rhythm. Jordan radiated absolute integrity because his entire career had been about playing music to the best of his ability and working on a sound that had begun in the world of Sonny Rollins, but had evolved into one of the most distinctive vessels of lyricism in the music. That sound contained a capacious ache reminiscent of Ben Webster, a tenor saxophonist who never seemed capable of expressing less than profound feeling. But Jordan's tone was purposely less smooth and the edge of metallic grain carried harsh memory and all that we would never know of the streets of Chicago, New York, and the venues of the many cities where the saxophonist had made his different stands. He had come up through heroin and now stood as a reliable witness whose testimony could bring much light to the ongoing trial of the world.

Harris was a small man with a head of such magnitude that anyone aware of Richard Wagner's cranium would think of the German composer whenever this professor of bebop appeared, leading his students, all of whom were part of his fan club of instrumentalists and singers. They would have been a cult if Harris was a different kind of a man. Harris never drank alcohol but was given to smoking even while playing, a habit that ended with a heart attack sometime later. He lived in the mansion of the jazz baroness out in the wilds of New Jersey. The home of the baroness had such a large number of feline creatures that Monk called it "catville." With his racing form in his pocket and his cigarette serving burning duty in the corner of his mouth, Harris was one of those men who never seemed to care about anything other than what he was involved in, most of which was music or his students or giving some sort of help to his friends.

The drummer who played with Jordan and Harris was Vernell Fournier, an innovator from New Orleans who had made his name with the seer of the modern jazz piano trio, Ahmad Jamal. Redman used Eddie Moore, who was a big black shadow casting personal variations on the patterns of Ed Blackwell. Blackwell was also from New Orleans and had been with Ornette Coleman at the emergence of his new style. Moore connected Redman's rhythm section to the beginnings of the music as much as his swing did to every school.

Walter Booker, whom we all joked was surely a descendant of George Washington, so much so that all one had to do to prove it was pull out a dollar bill and see if the bassist could deny it. Booker was perfectly sympathetic in his bass lines, which he felt should be delivered at a volume so low that he did not seem to be using an amplifier because, as he said: "That is how the bass is supposed to sound in this music." As the fine alto saxophonist Monty Waters said of the group: "It is perfect. Just to hear how Clifford phrases Bird's 'Quasimodo' is wonderful, each note so clear and expressive. Then that level of improvising that he and Barry do. What can you say? And, well you know, Dewey and I used to run the jam session at Bop City in San Francisco. Unlike a lot of these other people, I *know* Dewey can play. One time a guy came in who was working in a famous band and called for 'Cherokee' through the keys, all twelve of course. Dewey and I just looked at each other because we knew he thought he was going to pull something off, but he was throwing two rabbits in the briar patch. We bent his head a little that night."

It was always a real kick to see the beboppers pay closer attention when Freddie Simmons, who was from Philadelphia and could invent and invent and swing and swing, take off at the piano in Redman's band. Simmons was one of those unknown commodities that seemed to exist all over the country and always have—those players who can meet the moment with all of the aesthetic muscle that is needed in the context and shock the unnecessarily arrogant out of their pants. While Redman's long line and his rhythmic freedom were not as well appreciated as they might have been at first, he always closed off all carping when he went into a very slow blues that was heavy on the backbeat and thick with all of the Southwestern lore that produced the famous Texas tenors. By the end of that engagement, both schools of playing seemed much closer and more about the manner of achieving liberation, with or without chords, than about the question of freedom, which always arrived in the perfect guise of invented melody, answering Lester Young's question of whether or not you could sing a song as opposed to merely exhibit having practiced the saxophone.

Years later, John Hicks could be expected to come through the Kansas City barbecue joint on East 19th Street that is the Jazz Standard. He was downstairs in the club whenever someone of stature was there playing the piano. But this would be true whenever some jazz up on a high plane was supposed to be going on. With the smell of ribs and greens and potato salad wafting through the air, the serving staff far from obnoxious in the expected way of the old days, and the sound system quite good, which used to not be expected, and the fairly new convention of the piano being tuned, John Hicks almost always took a seat against the wall in the raised gallery at the back of the room, often in the company of his wife, who is also a musician. Except for answering a question now and again or responding to a greeting, he was always quiet and sat there listening intently with a glass of red wine rising to his lips occasionally.

Hicks was the superhero of New York piano in the middle eighties, an undeclared title that came to him after he left Betty Carter, or was fired because he had a drinking problem that could turn this intelligent, witty, and articulate man into a mumbler and a bumbler. But when his father died in St. Louis, Hicks disappeared for a while and returned to the scene wearing his father's suits and carrying a briefcase, as if to say that the screw-ups were behind him. From that point on, he began to march on the piano and light up one gig after another, playing with all the force of his church background brought into the more refined but equally torrid area of jazz that had been inspired by the example of John Coltrane's Quartet with pianist McCoy Tyner, the model for the Hicks style.

When Coltrane brought his group to Los Angeles, he played at Shelly's Manne Hole in Hollywood, a largely white joint. For the last few times, however, he changed venues to the black hustlers' hangout that was the It Club on Washington Boulevard, where white customers could almost always be sure they were being overcharged by the waitresses; and the saxophonist also did the weekend after-hours Friday and Saturday night shows at the Adams West. The Adams West was a movie theater at the western side of the black community that, between two and six a.m., drew jazz fans too young to get in the clubs and night people who preferred to relax in the comfortable seats with their paper cups and flasks at hand rather than be hustled into buying the night-club drinks that might be nearly devoid of liquor.

Coltrane was always a simply dressed and modestly handsome man who could have passed for a deacon on the way to a prayer meeting. He didn't have the look of special authority one saw in Miles Davis, Philly Joe Jones, Dizzy Gillespie, Art Blakey, Milt Jackson, Sonny Rollins, or Betty Carter. At best, he seemed like a humorless workman who had all of the details of the job he was about to do on his mind and had little interest in talking about anything outside of what he was about to do. Once he got to the bandstand, however, something unexpected happened.

On the first encounter, one could never believe the enormity of the force with which he and his musicians played. There was no talking. No announcements. I never saw Coltrane count off a tempo. He looked around, might smile at his drummer, then put the mouthpiece of his horn in the place where it would strain to travel known and unknown territory for perhaps a half an hour, sometimes giving the impression, at one of the peaks in his mountain range of an improvisation, that the horn was going to split from the heat traveling through it like the barrel of a machine gun that could no longer handle the froth of the sustained force passing through it.

What the saxophonist and his musicians did was beyond material and beyond logic. The music seemed more about the atomic presence of creation than its content. All of the scales and polyrhythms and advanced or simple harmonies were secondary to the power of four human burners with their flames turned all the way up. The meaning of the music? There may have been none other than some sort of charismatic paean to existence it-self, a sweeping sense of density, something like the spectacular motion of gases and liquids that beget solid forms. Yes, it seemed to be that elemental and that eternal, and as naïve as it might be, it gave us the irrational feeling that the men who made that sound were invincible, that they would not be taken down one by one like every great player and every person who had gone gently or accidentally, or resisting if not raging into the darkness before them. Black Elvin Jones, master of new triplet codes of independently coordinated rhythm, was back there grunting in a dark suit that was soon soaked, little Jimmy Garrison who could not be heard most of the time roared through his bass lines whenever audible, Tyner played the chords as if he was seeking a syncopated ring that both paralleled a gong while acting as a tonal extension of the drums. With this going on under him, behind him, or encircling his sound, Coltrane might rock and roll like a rhythm-and-blues player as he pushed his saxophone forward and drew it back to him, sometimes going down on one knee as his horn commenced testifying to something far beyond music but that could only be reached through it and could only achieve its goal with the molten goodwill of sympathetic players. To the unprepared, it might have sounded overstated, undisciplined, and hysterical, but it was not to become that until near the end, when the great quartet had been broken up by Coltrane's naïve submission to actual noise and incompetence. (Such sincere and overwrought mawkishness led to a recording like *Om*, which contains so much screaming and hollering that it was always a record with which one could *very* quickly clear the house after a party in Los Angeles had reached its peak and tiresome people were still hanging around, running their mouths and becoming unwanted pests; no exhausted beseeching could produce as prompt a stampeding exit as the sound of that recording.)

But in its great moments, the John Coltrane Quartet seemed to have multiplied its instrumentation to that three or four times its size, which was why its impact became so explosive: The pressure on the air was that of a big band at full blast. Many of its imitators, quite naturally, thought that playing loud and using modal forms would get the sound of that group onto their bandstands. Sorry. It wasn't about that.

Deep in the music was the result of Coltrane's vast experience. Slowly developing, the saxophonist had evolved at a much more casual pace than his predecessors, not truly coming into his own until he had passed his thirtieth birthday. His first presence outside of North Carolina was that of a lean Negro country boy knocking on the Philadelphia door of Benny Golson in the early forties. From that point on, he was often there for rehearsal, always ready to satisfy Golson's mother by playing "On the Sunny Side of the Street," which allowed him to display his emulation of Johnny Hodges, whom he once referred to as the world's greatest saxophonist. That must have shocked his British interviewer about twenty years later when the Coltrane Quartet was on a tour of Europe in the early sixties. This country Negro developed from walking the bars in Philadelphia with rhythm-and-blues bands to working with almost all of the great minds of jazz after 1945—Dizzy Gillespie, Tadd Dameron, Miles Davis, and Thelonious Monk, whose roots also went back to North Carolina and who might have been the finest musical mind of them all. All of that bandstand time, all of those rehearsals, the long discussions of music, and his obsessive studies had coalesced into an understanding of the fundamental elements of jazz, each of which was reinterpreted and, in its purest form, lay beneath, hovered over, and remained in position behind all of the innovations that he brought off *in conjunction with his players*: What they played, the interaction among them, was the real innovation, not the materials that they used, which largely included nothing of importance in themselves. Unlike the great compositions of Duke Ellington or Thelonious Monk, which would remain great *without* their creators, the greatness of John Coltrane's music is about *how* he and his musicians played together. I can see him now, on all of those bandstands with his quartet, as if he will never stop playing.

John Hicks carried a personal offshoot of that energy in his playing and swung until the cows came home if you didn't stop him. I first witnessed what he could do on his own at the Tin Palace, a club that had once been very beautiful, with polished wooden floors and a fine bar with mirrors on the walls, all of which depreciated under the ownership of an Irish guy who was hooked up with "the boys" and didn't care if it became a dive as long it served the purpose of laundering the money that was supposedly made in there. Things took one of those unusual twists that are common to New York when the club actually became profitable, which resulted in "an offering" that the backers in the shadows couldn't turn down. So in what eventually became a radiant rathole, Hicks started rising up on the piano bench as if possessed or looking for an angle from which he could throw more of his body weight into his attack. With broiling insistence, he pulled heat from his bass player and drummer, exhausting them by the end of the night. The tunes came one after the other with very little pause and the power of his time never lagged. On that night, I could tell that John Hicks was one of those players whose drive demanded that the men he hired be in shape and prepared to swing all night.

Some of the finest playing I heard from Hicks came in the quartets of Arthur Blythe and Pharaoh Sanders. Having first heard Blythe with Horace Tapscott when he was known as "Black Arthur," it was a pleasure to see his star rise in New York as he tested himself in a variety of contexts. Chico Hamilton had gone on record saying that he was the most talented saxophonist he had hired since Eric Dolphy, and Blythe had been well received by some of the press, especially Gary Giddins. His greatest moments came with the grand quartet he put together in which Hicks headed up a rhythm section that included bassist Fred Hopkins and drummer Steve McCall. For some reason, Blythe was never able to get CBS-Sony to record him in performance when his group played the Village Vanguard. Those are the vagaries of corporate shortsightedness; sometimes, especially in the world of the arts, artifacts that could easily be made permanent and become consistently profitable over the years are allowed to disappear into no more than the rightful legends of awesome memories.

However well I had heard Blythe play before, this rhythm section put raw meat on the table. Hicks was the T-bone, the one who held the tempos together and who brought out all of the jazz feeling in the other players, nudging Blythe deeper into the blues or encouraging his more lyrical inclinations and placing chords in the time that fanned the heat of the swing. Hopkins and McCall were the ones who polished the bottom of the sound and flayed the beat for the trio Air. They had taken the black New York avant-garde off guard when they came to town because Hopkins and McCall rattled whomever held onto the black nationalist convention by not only having white girlfriends but, what was truly out of the box, white women who were classy on the one hand, and strikingly fine on the other.

Gisela von Eiken, with whom Hopkins kept close company, made startlingly attractive jewelry out of thin metal wire and Bobby Kingsley, a very good photographer, was a statuesque looker capable of taming the savage beast of black nationalism in the interest of romantic fantasies. The reactions to Kingsley's form, face, and placid warmth always tickled McCall, who was old enough to be a bebopper and had been seasoned on those bandstands but was bringing an individual intelligence, power, and exquisite delicacy to free drumming. This shot him immediately to the first rank, with Rashied Ali, Andrew Cyrille, Sunny Murray, and Milford Graves, who ruled the Manhattan roost of that style. Hopkins had a big tone, inarguable command of rhythm, could create a bass line with or without chords, play in or out of time, and step on the swing pedal when it was called for. With the gully low sound of the blues just beneath the patina of his alto's tone and an unrivaled command of his flute among avant-garde players (especially since James Newton was in California), Henry Threadgill drew the third line that closed off the geometry of the triangle that was Air, a most impressive group.

But there was a chamber music quality as well—ambiguous Third Stream elements to Air that had no place on Arthur Blythe's bandstand. He was a much more powerful alto saxophonist than Threadgill. His sound was much larger, filled with more sensation, and he could rock the house when the swinging blues came down on him. There was no question that his time was more charismatic, and Blythe had developed a way of fusing his interest in the repetitions of African music with the drive of the jazz riff, which could result in overwhelmingly intense choruses of repeated figures and shoutingly inventive variations as his rhythm section bore down on him and the walls between audience disinterest and excitement were cracked wide open. The often glum staff of the Vanguard always perked up when Blythe and his men came into the club because they knew the air would take on that particular heartiness that it does when a band begins to swing for the stars and seems to lift a room up into another dimension. There's a record, but it's so far from the facts of the matter that it could be destroyed and we would lose nothing resembling what I am trying to recapture.

Pharaoh Sanders had not played in New York for a few years and decided to give the Tin Palace a whirl. He was not the thin, young black man I had first seen standing at the back of the It Club in a dark suit and a vest listening to John Coltrane play his cadenza on "I Want to Talk About You." I had been surprised at the time because Sanders had such a reputation and I still had not come to grips with the fact that what men could *do* did not necessarily make them look different from everyone else. Sanders seemed to savor every note that the older man played and had a smile of satisfaction on his face whenever emotion would physically move Coltrane so that his saxophone glinted under the lights as he appeared to vaguely tremble on the high bandstand in his country-boy Hush Puppies and wrinkled suit, obviously a man not given to gleaming sartorial concerns.

With his tenor in place, Coltrane performed as though alone at home and communing with the horn. He could have been letting the saxophone know that if it had secrets to tell him there was no getting away until he heard it come clean. So the unaccompanied solo was much like an aesthetic and technical interrogation. This was often the case when ambition and imagination colluded in the blues to be free that was Coltrane's central theme. But this desire for liberation was far beyond anything racial, though it swept the ethnic limits of the time along with everything else that was the duty of his persona to project, carry, and be burdened by. There were such things in what was a public statement made in a night club where hustlers were known to show off their finery and parade their whores.

This chamber music presentation of jazz in that bastion of spiritual stench was more than a little enthralling. One could witness the private intimacy of the great innovator's lyricism rising in the cadenza and hear the coating of romance as Coltrane floated harmonics out into the smoky air of the club. It seemed as if he was the recalling gasps of different lengths that were as beautiful as they were startling, the way that the unexpected sounds of a woman at close quarters can reveal legions of tales about desire, loneliness, and the possibility of freedom from the limitations of only knowing one's flesh alone. Such techniques fused to higher and more private meanings than anything that could be found in a music book or an exercise. That is what underlined Coltrane's status among musicians, so many of whom were reintroduced to the emotion of being enthralled students when they listened to him add more choices to what they already knew about music or about the saxophone or sensed about the life of any sensitive human being in the world.

The Pharaoh Sanders who came into the Tin Palace to play with John Hicks was another man from the second saxophone fiddle with Coltrane. He was humorous but stoic, said very little, was broader in size, and had behind him those last years when his mentor walked the earth, and Jimmy Garrison was disturbed by the younger saxophonist because, as he said: "He went all over the world screaming through his horn. Damn." Even down there on the Bowery, where the weights, disruptions, and muggings of dissipation showed themselves in the universal parade of tattered derelicts who might come marching, stumbling, running, or walking by the gallery windows that were open to the street, Sanders was by then known among his fans for his hit, "The Creator Has a Master Plan." That song offered a much more dreamy and less demanding vision of life than the one he had on his mind while with Coltrane, when it seemed as though the younger saxophonist was intent on blowing his horn apart or finding the most shocking sounds that it could make. All of the shouting and screaming through the horn had become a hot but comfortable part of his tonal palette, which no longer ignored the feeling of jazz rhythm or the sound of the blues. Sanders was now a reborn down-home house rocker who, with Hicks lit up beneath him, was about hard swinging. His work, like that of Ben Webster, tended to use few notes because that big broad sound had to be held in place, its vibrato raised and its beat given the leeway to stomping through swampland the way all backwoods players from the country were expected to do in their own individual ways.

Sanders was nothing if not a country Negro, whether he was dressed up in African regalia and shaking bells or chanting pentatonic riffs through the microphone. He was one of those Negroes who, apparently, had never existed before, the ones who were children of 1960s' black nationalism. I heard composer and conductor Butch Morris call them "country Africans." In other words, none of the books read or learned about through conversations focused on traditional African custom and religion, none of the studies of Egyptian history or Eastern thought, none of the Islamic leanings and swine-free diets, none of the interest in Third World customs or music or ritual dress had removed the deep imprint of the American South from these black people. All of the other stuff was no more than thick and colorful window dressing, at best.

Given that central quality, one understands why Coltrane loved Sanders: because their roots were so much alike. The writer Hattie Gossett remembers that "Coltrane was an interesting contradiction because he was corny-like. Very country. Backwoods. He was driving a Jaguar but he was still a country Negro. Suits didn't fit, white socks, pants too short. Then he would get up there and play all of this incredible music that was so complex you could get a headache from it if you weren't ready.

"Over at the Half Note on Hudson Street, where everybody in New York went to see what was *really* going on, Coltrane and McCoy, who was wearing those corny clothes, too, would be sitting outside the club in the car, like those country men do down South, talking to each other while everybody else is in the house at a party or something like that. Now Elvin Jones was soaking wet from all those drums he was playing and he was at the bar with his long black slender self, loud, just as loud as he could be and drinking tall ones of that gin. Yeah, baby, it was like *that*. Then there was the other one. Little Jimmy Garrison, who *always* seemed like he got the Holy Ghost when they were up there on that bandstand, and he would be moaning and grunting and all that. At the bar, Jimmy Garrison would be right there with Elvin and the musicians and the *people*. Not Coltrane, not McCoy; they were two country-style black men outside in the car."

Sanders was a continuation of that back-home spirit, and when he was inspired, he seemed about to start jumping up in the air as one arm rose and fell as he took the mike and gave his voice the same rough timbre we were used to on his horn, except that he would sing, "I got the blues!" Then it was all about to step deep into the briar patch of the groove as Idris Muhammad, a country Negro from New Orleans, laid one of those Crescent City street beats at an off angle in the swing and patted every phrase on the back with his bass drum as he escorted Sanders and Hicks deeper into the syncopation as big greasy Ray Drummond used the bass like a drum whose heads were made of four fat strings that had to be pulled in time. The listeners in the club couldn't get enough and the staff, which had become jaded and could be indifferent to someone who was not particularly creative, loved the band's dirty drawers. Sanders was one of the most popular musicians we hired and one of the most enjoyable musicians to hear because he reminded us all of no one else. He had the blues. He had the feeling. He had the spirit. He was a jazz musician.

But perhaps the strongest summoning of the Coltrane legacy that I heard from the younger generation was when Branford Marsalis played the old Bottom Line after he had left the Tonight Show to guitarist Kevin Eubanks, who proved on a nightly basis that the buffoon minstrel role can be continually updated: One neither needs to buck dance nor shuffle, just play the part of a laugh track ready to snicker, chuckle, snort, and guffaw whenever Jay Leno tells a good joke or a corny one. Good or bad doesn't matter: Laughing with minstrel intensity is the job. Some things never cease.

With all of that behind him, Marsalis was in the position to make a full-court move, except that one could not forget pianist Kenny Kirkland, who had been with the saxophonist from the point at which he left his younger brother's band to join Sting and then fly on his own. Kirkland was one of the fire spitters of the keyboard, a man from whose fingers came flames that consumed the notes. He also had the greatest drive and the richest rhythmic imagination of younger New York piano players. But poor Kirkland could never assert his talent apart from Marsalis because he was trapped in a death dance with dissipation. He was found dead, his body rotting after an overdose of cocaine that rumbled his bad heart to a stop. The door had been forced open at his place after the smell of his corpse had begun to disturb his neighbors. A hole that was a memorial to an irreplaceable talent opened in the potential of his instrument in the music of his generation.

It is perhaps because of the death of his friend that a certain gravity has come into Branford Marsalis's music. This deeper perception unites his work to that of every bebopper who has survived but will never forget all of the men and women pushed at an early age into the big sleep by the occupational hazards of the night life. (What, by the way, is the night? Is it a time, a color of the sky, an intermission from the sun, a chance to show off what electricity can do with the darkness, or is it, for most of us, a state of being in which all of our nocturnal inclinations can come up to the top?)

At the Bottom Line, Marsalis and his men were performing John Coltrane's extended religious work, A Love Supreme, a long-acknowledged classic over which listeners and musicians have been drooling for four decades. What the hell was he thinking about? There was danger there. Everyone knew he wasn't going to play the same notes that Coltrane did; nobody in jazz had ever put a repertoirial approach to a small-group piece that long. But if they improvised, then there would be no choice other than to compare their work to that which had pushed itself into the pantheon. So this was not an easy task; there was danger there.

What made the music work was that it sounded new because Marsalis's rhythmic complexity, which is second to none, had much more variety than Coltrane's because it was rooted in Sonny Rollins, the greatest titan of saxophone rhythm since Charlie Parker. That was not all. Marsalis also exuded the strength that goes beyond the hysteria common to the many lesser players caught in the sway of Coltrane. That control had thematic focus and brought a disciplined intensity to his spontaneous development of the work's four themes.

The most compelling aspect of the performance was that Marsalis's band nearly mirrored the impact of Coltrane's group because his drummer Jeff Watts, who naturally plays as loudly as a drum corps, created a tsunami of sound that pushed the saxophone up to the top of the band, since the horn would only be drowned out if it didn't get up over the swirling units of inflamed rhythms and simultaneous tempos with which the drums and cymbals closed off, or absorbed, all of the other sound space. When Marsalis made it to the peak of the drums, his notes were mobile but nearly unbearable and, as suspended as the thrilling image of a surfer who has somehow ascended to the top of a wave fully monstrous in its size, getting there because the strength of his balanced grace made it possible to use the power of the water until reaching the point at which the mighty liquid and the board upon which he stands unite the way a marvelous bird does with the wind, each becoming stronger in union because it is completely what the other is not.

This is the way Coltrane's band sounded in clubs, which is remarkable to hear from a group of musicians too young to have ever heard that ensemble but who captured its essence through a comprehensive understanding of the nature of its force. The performance so drained the audience that Marsalis made the right choice to close out with a sensually lumbering blues on which he relieved himself of all of the grease and gravy in his personality, conceiving a succession of one perfectly melodic and perfectly nasty but unclichéd blues phrase after another. The linear blues statements achieved elegance because each one arrived as though obvious pressure was a foreign concern. It was indigo musical sherbet to cleanse what we could call the palete of the typanic membrane. The blues rose like confetti going backwards, full of different colors and seeming to be the true identity of the air while in upward motion.

Not so long after that I had heard Charles Lloyd at the Blue Note, which had once done something no other club in New York could do. It had presented performers who had left jazz clubs behind them and were almost exclusively given to concert appearances. But money can change almost anything in human behavior. Their booking got more surprising when the owners of the Blue Note discovered that there were people in New York, New Jersey, and Connecticut who might be willing to pay fifty dollars or more to see someone like Sarah Vaughan, whom they had never been as close to as they might be in a club or could only recall experiencing her in a smaller room back in the day when she was black and fine but didn't know it. So the Blue Note had an exceptional roster of musicians until time began to wear it down and push those men and women into the long darkness from which we would never see them return. We then had to face the fact that nothing of individual human value can ever be replaced.

So when Charles Lloyd came into the Blue Note, I had no idea how he was going to sound. I had heard little of him during the height of his fame in the early sixties because he did most of his performing on the Eastern Seaboard, in Europe, and beyond. When I had met Lloyd in the early sixties, he was a tall Negro with a golden complexion who was playing with Chico Hamilton. I never caught him when he went on play with Cannonball Adderley and had not thought about him for years because Lloyd had retired from the music business at the top of the game and talked of moving back to the South and becoming a farmer. When I read that in an interview, I thought he had lost his mind. Those did not seem like the words of the resolute young man who had just graduated from the University of Southern California with a degree in music and stood with the relaxed confidence I had seen in educated Negroes all my life. At the time of meeting him, I was too young to associate advanced education with jazz musicians, which would have been a bit much, then or now. Like actors and dancers, musicians don't seem to need to know much about anything other than their craft. Which means what? An actor doesn't need to know much human psychology; his job is to make us believe in psychological states of being. If he can, that's enough. Let somebody else give us the theories about the workings of the human mind and the jungle of chameleons we know as motives and emotions. The same is true of musicians, especially the black ones, most of whom seem to have stopped reading books once they left grade school and depend mostly, as one hanger-on I know says, "on mother wit." To this day, I only know of two jazz musicians who have not only heard of but have read *Joseph and His Brothers*: Wynton Marsalis and Ariel Roland, a young bassist who works in the bebop underground of Manhattan.

When I met Lloyd again it was on September 11th and he was taking a walk on that worst day in New York history. The World Trade Center had fallen and Rudolph Giuliani, who had actually been thought dead, was back in charge, having been trapped for a while underground. Lloyd and I sat in front of a bakery in the West Village and he told me tragic and wonderful stories of the death of Billy Higgins and of his own early life in Los Angeles, when he had become acquainted with Ornette Coleman. The days of dope had destroyed the liver that Higgins was born with, and he had gotten a transplant, which did not take. But as luck will have it, a fresh liver arrived in the hospital on the same day and Higgins was taken upstairs and prepared for another operation. The second one worked.

I told Lloyd of the time that Cedar Walton was leading his trio at the old Sweet Basil on Seventh Avenue. Kenny Washington was playing the drums because Higgins was in California trying to get his health straight. Then Higgins came in the room to everyone's surprise. He brought the light with him, as usual. Washington demanded that he sit in on the drums. It was his gig, after all. Higgins sat in and, within one or two songs, he made Washington's drums and cymbals sound *exactly* as his did. This was quite a feat because neither those cymbals nor those drums were of the same timbre and of the same tuning as the one Higgins used. What a master. He did it all with his touch. When I turned around at the end of the set, the bar was full of drummers. Something had told them all to come to Sweet Basil. That something knew that Higgins was there.

On the bandstand at the Blue Note, Lloyd was in a high state of imagination. He played well all evening but the capper was an original called "Sweet Georgia Bright" that summarized much of what had happened in jazz over the last forty years. It began as an out-of-tempo duet with pianist Geri Allen that took a number of tonal directions, the melody appearing at first in snippets that gradually took on more presence until the whole line emerged and the two were joined by bassist Bob Hurst, drummer Eric Harland, and guitarist John Abercrombie. One could then hear the formal strength of Lloyd's imagination. What began as something resembling a chromatic etude gave way to a variety of little melodies that implied the theme, which Lloyd used to splinter and redirect whatever was going on when the band began to play on the theme. He would suddenly insert the song and begin swinging so hard the other musicians could hardly catch their breath, and then he would disappear. They continued playing and Lloyd would then duet with Allen, supported by bass and drums. Lloyd would drop out of the sound again, leaving the piano out there in trio.

Allen's invention was in high form as well and she not only got a number of colors from her keyboard but keyed into the rhythms of the drums and made dazzling variations on the ideas supplied by Hurst. As the fire rose, Lloyd came back in and took a long steaming feature on the tenor, bringing all the freedom that Coleman had given to the music while crossbreeding it with the detail that Coltrane was known for, focusing every bit of it with all of the Memphis underpinnings that the town had given in all of the ways that the South passes on greatness to its people.

It is also true that whenever I am in the Blue Note, I almost always think, at least fleetingly, of Billy Eckstine adjusting his suits and ties. I can see him up there on stage looking in the mirror across from the bandstand while his piano player of many years, Bobby Tucker, takes a transitional solo to bring him back in. Any time "Mr. B" was there, the room was full or very nearly. All of the old heads who had heard the singer many years ago when they were young did not swoon as they may have during the springtime of their lives, but, sometimes ruefully, nodded in recognition of how much can be evoked by a note or a word. Eckstine, his worn vibrato now like the surf at high tide, reminded them once again of how deathless certain experiences are and that they repeat themselves in different lives over and over.

Up the stairs in the dressing room between shows, Eckstine allowed himself to be surrounded by what could be the lower forces among the many. They had come to see the once-handsome man who had been the bronze matinee idol of the forties and fifties, so much of it due to a number of things—the pristinely masculine features, his light skin, the "good hair," and his remarkable baritone, the instrument with which he manhandled and manipulated the dross of sentimental love songs into golden romantic charms of melody. Those tunes aided many a man in slipping some young woman out of her underwear and made those enchanted young women feel free enough to bet on their hearts, usually a grand army of easily duped repositories of feeling that had no more than a fifty-fifty chance of being right in most cases.

Eckstine was the kind of Janus that one becomes used to in the world of jazz or any other art. As crude as he was elegant, Eckstine was also known among closest associates for knocking men as much as he was for charming away female inhibitions in his heyday: The overwhelmed might throw their moist drawers on the bandstand as they screamed his name. In his world and his time, Eckstine had been as big a scorcher of female souls as Caruso was on his first visit to America. Or so it seemed.

Never a serious swinger or a bluesman of more than middling depth, the singer felt that he something different, which made him the sole owner of all ballad material. He looked askance at any dark-skinned man trying to move in on his territory. That feeling lay beneath his bitterness toward Nat Cole, who was the first—and last—Negro singer to get a television show. Obliquely expressing that attitude, he could joke about big, black Joe Williams, saying that he had once told him: "I heard you singing that ballad and standing up there looking like the blues."

At any moment, uptown Harlem Negroes who were part of the old World War II 126th Street gang, crooks who hustled everything that could be hustled, would come in the dressing room bearing gifts. Mr. B had been their boy when he and they were young and wild. They and he had seen each other through many wardrobes, women, automobiles, and the gems that were supposed to distinguish those who were, if not aristocrats, players who knew how to win the game.

Mr. B watched them with that gaze of particular assessment as they paraded into his dressing room. All old men, they were usually very dark. Some had canes, others hobbled, some walked straight with an easy but sinister confidence. One with hair that looked like white steel wool coming from below the turned-down brim of his hat smiled with the ease of one who had long known power as he sat back in his mink coat and patent leather shoes. A hustling legend, he was fawned over by an Italian girl in a white sweater and white jeans. Her father was a Mafia man and he had told her about this great black gangster whom he had done business with back in the day and respected from the top of his head to the bottom of his feet. She gushed with every sentence, somewhat tongue-tied by drugs, and the old black king of his section of the shadow world of Harlem simply nodded as she went on and on. When she finally left the old man whom she found so magnetic, he described her as "a simple-minded bitch who couldn't keep her goddam mouth shut. I wouldn't let that bitch wipe my ass with her tongue." "Yes, you would," someone said and mass laughter boomed against the walls.

Eckstine could be taken into the dressing room's toilet for private gifts by two huge Italians who were built like metal pup tents and talked, as Lenny Bruce once said, "like tape recorders running backwards." They had served plenty of time but were clearly incorrigible. Wheezing and laughing, they were always ready to repeat the same sorts of brutal crimes that had shocked and disgusted the courts into handing down fierce sentences. In his broad, low laugh, Eckstine related how the two had demanded of one club owner that they have a ringside table and a bottle of the room's best champagne with four glasses waiting for them when they arrived with their wives. The club owner was surprised and asked Eckstine how these guys expected him, a man known to crowd audiences in like the contents of sardine cans, to give the four of them a table that could hold at least twelve. The singer told the club owner that if he didn't do as he was told, one night soon his club would be burned to the ground and he wouldn't have to worry about seating anybody else. Eckstine knew men who played rough, sometimes to the point of murder.

That is perhaps the reason, or part of it, why he could make those songs of love, romantic ambition, and erotic delicacy so real: He knew the dirt, the barbaric violence, and the decadence of the world so well that whatever was either clean or aspired to be had a shining reality to him. His gift was that he could make those things equally real to his listeners, using a baritone sound that was far more beautiful than that of Crosby or Sinatra, who always floated above him like two white kites held in place by the bigotry of the day. Yep, Eckstine had come through when there was no room for Negro matinee idols across ethnic lines. Still, he had become one among the Negro women of America and the white girls who might sneak out to hear him or collect pictures of the singer that they might stare at when home alone.

Mr. B had also led the first bebop big band, which included Charlie Parker, Dizzy Gillespie, Fats Navarro, Sarah Vaughan, Dexter Gordon, and Art Blakey. The bronze crooner had not only established his musical importance in the world of song and instrumental innovation, but also had many stories about how it actually was in the old days. There were certain tales that Art Blakey encouraged him to tell when the master drummer, who always carried himself like a king, came to the dressing room and sat in the corner laughing as the singer related the many fistfights and scuffles of one sort or another that Eckstine's refusal to accept insult from black or white had brought about.

One that Mr. B told was about the band being somewhere in the South during the forties when their bus had parked and the white bus driver drew the attention of a passing redneck. Joking, the good old boy said, "Looks to me like you got all the damn monkeys in Africa in them bus seats." Only Eckstine, Blakey, and one other musician were awake at the time. Eckstine bet the other musician that he could take him in one punch. The guy took the bet. As the redneck continued to look at the bus, Eckstine stepped off and rattled his cranium with a punch that took him all the way down. "Sumbitch was hanging off of a tree trunk, wasn't he, Bu?" the singer asked of Blakey. Laughing, Blakey, whose Muslim name was Buhaina, said, "Yeah. Dumb motherfucker."

Eckstine's legend was more raucous but no more steady in its stance against disrespect than that of Benny Carter, whom I had seen many times at the old Sweet Basil, at Carlos I, the Blue Note, or Iridium when it was across the street from Lincoln Center, which had been San Juan Hill at the time that Carter was a young knucklehead running the streets and playing with pistols.

Born in 1907, Carter was an elder statesman by the time I got to know him, but he was never one to take condescending treatment or disregard lightly. In Harlem during the 1930s, there had been a black cop who was jealous of musicians because they were always dressed so well and were walking around laughing and preening during the day while everybody else was at work. This officer of the law always looked for an excuse to run one of them in and, if challenged, would offer to take off his badge and go in the alley where the issue could be settled with knuckles. Forget an arrest.

Then came the day when the cop, more full of himself than usual, called Benny Carter out one afternoon as he was pausing to talk with some musician friends while on the way to a rehearsal. Carter, in a clipped tone, asked the men with whom he was talking to please hold his music and went with the cop into the alley, where he commenced to put his foot deep in the ass of the sore-headed bear who had removed his badge, put up his dukes, and stepped back, thinking he was ready to do a musician some damage. Hmmm. At a dance during World War II, someone asked Carter in an arrogant manner to play a tune. Carter coolly ignored him. The man was white, and became enraged and then dropped a penny in the bell of the bandleader's saxophone while he was playing. Carter removed the penny, leaped off the stage, knocked the man out, and dropped the coin on him. Another version is that he called Carter a racial slur, which brought about the same result. When I asked him about that, Carter said, "Well, if somebody calls you a nigger, you have no choice. You have to react."

In the eighties, when he began revisiting New York, Carter polished the crown that had been largely forgotten while he spent years in Hollywood writing for film and television and sometimes performing before the camera. In *The Snows of Kilimanjaro*, Ava Gardner asks, as the saxophonist performs with a lyrical, dancing sensuousness, "Doesn't that African have any piety?" All those years later, Carter resurrected satisfying memories of the special ease with which he could play the saxophone *and* the trumpet when he came Manhattan's way. He also presented the relaxed material he had written, almost all of it forming a collective swan song to the limitations of life that the people with whom he had grown up were forced to endure, here and there. One especially fine performance was with the American Jazz Orchestra in Cooper Union, where Abraham Lincoln had spoken. It was a rousing evening with Carter peeling off one high-browed and gut-bucket invention after another while John Lewis or Dick Katz beamed from the piano bench and master drummer Mel Lewis, always a super swinger, kept the reed section strutting and the brass popping.

Carter always brought much with his presence. He knew all of the great men of jazz when they had been young and full of energy and dreams. He knew how they dressed, how they talked, the way they played, and what made them special. I had never heard Coleman Hawkins, Ben Webster, or Johnny Hodges in person, which made the performances by Benny Carter that much more important. He was the last of those sequoias. As Rex Stewart wrote of the young Carter, he was a prankster and a man who played the saxophone as if looking for a lark, while his perfect pitch always gave him a grasp of the intellectual details of the music. The ghosts of Hawkins, Hodges, and Webster seemed to walk with him as he came on stage and let that suede panther of a tone out into the air. Carter had a superior technique of the caliber that was not supposed to have existed before the emergence of Charlie Parker. In his work, one heard a plush vibrato purring around and pouncing on his notes, which were always chosen with the infinitesimal deliberation of a past master who had heard the saxophone develop from a circus tool of barnyard eccentricity to an instrument as capable of expressing aristocratic inclinations as it was all of the low-down dirty blue memories that arrive from the innumerable alleys and boudoirs of the world.

The filmmaker Jean Renoir once said that the major question of the age was how to maintain primitive vitality in the face of sophistication. The playing of Benny Carter, like so much of the best of jazz, answered that question in spades. It had the strength and the smoothness that stood not only for the Harlem period of the 1930s when he came to early manhood, but all that Carter had added to his sound as he lived through, around, and close to that polyglot of things that impressed him as they do all artists, usually resulting in a vertical deepening of the expression, not a radical change of style.

Carter had the greater depth one would expect and even more confidence than one had heard in his earlier work. Still, the precision of execution did not mask the yearning that is at the center of so much American expression and so much of modern life. In Carter's swoops and purrs, the melodic imperatives laid down by Armstrong were given added dimension. The blues was not visited literally very often, but what Ellington called blue *moods* could always rise into an audible presence as so many instances of life came back, were reconsidered, and placed next to what Carter had become over the years. The musical muscle and the soaring articulation of intimate lyricism is easily discernible on "This Can't Be Love" and "Tenderly" from Carter's *3,4,5, The Verve Small Group Sessions,* studio dates from the early fifties that contain some of the most profound saxophone playing ever recorded. His every visit to New York was a gift of immeasurable magnitude.

At the Jazz Standard in the summer of 2005, I heard Charles McPherson, whom George Coleman refers to as "my hero." McPherson is probably the finest exponent of the language of Charlie Parker on the alto saxophone but he has accomplished a purely transcendent authority because he does not make much use of arpeggios. He does not play broken chords. Melody is his business and he uses the saxophone like a nail gun that turns the notes into small spears of feeling that he showers on the audience with an heroic certitude that is far from common. He is also a master of the unpredictable, bubbling rhythms that only Parker could invent, and there is a high-mindedness at the center of his work that always forces us to remember that there is something quite noble about improvising. The masculinity of his work never reminds one of a musclehead pumping iron with a saxophone in front of you. The essence of jazz masculinity is the fusion of the will to romance heard in all of the great ballads and the equal will to stand up to the substantial demands heard in any performance of difficult material. Pianist Ron Mathews, who was close to Monk, has become one of the men who makes jazz what it is because Mathews is almost always on top of the music and can be counted on to keep the ball in the air. A highly sophisticated improvisor, he was a perfect foil for McPherson, whose bebop is not at all polite and demands of his musicians a willingness to bring a wild and wooly quality to the harmony and the rhythm while pushing more depth into their melodic inventions. Bassist Peter Washington did not have enough heat in his tone the night I heard McPherson, but drummer Lewis Nash was all the way in there. His large and small reactions were always those of a great drummer whose taste was given its head while he worked first in New York with Betty Carter. It was quite uplifting.

Whenever I hear McCoy Tyner light up the bandstand at Iridium, or hear George Coleman and Harold Mabern put the pot on at Smoke, that remarkable neighborhood club on the Upper West Side, or even hear Wallace Roney at Iridium in midtown as he continues his ever more masterful personalization of the Miles Davis legacy, not to mention Sonny Rollins, the grand master himself, I eventually end up thinking about Tommy Flanagan. But it is always easy to think of him when I see the always-dapper Washington and the always-serious Nash.

I had often heard Peter Washington and Lewis Nash at the Vanguard in the trio of the irreplaceable Flanagan, who had long been highly regarded by fellow musicians but had spent much of his career in the bands of others. He had been featured on the piano when classic recordings were made, such as "Veird Blues" with Miles Davis and Sonny Rollins, *Saxophone Colossus*, with Sonny Rollins, and "Giant Steps," with John Coltrane. He was hired by Coleman Hawkins in the early 1960s, when the first mountain man of the tenor was performing and recording with the bravura, brusque lyricism, and harmonic finesse of a true phoenix. Flanagan once told a story about Hawkins during a small New Year's Eve party held at his home on a very cold night. Dexter Gordon turned up in a huge fur overcoat, a small-brimmed hat, and some white-soled loafers perfect for a day on a yacht. Flanagan recalled that Hawkins was speaking to him in his signal deep voice as they listened to a John Coltrane recording. Hawkins had the impression that the younger man sounded as if he was having mouthpiece trouble. "He sat back," Flanagan said, "took a sip of whatever he was drinking, and said that he figured Coltrane would soon be calling him to get some advice about that mouthpiece problem. That was something, but the real something was when the phone rang right after he said that and Hawk boomed out, like he was surprised, 'Did you say this is John Coltrane? I thought that was you.' Coleman Hawkins was something."

A well-read hanger-on had once taken too seriously a statement that Hawkins made about how he always knew what something was the *first* time he heard it. He scoffed at the idea that Hawkins would have had to learn "Giant Steps" and assumed Yusef Lateef was fudging the truth when he claimed that Hawkins had asked him if he could come to see Lateef and learn it. Flanagan said that sounded true to him, but then only those who learn what they learn inside of the music ever truly have a sense of what a man knows and what he doesn't know, or what he is willing to learn and how fast he can.

Hawkins had a strong position on the Mount Rushmore of jazz's musical intellectuals, but what is important about his last years were the towering performances with younger pianists like Tommy Flanagan and Barry Harris, who says of him, "I didn't know what Hawkins could do until I played with him. I only knew Charlie Parker. Hawkins didn't improvise choruses, like the rest of us. He improvised symphonic movements. He was incredible." Flanagan carried that legacy of immaculate form with him into his trio. The pianist formed that band after he had worked with Ella Fitzgerald for ten years, leaving in 1978 after a heart attack convinced him that, if he was going to go into the iron darkness, he should be leading his own band when he did.

Born in 1930, Flanagan was brought into music through his older brother, who took him to hear the musicians who played the legendary Paramount Theater in Detroit. But he was most excited listening to either the broadcasts or recordings of Billie Holiday. "I loved everything about the way she did music—her sound, her notes, her feeling. Her records were great. You could also hear Lester Young and Teddy Wilson and the other stars."

Indeed, there was a distinct similarity between the singer's work and the lilt of Flanagan's line, a beat that lazed just behind the tempo, an apologetic tenderness, the fusion of melancholy and awe, a prickly wit, then that melodic sureness and joy that gave his swing such accumulative substance. His very distinctive tone showed the influence not only of Holiday but also of jazz singing in general. Like Wilson and Monk especially, Flanagan was given to crooning effects achieved by manipulating the pedals, holding down keys long enough to sustain notes in decisively different ways, and working out inflections that evoke the voice—sighs, moans, swells, purrs, and the almost strangled hurts sometimes nearly indistinguishable from ecstasy. From Tatum, he learned that harmonic fluidity and surprising voicings could create accents in themselves by startling the listener's ear. The softer side of his piano tone and the breathiness of lyrical ideas that seemed to simmer up from the piano strings were informed by Wilson, but the stunning triplets and the lengthy melodic variations that snapped through the chords arrived by way of Charlie Parker and Bud Powell.

Flanagan's following grew at the Vanguard as he went through various fine musicians such as George Mraz, Art Taylor, Kenny Washington, and Al Foster until he settled on Peter Washington and Lewis Nash, who was with him almost to the end. There were many nights of superior improvising in the club and the band grew until they began to improvise unclichéd rhythms at the same time, something that one only hears when musicians have played together for such a serious number of jobs that they can, on the moment, intuit the same invention. Even then, it is rare, but you would hear it at least once a night from those three musicians.

So every appearance was something to see, but I found nothing more moving than the way Flanagan came back after another heart attack in the late eighties. He played for two weeks at the club and did not sound strong or himself for the first week, but by the second he was beginning to will his old authority into place and transform a lesser self into a fuller one. Words like courage and determination become thin if called upon to describe such a human effort, because all of jazz is about response and invention, which means that one has to regain those interplaying strengths, not merely the flexibility of weakened muscles. There can be no interruption between the brain and the body, the conception and the manner of execution. This means that it was no joke to sit there night after night as mind, passion, and artistry made their way up to a position of triumph that far exceeded something as mundane as survival. Humanity was shaking off the limitations of the flesh in the interest of a blues-informed statement that might not go on forever but reminded us of the aesthetic urge to give speech to existence and, even better, speak of it in the terms of song. Every last one of us who heard him stand up against the weights of life during those two weeks may be forgotten, but I doubt that any one of us will ever lose the memory of that inspired and inspiring engagement.

That was felt in a much different way when I was at the Jazz Standard one night to hear Lee Konitz, the last indisputable giant of the Lennie Tristano school. Konitz is almost always a thrilling player because his work is so free of cliches, his tone backs away from any overt versions of emotion based upon effect. It is a tabula rasa. *If you don't hear a melody, don't play*, might be his motto. Konitz is another of those small men whose fullsome spirits have made such a large place for them in jazz. He hates the expected but learned long ago how to avoid contrivance as he seeks something fresh. But as his confidence has grown over the years, he has become a more and more confident swinger. With the wonderful Matt Wilson drumming behind him, Konitz invented interconnected melody lines of glossy or astringent lyricism and put his foot firmly in the backside of the beat. The most uplifting moment came during "Cherokee," when something beyond nostalgia came alive and all of the victories and disappointments, the flesh and blood memories, and all of the rooms now gone lifted up into the present with the palpable quality only art makes possible.

I left Dizzy's Coca Cola Room one night in the fall of 2005 and felt that it was going to be good to get downtown and out of the first mall built in

Manhattan, which is in the Time Warner Building, part of Rudolph Giuliani's legacy to New York City. Everything was shining inside and the people had that look of awe, expectation, and the determination to become
part of something that always marks shoppers. Outside in Columbus Circle, the Manhattan air was rustling against itself as I hailed a cab. I was
shocked when I got in because I heard Louis Armstrong singing "Stardust"
from November of 1933, more than seventy years ago. I asked the cab driver, who was named Mark Carr, if that was on the radio, and he said no, it
was a CD that he had bought. I could not have been more shocked because
Carr was a young black man, which meant he was the last person I would
have expected to be listening to Louis Armstrong, given the great decay in
taste that one can witness everywhere in this dark age of hip hop. Elated by
that unexpected reemergence of aesthetic appreciation, I asked Carr what
had brought him to buy the recording and he said that he had seen the Ken
Burns television documentary *Jazz*, for which Wynton Marsalis, Albert
Murray, and I had been among the consultants. We never know how far the
concentric circles spread.

I asked Mark Carr to drop me off at the Village Vanguard. I was ready to
hear something. Bill Charlap, a thorough student of Tommy Flanagan, was
leading his trio, which included Peter Washington and Kenny Washington.
Charlap is one of the finest pianists in jazz and has the good fortune of
being the son of a songwriter father and a mother who is a singer of high-
quality American melody. So he understands the making of songs and the
nuances that singers bring to them. Those qualities make Charlap akin in
spirit to Flanagan, but his approach to the instrument is decidedly contemporary in that he, like a number of the younger players who have come forward over the last fifteen years or so, calls upon all of the styles of jazz at
will, which gives a greater breadth of rhythm to their phrasing and a much
more varied harmonic base to their work. It is another level of freedom because what Duke Ellington or Charles Mingus did in composition is now
done in improvisation. Everything from Morton to Bill Evans, Herbie
Nichols, Wynton Kelley, McCoy Tyner, Herbie Hancock, Andrew Hill,
and Keith Jarrett is available and might appear in any place and in any
order if that order will make for a coherent creation, which always achieves
balance through the weight and the elevation of individual taste.

The three played a version of "Israel" that was as good and free of the expected as the blues can get these days. Its scope of references and rhythmic
and harmonic forms provided a plain on which to build variations—some
old, some new, some unknown because they were invented combinations

of the past and present that were combined on the spot. The blues always goes as far back as one can remember and as far ahead as one can imagine. Of course, the name "Israel" should always emit a blues feeling because of what is going on in the world, but there was a great majesty to the performance, which swept together its many sources by an expanding and contracting melodic invention that called upon simple to dense chords, thick voicings, and ambivalent skeletal figures in the left hand that gave mystery to the sound. Charlap used the whole keyboard, from the tinkling top to the dark grunts in the lowest register. There was something stinging but also soaring about the fact that melancholy is somehow dignified by the thing to which it is responding, an emotional observation we often hear in the music of Ellington. One could always make up stories about anything entitled "Israel" because the very word resonates against so much of our rising and falling modern world since World War II. But there is always the hope that, however badly we have been treated or the mistakes that we have made in dealing with others, everything will be faced in full truth and then gotten past. High-minded dreamers dream a dream of that, anyway.

In the next set, Peter Washington, whom I first saw come to New York to play with Art Blakey, took over the music because his beat made him the leader. Washington is one of the great ones whom Blakey the lion breeder brought to us, like the Marsalis brothers, Terence Blanchard, Wallace Roney, Mulgrew Miller, and a number of the seasoned men who now stand tall as innovators or first-class jazz musicians. During that second set, Washington pulled those strings with the hectoring aggression one heard in Ray Brown, who often told Oscar Peterson and Ed Thigpen what to play through his bass line and his position in the time. One rarely hears Washington play the bass like that, but it must have been contagious because Kenny Washington rose up on those drums and began to take us down through the myriad timbres and strokes of percussive instigation that removed all doubt that he is one of the great scholars his instrument, and a pot-liquor poet when he feels it. Then Charlap relaxed and commenced to invent one stunning, deceptive, lyrical, and expansively witty improvisation after another. Those three were playing so well that they gave one definition of jazz that was as pure as it gets because it stood in for the spirit of all jazz styles.

I thought I would conclude things with a letter from a friend in Norway that I received last winter. It opened with: "First of all, thank you for seeing us in New York once again. We enjoyed it very much. It is so good that jazz is universal." Eva and her daughter Camilla had come to New

York in order to hear a blonde whom they were sure would surprise me because she was not a singer. The woman we were looking for is named Bodil
Niska and she plays tenor saxophone. We could not find out where she
was performing, but I received a CD in November that Eva referred to in
her letter by writing: "I decided to send you her latest record, just to give
you an example of her way of playing, since I mentioned the Ben Webster
influence to you."

The recording is entitled *Blue*, and Niska, living way over there in Norway, has found her personal expression in a sound derived from that of a
sore-headed bear of a Kansas City Negro known for the ferocity of his
swing, the delicacy of his ballads, and the vast delineation of aches and
memories he could bring to the blues. Webster was a big man known to
turn out bars and appear drunk at European airports with wilting bouquets,
weeping, as Betty Carter recalled, because he had just missed doing it right
once again. But there was no more heroic and operatic tenor saxophonist
than he and no one who could whisper the idealism of pure romance from
the saxophone as well Ben Webster could—or Rooster Ben as he was once
called. He had sat next to Johnny Hodges in Ellington's band, and had
gained much from the diminutive alto saxophonist who had been mentored
by the New Orleans roustabout and grand dreamer we knew as Sidney
Bechet, himself another sore-headed bear but one sent to Devil's Island for
having pulled one of the triggers in a Paris gunfight during rush hour.
Ellington called Bechet "the great originator," but he was just a head or two
or three below Louis Armstrong, who rose up from the Mississippi mud and
gave us the jazz sky of possibilities into which countless others could hang
their own stars. So when we hear Bodil Niska, this descendant of Vikings,
play pretty for the people in her own version of the way that Kansas City
Rooster Ben did, we come to understand once again what makes an art
great. It places local and long distance calls all over the world and people
pick up the aesthetic phone in places known for rice fields or deltas or
snowcapped mountains or plains or deserts or rain forests or fjords. That is
the ultimate proof of the universality of jazz and no better example of the
fact that jazz and the blues will remain right here, which is everywhere, inspiring whomever is moved by them. The blues is always for tomorrow.

Index